Advanced Strategies for Trophy Whitetails

Advanced Strategies for Trophy Whitetails

By David Morris

Long Beach, California

Bigfork, Montana

First Edition.

ISBN 1-57157-112-4

Library of Congress Catalog Card Number: 98-60864

10 9 8 7 6 5 4 3 2 1

Published jointly by Safari Press, Inc., P.O. Box 3095, Long Beach, CA 90803 and Venture Press, Bigfork, Montana. Designed and produced by Tom Bulloch, Woodland Park, Colorado. Readers wishing to receive the Safari Press catalog, featuring many fine books on big-game hunting, wingshooting and sporting firearms, should write to Safari Press at the above address or call (714) 894-9080 or visit our Web site at www.safaripress.com.

Dedication

To my brother, Flynn, as fine a big brother as a fellow
ever had, even though, for some strange reason, he had far rather hunt
white-wings than whitetails. And to Gary Schwarz and
Chuck Larsen, my main cohorts in whitetail mischief and my
brothers in our Lord Jesus Christ.

Acknowledgements

THE INFORMATION IN THIS BOOK represents not only what I've been able to learn firsthand, but also the cumulative knowledge and experiences of countless other people, far too many for me to name them all. But to each one, I express my appreciation. And to the following, I offer a special THANKS:

To my mother and daddy for keeping me in BBs, .22 cartridges and shotgun shells, a ceaseless and expensive task, back when the hope of ever *seeing* a whitetail was but the fanciful dreams of an imaginative youth.

To Steve Vaughn, my partner in Game & Fish Publications for nearly 25 great years, for his many contributions to my whitetail knowledge and opportunities. Among Steve's many other talents, he is one of the most innovative game managers in the country, as his pioneering work on food-source management at Fort Perry Plantation attests.

To Chuck Larsen, also my partner in Game & Fish, for his encouragement, true friendship and for making every one of the countless camps I've shared with him a genuine joy.

To Gary Schwarz, whose commitment to and knowledge of the whitetail and whitetail management are second to none, for his enduring friendship and for freely sharing with me his boundless enthusiasm and knowledge…and for recently helping me fulfill my dream of owning a South Texas ranch!

To Ludo Wurfbain, my patient partner in this book venture, and all his staff at Safari Press.

To my wife, Debbie, who not only hunts with me even when she'd rather be doing something else, but also cheerfully puts up with my year-round obsession...most of the time.

To my three daughters, two of whom—Jennifer and Kristin—enjoy hunting enough that they figure they get some return on my investment in the sport. My other daughter, Samantha (Sam), can't see what all the hunting hullabaloo is about but still goes along with it all quite merrily. A special thanks to Jennifer and Sam for their proofing help.

To all the staff at Game & Fish Publications, especially editorial director Ken Dunwoody and WHITETAIL editor Gordon Whittington, whose hard work makes it possible for me to chase trophy whitetails.

To all my other regular hunting buddies—George Cooper, Bobby Parker, Jr., Phil Reddock, Richard Jackson, Carroll Mann, Dick Idol, Randy Trice, Jim and David Goodchild, Roberto Chiappelloni, John Creamer, Max Corder, Pete Dunckle, Trey Morris, Melvin Osley, Eddie Spears, Wayne Shirey, Bryant and George Wright, Ray Perkins, Bill Jordan and David Blanton, the best manager I ever had at Burnt Pine Plantation and a special friend.

To James Kroll, who teaches me something new and interesting every time we're together.

To D'Arcy Echols and Tim McWhorter, my gun and shooting gurus.

To Tom Bulloch for his superb design and layout work on this and many other projects.

To Mike Biggs, the best whitetail photographer in the business, for allowing me to grace these pages with his put-you-there images.

To Troy Huffman, Glenn Hayes, Bill Draker and all the others whose excellent photos have made this a better book.

To Bruce and Dan Harrison for allowing me to hunt their fabulous Texas ranch for many memorable years, and to Bob Zaiglin for making it possible.

To Scott Taylor and Carl Frohaug, two of my favorite Canadian outfitters.

To Mike Harris and Nosler for helping with ballistic data.

And to all those I've missed who have helped make this book possible or ever shared in the whitetail experience with me. Thanks to all. It's been a blast!

Table of Contents

Introduction   X

SECTION I—HUNTING SMART...AND WHY YOU NEED TO

Chapter 1   Trophy Bucks Are "Hosses of a Different Color"   12
Chapter 2   The Strategy of Strategies   24

SECTION II—THE LAST BEST PLACES FOR TROPHIES

Chapter 3   Recipe for a Trophy   34
Chapter 4   Tale of the Tape—What the Record Book Says   50
Chapter 5   The Ground Rules for "Last Best Places"   58
Chapter 6   Texas/Mexico Brush Country—the Unlikely "Promised Land"   64
Chapter 7   The Plains and Prairies—Ribbons and Pockets of Greatness   74
Chapter 8   The Great Northwest—Land of Enchantment   80
Chapter 9   The North Country—the Tradition Lives On   84
Chapter 10   The Midwest—Land of the Giants   88
Chapter 11   Central Canada —Snow, Cold and Monsters   92

SECTION III—TURNING YOUR LAND INTO A LAST BEST PLACE

Chapter 12   A New Frontier in Private Land Management   100
Chapter 13   Better Nutrition—the Heart of Food-Source Management   116

Chapter 14 Putting the Strategy to Work—
            Real-Life Examples of Success   124

SECTION IV—WHEN-TO STRATEGIES

Chapter 15 Timing Is (Almost) Everything   140
Chapter 16 Understanding Fall Movement Patterns   148
Chapter 17 When Deer Move and Why   162
Chapter 18 Timing the Rut...and Unraveling Other
            Mysteries of the Sun and Moon   174
Chapter 19 Strategies for the Pre-Rut—Slow and Easy Does It   196
Chapter 20 Strategies for the Scraping Period of the Rut—
            Let the Festivities Begin   210
Chapter 21 Strategies for the Breeding Period—
            Heart of the Rut...and Trophy Success   226
Chapter 22 Strategies for the Post Rut—a Time of
            Hard-Earned Possibilities   240

SECTION V—STRATEGIES FOR THE HUNT

Chapter 23 Little Things That Make a "Big" Difference   254
Chapter 24 Rattling, Calls & Scents—Beyond the Basics   272
Chapter 25 Dressing for Hot Action in Extreme Cold   284
Chapter 26 Strategies for Top-End Bucks   298
Chapter 27 The Mystery of the Secretive Super Buck   310

SECTION VI—SHOOTING NEAR AND FAR...AND THE GEAR TO DO IT

Chapter 28 All-Purpose Sporters   334
Chapter 29 Long-Range Rifles   356

SECTION VII—CONCLUSION

Chapter 30 Trophy Hunting—the State of our Sport   388

Introduction

IN THE SECOND STAR TREK MOVIE, *The Wrath of Khan*, Captain Kirk finds himself and a small band of trekkers cut off from the Enterprise in a cavern miles beneath the surface of a hostile planet, seemingly doomed at the hands of their enemy Khan. There appears to be absolutely no way out. Almost as a last request, a lieutenant asks Kirk to tell how he overcame the Kobiashimeru Test (my best guess at spelling), a no-win test that had to be taken by all Star Fleet cadets. It seems Kirk is the only cadet to have ever come up with a winning solution to the no-win scenario. He answered that he had gone into the computer and rewritten the conditions of the test so that it was winnable!

In a game that was unwinnable as it stood, Kirk had changed the conditions and created a new playing field on which he had a chance to win. For most of us, that's exactly what we have to do if we are to consistently win at the game of trophy whitetail hunting. We have to change the playing field!

If the majority of hunters accepts whatever luck, fate, convenience or whatever lays in their lap, they are playing out a virtually unwinnable hand when it comes to taking big whitetails with any more frequency than a weekend golfer making a hole-in-one. It can happen but don't count on it. To swing the odds in a more favorable direction, the serious trophy hunter must take a page from Captain Kirk's playbook—he must change the playing field somehow. He has to break the inertia of the status quo and make something happen. He has to create a winnable scenario that puts him into a higher odds arena. He has to realistically assess his current state and carefully consider his options. Having done his homework, he must then develop strategies consistent with his goals, skills and resources. Hopefully, those strategies will land him on a playing field where success is within his grasp...if he does his part and a modicum of luck comes his way.

In whitetail hunting as in football, there are essentially two levels of strategies—game plans, which we'll call prehunt strategies, and play-calling, hereafter known as hunt strategies. As you might expect, prehunt strategies are all the plans and preparations made and implemented *before* the hunt ever begins. Hunt strategies are the maneuvers, both preplanned and impromptu, put into action once the hunt is underway.

The trophy hunter must be skilled in formulating both levels of strategies, but the emphasis of this book will be on the broader prehunt strategies. This is where the odds for success are established and the *opportunity* to incur a taxidermy bill is made or lost. Prehunt strategies will set the limits of the best case scenario before the hunter ever steps foot in the woods. What happens in the woods, the play-calling, only determines how much of the opportunity created by the game plan is taken off the table. Just as Kirk did in the no-win Kobiashimeru Test, I am a firm believer in stacking the odds so that I at least have a fighting chance to win. Sound prehunt strategies will do just that.

So, this is a book about strategies—game plans and play-calling; not tackling and blocking (tactics), though by necessity some of that is in here, too. In some ways, it's a sequel to my first book, *Hunting Trophy Whitetails*. Some of what is to follow is an update of and a more in-depth look at subjects covered in *Hunting Trophy Whitetails*. Much of it, however, is brand new stuff I've long wanted to talk about because it represents the very foundation of smart trophy whitetail hunting...and success. This book assumes the fundamental hunting skills are already in place, honed by long hours afield. I write this book for the hunter who is ready to use the greatest asset he has—his brain—in the pursuit of the greatest game animal on earth—the trophy whitetail deer!

Chapter One

Trophy Bucks Are "Hosses of a Different Color"

I PROBABLY FIRST BECAME CONVINCED that they were something extraordinary on a cold, windy afternoon in Georgia during the very early years of my hunting career. I already had several small and a couple of medium-sized bucks to my credit, but a really big buck still eluded me. I was in the process of helping my wife into a treestand high on a hill overlooking a recently harvested soybean field when I cast a casual glance toward another large beanfield several hundred yards to my left. Much to my surprise, a whopper buck was nervously trotting down a narrow hedgerow winding through the middle of the field.

Excitement got the best of me, and I foolishly launched a couple of absurdly long Hail Marys into the teeth of a 30-mph crosswind. Due to

You are looking at two animals so different from each other that they might as well be entirely different species. Which one had you rather bring home? No contest, is it? But, most bucks killed across America are yearlings like the one in front that never get a chance to grow up. Photo by Mike Biggs.

the wind and the distance, the buck had no idea where the shots came from and I had no idea where they went. Uncertain of where the danger lay, the buck ducked into the thin cover of the hedgerow and miraculously disappeared. Rifle ready, I waited for several minutes for the buck to show himself in the skimpy hedgerow but nothing moved not pushed by the wind.

Turning to my wife, I shouted above the wind, "He laid down in

My whitetail career was hardly off the ground when I began to realize that big mature bucks are the most reclusive and nocturnal of the species, a fact I am reminded of every time I hunt them. Photo by Troy Huffman.

the hedgerow. I'm going after him. Stay here and watch. Signal me if you see him."

With that, I departed posthaste for the hedgerow, checking back occasionally for a sign from my wife but receiving nothing more than a shoulder shrug. When I reached the hedgerow, I began my slow stalk well back from where the buck had disappeared, assured by my wife that he was still somewhere in that thin ribbon of brush. As I eased along, I began to doubt that a 200-pound-plus buck with sizable display of bone on his head could possibly hide in the scant cover afforded by the carpet of honeysuckle vines and the scattered persimmon and honey locust trees that made up this hedgerow. The farther I went, the more skeptical I became, despite my wife's assurance that the buck had not left that hedgerow.

Upon reaching the point where the buck had vanished, a shallow, honeysuckle-choked drainage ditch began to run through the center of the hedgerow, forcing me to proceed along the edge rather than through the center. Looking ahead, I could see that the hedgerow wound another

100 yards before petering out, leaving only the broomsedge and honey-suckle-rimmed ditch to make its way 75 yards to the thick pines beyond. If the buck was still around, and all evidence said he was, he had to be between me and the end of the hedgerow.

I proceeded on red alert but not without considerable skepticism. Yard after yard, nothing, not even an obvious place for a buck to hide. Frequent checks with my wife confirmed that the buck had not slipped out, at least via any visible route. I continued down the left side of the hedgerow until only 15 yards remained. Still no sign of the buck. I had all but given up when the ground in front of me erupted into a huge buck. There was no time to marvel over where he had come from. It was time to act!

The big buck immediately put the hedgerow between him and me, and I immediately set sail to remedy that. Brimming with anticipation, I knew I had him. With me right on his tail, there was no way the buck could cross that wide-open 75 yards to the woods without me getting off two or three good shots.

I burst forth from the hedgerow, head snapping left and right, ready to shoot...but the buck was nowhere to be seen. Frantic, I ran forward 10 yards for a better view. The soybean field remained empty. Desperate, I turned to my wife on the far hill for help. She held both arms straight in front of her and began pointing frantically toward the ground. Precious seconds passing, my mind raced. *The ground. He went in the ground?* Then, it hit me. The ditch!

Racing toward the ditch, my eyes futilely traced its course to the woods. Refusing to believe the buck had gotten away so completely unscathed, I half expected to find him burrowed up somewhere in the three-foot-deep crevice as I ran alongside it. But alas, the tracks told the story, almost as clearly as my wife, who had observed it all from her elevated vantage point, did later on!

Deep, spayed running tracks marred the full length of the silty ditch bottom. Hugging the ground, he had run flat out down that ditch, his well-adorned head held low and outstretched. The big buck had pulled off an impossible escape and denied me his presence on my trophy room wall when I had him cold! As I stood there and looked at those tracks, I realized for the first time that trophy bucks were something very special...and totally different from other deer.

EARLY SUSPICIONS

Oh, I was suspicious of them from the very beginning, even before that day long ago in Georgia. Even in my earliest days of deer hunting, I noticed that they were conspicuous by their absence. Not only did I not see or kill the bigger bucks I knew to be in the area, but seldom did the other hunters either, some of whom were far more experienced than I. I couldn't help but wonder why. The answers began to unfold in 1973, the year I founded Burnt Pine Plantation and first started watching them—no, more like studying them—in earnest.

During that first year, hardly a summer afternoon went by that didn't find me cruising the many soybean fields on the plantation. It didn't take long to realize trophy bucks were different from the rest of the clan.

> *The big bucks simply disappeared. If I hadn't seen them earlier myself, I would not have believed they were there.*

One of the first things I noticed was that I seldom got a really good look at them. They always seemed to come out late, be too far away or be running like a screaming banshee was after them. The does and lesser bucks—no problem looking them over. Not so with the big boys. Still, I had glimpsed enough trophy bucks by the end of that first summer to have high hopes when autumn finally cut through the Georgia heat and humidity. Surely, shooting a trophy would be no great feat with so many around. I was wrong.

I hunted nearly everyday that first deer season on Burnt Pine. Before the season had wound down, my earlier suspicions had been confirmed (in no small part by the buck that gave me the slip in the opening of this chapter)—trophy bucks were in a league of their own. As during the summer, the autumn soybean fields were well populated with deer, but only does and young bucks. The big bucks simply disappeared. If I hadn't seen them earlier myself, I would not have believed they were there. Only by a fluke did I blunder into one (actually, he blundered into me) late in the season while I sought relief and rest from long hours of stalking in a soaking drizzle. He just strolled up to me, looking almost as cold and wet as I felt. He was so surprised that he forgot to run; I was so surprised that I almost forgot to shoot.

When the next summer rolled around, I was more methodical in

Chuck Larsen approaches one of the many trophies taken on Burnt Pine Plantation during my 20 years as the managing partner of the 13,000-acre "deer-management laboratory." Photo by author.

my deer surveying. I spent more time sitting and glassing the beanfields and less time riding hurriedly from field to field. This gave me a chance to look over some excellent bucks. I got to where I could recognize specific bucks and came to know which fields they were using. By the time the leaves turned, I was familiar with a number of shooter bucks and confident that one or two would be mine by the close of season. Again, I underestimated my quarry.

Though I did manage to kill a respectable buck just off one of my favorite fields, he was a buck I had never seen before! To make matters worse, I didn't see a single one of the many big bucks I had whiled-away my summer afternoons earmarking for the fall! Oh, I saw plenty of smaller bucks, many of which were familiar, but the bigger bucks might as well have moved to China. Obviously, I was no deer hunting wizard at the time, but it was becoming abundantly clear that it wasn't just my ineptness—these trophy bucks were an entirely different breed of cat. The next few years would prove that conclusively.

GETTING THE GOODS ON 'EM

Burnt Pine was established as a commercial hunting plantation in Middle Georgia's deer-rich Piedmont Region. Its 13,000 acres were managed intensively for deer (and quail) through selective timbering, prescribed burning, agricultural crops and dozens of food plots. By the third

The remarkable whitetail can and does live right in the very shadow of man, and the big ones often do it without being detected! Photo by Troy Huffman.

year, our management program had readied the plantation for a full compliment of deer hunters.

Leading up to that first season of hunting, one of the jobs of the staff, which included two game biologists and several guides, was to survey the deer population. Among other things, they were to record the size, identifying characteristics and location of any notable bucks spotted. By summer's end, we had recorded an impressive array of sizable bucks, many of which could be positively identified if they showed up on the hanging pole. With an average of about 10 hunters per day booked throughout the seven-week season, we would surely have enough eyes (and guns) in the field to account for a significant proportion of the trophy bucks we knew were out there. But, my earlier experiences left me with some nagging concerns. Those concerns turned out to be well-founded.

Some very good bucks did, in fact, fall to our customers that season, but not as many as our sighting records led us to expect given the hunting pressure. Perhaps more significant, however, was the fact that we took relatively few of the trophy bucks we had previously identified and most of the trophies taken were unknown to us! In my mind, all doubts were removed about whether trophy bucks were altogether different from other deer. During that season, some clear patterns started to emerge about how to hunt trophy whitetails. Over the years, we tested and refined our ideas about those patterns and eventually developed techniques and strategies that significantly increased our chances to take mature bucks...but never guaranteed it.

During my 20 years with Burnt Pine, our customers harvested nearly 500 bucks meeting our minimum trophy age of 3 1/2 years old. We kept meticulous records. Every buck taken was aged, weighed and measured. The date, place and time he was shot and what he was doing were recorded. We even interviewed hunters after each half-day hunt and recorded what they saw. Bucks seen by our customers and staff were recorded and classified as 1 1/2, 2 1/2 or 3 1/2-year-olds...or if in doubt, as bucks of unknown age. Color-coded pins (different colors indicating different ages) representing each buck killed were posted on a wall-mounted aerial photograph of the plantation. This not only helped insure a well-distributed harvest, but also revealed much about buck movement patterns and preferred habitat. Out of all this, the amazing changes that take place in a hunted whitetail buck's behavior as he gets older became very apparent. They simply become a different animal—so different that they might as well be a separate species!

A WHOLE DIFFERENT CRITTER

The increasing difficulty associated with hunting a whitetail buck as he ages tells the story. At 1 1/2, the yearling is a pretty easy target. If he survives his first year, however, he doubles his proficiency at eluding a bullet. The big jump comes at 3 1/2, which is my designation for a mature buck and the minimum age I consider a buck worthy of true "trophy" status. Our records at Burnt Pine indicate that a 3 1/2-year-old buck is three times harder to get in the crosshairs than a 2 1/2! This means a 3 1/2 is six times harder to kill than a yearling! When you think about the relative scarcity of 3 1/2s in most places and how much harder they are to kill than the younger bucks, then it becomes obvious why the great majority of the bucks shot today are yearlings and 2 1/2s.

We were never able to accurately quantify how difficult it was to take bucks 4 1/2 and older. Frankly, we couldn't kill enough of them to obtain meaningful statistics. Certainly, another jump in elusiveness takes place at 4 1/2. At this age and beyond, survival becomes the buck's overriding priority. Most of his movement will take place under the cover of darkness or in the protection of thick cover. If pressured just a little, he will become almost totally nocturnal, which he tends to be anyway. About the only hope of encountering these older bucks during the hunting season comes when the rut temporarily erodes their defenses. If someone twisted my arm, I would have to say that by the time a buck reaches 5 1/2, normally his first year at peak size and in possession of full whitetail armament, he is at least twice as bullet-wise as a 3 1/2. Whatever the actual figure, he's more than enough challenge for the best we hunters can field!

If trophy whitetails are so different from other deer, then it should be obvious that they must be hunted differently. That became abundantly apparent on Burnt Pine. The basic tactics and hot hangouts for does and immature bucks just wouldn't get it for trophies. As we killed more mature bucks, we gradually began to see certain common denominators and patterns emerge. We recognized their extreme sensitivity to pressure. We saw their unique vulnerability during the rut. We learned that they liked thick cover and low light. In time, a fairly clear picture started to form, but the problem was that the picture was much clearer about what not to do if you were to have any hope of killing a trophy buck than what to do to assure success. In short, we eventually learned how not to shoot ourselves in the proverbial trophy hunting foot and what it took to have the best chance of cashing in on what we came to recognize as rather long odds in the most favorable of circumstances. We simply learned to play the odds. Occasionally we won; most often we didn't. That will always be the way of trophy whitetail hunting.

> *If trophy whitetails are so different from other deer, then it should be obvious that they must be hunted differently.*

While my education in the ways of trophy whitetails was underway at Burnt Pine, I took another giant step toward expanding my understanding of big bucks and my personal experience in hunting them. That step came with the startup of *North American WHITETAIL* magazine in

There's big...then there's BIG! This record-book 12-pointer was shot in the farm country of Saskatchewan. With 26 inches of mass per side, he is the most massive typical whitetail I've ever measured. Photo by author.

1982. Six years earlier in 1976, my partners and I had founded Game & Fish Publications and were already publishing state and regional hunting and fishing magazines throughout the country. As one of the owners and the editor of WHITETAIL, a whole new world of trophy hunting opened up to me. Not only did my job allow me to exchange ideas and information with hunters from across North America, it gave me the chance to actually hunt big whitetails throughout their range. Everything I saw and learned validated my experiences at Burnt Pine—the trophy whitetail was "a hoss of a different color."

All this raises the question of what is a trophy? For our purposes, we'll define a trophy as a mature buck, meaning at least 3 1/2 years old, with antlers large enough to rank him among the best bucks consistently taken in a given area. The last part of this definition guarantees he is special by his very rarity. Why 3 1/2 as the minimum age to rank "trophy" status? While it is true that bucks normally reach their greatest size between the ages of 5 1/2 and 7 1/2, only a small percentage of the bucks reach this age, largely because of hunting pressure. Bucks 5 1/2 and older

This buck is 3 1/2 years old, our minimum age for ranking trophy status. Note the straight belly line, the lack of depth in the neck and chest, the big eyes and slim face—all characteristics of a 3 1/2. Still, he has good headgear and is sharp enough to evade the best efforts of most hunters. But, give him two more years and he will be even bigger and smarter. Photo by Mike Biggs.

are practically non-existent in most deer populations, so to evaluate trophy prospects based on bucks of this age would eliminate most populations from consideration. On the other hand, bucks younger than 3 1/2 simply do not have the antler size or the survival savvy to be called "mature" or to be given the lofty label of "trophy" by serious hunters. But, a 3 1/2-year-old can have very impressive antlers and, especially when pressured, can exhibit the uncanny survival skills unique to the trophy whitetail buck.

One on one, the trophy whitetail is unquestionably one of the world's most challenging game animals. Think about it. As a species, the whitetail is among the most intelligent and adaptable of all animals. What other big game animal can prosper right under the nose of man? They live in thick cover, are all but nocturnal and are equipped with senses we humans cannot hope to match, especially hearing and smell. They are constantly wired and ready to jump out of their skin at the slightest provocation. And now, they've had a couple of hundred years of intense hunting pressure to hone their survival instincts to a fine edge, and that's the case with just your average, run-of-the-mill whitetail!

What about the smartest of the smart—trophy bucks? By nature, old, big-racked bucks are the most reclusive members of the clan. If that weren't enough, they've been made even more reclusive by being the most sought after of their species. It's literally a matter of get smart or get dead for trophy bucks. And, they've answered the call quite admirably—so admirably, in fact, that, except during the rut, they have very little in common with does or lesser bucks, either in their behavior or where they live. And now, over a quarter-century and 150 bucks later, I know beyond a doubt that unless you look at trophy hunting as unique unto itself you will remain mired in the deer hunting pack with slim hope of ever having your wife (or husband) complain about too many deer heads on the den wall.

> *One on one, the trophy whitetail is unquestionably one of the world's most challenging game animals.*

Chapter Two

The Strategy of Strategies

BILL STARED AT THE 12-POINTER, shook his head and repeated yet again, "Morris, you're one lucky rascal. Two years in a row you've killed a monster right here in your own backyard. How lucky can you be!"

Even as he spoke, my mind went back five years earlier to when I bought my small ranch in Montana. From the beginning, I had planned for and anticipated this day. I had searched long and hard for just the right tract of land located in prime deer country. Once I had found such a place and become thoroughly familiar with it, I had carefully planned every aspect of its improvement, from where my house would be to how I would access it for minimal disturbance of the game to the layout of the fields I intended to put in. Then, I had cleared two 15-acre meadows and planted them in clover and alfalfa. It was no accident that they were the only major food sources for two miles in three directions and for over 80 miles toward the mountain wilderness to the east. Before placing the deer stands overlooking the meadows, careful attention had been given to the

This 14-pointer's demise actually began over three years before I shot him, with the planting of two 15-acre clover and alfalfa food plots on my Montana ranch. Management is just one way to stack the odds of success in your favor before ever stepping foot in the woods. Photo by John Creamer.

prevailing wind direction, trails coming into the fields and an approach route to the stands that would not disturb the deer. The table set, I had known that in time the planning and the effort would translate into big bucks.

The payoff had not been long in coming. The first year, both my youngest and oldest daughters had taken their biggest bucks ever. The next season, my youngest daughter had topped her previous year's buck. The following fall, my wife had shot her highest scoring buck, a 150-class 13-pointer, and I had taken a 14-pointer grossing 179, concluding a three-year chase. Now, in the fourth year, I stood over a 12-pointer scoring a whopping 182 points!

"Yeah," Bill started again, "you're one lucky..." I stopped him before he could continue.

"You're right," I began, a little impatient to be hearing how lucky I was for the umpteenth time, "I'm lucky to have a place like this, and luck is always involved in killing a top-end buck. But the truth is, this buck and all the others we've taken here began their journey to the wall five years ago when I bought this ranch. And, every step I've taken since to enhance this the place for deer has brought this day a little closer."

Then, biting off my impatience, I agreed with him...again, "But, you're right. I am lucky to take such a great buck."

As he continued to recount my good fortune, I couldn't help but think that he could have done the same thing with the property he had purchased at the same time I bought mine. It, too, was situated in fine deer country, and he had the time and the resources to improve it for deer. Certainly, he considered himself a serious deer hunter, but the fact was that he hadn't done anything to improve his odds of success, either on his property or anywhere else. In fact, he didn't seem to plan ahead for deer season or even think about deer hunting until it was time to go deer hunting. As a result, every year he had bemoaned his bad luck...and my good luck.

You see, my friend failed to realize a key element of consistent hunting success—that developing and executing sound prehunt strategies can stack the odds in your favor well before the time to don your camouflage is even near. In fact, I personally think that putting into play well-conceived strategies in advance of the hunt is at least as important to success as what takes place in the field each fall, assuming the person is competent in basic hunting skills. Before I explain, first some definitions.

STRATEGIES VERSUS TACTICS

In deer hunting, we often hear the terms "strategies" and "tactics." They are sometimes interchangeable and are used in various ways. In our discussions, we need a definition that allows us to work off the same page. To that end, strategies are plans developed to create the greatest opportunity to succeed. Those plans can be developed well in advance of taking to the field, or they can be impromptu plans made during the hunt in response to new information and conditions. Tactics, on the other hand, are the techniques used in the field execution of strategies. This is the how-to legwork we're so familiar with.

In developing strategies, the hunter has the opportunity to bring

If you want to take bucks like this incredible double-drop-tined monster, you have to hunt where such animals live. Choosing the right place to invest your time is the first step in a trophy strategy. Photo by Mike Biggs.

his greatest weapon to bear—his brain! Planning, thinking, hunting smart—this is how good hunters become *successful* good hunters. The best astronaut in the world could not get into space without the preparations that precede the blastoff. True, hunting trophy bucks, though plenty difficult, is not space travel, but the principle is exactly the same. So here, we're going to focus on strategies and assume a would-be trophy hunter already has the basic hunting skills necessary to execute the plan once it is in place.

This is not to undermine the importance of tactics and field execution. Obviously, skilled hunters have a far better chance of buffaloing a wily old buck than the less skilled. But, I firmly believe that no hunter, no matter how skilled in the field, can consistently take trophy bucks without developing sound strategies. Unless you're one of the lucky few with fantastic trophy hunting at your doorstep, trophy bucks are just too rare and savvy for a hunter to pursue randomly and hope to consistently come out on top. Without taking steps to improve one's lot, the odds are usually so heavily stacked against the hunter that he has practically no chance of connecting. In this case, the best deer hunter doesn't have much more hope than the worst. Both are simply playing unreasonable odds. Sound strategies, however, create greater opportunity for success from the outset. Then when the skilled hunter takes to the field, he has a realistic crack at gathering a crowd around the bed of his pickup at day's end. On the other hand, though sound strategies greatly improve the picture for less competent hunters, if he lacks the skills to take advantage of his opportunity, his outlook remains pretty bleak.

Most hunters have limited time and money to invest in deer hunting. Given those limited resources and assuming they're serious about wanting to take trophy bucks with any kind of consistency, they would be wise to invest those limited resources in a way that maximizes their chances to come home with a trophy. Every time a hunter goes into the field, certain mathematical odds are at work. With trophy bucks, you can bet those odds are inherently slim and it is incumbent on the hunter to do everything he can to improve them. This is where well-thought-out strategies come into play. Good strategies will not guarantee consistent success, but their absence will all but guarantee consistent failure. From my experience, most hunters fall short in this strategic area and take to the field woefully ill-prepared to achieve a happy outcome.

PREHUNT STRATEGIES

As we've said, deer hunting strategies can be divided into two areas—prehunt and hunt strategies. Both are important, but if prehunt strategies don't create ample opportunity, hunt strategies, much like tactics, aren't going to make much difference. On the other hand, the opportunity afforded by prehunt strategies will amount to naught without solid hunt strategies, along with good tactical execution.

Prehunt strategies are the plans, decisions and preparations done in advance of the hunt that create fertile fields in which to plow. Certainly, *where* and *when* a hunter chooses to put in his time stand at the very top of prehunt strategies. No two factors bear more on his odds of success. Interesting enough, deer management, such as planting the two food plots on my Montana ranch I cited in the opening of this chap-

Every year, I plan my Canadian forays so that I begin hunting just as the rut fires off. Being in the right place won't do you a lot of good unless you are also there at the right time. I shot this 160-plus Saskatchewan 10-pointer in the heart of the rut, trophy hunting's prime time. Photo by Carl Frohaug.

ter, is becoming an evermore important prehunt strategy that can definitely change the playing field for the better. Actually, anything intentionally and thoughtfully done in advance to influence the outcome of the hunt qualifies as a prehunt strategy.

You can think of prehunt strategies in farming terms. It is exactly like a farmer who prepares and plants his field in the spring and returns in the fall to harvest his crop. Without the spring preparation and planting, what are the chances he would return to the field in the fall and find a good crop of, say, corn waiting for him? Very slim! It's the same with trophy whitetail hunting—if you don't plant some seeds ahead of time, the harvest is most likely going to be very lean in the fall.

Where-To

Nothing is more important in trophy hunting than where you hunt—plain and simple. Hunting in the best place possible is the greatest single step a hunter can take toward success. If you hunt where there are adequate numbers of bucks meeting your trophy standards, then you have a chance to kill one of those deer, provided you do your part. If there are no or very few trophies where you hunt, you're shot in the foot before you ever zip up your camouflage coveralls. A serious trophy hunter must carefully evaluate the trophy prospects where he hunts and decide if bucks meeting his standards are there in numbers sufficient to justify his time and resource investment. If not, he must look for the best alternative available given his constraints. We'll cover where-to in detail later.

When-To

I think the most underestimated prehunt consideration in trophy hunting is timing, i.e., when the hunter chooses to invest his limited days afield. As the saying goes, "timing is everything." Is this ever true in trophy hunting! Yet, many hopeful trophy hunters all but overlook its vital importance, even those who know how critical hunting the right place is. Sadly, if you hunt the right place at the wrong time, you have negated much of the advantage of the place. The end result of bad timing often is the same as hunting a bad place—either way, you go home empty-handed. Being around big bucks won't help if you can't see them, and you won't see them if you're there at the wrong time.

Timing a hunt for best results is more complicated than deciding where to hunt. Many factors come into play, such as food sources, hunting pressure, seasons, regulations, moon phases, habitat and the all-important rut, to name but a few. We'll talk much more about this later since big bucks hang in the balance of good timing decisions.

Management

As mentioned, deer management is another strategy plum ripe for the plucking. If a person is in position to improve his hunting lot through some type of management, the returns on investment can be great. Management can be directed toward producing more and/or larger trophies or aimed at increasing the visibility, thus huntability, of existing bucks, or some combination therein. Obviously, the scope and intensity of management can vary tremendously, depending on goals and resources. True, management has not historically been an option for most hunters, but that is about to change. New management strategies, especially food-source management, have put successful management, even on relatively small tracts, within the reach of a growing number of sportsmen.

In a way, deer management is related to where-to. How so? Through management, a hunter can make his own property *the place* to go for a trophy buck...and he can have lots of year-round enjoyment doing it! More to come on this later.

HUNT STRATEGIES

Hunt strategies are fluid, thought-out plans, based on an analysis of the overall situation and the most current information, aimed at maximizing the odds of success once the hunt is underway. Naturally, the better the information, the better the strategy.

Before I even take to the field, I usually start with an initial plan of pursuit based on what I already know or assume. I can do this because my advance research will have provided me with considerable information even if I've never been to that particular place. Chances are I'll have an idea about such things as the availability of food sources, the current stage of the rut, moon phase, hunting pressure, topography, cover, probable hunting techniques, hunting regulations, etc.

As the hunt progresses and new information comes in and/or conditions change, hunt strategies must evolve based on onsite realities. What the deer are doing will dictate most of the moves called for. Certain basics that affect deer behavior, such as the stage of the rut, feeding patterns, hunting pressure, weather, general travel patterns and herd density and composition, need to be sorted out and factored into the strategies as soon as possible. Obviously, this requires knowledge of deer behavior and deer patterns, which we'll delve into in coming chapters.

Plus, an analysis of the playing field must be made. What is the land like—its size, layout, topography, boundaries, natural barriers or bottlenecks, access roads or trails, food sources and habitat conditions? (Here, a topography map or aerial photo is invaluable.) How much pressure do the neighbors exert? Are there existing stands? If so, what's their hunting history, recent and past?

Even if the overall hunt strategy doesn't change, the hunter must constantly develop "mini-plans" during the ebb and flow of a hunt to react to day-by-day and minute-by-minute changes. For instance, say I'm hunting during the rut in the remote forestlands of western Montana. My initial hunt strategy might be to find recent logging operations and to

Sound strategies create opportunity for success, but the hunter still has to have the skills to cash in when the time comes. Photo by author.

quietly slip along associated logging roads, rattling when I find likely spots or rutting sign. After a couple of days, say I locate a fresh logging site where the deer are really concentrated and there are lots of running tracts, indicating rutting activity. Then my strategy may be modified to include sitting on this hotspot the last two hours of daylight while continuing my patrol the rest of the day. Say after hunting the fresh logging site two afternoons, I notice the prevailing wind is blowing my scent dangerously close to the area where most of the deer are coming from. If I move, I'll give up the only place in the cutover that offers good visibility. But, assume I also noticed that the afternoon thermals cause a near-reversal of the wind direction about an hour before dark each day. Another modification in strategy—I'll stay out of the logging area until about 45 minutes before dark to give the thermals a chance to change the wind direction in my favor. Then, I'll take up the vigil at the lookout point. Simple and logical...just the way sound strategies should be.

The hunter's abilities and physical limitations are factors in developing hunt strategies. Since hunters are not all equally adept, strategies must be tailored to the abilities of the individual. A strategy that's best for one may be a hopeless waste of time for another. Some hunters, for instance, don't have much of a chance of slipping up on deer and making a quick shot even if that is the odds-on call for the day. And, let's not forget the resources available to a hunter, such as portable stands, ATVs, the weapon, rattling antlers and, yes, even clothing. All these things play a role in shaping hunt strategies.

Finally, I should mention hunting regulations. There are places

where game regulations have a major effect, either beneficially or nega-
tively, on strategies. On the negative side, until recently in Saskatchewan, the outfitter/guide, no matter how incompetent he may be in
the woods, had to be at the hunter's side unless the hunter was on-stand,
in which case he had to stay put until picked up by his escort. This practically dictated stand-hunting as the only viable method of hunting, so
the strategy had to be built around that tactic, even if others offered
better odds. (I understand this regulation has been relaxed, but how the
relaxed version will ultimately be enforced remains to be seen.) On the
more liberal side, hunting from a vehicle is legal in Texas, thus the tradition of highracking. This is where a vehicle equipped with an elevated
platform moves slowly through the brush, allowing the mobile hunter to
look over a lot of country. Highracking is especially useful in quickly
gathering information about the nature of the habitat, the lay of the land,
deer behavior and travel patterns. Regulations *can* affect hunt strategies.

Sound strategies—that's were trophy hunting success begins. It
starts at the prehunt level, where the playing field is determined and
much of the potential for success is either created or lost. Then, the outcome shifts to what takes place in the field. Armed with the best information he can gather and a realistic evaluation of his skills and resources,
the hunter must now lay out the highest-odds strategies possible for the
hunt—or even the day, the hour and/or the minute—and always be ready
to adapt to new onsite realities. Then, the planning in place and the
table set for success, he must call on his tactical skills to turn trophy
potential into lots of inches of hard bone!

When it's all said and done, without a strategy derived from information, knowledge and experience, the hunter enters the domain of a
trophy buck without bringing his greatest weapon to bear—his brain!
And if he fails to take advantage of that asset and depends on nothing
more than blind luck to put a trophy whitetail in his sights, he can
probably get by with a shoe box as a trophy room!

Chapter Three

Recipe for a Trophy

Y BASIC STRATEGY FOR TROPHY
bucks is simple—I hunt the best places at the best times and then take
advantage of anything else I can to sway the odds my way. Nothing in
that strategy is more important than where I hunt. If I choose poorly on
that account, then it matters little what I do right from that point on.
You see, nobody, no matter how good he is, can kill something that isn't
there! And, where I choose to hunt determines what's there for me to
shoot. The only absolute prerequisite for killing a trophy whitetail is
being where there are trophy whitetails!

What constitutes a trophy varies by hunter. Every hunter must
decide for himself what size buck meets his personal trophy standards.
Once done, he must then realistically evaluate his chances of meeting his
standards where he hunts. Or, he can reverse the process—first evaluate
the trophy prospects where he hunts and then set his trophy standards
based on the largest buck he feels he has a reasonable chance to take
there. If the process leads a hunter to the conclusion that the size he is

Several mature bucks together in a field—this is a sight you cannot expect to see in heavily pressured areas. Hunting pressure is perhaps the greatest nemesis of trophy hunting throughout most of the country. Photo by Troy Huffman.

after is not available where he hunts, he must search elsewhere and be able to calculate his chances there.

This chapter is about laying the basic foundation for evaluating the trophy prospects for the purpose of mapping out a where-to strategy. However, as we cover all this, we will be discussing management and biological terms, definitions and principles that are integral to sound deer management, to which we will devote an entire section later. It is essential to gain a working understanding of these various elements of game management and biology, not only for the upcoming management section, but also so you can become the best hunter you can be...and to get the most enjoyment from the great sport of deer hunting.

In evaluating the trophy prospects, it is necessary that the hunter have a working understanding of what goes into growing trophy-sized bucks. Though many factors are involved, we'll quickly see that no one factor has a greater influence than hunting pressure. The relationship is simple—the greater the pressure, the poorer the trophy hunting. Because of the critical importance of hunting pressure and the need to quantify it, let's take a look at the characteristics of a deer herd subjected to different levels of pressure. The ills of excessive pressure will become obvious.

QUANTIFYING HUNTING PRESSURE

For our purposes, we'll categorize relative hunting pressure into three levels—light, moderate and heavy. After a quick look at the characteristics of each, you will probably have no trouble recognizing which is most applicable to your area. While game biologists do have ways of more accurately quantifying the effects of hunting pressure based on harvest data and scientific formulas, that kind of tedium is best left to the professionals. Fortunately, experience and a common-sense analysis of the hunting situation where you hunt will allow you to categorize the level of hunting pressure accurately enough to make a judgment about the trophy prospects.

A *lightly hunted* population is characterized by a high percentage of mature bucks, including some 5 1/2s, 6 1/2s and 7 1/2s. Less than 25 percent of the antlered bucks are harvested per year. The buck:doe ratio will be from 1:1.3 to 1:2. Competition between hunters is minimal. Deer move freely during prime daylight hours on somewhat predictable patterns. A distinct, competitive rut is accompanied by an abundance of buck sign and rutting activity. Today, only remote, protected or thinly populated areas have light hunting pressure.

Areas with *moderate hunting pressure* have a fair number of mature bucks. Most are 3 1/2s and 4 1/2s, but 5 1/2s and older are taken occasionally. Young bucks make up most of the harvest since from 30 to 65 percent of the antlered bucks are shot each year. Buck:doe ratios of 1:1.5 to 1:3 can be expected, depending on antlerless regulations and reproductive rates. Hunter competition is clearly evident, but enough solitude is possible for a "quality" experience. Deer movement is somewhat suppressed and altered, and overall daytime activity is largely limited to early morning and late afternoon hours. Mature bucks tend to be primarily nocturnal, especially outside the rut. The rut is fairly well defined but often sporadic. Buck sign is present and huntable, though inconsistent. Moderate pressure is the most prevalent trophy hunting situation in the U.S. today, and the quality of trophy hunting varies considerably depending on where in the moderate range a place falls.

In *heavy pressure* areas, mature bucks are outright rare, as you would expect when 65 to 95 percent of the antlered bucks are shot each year. The few mature bucks that do exist are nearly all 3 1/2s. A 5 1/2 or

Low hunting pressure usually means a distinct, competitive rut, the kind that trophy hunters long for. You can bet that a dispute over either a hot doe or who's boss is at the root of this fracas. Photo by Mike Biggs.

older is a real novelty. Yearling bucks make up the great majority of the harvest. The buck:doe ratio heavily favors does, and antlered bucks of any size are hard to pass up. Hunter competition is keen, and it is not easy for a hunter to distance himself from the presence or evidence of other hunters. Most natural deer activity is at night or very early or late in the day. Forced movement accounts for much of the harvest. The rut is a sad affair. Rutting activity and sign are spotty and inconsistent. Trophy hunting in heavily pressured areas is a most difficult game and pretty much limited to hunting a known buck or the most inaccessible areas.

THE BIG THREE

When trying to assess trophy prospects, there are basically three major questions that must be answered. *How many mature bucks are present? What is their size? How huntable are they?* Let's address each of these questions, but first, we need to distinguish between "adult," "mature" and "trophy" deer. We'll define "adult" as any deer 1 1/2 years old or older and "mature" as 3 1/2 and older. We've already defined "trophy" as a mature buck big enough to rank among the better bucks consistently taken in an area. Much of this chapter will focus on mature bucks since trophies are a natural byproduct of a population of mature bucks.

Overcrowding now vies with heavy pressure as the greatest detriment to buck quality. This buck, obviously not in the best condition, needs better food. More age won't allow him to grow much bigger antlers. Photo by Mike Biggs.

Also, a couple of other definitions will be helpful. One, what is a "fawn?" We'll define a fawn as a deer belonging to the youngest year-class in the herd. This means that deer less than one year old are termed "fawns." Once a new fawn crop comes along, the previous year's fawns are then termed "yearlings." So, deer from one to two years old are yearlings, or in deer management lingo, they are often referred to as 1 1/2-year-olds. Each subsequent year-class is referred to in half-year terms, i.e., 2 1/2, 3 1/2, 4 1/2, etc. Why the half-year designation? Because from a management standpoint, the key time and the usual interface point with man is the fall of the year, at which time deer, having normally been born in the late spring and early summer, are approximately a half-year past their birthday. Along these lines, the terms "fawn recruitment rate" or "reproductive rate" refer to the number of fawns entering the preseason fall population. "Fawn crop" often is used to mean the same thing, but that term more correctly refers to the number of fawns dropped during the fawning season.

The Number Of Mature Bucks Present

The number of mature bucks present is of paramount concern in evaluating trophy prospects. The more mature bucks present, the greater your chances of shooting a trophy. Essentially, three factors contribute to the number of mature bucks. One, the density of the deer population. Two, the buck:doe ratio. And three, the buck age structure. The latter two are largely determined by buck hunting pressure. Let's look at each.

Herd Density

Simple arithmetic tells us that greater deer densities should mean more mature bucks and greater odds of trophy success. If all things are equal, which is seldom the case, this is true. For instance, if two tracts of land have similar buck:doe ratios and buck age structures but one tract has twice as many deer as the other, the tract with twice as many deer should offer twice the odds of encountering a mature buck.

It is, however, possible to have too much of a good thing. In the above scenario, if the tract with twice as many deer is seriously over-crowded, then the tract with half as many deer may, in fact, offer better trophy hunting (at least in terms of buck size) despite having fewer mature bucks. Why? Because overpopulation reduces antler size due to poor nutrition. Nowadays, overcrowding has a major detrimental effect on buck size in many areas of the country, especially in the East and South. For the trophy hunter, the abundance of deer and where the herd stands relative to carrying capacity are both important concerns.

Of the factors affecting the number of mature bucks, I generally consider herd density to be the least important. However, there are a few places where overall deer numbers are so low as to be only marginally huntable. Examples can be seen on the fringes of the whitetail's range in such places as the northern forests of Canada and parts of Mexico. I have hunted wilderness areas in Canada where it literally took me a couple of days just to find deer tracks. Such extremely low populations are the exception, and ample numbers of deer exist just about everywhere white-tails are hunted.

The fact is that trophy hunting can be quite good even in relative-ly low populations. Interestingly, a low density actually offers a couple of significant advantages. One, it's easier to locate and pattern a specific buck. Two, rutting bucks often have to travel longer distances between doe groups, thus occasionally exposing themselves in daylight hours and perhaps even in the open. In any case, I would much rather hunt an area with few deer and a tight buck:doe ratio and good buck age structure than a high-density herd with a disproportionate number of does and a shot-down buck population.

Buck:Doe Ratio

The buck:doe ratio is nothing more than the ratio of adult bucks to adult does. It easily can be translated into percentages. For instance, a buck:doe ratio of 1:1 means 50 percent are bucks and 50 percent are does; a 1:2 translates into 33 percent bucks and 67 percent does; a 1:3 ratio results in 25 versus 75 percent; and so on. Excessive hunting pressure can play havoc on the buck:doe ratio, especially in herds with disproportionate pressure on bucks. Generally speaking, the buck:doe ratio is lower in lightly hunted populations and higher in heavily hunted herds.

It is a simple matter to see why the buck:doe ratio has a direct bearing on the number of bucks in the population. Assuming a tract of land is capable of carrying only so many deer without sacrificing size, then it's obviously to the trophy hunter's advantage to have as many bucks in that population as possible. The lower the buck:doe ratio, the greater the percentage and total number of bucks present. And, logic dictates that more bucks in a herd lead to a greater likelihood that mature bucks are present. As for does, it is only necessary to have enough to replenish deer losses each year, assuming the herd is at carrying capacity. A buck:doe ratio unnecessarily weighted toward does means space is occupied by does that could be filled by bucks.

Fawns are not included in the buck:doe ratio; therefore, the ratio between *antlered* and *antlerless* deer will reflect an even greater spread. If fawns, which obviously don't have antlers regardless of sex, are counted as "does," the antlered:antlerless ratio can actually be nearly twice as great as the true buck:doe ratio since a healthy herd can average a fawn per adult doe. As a result, a buck:doe ratio of, say, 1:3 could mean an antlered:antlerless ratio of around 1:6. Without taking this into account, antlerless sightings could give the wrong impression of the buck:doe ratio, which is normally determined in the fall when fawns are often mistaken for adult does.

Well-balanced herds have buck:doe ratios in the 1:1.3 to 1:2 range. Ratios around 1:1 are usually the byproduct of game management and are rarely, if ever, seen naturally in the wild. This is because natural mortality for bucks is higher than for does due to the physical toll the rut takes on bucks. (Bucks may lose 30 percent of their body weight in the rut from fighting, competitive stress and traveling long distances while eating very little.) A ratio over 1:3 almost always stems from disproportionate pressure on bucks.

I should add that it is possible for a herd with substantial pressure to still have a fairly tight buck:doe ratio if the harvest is more or less evenly distributed between bucks and does, or better yet, weighted toward does. There was time in Middle Georgia when I saw this. A five-deer limit, of which only two could be antlered bucks, and 25 either-sex days, most of which fell on weekends and holidays, encouraged a large doe harvest... and I might add, prodigious reproduction. As a result, the buck:doe ratio ranged from 1:1.5 to 1:1.8 even though pressure was moderately heavy.

I often hear about populations with extraordinarily high buck:doe ratios, like 1:10 or even higher. This, however, is only possible in a herd with heavy buck pressure and very little reproduction. Otherwise, the reproduction alone, which replenishes at a 1:1 ratio (actually, slightly more bucks are born than does), will pull the ratio back into more normal ranges. For instance, assume every adult buck is killed in a herd of 100 adult does and 80 fawns (a reasonable doe:fawn ratio in a healthy herd). The following fall, assuming no mortality to keep it simple, 40 does (half of the previous year's fawns) and 40 bucks would be added to the adult deer count, resulting in 40 bucks and 140 does. Even after all the adult bucks were killed the previous fall, this is still a buck:doe ratio of 1:3.5!

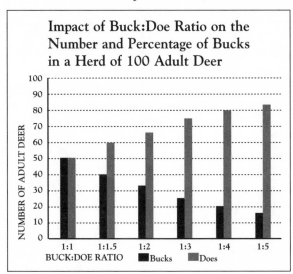

Impact of Buck:Doe Ratio on the Number and Percentage of Bucks in a Herd of 100 Adult Deer

However, if reproduction is lowered from overcrowding, depredation, natural disasters or the excessive harvest of fawns, especially buck fawns, then the buck:doe ratio can be worsened in the face of persistent, heavy buck pressure.

The importance of the sex ratio can be illustrated (see graph).

It doesn't take a brain surgeon to see why trophy hunting is better in populations with tight buck:doe ratios. Not only is the number of bucks higher at lower ratios, but a positive side benefit is a more competitive rut, the delight of every trophy hunter. More bucks and greater rutting competition—that's a good start to a hold'im-and-grin photo.

Buck Age Structure

The most damaging impact hunting pressure has on trophy hunting is seen in the buck age structure, which is simply the distribution of bucks throughout the various age classes. High hunting pressure reduces the number of bucks reaching maturity, thus lowering trophy prospects. Light hunting pressure assures plenty of mature bucks, greatly enhancing the trophy outlook. As we've defined trophy, a buck can't be a trophy unless he's mature and a buck can't reach maturity if he's killed at 1 1/2 or 2 1/2, as is the case over much of the whitetail's range. Age is, in fact, the most limiting factor in trophy production across the country, and hunting pressure more than anything else will determine how many bucks survive to maturity.

The graph below clearly shows the devastating effect pressure can have on age structure and why trophy hunting is difficult in heavily hunted areas. Nearly all the mature bucks are 3 1/2, and there are precious few of those. A 4 1/2 is a rare bird. I've hunted just such populations in the heavily pressured counties around Atlanta, Georgia, and the best a fellow can hope to do is come across any 3 1/2…then shoot fast!

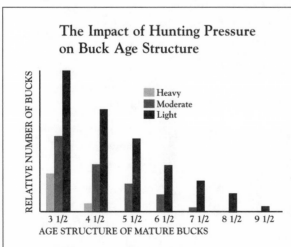

The graph illustrates the reasonable trophy prospects under moderate pressure, where enough bucks reach the older age classes to keep it interesting. Though 6 1/2-year-olds and over are in limited supply, a hunter who knows the country has a pretty good chance of sorting out a trophy buck in places with this level of pressure. Much of the Midwest, where short and/or restrictive firearms seasons are the norm, fits the description. The number of older age bucks in the light pressure scenario speaks for itself.

To summarize our discussion of the number of mature bucks present, herd density determines the total number of deer present. The buck:doe ratio determines how many of the deer are bucks. The buck age structure determines how many of the bucks are mature, which determines the number of trophies available.

The Size Of The Mature Bucks
Region-To-Region Size Differences

Most serious trophy hunters are well aware that great differences can exist from one region to another in the inherent size of bucks as a whole, even when average ages are the same. This size variance is where genetics and nutrition enter the picture…and as taxonomists would say, so do the subspecies differences. For the traveling hunter interested in hunting the biggest bucks available, this inherent regional size difference is an important consideration.

Once again, we'll use a graph to illustrate. For the sake of comparison, let's look at three different herds—one with inherently small deer, one with medium deer and one with large deer—and eliminate any age differences by assuming they are all subjected to the same hunting pressure.

In our example, the average size of mature bucks in the small deer region is 100. This would roughly correspond to, say, the Texas Hill Country. The medium region

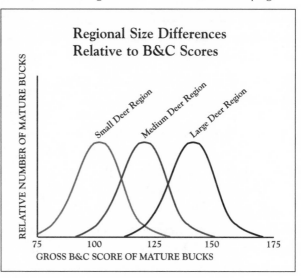

Regional Size Differences Relative to B&C Scores

RELATIVE NUMBER OF MATURE BUCKS

Small Deer Region / Medium Deer Region / Large Deer Region

75   100   125   150   175

GROSS B&C SCORE OF MATURE BUCKS

A badly skewed buck:doe ratio is a sure sign of excessive buck pressure and is certain to be accompanied by a poor buck age structure, a pitiful rut and sorry trophy hunting prospects. Photo by Mike Biggs.

average is 120, which would approximate some of the better areas of the South. The 140 average of the large deer region would approach that of the Midwest.

If you're interested in shooting a 150, where would you go? To the large deer region, of course. There is virtually no hope of shooting such a buck in the small deer region and a very slim chance of doing it in the medium deer region. Does that diminish the significance of a trophy in the small or medium regions? Absolutely not! A 130 in Georgia, for instance, is every bit the trophy a 150 is in Illinois since he would, at least in our example, represent the same minority percentage of the mature buck population. Yet, if your goal is a 150-plus buck, you're going to become very frustrated hunting him in South Carolina and downright confounded looking for him in the Texas Hill Country. Sure, a 150 is occasionally killed in both of these places, but the odds of any one individual doing it are something akin to winning the state lottery. Why fight the odds? Hunt where bucks of the size you hope to shoot live. You've still got to find and kill him, and when it comes to trophy whitetails, that's a tall enough order in the best of circumstances.

Factors Affecting Size At A Given Place

A growing number of serious trophy hunters are taking more then a passing interest in learning all they can about the three cornerstones of buck size—genetics, nutrition and age. Some are motivated by the knowledge that a better understanding of these factors not only enhances their enjoyment and success, but also better arms them in the fight to protect our sport. Others, and this number is swelling rapidly, have a practical need to thoroughly understand the workings of these factors—they are managing their own property for more and better bucks. Regardless of how one may use the information, all trophy hunters need to understand the role of age, nutrition and genetics. Let's see how they figure into the trophy prospects of a particular area.

Genetics determine the size potential of the bucks at any given age. The quality of nutrition determines how much of that size potential is actually realized at a given age. Finally, age is required for bucks to reach their maximum size under the existing genetic and nutritional realities. (In a later chapter about "secretive super bucks," we're going to look at two other factors that may well affect the antler size of an individual buck and why some bucks may sport their best racks when "on-the-mend" after what is normally considered peak antler years. But, the three factors discussed here remain the primary ones affecting antler size as a whole within a herd.)

The importance of genetics on antler size cannot be overstated, either in regards to its impact on an individual animal or on the collective potential of the herd. Genetics establish the ultimate potential for antler size before a buck ever eats a mouthful or lives one day. In reality, however, the genetic size potential of bucks is seldom achieved because of inadequate nutrition, largely from overcrowding, and/or the lack of age, mainly due to hunting pressure. It is even possible for the natural genetic potential of a herd to be eroded through the heavy, longterm harvest of the better-antlered bucks.

More and more across the whitetail's range, antlers, as well as body size, are shrinking because of poor nutrition. And in many cases, the habitat continues to be degraded as too many mouths vie for too little food year after year. The effect is cumulative and longterm. In too many areas, the quality of the habitat has been so severely damaged (and the carrying capacity reduced) that nothing short of a major die-off or a huge

Bucks like this 180-class Canadian giant killed by Ken Cantley are the product of herds with plenty of older bucks that have access to good vittles. It's unlikely that an out-of-balance herd would produce a trophy like this. Photo by author.

antlerless harvest, which would be politically unpalatable, will provide the time and relief necessary for the vegetation to fully recovery. From a trophy hunter's perspective, overcrowding has seriously cut into trophy prospects. How much? Just look back at the bucks that were killed in your own backyard when the herd was first expanding in your area. Some of those early bucks were giants by today's standards. Why? In all likelihood, better nutrition.

Unless we are in a position to manage property, the fact is that most of us can do little to change the existing genetic, nutritional and age status of a deer herd. Thus, while it is necessary to understand their roles, there is not much point in dwelling on the unrealized "potential" of a place. Rather, as we evaluate our hunting options, most of us are better served simply by determining the size of the mature bucks actually being taken in a given place and developing our where-to strategies based on that.

To that end, there are a couple of aspects of size that must be considered. The first is what we'll call the "average" size of mature bucks, though rather than a true average, it is actually the size representing the greatest number of bucks. Two, the "range of sizes" spanned by mature bucks within the herd. This second aspect, the size range, is a critical factor in determining the number of better-than-average mature bucks, i.e., trophy bucks, and the realistic top-end size. While nutrition and genetics play critical roles in the size attained by mature bucks at any particular location, the variable most often of foremost concern to trophy hunters when evaluating a particular place is the buck age structure, which is a function of hunting pressure.

The following graph, which is representative of a South Texas ranch, will show far better than words how the various levels of pressure affect the size, as well as numbers, of mature bucks in a given herd.

First, note the difference in the total number of mature bucks as revealed by the maximum height of the curve. Then, notice where each of the three curves peak along the horizontal size line. This represents the average size of mature bucks. On the light pressure curve, the average size is 130. On the moderate curve, it's in the low 120s. The heavy pressure curve peaks about 115. Why? In heavily pressured herds, most of its few mature bucks are only 3 1/2 years old. Under moderate pressure, there are

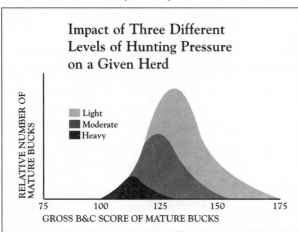

Impact of Three Different Levels of Hunting Pressure on a Given Herd

RELATIVE NUMBER OF MATURE BUCKS

Light
Moderate
Heavy

75   100   125   150   175
GROSS B&C SCORE OF MATURE BUCKS

more older, thus larger, bucks. In lightly hunted populations, all the mature age classes are represented. Since a buck is not normally as big at 3 1/2 or 4 1/2 as he will be at 5 1/2, 6 1/2 or 7 1/2, typically considered peak-antler years, it is easy to see why a population of bucks that averages older will also average larger.

For the serious trophy hunter, the range of sizes spanned is the telling feature, especially the right-hand extension of the curve. This defines the true trophy prospects by revealing the relative number and size of the larger-than-average bucks (i.e., trophies) and the top-end size.

The more the pressure, the less daylight movement and the less predictability in deer patterns.

In heavily hunted populations, almost any mature buck is a prize and holding out for a better-than-average one can be futile. Under moderate pressure, mature bucks are sufficiently abundant to justify passing an average mature buck in anticipation of a trophy eventually coming along, though the upper size is limited by a lower average age (and cropping of the better antlered bucks before they reach maximum size). In lightly hunted populations with a well-distributed buck age structure, the top-end size will be greater because of the increased presence of older, peak-sized bucks. Think of top-end bucks as the tip of a pyramid of mature bucks—as the pyramid's base of mature bucks shrinks or swells, so does the height of the peak. To have a few true top-end bucks, you have to have lots of mature bucks undergirding them. Only where the bucks are inherently very large, such as the Midwest and Central Canada, do younger mature bucks reach top-end size with any consistency.

Buck Huntability

Even when trophy bucks are present, the hunter still has to be able to kill them and the degree of difficulty in doing so varies from place to place. Buck huntability is a factor to be reckoned with, but it ranks well behind mature buck numbers and size in importance.

Many factors bear on buck huntability. For instance, timing of the season is a big one. If the hunting season fails to coincide with the rut, buck huntability is greatly reduced. Another factor is the herd density relative to the carrying capacity. In overcrowded herds, the incessant need for food makes deer easier to concentrate on food sources and more likely to move during daylight hours. Access to hunting land and the size of the properties that can be hunted by an individual also figure into huntability. Obviously, weather, moon phases and the like enter the picture, but these things have a temporary impact and that impact is essentially the same from place to place. There are, however, two overriding variables affecting buck huntability—hunting pressure (there it is again) and habitat conditions.

We've already talked about the negative effect hunting pressure has on deer activity, and we'll discuss it more in the upcoming chapter on deer movement. Suffice to say here, it both suppresses and alters movement. The more the pressure, the less daylight movement and the less predictability in deer patterns. Even rutting activity is suppressed by high pressure. Feeding patterns are affected to an even greater degree. The extent to which deer react to human pressure should not be underestimated.

The huntability of the habitat is also a consideration. Some places are inherently easy to hunt. Perhaps they offer quiet hunting routes, open lanes, fields, funnels, bottlenecks or other features that increase visibility or channel deer activity, greatly aiding the hunter in his trophy quest. Strategically located hills or bluffs, for instance, can be quite hunter-friendly. I once hunted an isolated string of hills in Mexico that ran through miles of great country, allowing me a bird's eye view of all the goings-on. In the Plains and Prairies, I've slipped along high bluffs overlooking riverbottoms that gave me an almost unobstructed view right into the thick cover below, making for a very effective hunt. On the other hand, some places are just plain hard to hunt. Thick cover, rough terrain, swamps, deep snow, inaccessibility, unbroken tracts of uniform cover, etc., can make for difficult hunting. Still, I much prefer tough hunting country with trophy bucks than easy country without them!

Chapter Four

Tale of the Tape– What the Record Book Says

I T'S ALWAYS GOOD TO USE HARD DATA to support assumptions. When it comes to the question of where the best places are for trophy bucks, we do have a standard reference we can look to for some hard facts. That reference is the Boone & Crockett (B&C) records, the official listing of the biggest bucks ever killed. I've used the B&C records as just such a reference in a couple of other books because it gives us some very useful information. However, the record book certainly does not tell us all we need to know about where trophies are found. Let me explain.

First, the number of bucks officially recorded does not necessarily even reflect the number of record animals that have been killed in a particular place. For instance, a comparatively small percentage of the "book" bucks shot in the Canadian provinces are ever entered in the B&C records. By contrast, in tradition-rich states like Wisconsin and Minnesota, where big buck shows and programs have been underway for years, few record-book deer go unrecognized.

Knowing where record-book bucks have been killed can tell us much about today's trophy prospects. Thomas Dellwo killed this 199 3/8-point typical in Missoula County, Montana, in 1974. Photo by Duncan Dobie, courtesy of North American WHITETAIL.

The fact that not all record bucks make it to official B&C status in Canada was driven home to me several years ago during a Manitoba hunt. A friend and I were looking over some new country when we saw a good buck cross a field and go into a woodlot. We stopped at the nearby farmhouse to ask permission to hunt the buck. The farmer, who was as friendly as could be, asked us what we were hunting.

"Whitetails," I said.

His response was immediate and adamant. "Not any of them 'round here. Only thing we got is jumpers."

Pointing, I persisted, "We just saw one over there in that field."

"Nope, that woulda been a jumper. Ain't no whitetails here, eh," he replied with a certain finality.

I guess I was a little slow on the uptake, but it finally hit me that a jumper was indeed a whitetail! So, I changed my approach.

"I guess he did look like a jumper. Mind if we hunt your woodlot?"

"Go ahead," he happily responded.

More to be friendly than anything else, I kept the conversation going. "Ever see any big jumpers around here?"

"Naw, all about the same. Oh, I guess we do see some nice'uns around. My boy killed one with peculiar horns last year. Wasn't that big, just peculiar. Round back of the barn, I think that's where we chunked it, eh."

My friend, who was a fledging hobby antler collector, had perked up at the prospects of a "peculiar" Canadian rack.

"Think we could see it?" he asked expectantly.

We proceeded around back of his barn, working our way through a graveyard of old farm equipment and discarded farm paraphernalia. The farmer finally bent over a tangled mass of rusted fencing wire and started jerking and grunting. A minute later, he produced the freeze-dried head of a buck…netting 209 non-typical! I know because my friend bought the rack for $50! The farmer seemed a little ashamed for taking so much money for a set of jumper antlers that "whatn't that big, just peculiar."

A heavily hunted place will see a much higher percentage of its big bucks shot each year and fewer carried over to provide good trophy hunting the following year.

It used to be that way in Canada, but it has changed some now. Still, many record bucks never make it to the hallowed ranks of B&C.

Hunting pressure is another reason the book may not tell the whole story of wherein lies the best chance to shoot a trophy. Where pressure is light, the record tally is achieved through harvesting a lower percentage of the available trophy bucks, leaving plenty of live big bucks to carry over to next year. On the other hand, a heavily hunted place will see a much higher percentage of its big bucks shot each year and fewer carried over to provide good trophy hunting the following year. For instance, New Brunswick and Mississippi both have about 27 bucks currently listed, but lightly hunted New Brunswick has achieved that number with far less pressure and has record bucks dying of old age there every year. Much heavier hunted Mississippi, on the other hand, has laid claim to its 27 B&Cs by mounting enough pressure to account for darn-near every record buck that walks that fine deer state in any given year. You can't hope to draw a bead on bucks that have already been shot; you need bucks that are still in the woods walking around. The record book won't always tell you where that is.

Also, our goal in this book is not to identify the best places to shoot a record buck. If a record buck is the only thing of interest, statistics already say you're playing in a game you're bound to lose. We're interested in identifying places that offer reasonable odds of yielding a trophy buck based on the size standards of the "collective universe of trophy hunters," which I can assure you is well below record size! Still, we can learn much from what the record book tells us. After all, a record buck is at the very top of the size pyramid, and for every book buck listed, many other great trophy bucks undergird that pyramid in that state or province. This fact alone dictates that we pay close attention to what the record book tells us.

(Note: All B&C data was compiled from the 3rd Edition *Records Of North American Whitetail Deer* by Dave Boland, one of the most prolific B&C scorers around.)

THE HOMES OF ALL-TIME B&C BUCKS

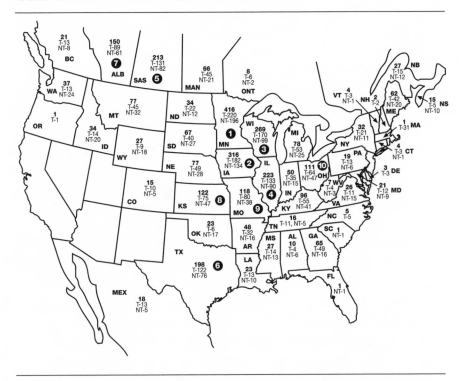

With 416 book bucks, Minnesota stands at the head of the record book and continues to turn out record bucks at an impressive clip. But,

Minnesota's top standing is being assaulted by a new challenger, Iowa, which out-produced Minnesota 219 to 162 from 1980 through 1994 and 88 to 54 in the last five years of that period. At 319 total record bucks, Iowa has just surpassed previous No.2 Wisconsin, which had held that position for decades. Wisconsin's 269 record bucks are enough to give it the No.3 position for now, but I look for it to drop back another slot soon because Illinois, currently No.4 at 223, is closing fast. In fact, Illinois has accounted for more B&C bucks than any other state in the '90s.

Regardless of the order of ranking, the four-state area of Iowa, Minnesota, Wisconsin and Illinois has accounted for 1,224 record bucks, an amazing 37 percent of the all-time total across the entire continent! In the United States only, these four states claim an overwhelming 44 percent of the record book! Throw in the neighboring states of Nebraska, Missouri, Indiana, Michigan and Ohio, and you've pretty well defined the hotbed of B&C production in the U.S. In fact, seven of the top 10 all-time B&C states or provinces are in the Midwest.

If seven of the top 10 B&C producers are in the Midwest, where are the other three? Two of them are right where you would expect—in Central Canada, namely Saskatchewan and Alberta. With 213 B&Cs, Saskatchewan holds the No.5 slot and is sure to move up. Saskatchewan's trophy potential was broadcast loud and clear in 1993 when Milo Hanson of Biggar, Saskatchewan, shot the new world-record typical, a wide 12-pointer scoring 213 5/8. Alberta has 150 B&Cs to its credit and now stands at No.7, though it is destined to a higher standing. And, the truth is that Saskatchewan and Alberta, as well as western Manitoba, are even better than the numbers reveal. A great number of the

A great number of Canada's bucks are never measured or registered with B&C...one Saskatchewan record-keeping organization has over 400 possible B&C bucks listed!

bucks killed there never see a tape, and many of those that are measured never are registered with B&C. One Saskatchewan record-keeping organization has over 400 possible B&C bucks listed! Undoubtedly, Central Canada ranks right at the pinnacle of giant whitetail regions.

At No.6 on the all-time list, Texas stands as an anomaly in the world of record whitetails, especially when you consider that most of its 198 record bucks came from hot, arid South Texas. The general trend is for buck size to increase as you move farther north into colder latitudes, but Texas defies that trend, at least in regards to antler size. This great deer state is unique...and one of the finest trophy hunting places in the world!

Georgia is also a bit of a trend-breaker. Its 65 record bucks completely overshadow the totals of the other Deep South states. Why is that? Almost certainly because of the successful stocking of inherently bigger Wisconsin and other northern deer into vacant habitat during the restoration years of the 1950s and '60s. Genetics do make a difference! Also, Ohio and Kentucky both stand out compared to their immediate neighbors. There's some sort of magic there.

TOP 20 RECENT PRODUCERS (1980-1994)

Location	No. of Bucks	Location	No. of Bucks
1. Iowa	219	11. Texas	56
2. Illinois	184	12. Michigan	45
3. Minnesota	162	13. Indiana	43
4. Wisconsin	113	14. Georgia	36
5. Saskatchewan	109	15. Manitoba	36
6. Kansas	101	16. Montana	29
7. Alberta	98	17. Nebraska	29
8. Missouri	82	18. Maine	26
9. Ohio	74	19. Idaho	23
10. Kentucky	67	20. Oklahoma	18

More than any other place in the U.S., B&C numbers probably do not accurately represent the trophy prospects in the northwestern states of Montana, Idaho and Washington. Even today, many of the record bucks killed there never make their way to the hallowed halls of Boone & Crockett. For instance, I personally knew of nine B&Cs killed in northwest Montana during a single season a few years ago. Only three of them were reported. Many unscored B&C contenders are hanging in service stations, bars and homes throughout the Northwest. Additionally, because of low hunting pressure, a relatively small percentage of the record bucks actually walking around in these states each year is killed.

It is interesting to note the strong tendency toward non-typicals in the northwestern U.S. Non-typicals actually outnumber typicals in

Wyoming, Idaho and Washington. Apparently, this area has a genetic disposition for non-typicals. The Canadian Maritime provinces of New Brunswick and Nova Scotia also have a disproportionate ratio of non-typicals, as do Oklahoma, Alabama and Virginia. For sheer numbers of non-typicals, however, the Midwest and Central Canada still dominate. The fact is that record non-typicals can come from almost anywhere since factors other than age, nutrition and genetics—i.e., factors like hormones and perhaps injury—appear to sometimes go into producing them.

Looking at "The Top 20 Recent Producers" listing (previous page), the emergence of the Midwest as the dominant trophy region in the U.S. becomes clear. I used the word "emergence" purposely. With the exception of Minnesota, Wisconsin and Michigan, the Midwest hardy even had huntable populations until well into the latter half of this century. Nearly 70 percent of Iowa's record bucks have been shot since 1980. Prior

HOMES OF THE WORLD'S BIGGEST

Typicals 190+	No.	Biggest	Non-typicals 240+	No.	Biggest
1. Iowa	11	201 4/8	1. Minnesota	9	268 5/8
2. Minnesota	10	202 0/8	2. Iowa	8	282 0/8
3. Saskatchewan	9	213 5/8	3. Saskatchewan	7	265 3/8
4. Illinois	6	204 4/8	4. Kansas	6	280 4/8
5. Alberta	5	204 2/8	5. Texas	5	286 0/8
6. Kansas	5	198 2/8	6. Alberta	5	279 6/8
7. Texas	5	196 4/8	7. Ohio	4	328 2/8
8. Indiana	5	195 1/8	8. Illinois	4	267 3/8
9. Wisconsin	3	206 1/8	9. Manitoba	3	258 4/8
10. Missouri	3	205 0/8	10. Virginia	3	257 4/8
11. Montana	2	199 3/8	11. S. Dakota	3	256 1/8
12. Maine	2	193 2/8	12. Montana	3	252 1/8
13. S. Dakota	2	193 0/8	13. New Brunswick	3	249 7/8
14. New York	1	198 3/8	14. Missouri	2	333 7/8
15. Manitoba	1	197 7/8	15. Louisiana	2	281 6/8
16. Nebraska	1	194 1/8	16. Nebraska	2	277 3/8
17. Nova Scotia	1	193 6/8	17. Nova Scotia	2	273 6/8
18. Michigan	1	193 2/8	18. Idaho	2	267 4/8
19. Wyoming	1	191 5/8	19. Maine	2	259 0/8
20. Kentucky	1	191 3/8	20. Wisconsin	2	245 0/8

to that time, Illinois only had 39 of its 316 record bucks! During the 15 years beginning in 1980, Indiana listed 43 of its 50 record bucks, and 20 of them were killed in the '90s! Before 1980, Kansas only had 21 book bucks! You see the pattern.

About the only real surprise in the recent top 20 may be Kentucky, which weighed in at No.10 with 67 entries. Remember, though, that Kentucky neighbors the Midwest. Man drew state lines; they mean nothing to deer. Also, Georgia, with 36 additions since 1980, is notable as the only Deep South state to make the top 20.

> *The record book tells us that the Midwest and Central Canada are home to the biggest bucks in the world.*

In "The Homes Of the World's Biggest" listing, only Texas interrupts the dominance of the Midwest and Central Canada in both the typical and non-typical rankings. In numbers and top-end size, Texas ranks near the top for typicals and non-typicals, again defying conventional wisdom that northern deer are always bigger. The tremendous size of bucks in Minnesota, Iowa, Illinois and Saskatchewan is clear. Kansas and Alberta also post impressive numbers for giants. The strength of the Northwest, Maine and Maine's neighbors to the north, the Canadian Maritime provinces, is evident. With five typicals over 190, Indiana is a better producer than its all-time numbers would indicate. For giant non-typicals, Ohio is noteworthy. Virginia and Louisiana come in surprisingly strong for world-class non-typicals with three and two, respectively.

In summary, what the record book tells us with clarity is that the Midwest and Central Canada are homes to the biggest bucks in the world. Despite Texas' arid, seemingly desolate landscape and southern location, this marvelous trophy state stacks up admirably with the best. But again, there's more to the trophy picture than just what the record book tells us, as we'll see in the following chapters.

Chapter Five

The Ground Rules for "Last Best Places"

Deer season is hardly over before I begin pondering my strategy for next year. And, it nearly always begins with the big question—*Where am I going to hunt?*

Many factors go into my final decision, which is made only after putting in the prerequisite research and legwork. What options are available? What are the size potential and the odds of success at each place? How much time and, in some cases, money can I spend? How's the timing relative to the rut and local hunting conditions? What are the seasons and regulations? How much flexibility is there in hunting tactics?

These and other considerations go into the mix. Certainly, as I'm sure you've surmised by now, right at the top of my list is the number and size of the trophy bucks likely to be found. Generally speaking, the more and the bigger, the better. However, there is a noteworthy exception to that rule I would like to discuss before moving on.

A buck scoring 150, such as this fine 11-pointer, is considered a trophy almost anywhere. In our "last best places" discussion, we'll be looking for places that can produce deer of this quality and better. Photo by Mike Biggs.

THERE'S NO PLACE LIKE HOME...MAYBE

The exception comes when someone hunts familiar territory, especially near his home. You see, it is possible for a hunter to have greater success year after year in a familiar place with lower trophy prospects than in a strange land with higher trophy prospects. Why? Because familiarity with the land and the deer on it gives him a huge edge, as does the sheer time he may be able to put in before and during the season. Not only can that edge translate into better odds of killing any trophy, it can bolster the chances that the trophy he takes near home will be more toward the upper-end of the relative trophy scale for that area. Of course, this scenario is predicated on the home tuff having sufficient, albeit less than the foreign soil, numbers of trophies and that some of them can satisfy the hunter's size standards. No amount of familiarity will overcome the absence of the very thing you're after.

> *It's possible for a hunter to have great success year after year in a familiar place, even if trophy prospects are lower.*

I have seen the advantages of home turf played out many times, both in my own hunting and that of others. I've lived in Montana long enough to hunt five seasons as a resident. During that time, I've killed two bucks in the 150s and a gross 179 and 182. The last two are certainly near top-end for the area. I can't claim that same relative success in the places I've traveled to and hunted, even though some of them have better trophy prospects than northwest Montana. I know many other hunters who work hard at home and consistently sort out better bucks than do others who travel to the best trophy areas on earth.

QUALIFICATIONS FOR CONSIDERATION

In the following chapters, we're going to look at the last best places for trophy bucks, but before we move on, I want to set some qualifications for our discussion. One, we're going to approach this on a big-picture level. We'll be looking at the major regions and states throughout North America that, as a whole, offer good trophy hunting. It is impossible to deal with all the exceptions that exist at a micro-level. As more and more management programs come onboard, especially in the South, the number of tract-by-tract exceptions will continue to grow.

Also, we're going to set high trophy standards for our discussions; otherwise, we'll have to cover too many places. Almost all trophy hunters, even those who can travel to the best places on earth, consider a buck grossing 150 to be big. To put a buck of that size into context, I seriously doubt whether more than two or three dozen 150-plus bucks are killed annually in my home state of Georgia, and that's out of an annual

Though the lure of big bucks in some faraway land may be strong, hunting near home has a couple of big pluses going for it, namely more hunting time and an intimate familiarity with the land and local deer. This Midwest bowhunter took full advantage of those pluses. Photo by Troy Huffman.

harvest of more than 350,000 deer in the best Deep South trophy state! (*WHITETAIL* magazine's Fort Perry Plantation in Southwest Georgia is about to raise those numbers significantly. We'll talk more about this unique management-research facility later.) A 150 is exceptional anywhere, and even the most serious trophy hunters recognize 150 as the hallowed mark for a trophy, much like the 10-pound mark is for largemouth bass. So, our discussion will center around places capable of producing bucks of that size and larger, though I will make passing comments on a couple of notable areas for trophies a bit under that mark.

What we've learned about the roles of the cornerstones for buck size—age, nutrition and genetics—will serve as the guiding parameters in our quest for trophy hotspots. For the necessary age, we need a population subjected to relatively low pressure. To realize a high nutritional plane, the area must have good inherent fertility and/or agriculture and the herd density must be maintained within the carrying capacity of the land. Then, because of our high trophy standards, the bucks must be inherently large. Wow! Our search has just been narrowed down! Increasingly, we're having to turn to management on private lands to meet this criteria, but happily, there are a few big chunks of "natural" trophy country left. Interestingly, most of them lie on the fringes of whitetail habitat, as we'll see.

NAMING NAMES

I'm going to come at this through the backdoor. First, let's talk about the places we can drop from consideration. Those places include much of the heart of U.S. whitetail country. Namely, the East, except for Maine, and the South. Most of the nation's deer live in these two regions, as do most of the people. This is not to say these regions don't offer great deer hunting; they do. They're just not great trophy places when your target is a 150. The main problems are heavy buck pressure and overcrowding. Some areas, particularly the sandy coastal regions, also fall short in the inherent fertility department. Though history tells us the genetic potential of these two regions is not quite up to that of some others, both are capable of turning out mighty fine bucks, including some well over 150. It's just that other factors are working against them.

Happily, there are a few big chunks of "natural" trophy country left. Interestingly, most of them lie on the fringes of whitetail habitat.

But, there is good news for these two regions—both have vast potential for intensive private land management for big bucks. Why do I say that? Several reasons—lots of arable private land, nearly all rural land is good whitetail habitat, a long growing season, plenty of rainfall and the potential for high reproduction. The South, as well as some Eastern states, has the additional advantages of long hunting seasons, liberal regulations and the potential to grow year-round agricultural crops attractive to deer. All these things are important elements in a revolutionary new private land management strategy that will bring amazing results on tracts as small as a few hundred acres. We'll talk about this benchmark new strategy in detail later in this book. Suffice to say, the trophy prospects on many private tracts in the South and East are destined to improve in the future with management.

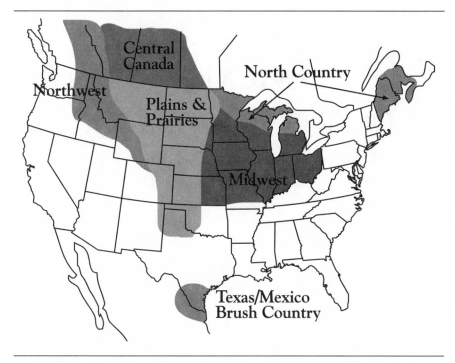

On to the places that do hold the potential to yield 150-class trophies. (See the accompanying map.) Let's identify them here, and then we'll talk about each in the following chapters. We'll group similar, contiguous areas together without regard to state or even country lines. The last best places for trophy bucks are the Texas/Mexico Brush Country, Plains and Prairies, Northwest, North Country, Midwest and Central Canada.

Every year, many 150-plus bucks are taken in these regions, but the trophy prospects are by no means the same in all the regions. There is great region-to-region variance in both the size potential and hunter success. A couple of them, namely the North Country and Northwest, are capable of producing huge bucks, but the odds that any given hunter, you for instance, could go there cold turkey and come home with a 150 are slim. Still, the bucks are there and that's our primary concern here.

Chapter Six

Texas/Mexico Brush Country–the Unlikely "Promised Land"

IF YOU DRAW A LINE ACROSS TEXAS from Corpus Christi northwest to San Antonio west to Del Rio, then everything south of that line would be what is appropriately called the "Brush Country." The Rio Grande River forms the western boundary of the Texas Brush Country, but its trademark habitat doesn't end there. It continues on about 75 miles inland into Mexico and forms what we'll call Mexico's Brush County. In this discussion, I'm going to primarily talk about South Texas, though some of what I have to say will apply directly to Mexico as well. After covering Texas, we'll briefly discuss hunting in Mexico and compare it to South Texas.

SOUTH TEXAS

For me, December 1982 marked the fulfillment of a lifelong dream—hunting the fabled Texas Brush Country. I had long read about the fabulous Texas ranches of whitetail legend and lore, ranches like the King, Kenedy, Piloncillo, East, Jones, Cameron and Maltsberger. I dared

At first glance, South Texas looks like a sea of dry brush that wouldn't support an anorexic rabbit, but is that ever a misconception! This semi-arid land is home to some of the finest trophy whitetail hunting in the world! Photo by Mike Biggs.

not hope that I would ever actually hunt such ranches, but in 1982, I found myself headed to the very heart of the Brush Country, to the Cameron Ranch no less! What I experienced there opened my eyes to a whole new world of deer hunting and began a love affair with South Texas that is unabated to this day!

The lure of South Texas has pulled me back there every year since 1982, and the Lord willing, I'll continue to return every December until the proverbial fat lady hits her high note. I've been lucky enough to hunt several of the top ranches in Texas, and I've never tired of hunting this hot, dusty land. In fact, if someone were to get me in a headlock, I would have to confess that South Texas is my favorite place to hunt whitetails, as evidenced by my recent purchase of a ranch there.

True, there are bigger bucks in other places, like Canada and the Midwest. And, there are places with more deer, like the Texas Hill Country or the riverbottoms of the Plains and Prairies. While the Brush Country may not have the very biggest bucks or the most deer, what it does have is *more big* bucks than any other place of like size on earth!

And, the top-end size, which pushes well into record-class, is plenty big enough for me! Plus, in my opinion, big Texas bucks are the most striking and handsome of all whitetails.

South Texas hunting is just plain enjoyable. The climate during the December and January rut is usually pleasant. Lots of other wildlife, such as javelina, coyotes, bobcats, wild hogs and a myriad of bird species, spice up the experience. The hunting options range the full spectrum, from stand-hunting to still-hunting from rattling to Texas' own unique tactic, high-racking (riding around in an elevated platform mounted on a vehicle, essentially a mobile treestand). The bucks are plentiful, big and, because of low pressure, usually doing the things that come natural. Because the deer-hunting tradition runs so deep, there's an excitement knowing you're part of a time-honored hunting culture shared by countless others who appreciate it as much as you do. All in all, hunting in South Texas is a unique experience.

A happy combination of factors contributes to South Texas' great hunting. To start with, the area consists primarily of large ranches, many 10,000 to 25,000 acres and some over 100,000. Many of these ranches have a history of zealously protecting and carefully managing their deer, resulting in low hunting pressure. And owing to a long tradition of trophy hunting, the South Texas harvest is the most selective anywhere. Hunters often look over many good bucks en route to something special. Few immature bucks are taken if any type of management is in place. As a result, the effective hunting pressure is even lower than the actual hunter-days applied. This makes for an excellent buck age structure and plenty of mature bucks.

In South Texas, few immature bucks are taken if any type of management is in place. As a result, the effective hunting pressure is even lower than the actual hunter-days applied.

There's another unique factor in South Texas' big-buck equation. Although the region supports a high deer population, periodic droughts and heavy predation, especially on fawns, tend to serve as a built-in mechanism to prevent overcrowding. As a result, relatively unhunted herds can stay in balance with their habitat, which allows for the virtual stockpiling of older, bigger bucks. This definitely is not the norm in most populations. You would have to look to the northern fringe areas, where

South Texas has put smiles on many a face by producing huge whitetail bucks like this impressive 170-class 11-pointer taken in Maverick County by ace trophy hunter Bobby Parker, Jr. Photo courtesy of Bobby Parker, Jr.

deer populations are limited by bitter cold and deep snow, to find a similar situation. This self-limiting population mechanism explains in part why some of the best trophy hunting today is on the fringe of the whitetail's range.

Additionally, when the Brush Country gets a little rain here and there, it is capable of providing excellent nutrition, which translates into high numbers of bigger deer. This hot, semi-desert land is covered with thorny brush that at first glance doesn't look like it would support an anorexic rabbit, but is that ever a wrong impression! The soil is very fertile, and the scraggly looking plants are deceptively nutritious. In fact, I know of no other place that can match the variety of native high-protein plant species found in the Brush Country. Add very good genetics to stout nutrition and lots of older bucks, and it's easy to see why South Texas is one of the premier destination spots for serious trophy hunters.

Along the lines of climate, nutrition and deer size, I want to expound on a unique aspect of South Texas. I don't know of any other

Hunters from all over the world travel to South Texas in hopes of bumping into a giant like this 200-plus non-typical. This fabled land is undoubtedly the most intensively managed region in the country, and whitetails are of major economic importance to landowners there. Photo by Mike Biggs.

deer population that regularly fluctuates as much in antler quality from one year to the next, even when the age structure remains essentially constant. South Texas is a boom-or-bust environment revolving around the abundance of rainfall. True, even in bad years, there are always good bucks in South Texas, but in good years, there are many great bucks there. Studies have shown that the difference in the average antler size of mature bucks between a good and bad year can be as much as 20 B&C points. That's a tremendous difference! But, what is most remarkable about South Texas is that one of the very worst years can be followed immediately by one of the best—all because of a big jump in the nutritional plane and the unique ability of South Texas deer to respond immediately to that better nutrition! Typically, recovery is a gradual process, taking place on a linear basis over years. Not so in South Texas.

Perhaps no two years better illustrate that point than 1996 and '97. The awful drought of 1996, among the worst in Texas history, resulted in one of the poorest antler years ever in South Texas. Only a mere handful of record-class bucks were killed, and most of them came off managed properties. Four of us from *WHITETAIL* magazine hunt a fabulous ranch in the Brush Country every year and usually take bucks in the

160 to 170-class. In 1996, only one buck in the 150s was killed. Hardly anything better was even seen. But ah, what a difference a year makes!

In 1997, abundant rains fell, especially in the critical springtime, and the antlers exploded in the well-watered Brush Country. On the same ranch we had hunted in '96, the four of us in 1997 killed three bucks over 170, two of which topped 180! The fourth guy eventually settled on a 10-pointer scoring 162 after passing up better ones. Statewide, the contrast between the two years was just as startling. Where only a handful of record-class bucks showed up in 1996, they were almost commonplace in 1997. Many deer contests saw all kinds of new records established, and the number of giant entries reached unheard of heights. In fact, more B&C bucks, over 30 by most counts, were killed in 1997 than during any other year previous, though many were not entered into the record books for ranch-security reasons. In essence, what we had in 1996 and '97 in Texas was one of the very worst years for antler growth followed the next year by one of the best. Biologically speaking, that is remarkable...and unique in the whitetail world.

What could explain this incredible one-year swing from very bad to very good? Two factors. One, the habitat is capable of yielding a tremendously high nutritional plane...when it gets rain. The capability is always there but the rain isn't. But when the rains come at the right time of year, a veritable explosion takes place in the nutrition available to deer. The brush puts on nutritious new growth and highly nutritious forbs and weeds seem to sprout up almost overnight. With well-timed rains, the fortunes of South Texas deer turn immediately from just getting by to prospering!

South Texas is a boom-or-bust environment revolving around the abundance of rainfall.

The second factor may seen obvious, but indeed, it is not a given. The deer of that semi-arid, boom-or-bust environment are uniquely adapted to maintain themselves at subsistence level during the hard times and to respond immediately and dramatically once rain creates surplus nutrition. In drought times, the surprisingly protein-rich brush becomes the mainstay of a reasonably sufficient nutritional plane, explaining why there are always a few good deer on the better ranches even in water-deficient years. Normally, during those drought times, the primary indexes of herd health—body and antler size and reproductive rate—drop and the deer seem to be in a holding pattern, awaiting rain. Then when it comes, the deer, like the parched land on which they live, seem to burst into renewed life, sparking with remarkable rapidity increased reproduction and body and antler size. Texas deer, like no other subspecies, are capable of immediately responding to surplus nutrition and, though they may be coming out of a stressed condition, using that surplus to restore themselves to a healthy state.

The management implications of that are enormous. If a land manager could provide his herd with surplus nutrition every year, then he could eliminate the boom-or-bust cycle to a great extent and take advantage of the tremendous potential of a herd geared toward an immediate and exaggerated response to surplus nutrition. More and more managers are realizing this and attempting to provide a consistent high nutritional plane year after year. Most efforts have been directed toward supplemental feeds and enhancing native habitat by mechanical means, i.e., roller-chopping and limited clearing, and managing cattle to minimize competition with deer. More recently, however, food plots, long thought to be impractical in that arid region, have begun to emerge as a tremendous new option to greatly elevate the nutritional plane of ranches. We'll talk more about this later when we get to our discussion of food-source management.

Ok, all that said, let's move on to what to expect in South Texas. But before we do, I want to point out that I will only be talking about the better ranches. Hunting quality varies considerably from tract to tract almost everywhere, but this is especially so in South Texas. The reason is deer management. Many ranches practice intense trophy management, sometimes including supplemental feeding and the use of game-proof fences to contain the herd. Others have more modest programs that limit harvests and promote quality to varying degrees. Some places have no management at all and have depleted buck populations.

What can you expect? To start with, it's probably safe to say that South Texas is the best place on earth for bucks scoring from 120 to 150, though you're starting to get into fairly rarified air as you approach 150. Some of the better riverbottom ranches in the Plains and Prairies region may top South Texas for bucks of that size, but the Plains and Prairies as a whole can't match the more widespread trophy output of South Texas.

By the time you get to 150-plus bucks, you're dealing with a rela-

You wouldn't have to get me in a headlock to squeeze the truth out—South Texas is my favorite place to hunt whitetails. This 26 1/2-inch wide, 180-class 12-pointer from Dimmit County, a top trophy producer, is just one of the many "big reasons" I have for feeling that way. Photo by Mark Lubin.

tively small percentage of all mature bucks. Yet, because of the sheer volume of mature bucks, South Texas still competes favorably with the giant buck regions of the Midwest and Central Canada for the number of 150s. Again, this only applies to the better ranches. If a ranch is hunted much and suffers from any significant "high-grading," 150s will be very hard to come by. That's why many of the commercial ranches in Texas, despite having lots of mature bucks, seldom yield 150s. A 150 represents a rather fragile upper-end resource in South Texas, and to have a reasonable crack at such a buck, you must hunt managed or big, lightly hunted ranches.

If 150s are a challenge, then you know 160-class bucks are going to be tough to come by in South Texas. Sure, one can show up on almost any ranch, but if you have specific designs on taking a 160 home, you've got to seek out the best ranches. Certainly, South Texas as a whole ranks behind the Midwest and Central Canada for bucks in the 160s. But if you're on just the right ranch...well, four of us from *WHITETAIL* maga-

John Teeter of North Carolina went to Mexico for one of its big bucks and was not disappointed. This 15-pointer grosses 196! Photo courtesy of John Teeter.

zine once killed four 160-plus bucks during a hunt on a huge, lightly hunted ranch! Such a feat would be difficult to pull off in either the Midwest or Canada. The high number of mature bucks, the large acreage, the light pressure and the hunting flexibility made it possible in South Texas…and the fact that 160s were there in the first place!

Unless you are hunting one of the best ranches in South Texas, to go there with the expectation of shooting a buck in the 170s is tantamount to expecting a new Corvette to appear in your garage because you found a four-leaf clover. But, stranger things have happened. After all, I've killed several 170s in South Texas! It's not impossible, but to have any realistic hope, you've got to skim off the top of the very best ranches in the state. When it comes to bucks of this size, South Texas doesn't stack up very well with the Midwest or Central Canada, either in terms of actual numbers or percentage of the buck kill. Still, South Texas does turn out plenty of book-class deer each year, especially when the rains hit right.

MEXICO

Let's now move across the Rio Grande River to Mexico. While much of what has been said about South Texas applies to Mexico, the land and the deer herds have been exploited more there. Plus, management is not nearly as widespread or as intense, although that's changing as more and more American influence filters down. Overall, trophy hunting in Mexico does not quite measure up to that of South Texas and there's even greater ranch-to-ranch variance in habitat quality and deer populations. It's possible to be standing on a virtual biological desert while just across the fence is a ranch teeming with good bucks. Choose well when you go to Mexico so that doesn't happen to you.

While Mexico does not have nearly as many mature bucks as South Texas, which reduces hunter success, the average size is at least as large.

Even on the better ranches, deer populations tend to run lower than in South Texas. The reason for this is twofold. One, the range has been grazed heavier by livestock and does not support as many deer. Two, poaching has been a long-standing problem. But, there is some good in all this. Since overcrowding is seldom a problem, bucks can reach impressive sizes if they live long enough. While Mexico does not have nearly as many mature bucks as South Texas, which reduces hunter success, the average size is at least as large. Heavier mass seems to be a common characteristic of the bigger bucks. Even if the odds of scoring on a 150-class buck fall below that of Texas, Mexico sometimes surprises hunters with a real upper-end buck. On the good ranches, a 150 is an ever-present possibility and hard hunting and time can yield 160-plus bucks. Beyond that, you're playing some pretty long odds, but one of the things I like about Mexico is that you never know what might walk out.

Chapter Seven

The Plains and Prairies–Ribbons and Pockets of Greatness

WHEN MOST EASTERN HUNTERS think of the Plains and Prairies, they see mule deer and antelope bouncing through vast wheat fields, shimmering grasslands or perhaps over rugged sagebrush-studded hills spider-webbed by coulees. Yes, that's a side of the Plains and Prairies region, but there's another side—the side that is home to some of the finest whitetail hunting in the country.

It's true that the great bulk of this region is primarily the domain of the mule deer, antelope and even the bison. They claim the drier upland areas without much of a challenge from the competitive whitetail. That is probably why many people are unaware that the whitetail deer also has an unyielding foothold in the wide-open spaces of America's midsection. But, the ever-adaptable whitetail has claimed for itself the

The fertile riverbottoms of the Plains and Prairies support some of the highest concentrations of whitetails in the world. Agriculture, especially when irrigated, is the key to these incredible populations. Photo by Mike Biggs.

best parts—the fertile, well-watered stream and riverbottoms and the fingers of cover radiating off them. In essence, whitetail populations are largely confined to ribbons of habitat in a vast, wide-open region otherwise largely devoid of whitetails.

Having said that, I must hasten to note some exceptions. One, whitetails have definitely begun their invasion into the uplands formally reserved for the mule deer. Whitetails are showing up in places you would think no self-respecting whitetail would ever show himself, like under a clump of sagebrush where the nearest thing to a tree is a fence post on the distant horizon. Yes, they're beginning to scatter out there, but we are not going to focus on the vagrant deer of the region, even though some of them are real whoppers!

The other notable exceptions to the waterway whitetails are the populations in the isolated mountain ranges scattered about the northern Plains and Prairies. Of the ones I am directly familiar with, the most noteworthy are the Bear Paw, Snowy and Sweetgrass mountains in Montana and the Black Hills shared by South Dakota and Wyoming. All these areas, and I'm sure others as well, offer good trophy whitetail hunting. From my experience, bucks in the Black Hills tend to run smaller than those in the Montana hills. You would be counted among the lucky few if you killed a 150 in the Black Hills, but that's not an unrealistic target in the Montana ranges, especially on the more protected ranches. In fact, the bucks in the isolated ranges of Montana are at least as big as those of the riverbottoms because overcrowding is less of a problem. However, because the riverbottoms support far more deer and because they are much more visible than those in the mountains, the chances of taking home a 150-plus buck are probably better along the watercourses. But despite lower hunter success, don't overlook the bucks in these isolated mountain ranges. Book deer are killed there every year.

The riverbottoms of the Plains and Prairies support some of the highest deer densities found anywhere, but only where agriculture is nearby. You see, the engine that drives the incredible deer production is the fertile agricultural fields often found in association with the riverbottoms. In areas without agriculture, deer densities are modest for the most part. Yet, where cover, usually in the form of cottonwoods, ash and willows, and agriculture come together in the right quantities, the number of deer can defy the imagination. I've hunted stretches of riverbottom that harbored close to a deer per acre! I've seen over 200 whitetails on a single 100-acre alfalfa field! From my observations, the highest densities and often the biggest bucks appear to be in association with irrigated alfalfa, which is a tremendous source of protein. I've also seen high populations in conjunction with sugar beets and grain crops.

> *The highest densities and often the biggest bucks appear to be in association with irrigated alfalfa, which is a tremendous source of protein.*

If you have ever doubted whether or not intensive farming, i.e., food-source management, for deer can make a difference in deer size and numbers, you have to look no further than the riverbottoms of the Plains and Prairies to see that the answer is a resounding "yes." The incredible concentrations around these food sources defy anything I have ever experienced in wild, unconfined herds. In a very real sense, riverbottom populations are not unlike high-fenced herds under intensive food-source management. After all, they are supported almost totally by agriculture and "confined" by both the open spaces and the localized nature of their food sources.

The incredible densities come with built-in problems, namely

*Throughout the Plains and Prairies—even in traditiional mule deer country—
are scattered mountain ranges that support good numbers of whitetails...and
some big ones. I shot this fine 9-pointer on Rocky Boy Indian Reservation in
central Montana's Bear Paw Mountains. Photo by Clinton Small.*

overcrowding. Too many deer leads to smaller bucks and all too often to
major die-offs. The riverbottoms are notorious for periodic outbreaks of a
disease known as "blue tongue," which can wipeout 50 percent or more of
a herd. It's a harsh way to control deer numbers, but restrictive hunting
regulations, the lack of access and sheer remoteness limit other control
measures. The die-offs do have the positive effect of bringing the herd

back in balance, thus pushing buck size back up. A visiting hunter would do well to check on when the last major die-off hit and try to time his hunt accordingly. Peak trophy production seems to occur from three to six years after a die-off. After that, overcrowding starts to take a toll on size. Frequently, die-offs cycle through the herd every six to eight years, or about the time the herd loses the retained immunity gained from the previous outbreak.

Peak trophy production seems to occur from three to six years after a die-off. After that, overcrowding takes its toll.

This is ranch country, and pressure, herd condition and habitat quality vary greatly from ranch to ranch. This is one of the problems in hunting this region. The good ranches are widely scattered, and it's hard for a visiting hunter to identify the better places and gain access. Because of the spotty nature of the resource, the whitetail outfitting industry is not very well developed.

The Plains and Prairies is perhaps the most huntable of all regions since the deer are largely confined to strips of cover and they feed mostly on open crop fields. Overall, pressure is low to low-moderate, but even at that, high huntability has generally reduced the number of mature bucks and the upper-end size. The top-end there is very fragile and can be hurt by a handful of hunters in only a couple of years, which has always been a problem for outfitters. Still, low pressure and high deer densities result in one of the highest localized populations of mature bucks to be found anywhere. For sheer numbers of mature bucks, only the famed ranches of Texas come close to the better Plains and Prairie ranches. But because the deer resource is far less widespread than in Texas, the region has always taken a backseat to the Lone Star State.

The high numbers of deer and the very predictable travel patterns make the Plains and Prairies one of the very best places in the world for bowhunters.

The high numbers of deer and the very predictable travel patterns make the Plains and Prairies one of the very best places in the world for bowhunters. My friend Bill Jordan of Realtree Outdoor Products takes a group of about eight outdoor writers to Montana's Milk River each year on a week-long bowhunt. Nearly everybody scores, and most of the bucks make the 125 (typical) minimum for the Pope & Young archery record book. I don't know of any other place where that can be done so consistently. But even in this phenomenal place, such success doesn't just happen. Bill and Realtree video producer David Blanton, who is himself a topnotch bowhunter, do a tremendous amount of advance scouting and stand work before the hunt so the odds are stacked in favor of success before the first arrow is drawn.

The great majority of mature bucks in the Plains and Prairies range from 120 to 140. Anything over 140 is a trophy, but because of the abundance of mature bucks, respectable numbers of 150s are produced. I once sat on an alfalfa field teeming with over 50 bucks, three of which topped 150. It doesn't get much better than that! It takes some hard looking for a 160, but they are present. A few book deer are shot there every year.

Overall, the Plains and Prairies region is one of the best places to tag a 125 to 150-point whitetail. For bucks in the 150s and 160s, the better ranches there rank on par with the better ranches in South Texas. Where overcrowding is not a problem and hunting pressure is minimal, the top-end can be even better! The only problem is finding and getting on one of the scattered "better" ranches. But, the effort can bring "big" returns!

Chapter Eight

The Great Northwest– Land of Enchantment

I've combined both the Canadian and the U.S. Rockies in this region because the trophy prospects north and south of the border are essentially the same. Only the eastern front of the Alberta Rockies, where massive bucks typical of farmland Canada are sometimes shot, edges ahead of the rest of the region in terms of top-end size. Also, hunting quality tends to tail off as you move farther west into British Columbia, Washington and Oregon, although Washington certainly gives up some fine whitetails. Generally, the best hunting in the region is found in Montana and Idaho.

For outright beauty, no place can top the Great Northwest. Snow-covered mountains, postcard valleys, crystal-clear rivers and streams, unspoiled forests and all the room to roam a person could ask for await

Hunting whitetails in grizzly country is certainly novel, and that's exactly what you can do in the Northwest. This is a vast, lightly hunted region with loads of public land and plenty of big whitetails. Photo by Troy Huffman.

hunters there. The whitetail shares this marvelous land with his cousins, the mule deer, elk and moose, as well as with sheep, goats, black bears and even grizzlies. This is the land of the great Rocky Mountains, and trophy whitetails call many of the valleys and associated hillsides home.

Huntability of the region varies widely, but on the whole, it's not an easy place to hunt. This is especially so in the expansive evergreen forests that make up so much of the region's deer habitat. In areas with agriculture, huntability is better since the deer are easier to pattern and

My wife, Debbie, shot this beautiful 150-class 13-pointer in Flathead County, Montana. Note the scope cut between her eyes. For a few minutes, we weren't sure who got the worst of the shot—Debbie or the buck. Photo by author.

expose themselves in and around the agricultural food sources. Additionally, deer densities, which could be described as moderate regionwide, can vary considerably even within local areas. Figuring out where the deer are and what they're doing can be an intimidating experience when someone first tackles this big, rugged, inaccessible country. The good news is that hunting pressure is fairly low throughout the region. Only the North Country is harder to hunt than the Northwest, but higher deer populations and lower hunting pressure in the Northwest contribute to higher hunter success.

Hunting deer in big, relatively uniform country without the concentrating effect of major food sources poses special challenges. Add to this the fact that the terrain, weather and cover conditions can be physically and mentally taxing. Given all this, you can see why I say that success here depends largely on the hunter's skill and physical condition. In the big-forest areas, lots of walking and looking are sometimes required to sort out a buck…and then you've still got to get him out. In western Montana where I live and hunt, I frequently walk 10 or more miles a day on whitetail excursions, looking, glassing, checking clearcuts, rattling, tracking or whatever else the circumstances at hand dictate. It's physically demanding, but it is one of my favorite ways to hunt whitetails. I don't know of any place I had rather be when the rut hits during the last week of November.

Overall, I would say mature bucks in the Northwest average a bit larger than those of South Texas or the Plains and Prairies, but because of lower densities and huntability, the chances of killing a trophy of almost any size are less. Most mature bucks in the Northwest are in the 120 to 140 range. A 140-plus buck is considered very respectable. Bucks in the 150s are in the upper-end range but are present in encouraging numbers. I consider 150 to be a reasonable target size for a serious trophy hunter with a week or so to spare during the rut.

Success here depends largely on the hunter's skill and physical condition.

Given time and luck, a 160-plus is a possibility. As you nudge into record-class (170s), the Northwest is pretty much on equal footing with Texas and the Plains and Prairies, but behind the Midwest and Central Canada. With the vast public holdings on the U.S. side, it is safe to say this area offers the best public-land hunting for trophy whitetails in the country.

Chapter Nine

The North Country–
the Tradition Lives On

"**N**ORTH COUNTRY," THE VERY
words conjure up images of vast evergreen forests, frigid mornings, deep snow, red-plaid-coated hunters armed with Savage 99s and, of course, giant bucks. More than anywhere else, this land, namely the great deer states of Minnesota, Wisconsin, Michigan and Maine, is steeped in deer-hunting tradition. Despite its fame, hunting in the North Country is not easy. Lots of snow, extreme cold, rugged terrain, vast, unbroken woodlands and low deer densities in many areas make hunting there among the hardest anywhere, but some of the world's biggest bucks call the place home.

I've combined a lot of country into this region, from northern Minnesota, Wisconsin and Michigan eastward to Maine, New Brunswick and Nova Scotia. While very different in history and culture, the hunting

The North Country can be a tough place to hunt, but the rewards can be "huge." Bucks like this 11-pointer from northern Wisconsin have earned this region a well-deserved reputation for trophy animals. Photo by Troy Huffman.

conditions, trophy prospects and hunting styles have much in common.

Note that I haven't included Ontario and Quebec in this discussion, even though they lie right across the border from some of the North Country's best states. Yet for reasons I've never fully understood, deer there do not reach the antler size of their U.S. counterparts. It must be a combination of the soils, genetics and perhaps weather, which is characterized by severe cold and deep snow. As you move farther east into the Maritime provinces, trophy size does increase once again, especially antler mass.

Basically, the North Country is an area of vast wilderness forests that was more suited to moose than whitetails before being disturbed by the hand of man. But when man's activities, namely farming, clearing and timbering, began to transform the comparatively sterile virgin forests into croplands or, as is more often the case, regrowth woodlands, the resident whitetail populations began to spread and prosper. Even today, deer are found in greatest abundance in areas where man has replaced the

This Minnesota buck, shot by James Rath in 1974, is almost impossibly big. He is a very symmetrical non-typical scoring 231 2/8. Over the years, some of the biggest whitetails in the world have come from the famed North Country. Photo courtesy of North American WHITETAIL.

mature forests with conditions more to the deer's liking. Clearcuts are an important hub of deer and hunting activity in many of the remote areas.

Hunting pressure in the region, much of which is open to public hunting, ranges from moderate in the southern reaches to low in the northern locales. Some places, particularly northern Maine and much of the Maritime provinces of Canada, hardly have any pressure. Obviously, low pressure means a good buck age structure. Yet, mature bucks are hard to find because deer densities are so low. But when you do come across a mature buck, chances are he'll be worth a visit to the local taxidermy shop. Rack size crowds that of the Midwest and Canadian farmlands, but in body weight, North Country deer don't take a backseat to any deer. Still, difficult hunting conditions and low numbers make a 140 a trophy.

While 150s there make up a higher percentage of the mature buck population than is so for Texas, the Plains and Prairies or the Northwest, the chances of killing a 150 in the North Country are less because of lower huntability and fewer deer. Still, 160-plus bucks are killed every year. Frankly, if a hunter can look over four or five mature bucks, one of them is likely to be a whopper. Just finding them is the problem. An aggressive, physically fit hunter has a definite edge when it comes to consistently ferreting out big bucks in this challenging land.

Part of the mystique of the North Country is the expectation that something huge can walk out at any time.

Part of the mystique of the North Country is the expectation that something huge can walk out at any time. Indeed, many book deer are shot in the region every year and some are world-class. In Minnesota and Wisconsin particularly, the top-end knows almost no limit, as the record books will attest. Northern Maine, New Brunswick and Nova Scotia, all of which are poured from the same mold, have a well-deserved reputation for huge bucks. Upper Michigan's top-end falls somewhere in the middle. Despite the hunter success being lower than the other trophy areas we'll discuss, the hope and anticipation that a giant buck may appear in your sights, as has happened so many times before, is reason enough to hunt this enticing region.

Chapter Ten

The Midwest–
Land of the Giants

W E'RE INTO SOME SERIOUS BIG BUCK country now. In fact, acre for acre, I believe the *better* areas of the Midwest harbor more world-class bucks than anywhere else, including Central Canada. Obviously, both Central Canada and the Midwest have the advantages of superior genetics, fertile soils and a great abundance of nutritious agricultural foods. But, the Midwest gains a slight edge in carrying capacity through a milder climate and a bit more cover in the agricultural areas. And, the crop mix common to the Midwest, namely corn and soybeans, may be a tad better for deer than the various small grains so predominate in Canada. Yet, we're splitting hairs. Anyway you look at it, these two similar areas are neck-to-neck in the race for the title of "the big buck capital of the world."

In much of the Midwest, and farmland Canada for that matter, the greatest limiting factor is cover, not food. Most often, deer densities vary according to available cover…and, to a degree, according to the rural human population. Midwest deer numbers range from fair to good where cover is in sufficient supply. Because of limited cover, the Midwest offers high huntability. Besides the Plains and Prairies, which in many respects

The Midwest is serious big buck country. This 200-point Ohio non-typical is representative of the giants for which this productive region is rightfully renown. Ohio, especially, is famous for world-class non-typicals. Photo courtesy of Abe Miller.

is very similar, I consider the Midwest to be the most huntable of all regions, at least when it comes to hunting an individual buck once he is located.

However, hunting in the Midwest is not without obstacles. While overall pressure is moderate, some areas are subjected to fairly heavy pressure. This has taken a toll on the number and age of the mature bucks in places. Also, short seasons, weapons restrictions and, in some cases, limited firearms seasons during the peak of rut all serve as roadblocks to easy hunting and throw the odds back in the buck's favor.

And while well-defined food sources, clear travel corridors and limited bedding options make patterning Midwest bucks fairly easy, there is a fly in the ointment—you may not have access to all or even most of a buck's homerange. You see, another drawback to hunting the Midwest is the fact that most landholdings are relatively small, usually less than a square mile. Thus, bucks may spend only part of their time on any given tract. At best, this can make patterning difficult. Plus, even in the Midwest, big bucks are not everywhere. They may be widely scattered among the many small farms, and unless you know there's a big buck on the tract you're hunting, you may be looking for something that's beyond your reach. All this means that seeing a big buck in the Midwest is not necessarily the problem; killing him may be.

In an earlier chapter, I said that a hunter familiar with his home turf has a better chance of killing a top-end buck, relative to his locale,

Lengthy bow seasons that often overlap the rut, plentiful major food sources and predictable deer travel patterns make the Midwest a mecca for serious bowhunters, who kill almost as many record-book bucks there as do firearms hunters. Photo by Troy Huffman.

on his own court than he would in a place he has to travel to reach. Nowhere is this more applicable than in the Midwest. Because of the need to hunt a specific farm (as opposed to an area) and preferably even a specific buck, the resident hunter has a great advantage over the visiting hunter in the Midwest. If I lived there, you would have a hard time prying me away until I had done all the damage I could in my backyard. I know of no other place where a hard-working resident hunter has such opportunity to find and hunt a particular big buck as in the Midwest, despite moderate hunting pressure and restrictive regulations.

For serious trophy bowhunters, the Midwest is the "Promised Land." Long bow seasons overlapping the rut, easily patterned bucks, relatively little competition from gun hunters and an abundance of big bucks make the Midwest the No.1 spot on the continent for giant bucks with a bow. The record books are full of Midwestern bucks that fell to bowhunters. In fact, bowhunters account for almost as many B&C bucks in the core Midwestern states as do gun hunters! Certainly, the opportunities created by ideal archery regulations and huntable country with plenty of oversized bucks have contributed to the incredible record for bow kills, but hunters still had to take advantage of the opportunities. And they did! The great archery hunting in the Midwest has given rise to a new breed of hunter who has refined his sport to a fine art. I consider the better Midwestern bowhunters to be among the best whitetail hunters in the world!

In the Midwest, a 140-class buck hardly turns the head of serious

A cornfield, a hunter armed with a shotgun and a whopper buck— all classic ingredients of a Midwest whitetail hunt. Photo by Tom Evans, courtesy of North American WHITETAIL.

trophy hunters. If a buck makes it to age four or five in this productive environment, he has a good chance of scoring 150 or even 160. Record-book bucks are there in numbers only Central Canada can rival. For 150-class bucks, I would have to give Texas and the Plains and Prairies an edge over the Midwest because of its restrictive regulations, especially during the rut, landownership patterns and hunting pressure. But, the tables turn for bucks topping 160. And, when the discussion enters the lofty reaches of record-class, the comparison with Texas and the Plains and Prairies ends.

All things considered, I think the top-end potential, especially for typicals, is at least as good in the Midwest as that of Central Canada... and that's saying a bunch! But when your individual chances of going home with a whopper from the Midwest are compared to doing so in Central Canada, I believe Canada has a distinct edge, at least for the visiting hunter. That edge, as we've said, has nothing to do with the number of big bucks present, but rather, it goes back to the fact that the Midwest operates under regulatory handicaps, without which, frankly, the giant bucks probably wouldn't exist there in the first place. But because you can hunt the Canadian rut with a rifle and have a little more room to roam, your chances of shooting a giant, at least with a gun, are better in the frigid land of our northern neighbor.

Chapter Eleven

Central Canada–
Snow, Cold
and Monsters

WHEN I FIRST STARTED HUNTING
Central Canada in the early '80s, trophy whitetail hunting was pretty
much a novelty among the residents, who mostly hunted for meat. There
was little technical expertise on the hows and wherefores of hunting big
whitetails. In fact, I hunted with one "guide" that didn't even know it
was whitetails that made the rubs and scrapes he so often saw in the
woods! The preferred local tactics were riding around in a pickup and
deer drives, methods that began to wear on the patience of the farmers
and the landowners as the number of nonresident hunters started to grow.
During those developing years of Canada's whitetail industry, hunter success was low, hunts were often poorly organized and executed and,
frankly, much of the hunting took place under questionable, if not outright illegal, circumstances.

Today, I am happy to report much improvement. Sure, some of the
old ills are still out there, but for the most part, Canada's whitetail industry is now on solid footing, although the threat of more restrictive nonresident regulations is ever-present. These days, hunter success is much
higher, the latest strategies and tactics are now commonplace among the
guides and outfitters and, best of all, hunts are run more professionally
and ethically. Still, hunting in Canada has plenty of challenges.

Whether talking about body or antler size, the fertile prairie land of Central Canada is home to huge bucks. This 9-pointer I shot in Saskatchewan scored 167 points and weighed 260 pounds, actually a rather average live weight for trophy bucks in that region. Photo by Brent Mitchell.

The area we're calling Central Canada stretches from the front face of the Rockies in Alberta eastward through Saskatchewan to a relatively small section of west-central Manitoba. Interestingly, the best whitetail country is not right next to the U.S. border but more toward the central part of the provinces. This is because much of the southern reaches are prairies or farmland lacking cover.

Central Canada is a frigid, snowy land where the arena for a trophy hunt can be great northern forests or small woodlots dotting expansive agricultural fields or a combination of big woods and agriculture. The region is characterized by fertile prairie soils, which lie at the root of the region's big deer capacity. The deer there are among the very largest in the world in both antler and body size. For antler mass, no other place can match it. Deer densities throughout much of the region are quite modest, and in some places, particularly in the more heavily forested areas, numbers can be downright low. Harsh winters, predation from coyotes and wolves and, in some farming areas, the lack of cover act to hold numbers down and prevent overcrowding. Generally, hunting in Central Canada is a game for the determined and stout-hearted, owing to relatively low deer densities, extreme cold, poor logistics and, in some cases, restrictive regulations and nocturnal tendencies in the deer, especially in the farmlands. Trophy hunting there is not unlike Babe Ruth's batting—there's a good chance of striking out but you never know when that long homerun may come along!

Hunting in Central Canada wears two distinctly different faces—agricultural hunting and forest hunting. Farmland hunting is very similar to the Midwest, and forest hunting is much like that of the North Country Region, i.e., low deer densities, large unbroken woodlands and rugged, inaccessible terrain. Assuming cover is in adequate supply, deer densities tend to be higher where the herd gets a nutritional boost from farm crops. Also, the bucks are larger, at least in rack size, and are easier to hunt where agriculture makes up part of their range. The good thing about the forest areas is that pressure tends to be lower there and deer tend to move more freely during the daylight hours. Some of the more populated or cover-short farm country has enough pressure to make age a problem in trophy production.

In our discussion of the Midwest, I said Central Canada had a distinct edge over the Midwest in trophy prospects. Besides Canada having more room to roam and fewer people, thus less pressure, I say this for two specific reasons. The first and the biggest edge is that Canada has a long rifle season that encompasses the rut. By contrast, the states of the Midwest have either very short rifle seasons or none at all, and if rifles are allowed, it's almost always outside the rut. The other big plus for Canada is currently limited only to Saskatchewan. I'm talking about baiting, a practice confined to the northern provincial forest, which also happens to be about the only area nonresidents are allowed to hunt in Saskatchewan presently. Before the purists among us start doing back flips over baiting, let's examine the circumstances.

Just north of the farm country, a vast belt of provincial forest (Crown Land) stretches across the province. Traditionally, this has been thought of as moose country. Until the last decade or so, very little whitetail hunting was done there. And for good reason—the numbers were so low and the country so vast, even the most dogged hunters could hardly

This is a sight you may never see again—four bucks grossing over 180, all killed within two days of each other on Saskatchewan's Mosquito Indian Reservation. Only in farm-country Canada! Photo by Derek Graham.

sort out a buck of any kind, let alone look over enough to have a legitimate chance at a big one. I know; I tried it! Hunting was easier in the farm country where deer were more numerous, could be concentrated on food sources and could be more easily patterned. So, the farm country was where residents and nonresidents alike hunted...until they started butting heads and the nonresidents were relegated to the Crown Land.

Since a sizable whitetail outfitting industry had sprung up by this time—in an area, I might add, where economic options were quite limited—the more determined outfitters scrambled to keep their livelihoods alive. Since visiting clients would not pay to hunt the provincial forest at the existing hunter success levels, they began trying to improve the odds by baiting, which was a legal but largely ignored tactic. As a result of baiting, the industry not only survived, it has flourished. Today, the number of outfitters has grown so large and their vested interest in the deer herd so great that vast areas are now under what could accurately be called a supplemental feeding program, and not just during hunting season but during all the stressful cold months. Because of this, the number of deer in the forest region has actually increased and hunter success there is the highest in Canada!

Essentially, hunters' money has bolstered the size and health of a deer population and created a prosperous new industry where none existed before. Unfortunately, some resent what's going on and are clamoring

Gary Raan shot this remarkable book-class, "handlebar" buck while hunting with outfitter Carl Frohaug in upper Saskatchewan. Photo by Carl Frohaug.

to stop baiting. Now, I'm not arguing for baiting as a widespread tactic. I would not even favor it in the farm country of Canada. But if baiting is stopped in Saskatchewan and nonresidents remain locked out of the farm country, the whitetail hunting industry in that providence will die.

What can a hunter expect in northern Saskatchewan? Well, to start with, hunting there is not easy. The logistics are a challenge, the weather is brutal, the hours are long and getting a crack at a trophy buck still requires plenty of hunting savvy. Big bucks seldom come right in and poke their faces in the grain pile. What bait really does is concentrate the doe groups and cause deer to establish more predictable travel patterns. These are huge advantages in unbroken expanses of woods with relatively few deer. Where the does are, the bucks will soon show up, especially as rut approaches. The bucks establish their rubs and scrapes around the bait sites. More often than not, the bucks visit the area to scent-check scrapes and trails leading to the bait site rather than to feed. Because of this, hunting bait is much like hunting a scapeline. Since big bucks usually don't come to the bait itself, the hunter must pay close attention to the entire area around his stand. Failure to do so costs countless hunters chances at big bucks they never even know are around. Of the seven bucks I've killed hunting near bait, only two actually came to the feed. All the rest were well away from the bait, and I would not have killed them had I not set the stand up to cover the entire area and had I not been paying attention.

Right now, the better hunts in Saskatchewan offer the highest odds of killing a 150 or 160-class buck of anywhere in the world. Yet, I believe the farmland hunts of Alberta may well offer a slightly better crack at 170-plus bucks. Let's talk about Alberta.

As the first Canadian province to really develop and promote non-resident whitetail hunting, Alberta has long enjoyed celebrity status among American hunters with dreams of giant whitetails. And why not? The place is home to some of the finest big buck hunting in the world! Much of the hunting takes place in the farmlands. For all practical purposes, Alberta offers the advantages of the U.S. Midwest without the restrictive regulations and the hunting pressure. That's saying a lot!

Alberta differs from Saskatchewan in two important ways. One, baiting is not allowed. Two, and most significant, nonresident hunting is permitted in the farmlands. The fact that baiting is not permitted makes hunting in the big woods areas of Alberta very dicey. Big bucks are there, just like in Saskatchewan, but without the benefits of baiting, hunter success is just too low for visiting hunters with limited time. In the farm country where bucks can be more easily patterned and hunted, baiting is not needed for reasonable hunter success. And, the farm country offers another advantage—better nutrition, which translates into bigger racks.

Over the years, it has become abundantly apparent that there is a difference in antlers between bucks with access to agriculture and those that live out their lives in woodlands. That difference, which can be measured in inches of antler, has its root in nutrition. Since 1983, I've taken over a dozen bucks in Central Canada and have been around when dozens of others were taken. While there are always plenty of exceptions, a clear pattern has emerged.

Deep-woods bucks without the benefit of farmland nutrition tend to have heavy, fairly narrow racks with relatively stubby main beams and tines. Inside spreads range from 16 to 18 inches. Seldom will a forest buck have an inside spread greater than 19 inches, and you would not need all the fingers on one hand to count the ones I've seen with inside spreads over 20 inches. Rather modest beam lengths of 20 to 22 inches are about normal for trophies shot there. Tines, while stout in mass, definitely run to the stubby side. You would be hard-pressed to find a true forest buck with 10-inch tines; in fact, I've never killed one with tines that long. I did once kill a buck *in* the provincial forest with 12-inch G-2s, but only the day before, I had seen him about a mile away—in an alfalfa field. Though I shot him in the forest, he was a farm-fed buck...and it showed.

The most outstanding characteristic of forest bucks is their mass. Many mature bucks have 20 or more inches of mass per side. I've shot several with 22 or 23 inches of mass on each beam and one with mass measurements of 25 and 26 inches! Mass like that adds 10 to 20 inches to the gross score over that of "normal" bucks with the same frame. For instance, the average 150-class Texas buck has about 16 inches of mass per side. Take that same 150 frame and increase the mass to 22 inches, and you've got a solid 160s buck. Well, that's how most forest bucks arrive at their high gross scores—through mass. Many deep-woods trophies grossing in the 150s and 160s sport 140s and 150s frames. This explains why they often score more than their appearance would indicate.

By contrast, farm bucks tend to have better developed beams and tines and have wider spreads. I have killed several farm bucks with tines over 10 inches and beams over 24 inches, even up to 26 inches. Inside spreads wider than 20 inches are relatively rare anywhere, but I've shot a couple of farmland bucks topping that and have seen several more killed by others. Antler mass on crop-fed bucks certainly doesn't take a back seat. The most massive typical buck I've ever seen was a book 12-pointer killed in the heart of Saskatchewan's farmland. Mass measurements on each side totaled over 26 inches! While forest bucks often appear to have greater mass, I doubt that is really the case. The more balanced dimensions of farmland bucks tend to lessen the impact of their outstanding mass.

By now, you're probably beginning to see why I said Alberta has a slight edge on Saskatchewan for 170-class bucks, at least as far as nonresidents are concerned. It is because nonresidents are largely restricted to forest hunting in Saskatchewan. In Alberta, they can and do hunt the farm country, where bucks have the nutritional benefits of agricultural crops...and the few extra inches that puts on antlers. For Saskatchewan residents who can hunt anywhere, Alberta holds no advantages. In fact, the edge goes back to Saskatchewan, as this province is the very epicenter of Canada's giant bucks.

From a nonresident standpoint, Alberta has one other leg up on Saskatchewan—nonresident pressure is spread over a much larger area. Visiting hunters can pursue big bucks throughout Alberta, and nonresident hunting pressure is spread out by means of a quota permit system for each zone. Still, hunting is not easy. Hunter success runs well below that

The hope of shooting a buck like this 15-pointer drives thousands of U.S. hunters to endure frigid weather and challenging logistics every year in Central Canada. I was the lucky one to tag this 187-point Alberta monster. Photo by author.

of Saskatchewan. Many visiting hunters in Alberta go home without a buck of any kind. Timing of the hunt is critical there. By far, the best time to hunt the farm country is during the rut. Even then, it's a crapshoot. But if your sights are set on a 170-class whitetail, I don't know of a better place than the farm country of Alberta. A couple of years ago, I rolled the dice in Alberta's Peace River Country and came up with a 15-pointer grossing 187! Last year, I came up empty on the same hunt. That's Alberta!

Lastly, brief words about Manitoba. Hunting there more closely resembles that of Alberta than Saskatchewan since baiting is not allowed and nonresident hunting is allowed in the farmlands. Manitoba's best big deer country is largely limited to the west-central part of the province, mainly the area around the town of Swan Plains. Generally speaking, hunting in Manitoba is not quite on par with that of either Alberta or Saskatchewan in terms of hunter success or buck size.

I've spent a lot of time talking about Central Canada because right now it represents the pinnacle of giant whitetail hunting. It's a unique place with tremendous mystique and virtually unlimited size potential. Yet, the kind of bucks that lure thousands of hunters there each year are relatively scarce even in this fabled land. Dream bucks are certainly present, but in reality, the great majority of Canadian trophies shot are in the 140s and 150s. Even there, a buck in the 160s gets everybody stirred up. And for every 150 or better buck shot in Central Canada, four or five hunters return home with dashed dreams. Still, there's always the hope that the next buck to step out just may be the buck of many lifetimes! Such is hunting in Central Canada.

Chapter Twelve

A New Frontier in Private Land Management

WHAT IF I TOLD YOU A MANAGEMENT strategy existed that could allow you to increase the number of deer on your property two or threefold, maybe more? What if I told you that same strategy could also increase your buck size to that of the best the area could produce? Then, what if I told you that your "more and bigger" deer could be contained within a relatively small area, perhaps seldom or never to leave your property?

"Yeah, right," you say, "and the IRS is going to waive my taxes next year!"

Sounds too good to be true, doesn't it? Well, innovative biologists and game managers across the country are snapping the shackles of so-called "conventional wisdom" and doing it! Best of all, you can too!

Now, wait a minute. Deer management in a where-to discussion? Are you serious? YES!

You see, management can be simply a way for you to shift a slice of the great trophy country now seemingly found only in faraway places to your own backyard! The where-to for trophy bucks can become your own property!

Before we look ahead to this groundbreaking new strategy, let's

Deer in many regions of the country have the age and genetics necessary to reach trophy proportions, but for them to reach the size of this great buck, quality nutrition is also required. Photo by Mike Biggs.

first look back so we can better understand from whence we've come and where we are today.

THE BIRTH OF "CONVENTIONAL WISDOM"

From the time the nationwide deer recovery first began in the mid-1900s until the expansion was more or less complete in the 1970s and '80s, management by game agencies correctly focused on protection. Later, as deer filled the available habitat, and in too many cases overfilled it, the strategy began to shift from protection to maintenance. In time, the goals became that of trying to control deer numbers, primarily through harvesting does, while maintaining maximum hunting opportunity for the greatest number of people. Worthy goals, but they seldom brought the most desirable results. Political constraints or the simple lack of control usually thwarted the goal of holding numbers down. The "chicken-in-every-pot" goal usually translated into excessive buck pressure. All too often, out-of-balance, overcrowded herds top heavy with does and seriously short of bucks, especially mature bucks, were the results.

Through all this, the game agencies and most professional biologists were trying to manage vast chunks of real estate—counties, regions, whole ecosystems and indeed entire states. With the responsibility of the overall resource resting on their shoulders, agencies did not have the time, money, personnel or, frankly, the mandate to manage individual tracts or invest in developing the techniques necessary to do so. As a result, their strategy was big picture. They were macro-managers. About the only real tool they had available was to control as best they could the number and sex of the deer harvested by regulating hunting pressure. Thus, most of the management advice they disseminated to private land managers paralleled their own experiences and dealt largely with harvest strategy and herd balance.

Because of their scant experience in managing individual tracts, or at least in managing them intensively, they placed relatively little emphasis on enhancing habitat or food availability and almost none on trying to significantly elevate the nutritional plane of the property. Since their experience with large tracts was rather superficial, their management perspective demanded lots of acreage to make a difference. And, habitat improvement on huge acreage was a matter of breadth not depth, thus only modest gains were feasible. From this environment evolved conventional wisdom—large tracts are necessary to manage deer; harvest manipulation through regulating hunting pressure is the most effective management tool; and about the only way to enhance carrying capacity is through the relatively wholesale management of natural habitat. While those conclusions are logical purely from a macro-manager's perspective, there's a whole lot more to the story when it comes to managing individual tracts.

A COLLISION COURSE

In a way, the quality of the resource and hunters' expectations have been on a collision course for a longtime. Hunters have been steadily advancing in experience, knowledge and standards, while the deer resource has been slipping in some important ways by which a growing number of hunters now measure the health of a herd. Certainly, overcrowding and poor herd balance head the list of threats. Too many deer results in smaller deer, lower reproduction, susceptibility to stress, para-

Any management program must include a strategy to maintain herd balance, a big part of which should be cropping does to hold numbers down and to maintain a tight buck:doe ratio. Pat Shirey proudly shows off her first deer, and the smile on her face proves that doe hunting can be fun and rewarding. Photo by Lawrence Wood.

sites and diseases, greater human/deer conflicts and long-term damage to the habitat, which leads to an inevitable lowering of the carrying capacity. Poor balance, usually as a result of overharvesting bucks and underharvesting does, leaves herds depleted of bucks, especially mature ones, and top heavy with does. Not only is this very bad for deer, but it has left today's demanding whitetail hunter frustrated and determined to find ways to improve the health of the deer herd and the state of his sport.

To understand why the modern deer hunter is more discriminating than ever before and why he wants more from his chosen sport than is now being realized, it is necessary to look at from where he has come. It is said that there are typically four stages in the evolution of a deer hunter. The first, as you would expect for a beginner, is simply to kill any legal buck. Size does not matter. The second stage is to take as many deer as possible. When sufficient numbers have been tallied, the third stage follows when the hunter begins seeking more challenge by taking deer with different type weapons, i.e., bow, muzzleloader, handgun, etc. The last stage is reached when the hunter shifts his focus to the wisest and most challenging of the clan—the trophy buck.

Certainly, this pattern is representative of countless modern hunters, especially the myriad "baby boomers" who began hunting during the herd expansion years of the '60s, '70s and early '80s. The fact that so many hunters today have so much experience lies at the root of the rub— many hunters have now reached the so-called trophy stage and are only interested in hunting good mature bucks, not just in killing any buck.

Overcrowding is a serious problem in many regions, particularly in the East and South. Undernourished bucks like this one are but a pale shadow of their true potential. Photo by Mike Biggs.

This goal is inconsistent with the realities of most deer herds today. Frustration is the result. Now for the good news—the future can be better!

Based on everything I've seen, there is a fifth stage in the evolution of a deer hunter. It offers hope for the frustrated and, I'm happy to report, for the well-being of our deer herd. This fifth stage stems from a commitment to the sport and a sincere interest in the welfare of the whitetail. Yes, it is motivated by a love of hunting, the desire to see more good bucks and the hope of harvesting big, mature bucks, but its end is a healthy, vigorous herd and a bright future for our sport. The fifth stage is an action stage that calls for getting involved to bring solutions. I am speaking of management—more specifically, the kind that restores nature's original management scheme for the whitetail, when *nonselective* predators held the whitetail in-check with its habitat, resulting in healthy, balanced herds with tight buck:doe ratios and well-distributed age classes.

Society as a whole began the disruption of this natural scheme by demanding the elimination of the large predators. We hunters, often under the auspices of misdirected policies, contributed to further imbalance by a selective and excessive harvest of bucks while leaving the does largely unchecked to reproduce beyond the ability of the habitat to support them. *So, in the natural whitetail herd, we find the baseline objective for modern game management—a balanced, healthy population with a tight buck:doe ratio and plenty of mature bucks that is maintained within the carrying capacity of the land by a near-equal harvest of bucks and does.*

Does man have a role in returning deer herds to a natural balance and maintaining them there? Of course, only it's not just a role; it's an obligation. The large predators that once "managed" the deer herds are no longer tolerated in close proximity to man, which happens to be where most whitetails live. Man must assume the role of game manager to help restore our herds to a healthy state and then maintain them there. Hunting is one of the primary and most essential tools in his management arsenal...and I might add, the one that provides the economic clot to make it all possible!

A hunter's involvement in management can be direct and focused, like working to improve the deer herd on a particular tract of land. Or, it can be indirect and broad, such as educating himself in the principles of game management in order to do what's "right" in his role as a hunter or to encourage agency game managers to act in the best interest of the resource. The truth is that every time a hunter pulls the trigger on a deer he is "managing." Without knowledge, he cannot know whether his "management" is good or bad. Regardless of the level of involvement in management or the motivation, all hunters need to be a part of securing a better future for both the whitetail and the sport through promoting a healthier herd. If the desire and the means to accomplish this goal are present, as I believe, then a positive change is within our grasp.

THE BEGINNING OF SOMETHING NEW

Necessity is indeed the mother of invention. In the face of declining quality in the country's deer herds from both too many deer and an excessive buck harvest, a handful of innovative private landowners and managers said "enough!" They started looking at what they could do to grow bigger bucks back on the old homestead. We at WHITETAIL magazine were counted among that number. Thus was born Georgia's Fort Perry Plantation, WHITETAIL's 2,000-acre management research facility directed by Steve Vaughn. From the outset, Steve wanted WHITETAIL to begin looking at ways for the average landowner, not just someone with vast holdings, to produce a healthy herd with more and bigger bucks.

Because limitations exist in every deer herd, WHITETAIL's goal was to intensify management efforts to achieve maximum results with limited land and resources. What WHITETAIL found after 10 years of research and management at Fort Perry is a bold new management strategy that has thrust nutrition into the limelight as a powerful untapped tool for altering the face of private land deer management for the better...and bigger! Plus, Steve's original hope was realized—this commonsense nutritional strategy will work on tracts once thought to be too small for an effective program and/or on marginal land with low inherent carrying capacity! In other words, it'll work on your property. And, we at WHITE-TAIL are committed to telling you how, thus the greatly expanded management coverage in our magazine and the chapter you are now reading.

This management concept is certainly not limited to Georgia or even the South. It'll work to some degree or in some form throughout the whitetail's range, as evidenced by the fact that many other managers throughout the country are also pushing the deer management envelope to new levels through better nutrition. People like Dr. Gary Schwarz of El Tecomate Ranch in South Texas and Jackie Brittingham of Briarwood Ranch in Illinois, to name but a couple, have fashioned their own successful food-centered strategies. Like Fort Perry, many of these other places are blowing the top off what was once thought to be the limits of possibilities. All in all, better nutrition is opening the door to great homegrown hunting to almost anyone with a decent slice of deer country.

We have long known that quality nutrition is key for a healthy herd and that nutritious food increases deer size and numbers. For size, the agricultural crops of the fertile farmlands of the Midwest or Central Canada provided a case in point. For numbers, the proof could be seen in the incredible deer densities found in association with the irrigated alfalfa fields along the otherwise lightly populated riverbottoms of the Plains and Prairies. Certainly, progressive Texas ranchers, who have always set the pace in private land deer management, have incorporated enhanced nutrition, usually direct feeding, into their management for years. Yet, only recently have we come to fully understand the degree to which the private land manager can elevate the quality of nutrition on his property and the astounding impact it can have on his herd.

Deer are like any other animal—meet their basic requirements for life, i.e., food, water and cover, and they thrive in good health, reach large size and reproduce abundantly. Think of them as little cows in this regard. Ranchers have always operated in the sure knowledge that more and better (nutritious) feed allows more and healthier cows to be supported on a given acreage. Assuming water and cover are in adequate supply, exactly the same principle applies to deer—the more and better the food, the more and bigger the deer.

That fact is the beginning point for our new strategy, but let's take it one step further. What if all the deer's needs, including a ready supply of preferred, highly nutritious food, were met in a relatively small area? Doesn't logic say the deer would stay close by rather than wander off to where pickings are poorer? If the answer is yes, and it is, then you have the final block in the foundation of a new management strategy. Namely, provide deer with a localized supply of more and better food, along with nearby cover and water, and you get more and bigger deer that hold tight in the area. Does it really work? A resounding YES!

Sounds simple, doesn't it? In concept, it is. Yet, it marks a major turning point for deer hunters, from a reactive role in game management to a proactive role. This strategy will empower private land managers across the continent to take charge of deer management on their property and to determine their own hunting destiny...while contributing to a healthier deer herd! That's saying a lot!

A NEW FRONTIER IN DEER MANAGEMENT

Let's now lay out this new strategy, which we'll call "food-source management," and discuss its various aspects. Here's the program in a nutshell: *Provide attractive, highly nutritious, concentrated food sources through agricultural plantings and/or direct feeding, preferably on a year-round basis, for the purpose of increasing deer numbers and size and holding the deer in a relatively confined area. Then, implement a harvest strategy that maintains the deer density within carrying capacity to allow for maximum body and antler size and peak reproduction and that promotes a low buck:doe ratio and a good buck age structure.*

This strategy revolves around nutrition, herd balance and people, specifically their goals and resources. For now, we'll focus on the first two.

Nutrition Is The Key

The heart and soul of this program is obviously enhanced nutrition through a concentrated, favored food source. The goal is twofold—

increased nutrition and high attraction. Hunters have long used food plots and direct feeding to attract deer for viewing and harvesting, and while that remains an important benefit of this program, what we're talking about here goes far beyond that.

More And Better Food

The first goal is to substantially elevate the quality of nutrition available to the herd so that deer numbers, size and reproduction increase as a byproduct of a healthier herd. Yes, this takes a serious commitment, but it is well within the reach of most landowners and managers who are already trying to manage their deer.

To receive maximum benefits, nutritional needs must be met year-round. In the spring and summer, the greatest need is for protein to rebuild rut and winter-depleted muscle, to grow new antlers and to nourish developing fetuses or fawns. During the fall and winter, deer need carbohydrates to supply energy and maintain body fat so minimal muscle is burned. So, we can divide the four seasons into two distinct times—warm (spring and summer) and cool (fall and winter) periods.

Almost anywhere arable land is found, the warm-period need for protein can be met to a large degree through agricultural plantings, primarily legumes of some sort. Agriculture in the form of corn or small grains can also provide carbohydrates during the cool period in areas where snow doesn't accumulate too deeply. In non-arable or heavy snow regions, direct feeding of, say, high-protein pellets or corn (carbohydrates) may be necessary to provide the required nutrition.

The whitetail is hardy, adaptable and equipped to withstand all but the harshest conditions nature throws at him. For instance, as an adaptation to counter the physical drain of fall and winter, deer enter the fall with heavy fat reserves and shift to a low-energy, maintenance existence during the winter. As a result, they can get through the winter on relatively slim rations, though at a cost. Yet, despite their hardiness, whitetails respond favorably to any help that comes their way during either the warm or cool season. Obviously, improving their lot year-round is best, but if a year-round program is not practical, some gains can be acheived by meeting the nutritional needs of either season. Which is most important? It depends on the area, but generally, I'd have to say protein during the growing season is most beneficial. We'll talk more about this later.

Food-source management is a strategy aimed at greatly enhancing the nutritional plane of a tract. Depending on the scope of the program, it is possible to increase both the size and number of bucks significantly. Agriculture lies at the root of this management strategy. Photo by Troy Huffman.

How much can nutritious, major food sources increase the number and size of the deer on your property? That depends on many factors, not the least of which is the property and the nature and extent of the food sources. The increase in number and size we've seen at Fort Perry has defied anything we thought possible! The same is true on many other food-source programs. On El Tecomate Ranch, though only about 3,000 acres, Gary Schwarz and his family have consistently dominated Texas' big bucks contests! Plus, Gary is carrying roughly a deer per six acres…in country with a natural carrying capacity of about a deer per 25 acres! Under an intensive program, I'm being conservative to say the number of deer that can be carried in maximum health can be doubled, tripled or even quadrupled. We're doing that and more at Fort Perry!

A good way to get a handle of the size potential on your property is to look back on the deer that were killed during the heyday years of big bucks when the herd was first expanding. This was when the herd was still below the inherent carrying capacity of the land and prime native foods were most abundant, allowing the deer to reach their greatest size on *natural habitat*. But, food-source management has the potential to improve nutrition far beyond what was ever possible with natural habitat.

Attraction

A requirement for a successful management program is some level of control over the herd so that outside losses are reduced to an acceptable level. Otherwise, the manager will be pouring nutrition into bucks the neighbors will be shooting, probably before they're old enough to be big. Traditionally, this control has been achieved either through a vast land base, usually several thousand acres, or by a game-proof fence. Some lucky landowners have natural barriers, such as rivers or lakes, perhaps busy freeways or, in the case of the riverbottom habitat in the Plains and Prairies, even wide-open spaces to help contain the deer. And, a few have good neighbors or adjoin unhunted or inaccessible tracts so that the deer can leave the managed property without suffering unnatural losses. Whatever the means, a manager must have some level of control over his deer. That usually means keeping them on his property as much as possible. Without thousands of acres or physical barriers of some kind, how can that be done? Lots of good food!

That leads us to the second objective of a nutritional strategy—to make the food source so attractive that, assuming water and cover needs are met, the deer will stay in relatively close proximity to it, thereby spending the great majority of their time on the managed land and under the control of the manager. This places certain requirements on the nature of the food source, especially as it relates to managing tracts of limited size.

The food source must be confined to a specific area, such as a food plot or feeding station, be highly favored by deer and provide the bulk of their nutritional needs. Meeting these three requirements allows the land manager to specifically locate his food sources so that deer activity is contained to his property to the greatest extent possible. Not only does natural habitat management have less potential to increase carrying capacity, it does not concentrate the deer around a focal point. Thus, it fails to deliver the critical advantage of herd containment so essential on smaller tracts.

How tight can major food sources hold deer? Again, many factors go into this equation, such as the part of the country, cover conditions, hunting pressure and time of year. Certainly, the quality, volume and nature of the food sources are important. For instance, deer simply like some foods better than others. Additionally, the longer food sources are in place, the closer deer tend to stay to them. Why? Deer become increasingly accustomed to and dependent upon the food sources, and perhaps more importantly, the fawns raised on the food sources will "imprint" on the area and claim it as their own.

So, what can we expect? Based on research conducted on Tecomate Ranch by Dr. Tim Fulbright of the Caesar Kleberg Wildlife Research Institute, indications are that deer dependent on established major food sources, in this case food plots rather than direct feed, spend about 95 percent of their time within a half-mile of the food sources. Better yet, that same research shows that most of that time is spent within a quarter-mile of the food source! Our experience on Fort Perry bears out these numbers.

All of a sudden, it comes together! More and bigger bucks, which *can* be contained in a relatively small area! Presto, trophy buck management is possible on smaller tracts than ever thought possible...without a high-fence.

Another big plus of preferred major food sources is that they allow deer to be seen and enjoyed consistently at predictable places. This offers obvious hunting advantages, but the management benefits may be even greater, particularly when trying to census the herd or harvest just the right animals. Certainly, one of the greatest pluses this program offers is the year-round enjoyment and satisfaction of just watching deer do their thing and seeing the herd and individual bucks get better and better year after year.

Herd Management

The second and more traditional aspect of this food-source strategy calls for managing the herd, just as any serious management plan would. The goal is to control the number of deer and to maintain a tight buck:doe ratio and good buck age structure through a balanced harvest strategy.

What is the right number of deer for your property? The simple answer is the most the place can sustain at your level of management while still achieving maximum body and antler size and peak reproduction. You'll have to determine what that is on your property under your program.

Buck age structure is simply the distribution of bucks throughout

Does quality nutrition make a difference? Young Taylor Schuster thinks so. He killed this 188-point non-typical on South Texas' Tecomate Ranch, which is leading the way in agricultural-based nutrition in that part of the world. Generally, the better the food, the bigger the bucks. Photo by author.

the various age classes. What's a good buck age structure? That depends on the harvest strategy, which depends on the desires of the manager. A trophy buck program requires that as many bucks as possible be allowed to reach the mature age classes, which means protecting 1 1/2s and 2 1/2s. Once they reach maturity, the manager has to decide how many and what size/age are to be taken. His decision will determine the buck age structure and the nature of his program. For instance, if the goal is top-end bucks, the herd must have a good representation of older, peak-antler-aged bucks, i.e., 5 1/2 to 7 1/2. If a heavier harvest targeting any mature buck is the goal, then the mature age structure will likely consist primarily of 3 1/2s and 4 1/2s.

What is the ideal buck:doe ratio? That's the manager's call.

Harvest objectives certainly figure into it. The general goal is to move toward a one-to-one ratio of adult bucks to adult does, but this is seldom achieved. In the real world, something around 1:1.2 to 1:1.5 is more realistic. Philosophically, you want the herd to consist of as many bucks as possible and only enough does to replace the previous year's losses. In practice, the problem is seldom too few does.

What about genetics? That's always one of the first questions to arise in a trophy program. Frankly, I think the infatuation with genetics stems from the fact that many people believe it offers a quick fix for bigger bucks. It doesn't. The truth is that the deer on your property have far greater genetic potential than you think. If bucks of a size you would be happy with have ever been killed in your area, then your deer undoubtedly have the genetic potential to realize your trophy dreams...if you provide them with quality nutrition and time to grow up. Actually, it may be possible to grow even bigger bucks than ever before. Why? Because the improved nutritional plane possible under an intense program can provide higher quality nutrition than the natural habitat was *ever* capable of yielding. This allows bucks to acheive even more of their genetic potential (meaning, get bigger) than ever before.

And, an ongoing high nutritional plane may well bring another factor into play that leads to greater size than thought possible. Gary Schwarz first brought this theory to my attention. He had come across a study reported in the 1986 *Wildlife Society Bulletin* that dealt with why the antlers of red stag and roe deer in Europe were so much smaller than those in museums from medieval times. Though the study was conducted before World War II by a European scientist named Franz Vogt, it wasn't brought to the attention of the American community until scientist Valerius Geist published the 1986 paper reporting on the results of Vogt's study.

Essentially, Vogt believed that the effects of poor nutrition over many generations acted to suppress the potential for full genetic expression in antler and body size. (We'll just focus on antler size.) He wasn't just saying the antlers were smaller on a particular animal because of poor nutrition; he believed the genetic potential for size had actually been eroded as an adaptation to long-term malnutrition. He also theorized that with the availability of optimum nutrition, the suppression of antler size could be reversed over many generations. His studies eventually proved his theory correct! In five to seven generations under high nutrition, Vogt overcame the genetic suppression and released the full genetic potential of the animals, producing red stags equal in size to those of medieval times! And, whitetails will respond the same way!

First, get good nutrition to your *balanced* herd, then tweak genetics through controlled harvests.

How Much Land Is Needed?

While food-source management is simple, thought, time, money and work are required to put it into practice. Many decisions must be made along the way. Ultimately, the shape of the program will be determined by the resources available and the goals of the people involved. Let's spend a moment on one of the most important resources—the land.

The most often-asked question about this program is how much land does it take? The answer is NOT AS MUCH AS YOU THINK! Food-source management can improve your hunting to some degree even if you only have a few acres. The least you can do is attract deer to your food source, even if you can't keep them on your place or significantly improve the nutritional plane. But, that's not really taking advantage of the nutritional benefits so key to the program. To accomplish this, land size does come into play, but perhaps not in the most obvious way.

You can't think of this program only in terms of how much land you own. You have to look at the overall area, whether you own it or not, used by the deer feeding on your food sources. We'll call this the "managed or protected" area. Obviously, this area cannot have heavy, indiscriminate hunting pressure if the program is going to be successful, thus the name. It is this acreage that is important.

What size managed area is necessary? Earlier we said that deer tend to spend 95 percent of their time within a half-mile of a major food source. Using this half-mile as the distance from a food source that would allow reasonable control over the herd, we can come up with an acreage parameter for the protected area. Assuming centrally located food sources, a protected half-mile radius around the food sources would result in roughly a square-mile area, or 640 acres. Though that will not give full control of the herd, it's a good rule-of-thumb for the minimum protected area required for an effective program...if the neighbor situation is not intolerable. (Mere acreage is not the only concern—so is maintaining the half-mile distance from a food source to a bad neighbor. The shape of the land factors in here.) Obviously, the larger the protected zone, the greater the control over the herd.

As we said, you don't have to own the entire protected zone to receive its benefits. True, it's best to own as much of the impacted area as possible to fully control it, but with the right neighbors, the program can be successful when you own only a part of the managed area. Since you have the food sources, the deer will end up under your dominion sooner or later. So, if your neighbors won't shoot your deer before they get big, your program will fly when you own only part of the managed land.

From all this, you can see how the right 50 or 100 acres could keep a family in taxidermy bills. My 80-acre "ranch" in Montana sits in the middle of inaccessible, lightly hunted national forest land, and my two 15-acre clover meadows are the hub of local deer activity. I know others who manage even less land to amazing effect. One is a 10-acre tract next to a large, unhunted utility holding. You wouldn't believe the huge bucks that have come off that tiny tract over the years!

What would be the ideal size to manage? Again, it depends, but all things considered, the ideal size to fully exploit the concept is from 1,000 to 3,000 acres, sizes well below that once thought to be necessary for an effective program. Anything less than 1,000 acres stands to suffer significant losses to hunting neighbors. Anything more than 3,000 acres presents daunting logistical challenges, both from the standpoint of nutrition and herd control. Certainly, commercial or large-scale programs can be successfully implemented on tracts as large as the involved parties are willing to take on.

There you have it—an overview of a strategy that promises to change the way we look at private land management. If it sounds like I'm excited about this concept, it's only because I am! I know it'll work. And in the next chapter, we're going to look into the workings of this strategy and see exactly why it truly has the potential of turning your property into a "last best place."

Chapter Thirteen

Better Nutrition– the Heart of Food-Source Management

 S IMPLE IS ALWAYS BEST. AND AS WE look at the nuts and bolts of food-source management, I hope and believe that you'll think the whole thing is simple, perhaps even obvious. If so, then it's got a chance of flying when you take the concept to the field. I really think the beauty of this strategy lies in its simplicity and logic.

Well, let's now get right into the heart of food-source management—its nutritional side. The goal here is to explain how and why it works and layout the seasonal nutritional needs of the whitetail so the whole thing makes complete sense.

HOW AND WHY FOOD-SOURCE MANAGEMENT WORKS

We need to start with some assumptions. First, a deer eats about 8 to 10 pounds of food a day. We'll use an average of nine pounds. If you multiply nine pounds times the number of days in a year (365), that'll give you the annual average food consumption for one deer, which we'll round off to 3,000 pounds. Now, let's assume that the natural habitat can grow about 300 pounds of *good* deer food per acre over the course of a year, which is realistic for much of the South and East. Studies have shown that deer can eat only about half of the available food without

In food-source management, the basic nutritional strategy calls for high-protein forages, mainly legumes of some type, in the spring and summer, when antler growth and the demands of fawning place high nutritional requirements on both bucks and does. These bucks sure like the program. Photo by Troy Huffman.

seriously damaging the habitat. (You can see how carrying capacity is determined.) So, about 150 pounds of good deer food are available per acre of natural habitat. To determine how many acres are necessary to support one deer, we simply divide the annual poundage of food consumed by one deer (3,000) by the poundage of food an acre of habitat can produce without suffering damage (150). That tells us that the carrying capacity is a deer per 20 acres, about what might be expected for a place under a *good* natural habitat management program.

If that level of carrying capacity is not sufficient to meet the goals of those involved with the property, there are four options—lower the goals, reduce the number of participants, continue on frustrated or elevate the carrying capacity. Not surprisingly, most private landowners don't like the first three options. More and bigger deer from increased carrying capacity sounds a lot better.

Better Nutrition, Higher Carrying Capacity

There is more than one way to increase carrying capacity. The traditional method is to improve the natural habitat, and there's not a thing wrong with that. In fact, all reasonable steps need to be made to improve natural habitat. However, this strategy has some limitations. First, it takes

In the cool season, winter-greens, such as rye, oats, wheat and other small grains, can be important sources of needed carbohydrates so deer won't have to burn so much fat and muscle for energy. Photo by Troy Huffman.

time, perhaps several years, to effect wholesale habitat improvement. Second, landowners might not be willing to allow what it would take. The key is to get more sunlight to the forest floor and to regenerate early succession-al growth. That takes some fairly drastic mechanical measures, such as prescribed burning, thinning timber, creating edge through clearing, etc. Such major habitat alterations might not sit well with the landowner. Third, the level to which the carrying capacity can be increased through manipulating natural habitat is somewhat limited, short of practically clearcutting. Also, natural habitat improvement will not deliver two important advantages found in the concentrated food sources associated with the strategy we're discussing here—one, increased deer visibility and huntability; two, the ability to hold deer in a localized area.

Increasing carrying capacity through enhanced nutrition lies at the heart of food-source management. This is accomplished through nutri-tious agricultural crops and/or direct feeding. Our focus here will be on agriculture, by far the preferred and more desirable of the two options. In places with tillable land, literally tons of highly nutritious deer food can be grown per acre. For instance, a year-round food-plot program can pro-duce up to 10,000 pounds of deer food per acre, all of which can be at least as nutritious as the very best nature provides. That's more high-qual-ity deer food than 70 acres of natural habitat normally produces since all of the agricultural crop theoretically could be consumed by deer without hurting a thing! Put another way, one acre of year-round food plot can meet all the annual nutritional needs of 3.5 deer! That's production! Compare that to 20 acres of natural habitat to support one deer. And remember, all of the agricultural food can be top-rate. The huge advantages of food-source management should be abundantly apparent.

To illustrate, let's assume a 2,000-acre club wants to carry 200 deer, about twice what the property can support under natural habitat management. Let's assume the club members want their deer to reach the greatest size possible. So, they design a year-round agricultural program to provide 100 percent of the deer's nutritional requirements, realizing, of course, that the deer will continue some browsing on natural vegetation even with a table full of deer delicacies. It's an easy exercise to determine how many acres of food plots are needed to support 200 deer. Simply divide the number of deer to be carried (200) by the number of deer an acre of food plot will carry (3.5), and you get the required acreage of agriculture. In this case, about 60 acres.

Yes, 60 acres of year-round food plots (assuming the right crops are planted with the right farming techniques) can meet all the nutritional requirements of 200 deer. That's a program a club can get started right away quite cost effectively and with minimum startup hassles. And does it ever work! That number, 3.5 deer per acre of food plot, is exactly what we're supporting on food plots at Fort Perry...and have been for years! If you want to carry more deer, it's almost as simple as doing the math and adding the necessary acres of food plots. Of course, there's a limit to how high you might want to push the herd, but it's well up there if nutritious food is in abundant supply.

In areas with high inherent carrying capacity, the native habitat can pick up more of the slack and reduce the number of acres required to get to the same number. For instance, Gary Schwarz's El Tecomate Ranch lies in prime South Texas Brush Country, where the natural habitat is inherently productive. Because of the support he gets from nutritious native vegetation, Gary, with a little help from supplemental feeding, is able to support over four deer per acre of food plot, even though he only double-crops about half his acreage each year.

SEASONAL NUTRITIONAL NEEDS OF THE WHITETAIL

In order to formulate a nutritional strategy (plan) for whitetails, it is necessary to know their seasonal nutritional needs. Biologists and scientists can get into tedious detail on this subject, but from the game manager's perspective, it's really quite simple.

From a timing standpoint, bucks and does have quite similar nutritional needs, but for very different reasons. Basically, they both have two distinct periods with specific nutritional requirements—during one period, they require protein; during the other, carbohydrates. Generally, when bucks have the highest need for protein, so do does. The same is true for carbohydrates. Convenient, isn't it? It is, however, no accident. The needs of the deer are adapted to when nature supplies the appropriate nutrition in greatest abundance. During the spring and summer, plant growth is underway and protein production is at its peak. During the fall and winter, plant growth is largely complete and plants have produced carbohydrate-rich mast and seeds. Even the leaves of many plants are high in energy-yielding sugars and carbohydrates in the fall. Interestingly enough, the whitetail's need for protein is highest in the spring and summer and is greatest for carbohydrates in the fall and winter.

Two Seasons, Two Nutritional Needs

Let's divide the year into two parts based on the whitetail's nutritional needs. We'll call one the cool season, meaning fall and winter. The other, the warm season, is spring and summer. During the warm season, bucks have either just begun or are about to begin their annual antler growth cycle. Not only that, they have just come through the winter and need to rebuild the muscle and mass lost during the rigors of rut and winter. From early spring all the way through the summer, protein is of utmost importance in both growing antlers and rebuilding muscle and body mass. If protein is in short supply, the body gets first dibs on what's available, and whatever antler growth is lost while the body recovers is lost for good, at the cost of antler size in the coming fall. For bucks, the rule of thumb is that they need a high-protein diet, ideally consisting of at least 16 percent protein, from the time they lose their antlers in late winter/early spring until they shed their velvet during early fall.

During this same warm period, does also need a high-protein diet. Like bucks, they must regain the muscle and body mass lost during the winter. And also like bucks, they need to nourish something growing very rapidly—fast-developing fetuses. Nature has worked it out so that fetuses don't grow much from conception until about the onset of spring, but from that time on, fetuses rapidly develop into the full-pledged fawns that will be born in late spring or early summer. And of course, the nutritional drain on does doesn't end with the birth of a fawn. Nursing continues all summer and places great demands on does, requiring that they essentially have to eat for two. Protein is the primary nutritional requirement for does from the beginning of spring until weaning time in early fall, about the same time bucks shed their velvet.

The cool season places similar demands on both bucks and does. The name of the game now is not building muscle or body mass as much as it is trying not to lose what they already have. Between the heightened activity of the rut and the caloric demands of the cold, deer need an outside energy source to burn rather than burning muscle and consuming their body reserves. This is especially so with bucks during the rut. Growth is not the issue during the cool period, energy and maintenance are. Thus, protein requirements are much lower, but carbohydrates are now needed in greater supply. From the manager's standpoint, the better shape the deer come through the winter, the more of the spring's early protein can go to antler growth in bucks and fetal development in does, which, of course, ultimately contributes to antler size and fawn survival.

Meeting Seasonal Nutritional Needs

Understanding the seasonal nutritional needs of the whitetail makes it relatively easy to develop a nutritional strategy for a management program. The basic strategy is to provide a source of high-protein feed beginning in spring (corresponding to antler-drop) and continuing through summer (to velvet-shedding). Then, from the start of fall through winter, provide a carbohydrate-rich food source. Ideally, all or most of this strategy can be carried out through agriculture. If not, direct feeding is an option, at least as a supplement. It's a simple strategy really.

Since the best way to meet the whitetail's nutritional needs is agriculture, then let's apply an agricultural strategy. The warm-season protein requirements can best be met by planting some type of legume. Legumes are nitrogen-fixing plants, meaning they take nitrogen from the air and, with the help of bacteria in their roots, put nitrogen back into the soil. Since nitrogen is one of the essential nutrients for plant growth, legumes are natural soil-builders. Legumes are typically warm-season plants and are characterized by having seeds that grow in pods. Peas, clovers and beans, including soybeans, are legumes. There are many types of legumes suitable for deer, and almost anywhere whitetails are found, some kind of legume will grow. Some are annuals, meaning they grow for one season then die, and some are perennials lasting for years. But, the one thing legumes have in common of particular interest to us is that they are typically very high in protein. So, some type of clover, pea or bean, either an annual or a perennial, is probably the best source of agricultural protein for deer anywhere in the U.S.

If direct feeding is required during the warm season, either as a primary or supplemental source of protein, the usual answer is high-protein pellets, of which there are many choices suitable for deer on the market. Natural and less expensive options, such as soybeans and cottonseeds, may be available locally. Deer normally have to be trained over time to eat both pellets and other feeds they have no previous experienced with.

What about carbohydrates? In warmer climes where cool-season agriculture is an option, small grains that grow in winter, such as rye, wheat and oats, are excellent sources of carbohydrates. Some warm-season crops harvested in the fall, such as corn and small grains, can continue to be a valuable source of carbohydrates well into winter. However, agriculture may not be a total solution in cold regions, in which case direct feeding is probably the best alternative. Corn, which is cheap and readily available, is hard to beat as a direct carbohydrate source. In some areas, such as high acorn-producing locales, mast production can be encouraged by reducing competition and by fertilizing, thus offering some natural carbohydrate support.

Is a nutritional program worthwhile if cool-season feeds aren't included? For instance, will planting a warm-season high-protein crop do any good if a winter carbohydrate source isn't provided? The answer is yes! Everything that elevates the nutritional plane helps deer. Obviously, the more the nutritional plane is elevated, the more gains are realized. Even cool-weather carbohydrate feeding alone helps some, but not to the same degree as a warm-season high-protein source. Deer, especially those in cold climates, are adapted to survive the cold times with minimum nutritional intake. The strategy is to bulk-up as much as possible in the summer and fall in preparation of having to burn body reserves of fat and eventually muscle to carry them through. Plus, they have adopted an energy-conserving lifestyle during the cold times. Barring extreme conditions, they can get through the winter in decent shape, but every pound of muscle that is preserved by having sufficient energy-providing carbohy-

Food plots have long been used to attract deer for viewing or hunting, but food-source management goes far beyond this. Intensive management can provide the bulk of a herd's annual nutritional needs, but to do that, you have to forget food plots in the traditional sense—what we're talking about is farming for deer...and keeping the table well-set year-round. Photo by Mike Biggs.

drates available adds to the overall health of the herd, the antler development of bucks, the fawning success of does and the survival rate of fawns.

One other question often arises. Which is better, annuals or perennials, particularly in regards to legumes since perennial carbohydrate options are somewhat limited? The answer depends on many factors, like the amount of tillable farmland available, budget, goals, soils, topography, the list goes on. The choice lies with the manager, but generally speaking, annuals produce more tonnage and allow for easier weed control. Plus, double-cropping both warm and cool-season crops on the same acreage cuts down on the acreage of farmland necessary for the program, an important consideration on many properties.

Yes, it really is quite simple and logical isn't it? That is why it works! And in the next chapter, we're going to see the strategy at work on two very different places—Fort Perry in Georgia and El Tecomate Ranch in South Texas. The exact same principles are at work in both programs, but because of climatic and habitat differences, the way the programs are executed is very different. The results, however, are the same—lots of big bucks!

Chapter Fourteen

Putting the Strategy to Work–Real-Life Examples of Success

THE BASIC NUTRITIONAL STRATEGY for whitetail management is essentially the same everywhere, but how that strategy is carried out will vary greatly from place to place, whether by choice of the managers or by the dictates of the place, climate, soils, resources, regulations or circumstances. The options are limitless, yet the underlying principles remain steadfast. With that, we're going to head to the field and look at two successful but different real-life examples of how this strategy is executed.

We'll first look at *WHITETAIL's* Fort Perry Plantation. Then, we'll go to El Tecomate Ranch in arid South Texas, where Dr. Gary Schwarz has developed an agricultural-based nutritional program in a place where dependable crops *supposedly* can't be grown. These two examples well-illustrate a wide range of innovative and practical ways the nutritional cat can be skinned. I could have easily chosen other examples in Michigan, Wisconsin, Illinois, Mississippi, Louisiana, Florida or a number of other states. The main thing our two Southern examples won't address is the snow limitations prevalent in northern climes, where cool-season nutrition normally must be met by direct feeding rather than agri-

More and bigger bucks is what food-source management is all about. The game manager can pick from a wide range of management options and make his program as intensive, or as basic, as he likes. Photo by Mike Biggs.

culture. We will, however, briefly cover supplemental feeding that will be applicable everywhere.

While our discussions here will focus mostly on the nutritional side of management, I want to point out that both Fort Perry and Tecomate have specific herd management strategies, as must any successful program. But here, the purpose is to clearly establish the exciting new concept of nutritional-based management, not to delve into the intricacies of all aspects of game management in every part of the country under every circumstance. That would require a whole book dedicated solely to management. For now, we're just going to look at two successful food-source management programs as examples of what will work. They will clearly illustrate the nature of the management concept and what is possible. We've got a lot of ground to cover so we'll be speaking in plain English and get right to the point.

THE FORT PERRY PLANTATION STRATEGY

Under the direction of Steve Vaughn, WHITETAIL magazine has fashioned 2,000-acre Fort Perry Plantation in southwest Georgia into a management research facility. Since its beginning a decade ago, Fort Perry has continually experimented with ways of increasing the produc-

The South is not known for big bucks, but Fort Perry Plantation, North American WHITE-TAIL's 2,000-acre management-research facility, has pushed the trophy possibilities envelope to a whole new level through its pioneering work in food-source management. Photo by Mike Biggs.

tivity of private lands through intensive management, focusing largely on enhancing the nutritional plane. That effort has resulted in a food-source strategy that yields BIG results, and best of all, it's a strategy the average landowner can cash in on.

The working concept behind this program is applicable almost anywhere, but the particulars may not be the best for your land or your circumstances. In fact, the time may come when we find a better way to elevate our own nutritional plane on Fort Perry. But for now, we offer this program in its most basic form as an example of a strategy that, in terms of both deer numbers and size, brings nothing short of astounding results.

How astounding? As for numbers, we're supporting several times the number of animals possible on unmanaged habitat. We'll just call it more than a deer per five acres! As for size, if I told you the actual truth, you wouldn't believe it. I wouldn't have believed it had I not seen the animals for myself. As I write this, our program has just reached the point that we're ready to begin harvesting bucks. By the time you read this, we will have data on antler and body size for harvested bucks, but as for now, we'll have to go on sheds, pickups, survey photos and field-judging. From that, I can tell you conservatively that practically all of Fort Perry's 3 1/2-year-olds and older score above 150 and some push *well* past 170! How did we get them there? Let's see.

Overview

First, let's look at a simple overview of the program on Fort Perry.

Fort Perry's intensive year-round agricultural program, consisting mainly of cowpeas in the warm season and rye and clover in the cool season, has greatly elevated the nutritional plane of the property. The land is now carrying several times the number of deer possible with only natural habitat management, and even this 160-class 9-pointer would not rank among the better mature bucks roaming the property. More and better food is the key. Photo by author.

Agriculture is the heart of our nutritional strategy, though we do backup the crops with free-choice supplemental feed. We also fertilize selective natural habitat to enhance browse production. About 10 percent of our acreage is devoted to food plots ranging in size from 5 to 50 acres. We double-crop our fields with warm and cool-season crops. Fort Perry has deep, sandy, relatively infertile soils, and if we can grow good crops, most any place can. We are able to do it because we soil test, apply the recommended treatments of fertilizer and lime and employ sound farming techniques, including weed-control practices. All these things are important for maximum efficiency. However, farming for the purpose of growing deer feed doesn't require the level of sophistication demanded by commercial farming. Still, the better job you do, the more returns you'll see.

I should also point out that with its long growing season, abundant rainfall and tillable (though infertile) soil Fort Perry, like much of the South, is conducive to a straightforward, efficient and rather economical food-plot program. You'll see just how comparatively user-friendly

Cowpeas are the primary warm-season protein source for Fort Perry deer. Food plots like this one provide literally tons of highly nutritious feed, enough, in fact, for one acre of year-round food plot to support 3.5 deer in prime condition. That changes the rules on private-land management. Photo by Steve Vaughn.

Southern farming really is when we look at what's necessary to pull off an agricultural-based program on El Tecomate Ranch in arid South Texas.

Warm-Season Plots

Now on to the specifics of Fort Perry's program. We'll start with the warm-season planting. Though we have experimented with various clovers and soybeans, the legume we've settled on as our staple is iron-clay cowpeas—a high-yield, high-protein annual legume that our deer really find to their liking. Using "no-till" farming techniques, we plant about a bushel of cowpeas per acre right over the winter grain, after mowing it down. (No-tilling is our choice; it certainly doesn't have to be done that way.) Planting usually begins in early May when the soil temperature reaches 70 degrees.

As soon as the tender young peas come out of the ground, deer take to them. They are vulnerable to over-browsing at this time on small plots, but on Fort Perry, we have thus far been able to overwhelm them

What a mainframe on Chuck Larsen's 25-inch, 172-point South Texas monster! Photo by author.

This Saskatchewan brute topped 350 pounds, but he's not the heaviest buck I've ever shot there—a 400-pounder is! Photo by Carl Frohaug.

This photo captures something of the mystique surrounding trophy whitetail hunting. Photo by Mike Biggs.

Every time a hunter sees a doe, this is what he hopes will be following her. Photo by Troy Huffman.

Eating time for this massive-tined buck. Photo by Mike Biggs.

Now's the time to lose the rattling horns and grab the rifle. Photo by Mike Biggs.

This early season jousting is not yet for all the marbles, as it will be once breeding rights are on the line. Photo by Mike Biggs.

As the saying goes, "No pain, no gain." Well, sometimes cold-weather hunting deals out plenty of pain…and gain. Photo by Carl Frohaug.

After almost getting him during each of the two previous seasons, I finally tagged this 179-point Montana buck in the waning minutes of the third season of pursuit. Photo by John Creamer.

Drop-tines everywhere! On this buck, I'd just come up shooting! Photo by Mike Biggs.

There's 220 inches of bone on this buck's head. Photo by Mike Biggs.

I was out scouting right after a tremendous Montana blizzard when this 182-point buck surprised me…and I him! Photo by Debbie Morris.

A 10-pointer grossing 179 and my trusty 7mm Rem. Mag., which felled the big buck. Photo by author.

A symmetrical typical 12-pointer on red alert. Photo by Mike Biggs.

A most interesting rack on this early pre-rut buck. Photo by Mike Biggs.

This buck is venting his aggression and readying himself for the fall wars. Photo by Mike Biggs.

A classic wide-racked South Texas trophy. I stopped this 180-class 12-pointer short during his mid-morning scraping rounds. Photo by Mark Lubin.

Whitetail hunting's bewitching hour. Photo by Mike Biggs.

with acreage. Otherwise, the young peas, especially those on small plots of less than five acres, would have to be protected, i.e., fenced off, during the first few weeks after emerging.

Cool-Season Plots

Our cool-weather planting is actually designed to provide not only fall and winter carbohydrates, but also to carryover into the warm season and kick in some early protein. We accomplish this by planting a mixture of rye (the carbohydrate producer) and two varieties of clover—crimson and arrowleaf clover. Crimson's growth takes off in the early spring about the time bucks drop their antlers. Arrowleaf comes on a little later and produces until the cowpeas are planted. The clovers provide a critical source of protein early in the spring when both does and bucks have a very high demand for it. We plant our rye (no-tilled behind the "scalped" cowpeas) around the first of October at a rate of a bushel an acre in combination with about 10-20 pounds per acre of the two clovers.

Supplemental Backup

As noted earlier, to guarantee a constant source of both protein and carbohydrates, we back up our agricultural crops with year-round, free-choice supplemental feed. Basically, it's a safety net for the agriculture, mostly for the transition periods between crops but also in the event of poor crop production from drought or any other reason. From the time bucks drop their antlers in the late winter/early spring, we feed high-protein pellets, often mixed with corn early in the transition. Once bucks begin velvet-shedding in early fall, we shift over to corn. We normally see our greatest supplemental feed use in May when the does are heavy with fawns and don't like to move very far to feed. As for overall supplemental feed use, it comes in a very distant second to agriculture, which supplies the bulk of the nutritional requirements for Fort Perry deer.

Summary

The Fort Perry program is surprisingly simple isn't it? But, what it has done for that deer herd would have been thought impossible just a few years ago. It's safe to say that for both size and numbers the Fort Perry herd will rival any in the entire country! It was all made possible because of a management plan that has greatly increased the amount and quality of food available to the deer. As a result, deer size has soared and carrying capacity has increased to several times that of the natural habitat...while the quality of the natural browse has actually improved! That's progress any way you look at it.

EL TECOMATE RANCH STRATEGY

Before 1995, I thought I had met the nuttiest of the country's deer nuts. I couldn't imagine anyone crazier about the whitetail deer than folks like Bobby Parker, Jr., Steve Vaughn, James Kroll, Dick Idol, Jackie Brittingham, Scott Taylor, Gordon Whittington, George Cooper, Bill Jordan, Chuck Larsen, Greg Miller, David Foster, to name but a few of the many whitetail junkies I've crossed paths with. Not withstanding my wife's opinion of me, I figured these guys were the most smitten of the smitten. Then, I met Dr. Gary Schwarz...

Gary is an oral maxillofacial surgeon by profession, and an excellent one, but by love and by choice, he is one of the most dedicated, knowledgeable and innovative deer managers in the country. And as his accomplishments on El Tecomate Ranch in South Texas attest, he is one of the most successful.

One of the great things about Gary's success story is that he started with nothing, not even an acre or a dollar to buy it with. While still in dental school, Gary, along with a handful of friends, borrowed money to buy his first ranchland. Over time, using conservation easements to provide tax relief to help in the purchase of ranchland and to assure the longterm protection of the natural habitat, he added more acreage, some his own and some with partners. Today, Gary's personal acreage, El Tecomate, totals about 3,000 acres.

Making The Desert Bloom

In the country's most intensively managed state, Gary is Texas' undisputed leader in food-plot-based nutrition. His ascension to that position took time, creativity, hard work and a lot of experimenting, often in the face of steadfast insistence that what he was trying to do with food plots would not work. And, the skepticism was not without basis. The fact is that there are few places where consistently growing decent crops represents a greater challenge than in hot, dry South Texas.

Need proof that better nutrition really makes a difference? Here's 215 points of proof! This awesome 30-inch buck, appropriately called "Heart Attack," was produced by Gary Schwarz's food-plot program on Tecomate Ranch. With a typical 10-point frame scoring over 190 points, this buck could be the largest "basic 10" ever known from the state of Texas. Photo by Bill Draker.

That is one of the reasons I picked Tecomate as an example—if agricultural food-source management will work there, it'll work practically anywhere. And as Gary has proven, does it ever work there!

In recent years, Gary's nutritional program on El Tecomate has produced buck after buck winning top honors in Texas' many big buck contests. His success has even been documented scientifically by comparing the body and antler size of his bucks to those of neighboring leaseholders who have the same herd management strategy but no nutritional program beyond natural habitat management. The results have been nothing short of startling. In a three-year comparison of mature bucks, Gary's bucks averaged 20 B&C points larger and 26 pounds heavier than those of like ages on neighboring leases! Twenty B&C points—that's the difference between a 140 and a 160 or a 150 and a 170! To a trophy hunter, that's all the difference in the world! And, the study was conducted four years ago. Today, the difference is even greater!

Gary's success with food plots on Tecomate has drawn so much attention that he was literally forced into starting a seed company to help others obtain both the drought-tolerate seeds and the expertise in dryland farming necessary to put food plots to work on their property.

> *No matter where you are, herd management principles remain the same, but how you get nutrition to the deer definitely varies by locale.*

Joining forces with Fred Schuster, a professional farmer in the Rio Grande Valley, and Dr. Tim Fulbright, a wildlife biologist and range scientist with the Caesar Kleberg Wildlife Research Institute, Gary put together a team committed to helping the private land manager succeed. Thus was born the Tecomate Seed Company (Route 2, Box 77A, San Juan, TX 78589, 1-800-332-4054) headed up by Fred Schuster. Since its inception in 1993, Tecomate Seed Company has led the charge in food-plot management in Texas.

How did Gary achieve the kind of results that has caused even the diehards in the great deer state of Texas to sit up and take notice? Interestingly, the overall strategy is essentially the same as that of Fort Perry and any number of other successful programs I'm familiar with, validating the underlying principles of food-source management. Gary's program revolves around meeting the year-round nutritional needs of deer with cool and warm-season food plots. What makes Gary's program different is how he has to go about it. Every region of the country has certain farming limitations that must be overcome to maximize food-plot production. In the South, it's often acidic soils and infertility, solved by liming and fertilizing. In South Texas, it's a lack of moisture, solved by a combination of drought-tolerate plants and moisture-conserving farming techniques. Of course, no matter where you are, herd management principles remain the same, but how you get nutrition to the deer definitely varies by locale, as we're about to see.

Searching For The "Magic Bean"

Gary, being a farmer and rancher at heart, was quick to recognize the need to provide year-round nutrition and the potential to accomplish

When Gary first started trying to grow food plots in arid South Texas, he experimented with all kinds of legumes in search of a warm-season, high-protein food source that would prosper in the hot, dry conditions there. He found his answer in Australia in the form of a remarkable legume called lablab. I took this photo of Gary in a stand of lablab in late December, after the deer had fed on it since the previous April and after summer's heat had done its worse.

this with agricultural plantings. So, in hopes of finding a warm-season protein source, he began experimenting with readily available plants, such as cowpeas, soybeans, alfalfas and clovers, using standard farming techniques. At best, he met with only modest success. It became obvious that South Texas' hot, arid climate called for plants suited to dry-land farming in this demanding environment. His quest for such plants eventually led him to Australia and a drought-resistant forage legume called lablab, which is similar to cowpeas and soybeans. Subsequent testing revealed that lablab was indeed an excellent choice for the region. Deer eagerly consumed the high-protein plant and flourished on it.

Interestingly, what at first might seem like a negative regarding lablab actually turns out to be a positive. Gary intentionally selected a variety of forage lablab, now trademarked Tecomate Lablab, that does *not* tend to go to seed in South Texas. Even the little blooming that does take place occurs in December. What's the significance of this? Once an

133

annual plant goes to seed, it loses much of its nutritional punch, having completed its mission in life. Cowpeas go to seed in 80 to 90 days. Lablab, which can be planted as early as late February in South Texas, will continue to provide nutritious feed into December or until the first frost hits, which seldom occurs before late November. As a result, lablab keeps on ginning for eight or nine months. Yeah, Gary has to buy his seeds from Australia, but he figures the tradeoffs are well worth it.

A "reversible," mesh-wire fence keeps deer out and prevents over-grazing when the plants first emerge and can then be raised to allow deer to come under the fence when the plants mature.

Still, even with lablab in-hand, there were hurdles to overcome. One, farming techniques had to be refined to maximize the use of the limited water available. (We'll talk about this shortly.) Two, lablab, like other dicotyleton plants such as soybeans and cowpeas whose growing point is above ground, was vulnerable to overgrazing during the first few weeks after emerging. Of course, the overgrazing problem during the sensitive first weeks could be moderated by either lowering deer numbers, an idea inconsistent with objectives, or by planting enough acreage to spread grazing pressure so damage is minimal. The latter solution is what we opted for at Fort Perry, but that wasn't an option for Gary because of limited tillable land on his property. To keep the deer out during the critical three or four weeks lablab is vulnerable, Gary had to employ a "reversible," mesh-wire high-fence. After experimenting with several versions, he settled on a six-foot, five-inch-high fence consisting of a 32-inch lower section and a 47-inch upper section with two inches of overlap. When the plants are large enough to withstand heavy grazing, the lower panel can be *raised* to let the deer come *under* the fence.

Gary went about meeting the cool-season requirements in much the same fashion as the warm—he searched for better-suited plants and experimented...a lot. In time, he came up with several options that could answer the call and finally settled on one mix as the staple on his ranch—for now. It's something he calls Tecomate Duel Deer Mix. The mixture consists of several types of winter grasses, including wheat, triticali, ryegrass and oats, and various legumes such as Austrian winter peas, clovers, vetches and even alfalfa. With this mix, the grasses address win-

On both Fort Perry and Tecomate, serious farming techniques are employed, and the results are nothing short of incredible. Photo by Glenn Hayes.

ter carbohydrate needs and the legumes provide a leg-up on early spring protein requirements.

Now, just a word on Gary's supplemental feeding strategy. He does backup his agricultural crops with free-choice supplemental feed—soybeans and high-protein pellets in the warm season and corn and some pellets in the cool season. However, Gary views the supplemental feed purely as a safety net. He says he would not use it at all if he could put more acres in agricultural crops, but limited tillable ground limits his food-plot acreage to just over four percent of his total area. In short, agriculture is the heart of his program, as it is at Fort Perry.

Before we look at an overview of Gary's basic program, I should say that what we're going to talk about is just one of several configurations that will work to some degree. Gary has other plants and mixes on the market that have proven themselves. For instance, he has a warm-season plant called Tecomate DQP, which stands for deer and quail peas. This crawling, vining-type legume offers over 20 percent protein, isn't vulnerable to early overgrazing and will even carryover in South Texas if temperatures don't fall below 28 degrees. It is an especially good choice when putting up reversible fences is not an option, but lablab, when farmed

A picture is indeed worth a thousand words—a week on Tecomate Ranch! These are obviously some well-fed whitetails. Photo by Glenn Hayes.

correctly, is even better in South Texas. Therefore, that's what we're going to look at in our example. Also, Gary has several other plants and mixes still in the experimental stage that hold great promise. Something may eventually come along that will prove better than the lablab and Duel Deer Mix combination that we're going to look at in this chapter. The real point here is to see how one manager, in this case Gary Schwarz, has met the challenge of better nutrition. The specifics of what he did and how he did it may or may not be applicable to you, but the principles will be.

Banking Moisture

Right up front, Gary had to find a way to overcome the greatest challenge of growing food-plots in South Texas—a shortage of water. This required special farming techniques, some of which could be extracted from traditional farming methodology. Some had to be developed for the purpose. Thus combining some old and some new, Gary came up with his own strategy for "banking water." At its heart is deep tillage of the soil, creating a 16 to 20-inch layer of soft, absorbent soil. This layer, which is prepared weeks and even months ahead of planting time, serves as a sponge that allows the moisture from the occasional rains to be soaked up and preserved above the hardpan but below the level where the scorching sun and drying wind can quickly suck it away. Even as little as one inch of rain on this absorbent layer of soil can be enough to produce a good crop of lablab. Gary points out that sandy, loamy soils are best for banking moisture. Heavy clay soils require irrigation or more rain.

The Program At Work

Gary normally plants lablab as soon as the danger of freezing is over in late February or early March. The deep tillage in preparation for late winter/early spring planting is done from mid-August through December, but the gamble increases as more time passes. After deep tillage, the field awaits the rain. When it comes, Gary lightly tills the plot again with a field cultivator or a disc to "seal" the moisture in and control weeds that would draw out precious moisture. If necessary, this is when he also applies a herbicide to prevent the germination of grasses and certain weeds. When the time is right, he plants the lablab with a row-crop planter at a rate of a seed per 8 to 12 inches (8 to 10 pounds per acre). The protective fence is lowered to keep the deer out for three to four weeks until the lablab is well-leafed and going strong.

Gary came up with his own strategy for "banking water," overcoming the greatest challenge of growing food plots in South Texas.

In order for lablab's protein to be available during the critical early antler-growing phase, Gary tries to have the field ready for grazing by the first two weeks of April. To encourage more rapid growth and curb weed competition, he normally will cultivate the crop a time or two. The result is a stand of up to 8,000 pounds per acre of highly digestible, 25 to 30-percent protein plants that will put bigger antlers on more bucks...and this in a region once thought to be incapable of consistently growing a warm-season crop!

You may have figured out that the need to bank moisture prior to the spring lablab planting seriously curtails the ability to double-crop warm- and cool-season crops on the same acreage, as we do routinely on Fort Perry. During wet years, double-cropping can certainly be done. The problem is that you can't know in advance when it's possible. So, Gary faces a decision. He can plant a winter crop prior to planting lablab and take a chance that sufficient winter and spring rains will fall to replace the moisture used by the winter crops. Or, he can play it safe and plant

137

the winter crop on different acreage, allowing the waiting lablab field to bank moisture for the spring planting. Gary has done it both ways but prefers to bank moisture to maximize lablab success. This requires more land for food plots, but happily, a good field of lablab goes a long way in inherently productive South Texas.

The cool-season planting of Duel Deer Mix is not quite as critical as the warm-season planting. The cooler weather stretches out the moisture a bit more. Still, moisture conservation is important. Gary's best success comes when he deep tills the soil in mid-August through September to capture the fall moisture prior to planting Duel Deer Mix (using a grain drill and a planting rate of about 30 pounds/acre) in November or December. Why so late a planting? Earlier plantings, while feasible in cooler, wetter climates, are likely to suffer from heat and the lack of moisture in South Texas. By waiting, much higher productivity can be expected. True, the benefits of the plot as an attractant during the early part of hunting season are lost, but the primary goal is nutrition, which is delivered in greater doses by planting later when conditions are better.

Food-source management brings you something entirely new—control over your deer herd and hunting future!

Even in South Texas, it is possible, even practical, to follow a warm-season crop with a cool-season one. To start with, the warm-season crop can be plowed under and deep tillage done in, say, September, leaving time to bank moisture before the late fall planting. Gary frequently does this. Sometimes, however, Gary will let the lablab stay later into the fall and plow it under just prior to planting Duel Deer Mix. Moisture is the deciding factor. It's the manager's call to make.

By the way, because of the grass/legume formula of Duel Deer Mix, it is an effective all-season crop and can be left in production practically all year, to be plowed under the subsequent fall in preparation for a lablab planting in February. Rotating crops on a field is also helpful in preventing root rot in lablab, and other legumes, and helps the soil as well.

So there you have it—the food-plot strategy for El Tecomate Ranch. Yes, it takes a lot of work to pull it off, especially when first getting set up. But think about what it produces. A 20-acre lablab plot is capable of yielding up to 160,000 pounds of highly nutritious deer feed! That's 80 tons! At $300 a ton, an equivalent amount of high-protein pellets would cost $24,000...and would not bring the same results! Once everything is set up, the annual cost of planting is a fraction of that. With a little more than four percent of El Tecomate in food plots, Gary is supporting a deer per six acres at jumbo body and antler sizes. Is it worth it? Gary thinks so...and so do a growing number of people both in Texas and across the country.

You Have Options

Yes, food-source management brings you something entirely new—control over your deer herd and hunting future! You can pick from a wide menu of options and match the depth and breadth of your management plan to your objectives and resources. All options are open, from the most basic first step—a food source aimed primarily at attracting deer for viewing and harvesting—to going all the way with an intensive year-round feeding program and a carefully regulated harvest aimed at achieving precise herd balance. And, anyone with a sizable chunk of deer country, a desire to improve his deer hunting lot and a commitment to improving the health of his deer herd can make a difference. Whatever you choose, whatever progress you make, you will have the satisfaction of knowing that it all came to pass because you cared enough to make it happen!

Chapter Fifteen

Timing Is (Almost) Everything

T

IMING IS EVERYTHING IN WHITETAIL
hunting…assuming, of course, you're hunting in the right place to start
with. Being in the right place at the wrong time is little different from
simply being in the wrong place! I learned this by hunting at the wrong
time! And being hardheaded, it seems I occasionally have to be reminded
of this crucial fact again. I got just such a reminder a few years ago on one
of the best ranches in Texas.

From previous experiences on "trophy hunts" during the peak-rut
third week of December, we knew loads of big bucks roamed the sea of
brush on this fabulous ranch. On the strength of that fact, three of us
from WHITETAIL magazine took our wives there on Thanksgiving
weekend for what the ranch manager called a "ladies-only management-
buck hunt." The women folk could shoot the biggest basic 8-pointer they
could find. Sure, we all knew late November was well ahead of the rut
and that hunting would be tougher then. Still, we expected to see plenty
of big, mature bucks. It would simply be a matter of putting in the prerequisite time before a whopper 8-pointer showed. Our assumption was
in error!

As it turned out, there was nothing simple about finding a mature
buck of any kind. The hot, dry brush seemed to be practically devoid of
life on four legs. Our wives soon got tired of hearing tales about what we
had seen on previous December excursions. Had it not been for a buck

140

A double-drop-tined buck is the dream of nearly all trophy whitetail hunters. Tom Brooks killed this one because he made plans to be in the right place, Saskatchewan, at the right time, the peak of rut. Photo by author.

Louisa Vaughn caught snoozing in his bed during the midday heat, we would have all returned home with nothing more than disgruntled spouses.

Great ranch; bad timing!

I knew better than go after mature whitetails during a low-odds time with no extenuating circumstances to swing the odds back my way, even if convenience, expediency or comfort argued otherwise. Even before that Texas trip, I had learned that lesson over and over, like during my early runs at those elusive Canadian giants. Actually, a bad experience on my second hunt ever to the frigid land of our northern neighbors caused me to override my normal rut-timing policies on subsequent hunts up there in favor of trying to survive the experience with all my digits still intact. That particular ill-fated hunt took place during late November in Manitoba, and not once the entire week did the mercury top minus 10! Being a thin-blooded Georgian, I'd never seen cold like that, and having experienced it once, I wasn't anxious to ever see it again! With that experience "frozen" into my memory, the opening week of season got the nod on my next hunts in hopes of avoiding the extreme cold. Well, I did avoid the cold...and the bigger bucks as well!

As is still the case, Canada's first week of season fell well before the rut, and the mature bucks simply weren't moving then. I made the early hunt two or three times. Each time, I would return home with whatever modicum of success I had been able to scratch out, only to hear tales of big bucks running wild later during the rut. It didn't take too much of that to motivate me to learn how to dress for the cold. Ditching my Southern attire of layered flannels and cottons, I suited up for a polar expedition, gritted my teeth and weathered the stinging bite of mid and late November for a chance at the rut-crazed giants. That extra two or three weeks transformed the place completely from what I had seen in late October and my fortunes soared!

Same place; better timing!

When the long-anticipated opening of Kansas to nonresident whitetail hunting finally came about in 1994, there was a mad rush among serious hunters to procure one of the few hundred tags issued. I was among those in the rush and was fortunate enough to draw a tag. I had heard the stories about the monster bucks in this great state and was anxious to hunt there. But, I had a lingering doubt as to how it was all going to turn out. Why? The gun season took place well after the rut. I knew the post-rut was going to be a difficult time to hunt these farmland bucks. They were sure to have curtailed their earlier ramblings and were likely to be holed up as they recovered from the rigors of the rut. Despite my concerns, the incredible stories the outfitter was telling me of big bucks freely roaming about renewed my hope, though past experience with the post-rut gave me plenty of reasons to worry.

When the time for the hunt rolled around, seven of us ascended on our camp with high expectations. Those expectations were fueled by continued tales of the big bucks that had been seen just days and weeks before. A brief afternoon scouting trip revealed awesome rubs and scrapes to back up the tales, but the age of the rubs and scrapes heightened my anxiety about our timing. Everything I knew about timing told me we should have been there two or three weeks earlier during archery season when the rut was underway. Still, I hoped.

I would like to say that the hunt was replete with huge bucks run-

ning to and fro, but alas, it did not happen that way. Indeed, I didn't even
see a deer until the fourth day. Weathering big buck sign mocked me as I
hunted denuded hardwood bottoms and green fields practically void of
fresh tracks. All the places big bucks had been seen earlier now were
devoid of any deer activity. The story was the same for everybody.
Coyotes, bobcats, hawks and turkeys were usually the highlights of our
nightly reports.

On the next to the last day, my Florida hunting buddy, George
Cooper, abandoned his stand and began to ramble around in frustration.
As he stood on a bluff overlooking a cedar thicket at the head of a long
draw, a buck's nerves gave way and he bounded into the prairies. George
made a 200-yard offhand shot on the 155-class 8-pointer, making George
the hero of our little camp. The final day was spent pushing the thickest
cover we could find. By forcing movement, we began to see deer, though
not the kind we had trekked to Kansas in hopes of. When the hunt
ended, I had used my all-time luckiest shot on a high-140s 8-pointer hell-
bent for some place in Nebraska. Five others went home empty-handed.

Upon returning to the office of WHITETAIL magazine, the calls
began coming in from others who had hunted Kansas on its grand opening. The reports were the same—huge buck sign everywhere but no bodies to go with it. Sure, the odd good buck was killed, but almost without
exception, they fell to forced movement or some kind of fluke. For
instance, one guy had killed a high-160s 10-pointer while walking back
to his pickup after a morning's hunt. He had parked his truck a half-mile
out in the prairies to avoid alerting the deer he planned to hunt in the
distant wooded draw. As he ambled back to his pickup, he happened to
notice something resembling a set of antlers silhouetted above the grass
under a lone cedar tree about 200 yards from his truck. A hunkered-down
sneak on the possible rack ended with the biggest buck of his life.

The post-rut in Kansas had proven to be an awful lot like the post-
rut everywhere else—slow! The problem wasn't a lack of big bucks; it was
bad timing!

THE RUT IS THE KEY

I believe poor timing is one of the most common and costly mistakes made by even serious trophy hunters. Timing a hunt for maximum

Being in the right place is one thing, but you also have to be there at the right time. Advance planning will help. Photo by Troy Huffman.

odds of success is absolutely essential if you want to consistently return home with happy results. It's not enough just to be in a good place; you also have to be there at the right time. When that right time occurs varies based on many different factors. Paramount among those factors is time of year relative to the rut. The rut is the very centerpiece of all fall whitetail activity, and in one way or the other, it influences what deer are doing throughout the entire fall. It is imperative for a serious trophy hunter to understand the pattern of fall deer activity associated with the rut. Timing your hunts starts with that understanding.

Fall is a time of change, even upheaval, for the whitetail. The weather, food sources and habitat are all in a state of flux throughout much of the fall. Most of all, the animals themselves are undergoing major metabolic and behavioral changes as they prepare for the onset of the most chaotic and drastic behavioral shift of the entire year—the rut. The fact is that from the time of velvet-shedding in the late summer/early fall until antler-shedding in the winter, nearly all whitetail activity, especially that of bucks, revolves around the rut, either preparing for it, participating in it or getting over it. (Note: While I refer to the time span we're discussing as the fall, we're actually talking about the entire time bucks have hard antlers, even though that time may encompass parts of summer, fall and winter.)

Fortunately for the hunter, the general pattern of changes in fall deer behavior and activity is predictable and common to all North

American whitetail populations to some degree. Yet, exactly how this pattern is played out at any given place depends on the conditions unique to that place. Certain outside influences, some local, others broad-based, can and do cause local variances in the overall pattern. The savvy hunter, however, can recognize these factors and quite accurately predict how they will affect deer activity. Thus, by understanding the general fall activity pattern and factoring in the outside influences, it is possible for a hunter to anticipate what deer will be doing at any given time where he hunts and plan his time afield accordingly.

This brings us back to the fact that the fall activity pattern keys off the rut. Thus, as logic would dictate, precisely when the pattern is played out depends on when the rut takes place, which varies greatly across the continent. For instance, the rut begins in early September in South Florida, late October in Hill Country Texas, mid-November in Wisconsin, mid-December in South Texas and late January in South Alabama. Since the fall activity pattern keys off the rut dates, a shift of as much as several months in the timing of the various stages of the pattern is to be expected across the whitetail's range. So, in order to anticipate where in the overall fall activity pattern a local deer population is at any given time, one of the first things a serious whitetail hunter must do is *find out when the rut takes place* where he plans to hunt.

FALL MOVEMENT PATTERNS

Since the rut is the centerpiece of fall deer activity, I view everything relative to the rut. There's the rut, and then there are the times preceding and following the rut. Thus, we can logically break the fall into the three segments—pre-rut, rut and post-rut. But, does this segmentation allow for adequate identification of all the fall deer movement patterns? Close but not quite.

In my first book, *Hunting Trophy Whitetails,* I divided the fall into four activity periods—the pre-rut, the scraping period of the rut, the breeding period of the rut and the post-rut. Those four periods, two of which are divisions of the all-important rut, certainly represent the main activity periods. However, because precise timing is so critical for maximum odds of success, especially during the harder-to-hunt pre-rut and post-rut periods, we will further subdivide these two periods into what I call "phases" based on certain clear activity patterns within each. The pre-rut period can be divided into three phases—summer transition, core-area feeding and lull phases. The post-rut period divides into the waning rut, recovery and feeding phases. We'll keep the same two divisions of the rut—scraping and breeding periods.

To illustrate a "typical" timeline for the fall activity pattern, let's lay it out graphically. We'll assume the breeding period, from which everything else keys, begins in mid November. This rut date would correspond to the timing of the rut throughout much of the central and northern U.S. and Canada. I want to point out that what we're talking about here is the activity and behavioral patterns apparent to the hunter and not necessarily exactly what's going on purely from a biological standpoint. For instance, the duration of our breeding period will be about two weeks, but in reality, some breeding will take place over a much wider time span than that. However, what the hunter might call the "peak of rut" usually lasts two weeks or less. Only the behavior and activity that translates into hunting opportunity is of concern here. Also, some periods and phases have well-defined beginning and ending points; others more or less "fade" in and out. Some are fairly consistent in duration; others are more variable. We'll discuss the various aspects of each in detail later.

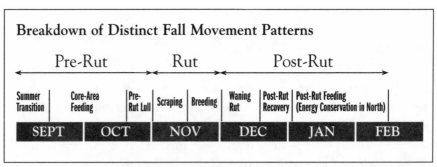

Breakdown of Distinct Fall Movement Patterns

	Pre-Rut			Rut		Post-Rut		
Summer Transition	Core-Area Feeding	Pre-Rut Lull	Scraping	Breeding	Waning Rut	Post-Rut Recovery	Post-Rut Feeding (Energy Conservation in North)	
SEPT	OCT		NOV		DEC		JAN	FEB

Each period and phase represents a time of predictable deer activity seen to some degree wherever whitetails are found. And, each offers the hunter certain opportunities and poses certain obstacles. Yet, almost without exception, the greatest chance for success is during the two rut periods. Why? Big, mature bucks are by nature nocturnal and secretive. Unless something spurs them to move, they seldom expose themselves during daylight hours under normal circumstances, making them exceedingly difficult to hunt. Obviously movement can be forced, i.e., deer drives or incidental pressure from hunters, but trophy hunters are more interested in voluntary movement. The greatest single factor that can prompt a mature buck to willingly leave the security of cover in the fall and move about during shooting light is the sense-blinding lure of the rut! This ritual of passion-driven madness is the only time mature bucks cast aside their usual caution, perhaps better described as paranoia, and expose themselves with any degree of regularity to the dangers of the world, including the hunter's bullet or arrow. No other time compares to the rut when mature whitetails are the target!

Yet, the rut is rather short-lived, and by necessity, whitetail hunting must often take place outside this prime time. Therefore, the hunter must be able to evaluate his chances during the other times as well. How much potential a particular phase in the pre-rut or post-rut may hold depends to a great degree on the presence or absence of the outside influences mentioned earlier. Foremost among these influences are hunting pressure, which generally serves to negate potential, and major food sources, the presence of which can greatly bolster the odds of success outside the rut. Other influences that also come into play when timing a hunt are the hunting techniques employed, hunter skill, time available, herd composition, cover conditions, hunting regulations, expected weather conditions, size and nature of the property to be hunted, mobility and accessibility, to name but a few. These and other factors can greatly affect local huntability and odds for success at any given time. It should be obvious that the hunter must have a broad understanding of both the overall fall activity patterns and the many outside factors affecting local activity at a particular time. In the following chapters, we will look at both.

Until now, we've talked mostly about the big-picture movement pattern and factors that affect that pattern. Besides these big-picture or macro patterns, there are also influences that affect the relative level of day-to-day deer movement. At the forefront of these considerations are weather conditions, moon phases and, here it is again, hunting pressure. While choosing the best timing for a hunt is more dependant on the factors affecting the long-term movement pattern, a hunter's ability to predict short-term movement intensity and to truly understand what deer are doing depends on knowing what motivates deer on both the macro and micro level. We'll round out our timing picture by also taking a look at the factors affecting day-to-day deer movement later in this section.

Chapter Sixteen

Understanding Fall Movement Patterns

Whuen I'm CONTEMPLATING THE timing of a hunt, I have a process I go through. It's really quite simple. I first determine what the hunting situation is where I'm going to hunt. That involves all the outside factors discussed earlier—hunting pressure, presence of major food sources, hunting techniques to be employed, skill, time available, herd composition, cover conditions, hunting regulations, expected weather, size and nature of the hunted property, mobility, accessibility, etc. Then, I figure out when the rut is going to hit. Next, I match all this up with the fall movement pattern. From this, a pretty clear picture should be formed of when the best time to hunt there will be. After working my schedule into the formula, the dates are set.

Of course, knowledge of fall activity patterns and the ability to anticipate what the deer will be doing at various times during the fall are at the hub of this process. To that end, let's rather briefly walk through the fall activity periods in sequence. Remember, the patterns discussed here represent the ideal and we're only concerned about mature bucks. Young bucks don't follow this pattern, nor do does. Certain factors, most notably excessive hunting pressure, can disrupt normal deer activity.

The one in focus is the key to your fall hunting success. Hot does lure big bucks into places they would never go on their own...like into your rifle sights. The rut is the centerpiece of fall movement patterns. Photo by Mike Biggs.

THE PRE-RUT

The approach of fall marks major changes in the bucks' world. After a leisurely summer spent in bachelor groups, usually consisting of similar-aged bucks, though bucks of different ages will often buddy-up, a transformation begins in bucks. Triggered by changes in daylength, the testicles, which have been quite literally out of sight and out of mind, begin to swell and drop back into the scrotum. With this comes increasing production of hormones, most notably the male hormone testosterone. This powerful hormone coursing their veins, both physical and mental changes are initiated in bucks. Their velvet-covered antlers hard-

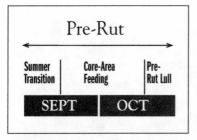

en. Soon thereafter, the velvet dries and, with a little help from the buck, is shed. Even as these physical changes are occurring, the bucks' passive attitude and social tolerances also begin to undergo transformation. These changes, marked by the shedding of velvet, usher in the beginning of the pre-rut period, which occurs in early to mid-September over most of the country.

Summer Transition Phase

The first two weeks or so of the pre-rut make up what we're calling the summer transition phase. Essentially, this phase is just what the name implies—a time of transition from the summer pattern to the fall, rut-governed pattern. This phase starts out with the bucks doing pretty much the same thing they did all summer, namely feeding early and late on the best food sources around and resting in cool, protected places during the heat of day. The bucks really pack in the food now. Most food sources continue to be the same ones they depended on during the summer since the shift to fall sources has not yet taken place. Though their relatively slow-paced lifestyle still revolves around food, security and comfort, the occasional bout with saplings using their newly battle-ready headgear attests to the accelerating pace of the bucks' hormone-driven internal clock. Soon after the start of this phase, the heretofore chummy bucks within the bachelor groups start looking crossways at each other. Aggression begins to mount, and bucks start posturing and vying for dominance in an effort to finely tune a hierarchy largely already established. They become increasingly intolerant of each other's company, leading into part two of the pre-rut.

The Core-Area Feeding Phase

The core-area feeding phase kicks off when the bachelor groups begin to breakup. About two or three weeks into the pre-rut, bucks, especially the older ones, begin to gradually separate and retire to their own core area, chosen largely based on security and seclusion. Some bucks may continue to chum around with one or two of their old running buddies for a while even after breakup begins, but they too will soon grow

Rutting activity is not the only thing that can put a big buck in front of you. Special circumstances and conditions can create opportunities outside the rut. During a hot, dry fall in South Texas, George Cooper shot this 160-class 10-pointer at a waterhole before the rut kicked in. Photo by author.

tired of each other's company. Yearling and younger bucks often stay banned together much longer, having not yet adopted the behavioral traits of mature whitetails.

Once in their core area, bucks settle into a feeding/resting routine. Most of their movement is from their bedding area to feeding grounds and back again. In their core area and along their rather predictable travel routes, rising testosterone levels prompt them to hone their fighting skills on bushes and small trees and engage in some preliminary "pawing." During this time, mature bucks are largely solitary and reclusive, moving mostly in low light and at night. On the positive side, their feeding routine is often somewhat predictable, though they will sometimes inexplicably change feeding locations. They have little interest in does and don't intentionally interact with the doe groups, though they may feed on the same food sources. Younger bucks, however, tend to hang around the doe groups, mainly because the does are usually near major food sources.

Though bucks normally come into the pre-rut in good physical

The scraping period of the rut represents a unique time to hunt a particular buck. For a short time, mature bucks follow a predictable routine of checking and making breeding scrapes and rubs. This buck is hard at work on a scrape, which nearly always will be located along an edge. Photo by Troy Huffman.

condition from a summer of feeding, they continue to build fat reserves and body mass in anticipation of the challenges of the rut and winter ahead. As nature's economy would have it, fall foods such as acorns, the various other mast crops, agricultural crops and even the leaves of some trees and plants are particularly high in carbohydrates, contributing to the buildup of fat reserves.

All the time the bucks are feeding on the abundance of fall, another factor is also contributing to their bulk and their progress toward the battle-ready physique characteristic of the coming rut. That factor is hormones. Testosterone has the same amplifying effect on bulk that steroids have on an athlete. As the days pass leading toward the rut, hormone levels continue to increase, as does aggression, and the combination of abundant food, hormones and exercise from mock fights and rubbing all contribute to the bulking process, which sharply accelerates as the rut nears.

The Pre-Rut Lull

Throughout the core-area feeding phase, mature bucks spend most of their time in and around their core area, leaving only to feed or water. As the pre-rut period draws to a close, their homebody tendency reaches its zenith in what I call the pre-rut lull. They are now in prime condition and carry maximum body mass. They begin to lose interest in food and become more and more distracted by things to come, though they are not yet ready to begin their rut-related ramblings. Gradually, their usual feeding pattern begins to breakdown. They stick close to home, venting mounting aggression on nearby saplings and trees. For a brief time, perhaps a week or two, bucks become reclusive, staying mostly in and around their core areas as hormones and stepped-up rubbing put the finishing touches on their thick-necked physique. From a travel standpoint, this pre-rut lull is truly the calm before the storm.

There may well be scientific reasons for this pre-rut lull. Namely, this downtime is almost certainly tied, at least in part, to how moon phases play into the timing of the rut. Moon light, or in this case the lack thereof, may well trigger hormonal responses that actually suppress deer activity during the time just prior to the start of the scraping period. We'll talk about the moon's role in the timing of the rut in a later chapter.

By the end of the pre-rut period, mounting restlessness takes feet and bucks begin to expand their travels, laying down more serious rubs and scrapes. Aggression and lust grow. Feeding takes a backseat as the bucks shift their focus from food to females. With that, the pre-rut has ended and the rut has begun.

THE SCRAPING PERIOD OF THE RUT

Assuming a mid-November breeding startup, you can expect the scraping period to more or less osmosis out of the pre-rut around the first of November. Although I've seen significant scraping activity three or more weeks before the start of breeding, experience leads me to believe that the serious, consistent scraping characterizing this period lasts about two weeks. Activity during the first week normally builds gradually, but I've occasionally seen the symptoms of the pre-rut lull carryover into the first week. The real festivities don't usually crank off until about a week before breeding starts.

The scraping period is marked by an increase in scraping and rubbing activity (usually in and around doe concentrations), much increased buck travel and heightened buck aggression. Bucks start out the scraping period using their core area as the base of operations. Instead of traveling mostly to and from their feeding grounds as they did during the pre-rut, their destination is now doe groups, some of which may be a mile, two miles or even more from their core area. Bucks make scouting passes through the home ranges of doe groups, locating the high-activity areas and checking out the territory, especially the "traditional scraping areas" where mature bucks make breeding scrapes and rubs year after year. On these early runs, the bucks make preliminary "test" scrapes and rubs, usually in the traditional scraping areas, and may even feed a bit on nearby major food sources.

A few days into the scraping period, the bucks start their work in earnest. Their route and routine now pretty well established, the bucks begin making serious breeding scrapes. These are no longer the haphazard, poorly formed pawings of weeks goneby. Breeding scrapes are large, perhaps two to five feet in diameter, well-defined, oval-shaped areas pawed completely clean of leaves and debris. About 4 to 4 1/2 feet above the scrape, there will almost invariably be a mangled and broken overhanging limb made that way by the buck's sometimes violet attempt to leave his scent on the limb from his forehead and/or preorbital glands. Even his mouth gets into the action as he frequently bites the branches and pulls them through his mouth. The ground in the scrape will be "plowed up," damp and often musty smelling. This odor is because both bucks and does urinate over their tarsal glands (located on their hind legs) onto the scrape, leaving their "calling card" for a would-be mate. Often, scrapes will be strung together forming a "scrapeline."

Breeding rubs are usually in association with breeding scrapes. Hormones running high, bucks work themselves into a lather when engaged in the serious work of setting the bait for a hot doe. At some point, they release their pint-up frustration on nearby bushes and trees, often shredding or maybe even breaking in two their chosen target. Like scrapes, several rubs are usually together, forming a rubline. Also like scrapes, rubs are both visual and scent-markers.

Rubs and scrapes are practically always found along an edge of some type, often near major food sources, if present. Seldom-used logging roads, the edge of clearings and fields, old homesites, the break between two timber types and stream and lake edges are favored places for scrapes and rubs. One of the very best places to check is where you've seen them in years past. Barring changes in the habitat, these traditional scraping areas will be used year after year and probably by more than one buck. Even if a good buck has been shot there, don't give up on the place.

Either others are around or another will soon show up.

Just a word about the incredible importance of scent and chemical communication in whitetails. They are marvelously equipped to both detect and distribute scent. They have noses that will make a bloodhound pea-green with envy, and their head, feet and legs are adorned with an array of scent glands, not to mention the scenting capabilities of their urine and saliva. Everything they do has purpose. Rubs, scrapes, licking branches, the rub-urination behavior and even their tracks all leave scent that communicates something very specific to other deer, like the identity of the marking animal, its dominance status, its breeding readiness, etc.

In many cases, it even goes beyond communication in the classic sense. Scent or chemicals called pheromones can actually cause involuntary responses in other deer. For instance, biologists now believe that the scent left on, say, breeding rubs made by dominant bucks can trigger the onset of estrus in a near-ready doe and actually suppress the breeding urge of subdominant bucks! Signpost rubs, which are large rubs made and frequently worked by dominant bucks, as well as other bucks, are major communication points. Signpost rubs—some of which are used for generations—are usually located in social hubs, at staging areas, in and around preferred core areas or at other strategic points.

Back to the scraping period. Growing aggression now leads to challenges and fights between bucks of similar size. Mature bucks are now ranging well beyond their familiar territory where a hierarchy has been established among area bucks. During their travels, they encounter other mature bucks that offer challenge. Threats and posturing—hackles up and ears back—usually settle the matter, and when that doesn't work, fights breakout. Some can be serious, but the most violent fights come during the breeding period when a hot doe is the direct prize.

Once bucks start scraping in earnest, the pace of the deer world really picks up. The mature bucks begin a somewhat predictable routine (though the predictable part is relatively short-lived) of making, checking and maintaining scrapes at the social hubs of the various doe groups. The younger bucks randomly work the doe groups and make half-baked scrapes, usually near the major feeding areas, and check the scrapes of the mature bucks, hoping to get in on whatever action may occur. Does continue to feed, but their schedule becomes more and more disrupted by their own restlessness and by the evermore persistent bucks. The near-steaming pot of flurried activity may well be further stirred by the odd early doe coming into heat.

In addition to working their scrapes, bucks begin seeking out does in hopes of catching their first whiff of the coming estrus. The does, their tails tucked and their bodies hunched and low to the ground, scurry away from their impassioned suitors. Should the doe urinate, the buck excitedly sniffs or licks the discharge, sometimes raising his head high, curling his upper lip and placing the discharge on a small apparatus on the roof of his mouth called the Jacobson's organ. "Flehmening," as it is called, is a common behavior in hoofed animals and is apparently associated with determining the breeding readiness of the doe and/or encouraging it in the buck.

Within a few days of the beginning of widespread scraping, the promising scent of soon-to-be-ready does permeates the air, perhaps first picked up by the bucks at their scrapes. This alluring scent disrupts the bucks' travel routine and rewrites their schedule. They start to spend less time working their scrapes and more time actually checking out does. Their travels become less predictable. The bucks spend more time near the doe groups, even bedding near them, returning to their core area less frequently. They travel feverishly from one doe group to another, seeking the receptive doe they know will soon appear. They eagerly check each doe they encounter. The madding scent of approaching wholesale estrus finally fills the woods. Then, with the first wave of hot does comes the frenzied start of the breeding period.

THE BREEDING PERIOD OF THE RUT

For two days now, that almost-ready scent has been in the air, driving the buck to seek its source at any cost. In the merging light of first dawn, he alternately trots and walks down the familiar trail that will take him to his scrapes in the small clearing near the edge of the cornfield. In a stiff-legged trot, he covers the last 50 yards to the washtub-sized scrape. Even before he noses the wet, freshly turned soil, his eyes wall with excitement. It's there, fuming up from his scrape—the siren-scent of a doe fully in estrus, ready to breed. Nose to the ground, the buck frantically sweeps back and forth in search of the departing trail. In seconds, he hits it, lock-

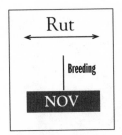

ing onto the mind-blinding scent with unwavering certainty. Intent on one thing, he goes off in a stiff, short-gaited trot. The trail takes him into the corn-field and on through a large fallow field. The buck gives no heed to the strangeness of being in the broad open in full daylight. His mind is on one thing—the doe that left her calling card in his scrape. Unerringly, his nose takes him to her. Two small bucks have already found her. He rushes in and scatters them and then turns to the doe. She is ready but teasingly unwilling to accept his advances. A chase ensues. The same scene is being played out throughout the land. The first major wave of does has entered estrus and the breeding festivities are underway.

Before proceeding, let's explore some basics about the breeding period. This period does, in fact, come on rather suddenly when the first big wave of does enters estrus. True, a few does come into heat earlier and some later than the majority, but it's the first big wave, made up primarily of does 2 1/2 years old and older, that brings on the frenzied breeding activity known as the "peak of rut." This critical time, which lasts about two weeks, is what we define as the breeding period and is of the utmost importance to hunters. All things being equal, the heaviest breeding activity takes place during the first week or so and then tails off after that.

Obviously, some does are bred after our two-week breeding period. A few are, of course, simply latecomers from the primary rut. Then, about 26 days after the start of peak rut, a second and much smaller group of does, consisting mostly of 1 1/2-year-olds but also including older does that didn't conceive the first go-around, will enter estrus and trigger what is called the "secondary rut." This occurs during what we've designated as the post-rut period. Additionally, 26 or so days later a minor "tertiary rut" occurs when six-month-old fawns enter estrus for the first time, which will include from 20 to 50 percent of the fawns in a healthy herd. As far as the hunter is concerned, both the secondary and tertiary ruts are of far less importance than the peak-breeding period. In most places, hunters are hard-pressed to even see evidence of the secondary and tertiary ruts.

As we've said, the timing of the breeding period varies greatly throughout the whitetail's range. Certainly, November is the main month for breeding across the country, but over our vast land, breeding can begin as early as August or as late as February. When the peak of the rut

Understanding fall movement patterns is critical to trophy success. Max Corder (right) and Carl Frohaug put their heads together to figure out this record-class Canadian buck, who was preoccupied by the rut. Photo by author.

occurs is determined by nature in order for the fawns to be born at a time that allows for maximum survival. It is incumbent on every hunter to find out when the breeding window is where he hunts. We'll talk more about the timing of the rut in a later chapter.

A doe will start showing signs—urinating on her tarsal glands and emitting the telltale scent—of approaching estrus a day or two before she's actually ready. She will become restless and scorn the company of other does. She may well begin seeking out a buck by visiting scrapes. Most experts now agree that the dominant or alpha doe will seek out the dominant buck in the area and do her part in warding off the advances of the lesser bucks. One thing is for certain—her siren scent will soon find its way to the nostrils of a lovesick buck. When it does, scant time will pass before he finds her. If he is able to fend off other bucks, he may remain with her until she goes out of estrus, which only lasts 24 hours. Or after doing his duty, usually more than once, he may move on after a short while in search of another receptive doe, revisiting doe groups or his scrapes if he doesn't come across a hot doe right away. It is not uncommon for more than one buck to breed a hot doe, but in most cases, the dominant bucks get first crack at her.

When the first wave of does come into heat, the normally ordered life of the whitetail deer turns to chaos. Predictable travel and movement patterns are a thing of the past. Bucks lower their defenses to a degree unlike any other time. They can be so totally obsessed by the breeding urge as to appear plain stupid. They may move at any hour of the day and expose themselves in ways and places unthinkable outside the breeding period. Bucks, even the wise, mature ones, now may blindly follow the harrowed does wherever they lead them, shadowing their every move.

As I said, dominant bucks get first choice of the hot does. In lightly hunted populations with low buck:doe ratios and good buck age structures, the young and subdominant bucks spend much of their time watching from the sidelines in utter frustration as the dominant bucks get most of the action. I've seen as many as a half-dozen subordinate bucks look on longingly as the big boy feverishly guards his lady and fends off persistent advances from the lesser hopefuls. At times, it seems that the doe actually enjoys exasperating her suitor by trying to break free of his defenses. In such cases, the buck will often work the doe back into position exactly like a quarter horse works a cow. To avoid competitive situations, bucks will frequently take control and drive the doe off to isolated spots, which accounts in part for some of the absurd places bucks are sometimes found during the breeding period.

A bunch of lovestruck males and a few willing females are a sure formula for a fight, especially when you consider the ladies are only willing once a year! This is certainly the case with bucks during the breeding period. The most serious fights of the year occur now when two dominant bucks lay claim to the same hot doe. Most fights are short and end in nothing more than damaged pride or chipped antlers, but occasionally, sex-driven battles can be to the death. I've witnessed a couple such battles, and the fury of the fracas is an awesome thing to behold. In the carcass of the loser, I've seen the aftermath of many more. A many a good male, deer and otherwise, has cashed in his chips trying to win the favor of a flirtatious beauty.

Toward the end of the breeding period, the hectic pace begins to wane. The number of does in estrus declines, and the fervor of the bucks abates, their pent-up lust now partially satisfied. Weariness, lack of food and often injury sap the bucks' enthusiasm and energy. Gradually, the initial big wave of does passes through the first cycle and the breeding period, i.e., the peak of the rut, draws to an end.

THE POST-RUT PERIOD

The Waning Rut

The post-rut period can be divided into three phases. The first is what I call the "waning rut." This phase includes both the tail-off breeding activity from the peak rut and the relatively minor secondary rut. The

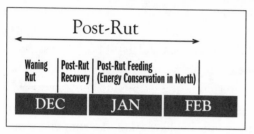

waning rut occurs during the first three weeks of the post-rut period, but it is only a pale shadow of the breeding period. General deer movement now is far less than during the peak-breeding time, and both fresh sign and visible rutting activity are greatly reduced. Much of the activity takes place at night as a result of the cumulative effects of growing weariness and ongoing hunting pressure. Still, the waning rut likely offers hunters their best chance of success during the post-rut period, meager though it may be.

The Recovery Phase

Next comes the recovery phase, so designated because this is a time of recuperation for rut-spent bucks. As the waning rut plays out, bucks begin to spend more and more time resting. Bucks, now weary and perhaps 20 to 30 percent lighter from their relentless pace, lay up in thick cover and begin a slow recuperation from the rigors of the rut, only to be rousted from their convalescence by the lure of a last fling. Although does, fawns and young bucks come through rut in better shape than mature bucks, they also rest more now, but generally near major food sources where they can feed early and late in the day or at night. Most feeding by the older bucks takes place near their beds, which is likely to be back in their core area. During the recovery phase, which usually lasts a week or two, it can appear as if mature bucks have completely disappeared.

Actually, this phase might be more accurately termed a phenomenon. Why? While it's something that happens every year, its sequence and exact timing tend to shift around from year to year. During some seasons, this time of buck disappearance occurs on cue after the waning rut plays out in three or so weeks. Other years, the bucks' disappearing act is most evident *during* the waning rut, or at least during part of it. For a long time, this shifting around really confounded me, but gradually, I began to see that the moon's affect on the timing of the rut played prominently into when this phase hit. We'll talk more about this later. Suffice to say that the recovery phase usually is most manifest sometime around three or four weeks into the post-rut period.

Post-Rut Feeding

The third phase, post-rut feeding, occurs when the last vestiges of rutting activities have wound down and the somewhat rested bucks return to a feeding pattern. Gaunt and facing coming winter, they need to nourish themselves. Gradually, they begin to venture farther and farther out in search of quality food. If a major food source is nearby, they will end up there. In the absence of concentrated food sources, they range out and forage the best they can. The feeding pattern is much like the pre-rut, except the bucks are now more lethargic and nocturnal. Because food sources are fewer and more localized this time of year, longer distances often must be traveled to reach prime food sources. Thus, to conserve energy, bucks will frequently abandon their core areas now in search of food.

Deer are very energy efficient during this time, especially in northern climates. If food sources aren't available that offer good returns on their energy investment, they'll opt to conserve energy rather than expend more than they take in trying to feed. In harsh, snow climes, bucks, as well as other deer, will actually forego aggressive feeding attempts in favor of an energy-saving holding pattern, usually in some type of thermal cover. In its most classic form, this behavior is known as "yarding," though less obvious forms of energy-conserving behavior most often take place. Whatever form of energy management they choose— feeding and/or conserving—the pattern will continue until the bucks drop their antlers, which signals the end of the post-rut period.

From this look at the fall activity patterns of the whitetail, it should be abundantly clear that the rut represents the very best time to shoot a buck, especially a trophy. Also, it should be obvious that timing the key breeding period of the rut as accurately as possible is essential to a fall hunting strategy. Given that, before we delve into the pre-rut and post-rut periods, let's look first at the factors affecting the timing and intensity of the rut.

Chapter Seventeen

When Deer Move and Why

 IN MY BOOK, *HUNTING TROPHY Whitetails*, I covered the factors affecting day-to-day deer movement in great depth. My intent here is to capsulize that information as an aid in developing a timing strategy. The long-term strategy is best played out in the field when we are equipped to adapt that strategy to the day-to-day variables that may affect deer movement and behavior. Given that, we need to have a solid working understanding of the many factors that influence deer movement.

From the hunter's standpoint, there are three forms of deer movement—forced, rutting and feeding movement. Movement forced upon the deer by outside disturbances, either man-caused or otherwise, has no bearing on natural deer activity and is not of concern to us here. Rutting movement, which is of paramount importance to trophy hunters, is any deer activity centered on breeding and the breeding ritual. Feeding movement is activity associated with a deer's ongoing need to feed itself.

Certain conditions are conducive to good deer movement. One of the best, especially for big bucks, is a light drizzle, which was falling when Bobby Parker, Sr. shot this fine Texas whitetail. Photo by Bobby Parker, Jr.

NON-WEATHER FACTORS

Hunting Pressure

Of the non-weather factors affecting deer movement, hunting pressure has to be near the top in most places. The whitetail deer is very intelligent and adaptable, and the speed and degree to which it reacts to hunting pressure, i.e., man's sudden, disruptive intrusion into his domain, is amazing. Almost overnight, they will alter their normal behavior to avoid exposure to man by either shifting their activities to thicker cover, becoming more nocturnal, relocating to quieter areas or trying some combination thereof. Even moderate hunting pressure will quickly and substantially alter deer behavior and shift movement to the low-light hours and night. Heavy pressure can entirely disrupt behavioral patterns and make deer, especially older bucks, almost totally nocturnal. Yes, hunting is a key controlling factor in deer movement and can override nearly all other factors.

Other forms of human intrusion, such as logging and farming, also can temporarily change behavior, but it amazes me how discerning deer seem to be about the benevolent intent of such activities. In Montana, I seek out active timber operations and have actually hunted deer in the mist of ongoing logging operations. Deer love to browse the slash from such operations. Even if the deer shy away when the logging is underway, they pour into the area as soon as the echo from the skitters and chainsaws fades away at day's end. Predators, such as wolves and feral dogs, also can impact deer movement. In Canada, I've seen deer behavior change abruptly when a pack of wolves moves into the area. Free-ranging dogs can have much the same effect.

Rutting And Feeding Movement

You may wonder why I've included rutting and feeding movement among the factors affecting deer movement since they are basic forms of movement. The reason is twofold. One, the level of the two forms of movement obviously varies by time of year, thus affecting activity on any given day. Two, and possibly less obvious, not all rutting and feeding movement is created equal. Rutting intensity varies by locale based on herd composition and range conditions, as we've discussed previously. True, the rut is always the time of peak deer activity everywhere, particularly for bucks, but the amount of activity is not necessarily the same from one tract to another on any given day. Healthy, balanced herds with low buck:doe ratios and good buck age structures will exhibit greater rutting activity than those out of balance.

The same variability exists in feeding activity. Two factors are the main players in this tract-to-tract variance. One is deer density relative to carrying capacity, i.e., overcrowding. Nutritionally stressed deer must feed longer and more often to maintain themselves, resulting in more daytime feeding. Conversely, well-fed deer don't have to feed as often or as long and are more selective about when they feed, generally leaning toward the nocturnal. During the early years on Burnt Pine Plantation, our deer herd was well under carrying capacity and the deer visited our many lush food plots sparingly during the day. It wasn't until the herd grew beyond carrying capacity did the pinch of hunger from too many mouths drive the deer to food plots consistently during daylight. Then, food plots became the centerpoint of our afternoon hunting strategy. That doesn't mean that deer only use food plots or agriculture when stressed, only that the level of daytime use is generally greater when food is in short supply.

The other factor affecting feeding activity is that old familiar one—major food sources. Where concentrated food sources exist, visible feeding activity is greater, and visibility is what really matters to hunters. For instance, I have two friends in Texas who both own ranches with very similar deer populations. One, however, plants winter food plots; the other doesn't. During the rut, they both do well, but after the rut, you are hard pressed to find good bucks on the ranch without food plots. While on the other ranch, post-rut hunting (the food plots aren't usually up very well during the pre-rut) is quite good as the hungry bucks feed on the easy pickings in the food plots. Thus, we can see how food sources can be a factor in day-to-day movement and hunting plans.

I should again mention that feeding activity is less likely to put a big buck in your sights than rutting movement and is more easily disrupted by hunting pressure, adverse weather conditions, etc.

The Moon

In the next chapter, we're going to cover the moon's effect on the rut in detail so we won't get much into that here. Suffice to say that rutting activity is intensified when the full moon coincides with the traditional peak of rut. When the full moon hits outside the peak-rut window, particularly on the front side, the rut is "pulled" toward the moon, spread out and reduced in intensity.

When the full moon and peak-rut window overlap, daytime movement follows a predictable pattern. Normally, expect early morning and late afternoon rutting activity to be so-so then, though huntable activity can take place any time of day. Interestingly, from about 10 a.m. to 1 p.m. can be an especially good time for catching amorous bucks seeking female companionship. Over the years, I have killed several trophy bucks during this midday window on full moons in the rut and make it a point to be in the middle of high-use deer areas during this time.

When the rut is not underway, I had just about as soon ice-skate barefooted as hunt the full moon. It is my opinion that the full moon suppresses feeding movement during the prime early morning and late afternoon hours, presumably because of stepped up nighttime activity. There is some midday feeding during the full moon (deer tend to feed every four to six hours), but deer, especially big bucks, aren't going to travel very far to feed in broad daylight or expose themselves much. Unless you're sitting right on top of them when they get up to eat, you aren't going to see much evidence of midday feeding. Don't count on it to put many big bucks in front of you.

The new, or dark, moon brings on a different daytime movement pattern. Whether feeding or rutting movement, most activity tends to take place during the naturally prime early and late hours, with relatively little midday activity. The result is concentrated and predictable movement that works to the hunter's advantage…when hunting feeding deer. During the peak of rut, however, I'll still take a full moon over any other.

There's logic in why the daytime movement patterns of deer on the new and full moons follow this apparent course. I'll explain the logic, but I have to tell you it may not be so simple. The logic is built on two assumptions. One, the full moon sways the deer's daily internal clock so that his "business" is largely taken care of at night. A new moon has the opposite effect—low nightly activity and greater daytime movement. (We'll talk more about all this in the next chapter.) Assumption two: The whitetail has a rumen in which he stores food for future digestion, and the rumen needs to be replenished every four to six hours. In fact, whitetails appear to generally follow a four to six-hour activity cycle throughout the 24-hour day, even though some of the cycle involves much greater levels of activity. Even in the rut, the stirring of the rumen may prompt deer to get up and move, possibly to engage in rutting activity, even if they don't feed much.

Given all this, let's assume a deer on a full moon is busy about his affairs right up to daybreak, say 6 a.m., then lies down. About four to six

Hunters can spend their time afield more profitably if they understand the factors that make for good, and poor, buck movement. A mature buck like this doesn't just happen to be out in the open. Photo by Troy Huffman.

hours later, he'll need to feed again, or at least is prompted to do so. That means he'll get up sometime between 10 a.m. and noon, which frequently happens during a full moon. That midday foray will pretty much hold him until dark, when light of the full moon will once again direct his nighttime excursions.

Now for the dark moon. The theory has it that deer don't tend to feed, or engage in rutting activity, as much at night and wait for first light to get back to serious business, like filling their rumen. Assume they feed or otherwise remain active until about 9 or 10 a.m. before lying down. That would mean that they don't have to get up again for supplies until about 3 or 4 p.m. Yes, a little early to begin afternoon shopping but close enough to the prime late afternoon hours.

Simple logic would have it that the light at night allows deer to see better; thus, they can better carryon their activities. I don't believe it's that simple. I've seen deer moving and feeding on dark moons. And, I've seen them laying around like bloated cows on full moons. There are undoubtedly more factors at play than just better visibility. I don't doubt that light is the key, but not because it enhances sight. I believe that bright full-moon light and the darkness on the new moon somehow prompt the deer's internal clock toward a particular movement pattern. This pattern manifests itself in the way we've described but is more complicated than first it would seem. We'll discuss a possible explanation for all this in the next chapter, but for now, a simple light-based logic seems to lead to the right conclusion, whether or not it's for the right reasons. Given that, does the same logic lead to predictable daytime patterns during the other two moon phases? Let's see.

The first-quarter moon sheds its light, albeit modest, during the first half of the night and is dark the latter half, meaning the deer should feed early in the morning and not so much in the late afternoon. Conversely, the third-quarter nights are lit by the moon from about midnight to dawn, leading to expectations of slow early morning activity, some midday action and good late afternoon movement. I've sure seen this pattern at work...and not! Frankly, I don't think the light of the quarter moons (which are actually half lit moons) is all that big a deal in the lives of deer. Generally, I view quarter moons as relatively benign factors in the movement scheme. Plus, I am certain that other factors easily override the effects of the quarter moons. However, I must admit to having a prejudice against hunting first-quarter moons, when overall deer activity seems to be poorest.

WEATHER

On Burnt Pine Plantation, I conducted extensive studies on deer movement for years. I collected every imaginable kind of data from our hunts and compared it against every parameter I could think of that might influence deer movement. Much of that effort was focused on how weather conditions affected day-to-day activity. After a few years, I pretty well had Georgia movement patterns pegged. But alas, as my travels and experiences broadened, I found that my Georgia trends didn't always wash with the realities of the new places. I went back to the drawing board, hoping to find a common thread that would unravel the movement riddle anywhere I hunted. In time, I found the common thread, but what it told me was that every place is different...but also the same! Let me explain.

The guiding principle to deer movement is so obvious and simple I should have recognized it earlier. It is this: All things being equal, deer move best when weather conditions are the most comfortable and invigorating for them relative to what they are used to and what they are prepared to face. There are certain weather conditions that cause deer to "feel good" and be more active.

Both being warm-blooded, a deer's "comfort zone" and ours share certain similarities, but they are also different, at least in degrees. To start with, whitetails are accustomed to being out in the cold and are better equipped to face it. Therefore, they not only can tolerate more cold, but they are comfortable in lower temperatures than we are. We can dress up or down for the weather, but deer can't. Once they don their winter coats and layer-up with fat to face the coming winter, they are "dressed" for the cold. Since they can't shed their coat, warm weather is uncomfortable for them. Yet, extreme cold relative to that region and that time of the year is at best unpleasant. Thus, both unseasonably warm weather and unusual cold curtail deer movement. Conditions in the comfort zone, which varies by region, encourage good deer movement. Once I understood this, deer movement patterns from Texas to Canada fell into place...mostly.

Obviously, it is difficult to draw ironclad conclusions about the ideal comfort zone for good deer movement for every region in North America. It's all relative to what's "normal" for that region. Mexico and Canada, for example, could not be more different in their norms. The burden, then, falls on the individual hunter to determine what specific conditions make up the comfort zone for good deer movement where he hunts. However, some general principles can be identified regarding relative weather conditions and deer movement that can be applied most any place. Let's look briefly at some of them.

Temperature

Without question, temperature is one of the most important factors governing day-to-day deer movement. Generally, deer movement is best when the temperature for a given place and date is at or below normal. If it's warmer than normal, expect poor movement. Even seasonable weather is too warm for my taste...and usually the deer's. Cooler weather invigorates deer and causes them to move more during the day. Cooler than normal temperatures are particularly critical to rutting movement. Warm weather will shut down rutting movement even faster than feeding activity.

At what point does the temperature fall below the deer's comfort zone and curtail movement? Clearly, that too-cold mark varies greatly across the whitetail's range. On Burnt Pine Plantation in Middle Georgia, activity slowed when the mercury dropped into the teens. In South Texas, that number is higher, probably in the upper 20s. In Canada, it's somewhere around minus 20 degrees. Anything you recognize as being extremely cold for that area threatens to be too cold for good deer movement. Still, I had much rather hunt when it's too cold than too warm.

Relative Humidity

Relative humidity is a player in deer movement. We're all familiar with the difference in how we feel cold or heat in dry versus humid conditions. Essentially, humidity seems to have the same effect on deer. High humidity tends to narrow the comfort zone for deer, though I believe its effect is much greater on the warm end of the spectrum. Heat is much more oppressive and energy-sapping when accompanied by high humidity. Having moved from humid Georgia to dry Montana, I can tell you that 25 degrees, for instance, in Montana is quite invigorating and comfortable for outdoor activities, but that same temperature in Georgia chills to the very bone.

Hot, humid weather makes for very difficult hunting and tends to bring deer movement to a halt. String several such days together, and the deer sometimes seem to virtually disappear. However, once these conditions give way to cooler, drier weather with the passage of a cold front, deer activity peaks.

Drizzle, Rain And Snow

There is one very notable exception to the trend of warm weather and high humidity leading to poor movement. That exception is a light, steady drizzle, or even a substantial mist. Wise old bucks are less wary and more likely to leave thick cover on such days. Maybe it is the low-light

I caught this 24-inch, 160-class 9-pointer scouting for does around a windmill at midday on a full moon. I was there because I knew from experience that hot, dry conditions and a full moon in the rut were conditions ripe for midday movement near water in South Texas. Photo by Richard Jackson.

conditions combined with the cooling effect of the drizzle and the quiet, soothing nature of the wet woods that cause good movement during a drizzle. Whatever the reasons, this can be an excellent time to shoot a trophy whitetail. The best time to hunt drizzling rain is the first day it starts. After that, movement becomes spotty. Like people, deer tire of it.

When drizzle becomes rain, it loses its magic. Heavy rain sends them to the cover of thickets, preferably evergreens. Generally, the longer rain persists, the poorer the movement. When the rain stops, even for brief periods, deer often move around.

Deer react to snowfall in pretty much the same way they do rainfall. A light snowfall is a good time for deer movement, especially that of mature bucks. During periods of heavy snowfall, activity is slowed and deer seek cover. For some reason, the resumption of deer movement seems to be delayed a day or so after a heavy snowfall. It's almost as though they don't want to be the first to make tracks. But within a day or two, action usually comes on strong.

Wind

Wind is a factor in deer movement. The harder the wind blows, the less deer move. The noise and movement created by high winds make deer nervous and impair their senses. Light to moderate wind, provided it is reasonably steady in velocity and direction, doesn't hamper movement much. In areas where wind is the norm rather than the exception, such as the Plains and Prairies region, it has little effect on deer movement.

Barometric Pressure

In deer movement, barometric pressure is probably more a symptom than a cause. Essentially, it's an early alarm system that forecasts coming weather changes, some of which deer react to in advance. Generally, deer movement is best on an unstable barometer or during high pressure, which in the fall is often associated with cool, dry air. A falling barometer normally forebodes bad weather; a rising barometer usually promises improving weather. In both cases, deer will sometimes move in advance of the visible change; however, my experience has been that deer movement *after* a weather change is far greater than before. The severity of the system will determine the level of pre-frontal and post-frontal deer movement.

Nothing can spark deer movement like a major weather change, especially one bringing in colder temperatures.

This is a good time to point out that nothing can spark deer movement like a major weather change, especially one bringing in colder temperatures. I spend a lot of my worry time in the fall anxiously awaiting the arrival of just such fronts. Major changes to the cold side can really cause an explosion in activity, especially rutting activity.

SUMMARY

Best Movement
- Low to moderate hunting pressure.
- Rut approaching or underway.
- Good buck age structure and low buck:doe ratio. (Increases rutting activity only.)
- The presence of concentrated major food sources.

- Dense deer populations. (Increases daytime feeding activity.)
- Temperatures in the "comfort zone" of deer, meaning normal or below for the date.
- Low relative humidity. (60 percent or less, depending on what is normal for the area.)
- Light drizzle or light snow. (An exception to the humidity/temperature pattern.)
- No or light, steady wind.
- Dropping or rising barometric pressure or steady high.
- Major weather changes, especially those ushering in colder air.
- Clearing weather immediately after a prolonged rain.
- A day or two after major snowfalls.
- New moon for predictable early and late feeding activity.
- Full moon and the days immediately thereafter for rutting activity during peak rut.

Poorest Movement
- High hunting pressure.
- A lack of concentrated food sources.
- Poor age structure and high buck:doe ratio. (Adversely affects rutting movement.)
- Low deer densities. (Feeding activity less visible.)
- Temperatures above (worst) or below the deer's "comfort zone."
- Successive days of hot, humid weather is the worst.
- High relative humidity. (60 percent or more, depending on what's normal for the area.)
- Heavy rain or heavy snow.
- High, gusty and/or variable winds. (Where high winds are not normal.)
- Low barometric pressure. (Often accompanies turbulent or warm, humid weather.)
- Full moon when depending on feeding activity.

All this said, you must remember that no one factor controls deer movement. Several factors are almost always acting in combination. Yet, the general patterns are there and knowing them will make your days afield more successful.

173

Chapter Eighteen

Timing the Rut...and Unraveling Other Mysteries of the Sun and Moon

THESE NUMBERS MIGHT DISCOURAGE some. Others may find hope in them. Whatever your view, they're true nonetheless. We might as well know it up front and accept it. That way, we can turn it to our advantage, or if necessary, plan around it as best we can. What numbers am I speaking of? Of the 500 or so mature bucks harvested during my 20-years at Burnt Pine Plantation, 75 percent of them were taken during the two-week period between November 1 and 14, even though these two weeks only represented 29 percent of the seven-week season and pressure was fairly evenly spread throughout the season. Furthermore, almost 50 percent of them were taken during the week spanning November 3 and 9, which only represented 14 percent of the total season!

What gives? The rut! You can shake it up anyway you like, but this one fact remains—the rut is the best time to shoot a trophy whitetail. Mature bucks are so much more vulnerable during this time that we at Burnt Pine viewed their rather sudden appearance in the harvest as the

A full moon and a good buck on the prowl—this is a scene likely to be played out during the rut. The moon definitely has a part in the timing and intensity of the breeding ritual…and in a wise hunter's plans. Photo by Mike Biggs.

best indicator of when the rut was underway.

In Middle Georgia, the annual rutting ritual normally hits full swing the first two weeks of November. Over the years, we grew to expect the peak of rut to kickoff around November 3 and hot action to continue for about a week before tailing off. Some years, the pattern held better than during others. Occasionally, we would see the timing of the hottest rutting activity shift a bit either way. Once in a while, classic rutting activity would crank-up the last of October. Other years might have seen the rutting ritual start slower and extend later than usual, perhaps almost to Thanksgiving. More often than not, these shifts from traditional peak-rut dates seemed to be accompanied by an unwelcome side effect—a less intense, more spread-out rut. But over the long haul, the timing and nature of the rut were basically variations off a dependable central theme. Yet, for the serious trophy hunter, being able to predict both the timing of the central theme and when variations off that central theme are likely to take place are crucial to consistent success.

I need to warn you that we're not dealing in absolutes here. We're not going to be able to cram the whitetail rut into a perfect little box. The animal is too complex for that. Besides, this is not a one-factor-controls-all kind of thing. Many factors come into play, some innate, some environmental and some circumstantial. Still, we can come up with some practical parameters and a solid understanding of the major players in rut-timing that will serve you well when trying to time your hunt to correspond with the rut or develop an overall fall strategy.

THE OVERALL CONCEPT

I'm going to start by getting the cart ahead of the horse. Right up front, I'm going to lay out the general concept in the simplest way I can. I feel this is necessary in order to set the proper context for what is to follow…and because what is coming can get a little complicated. But first, a qualification.

When talking about the rut, there are really two different aspects—the ritual activity associated with the rut and breeding per se. We hunters are more interested in the ritual activity, i.e., the deer movement associated with traveling, scraping, rubbing, chasing, trailing, etc., than in the breeding. True, the two normally go hand-in-hand but not always. It is possible for breeding to be underway with little accompanying ritual activity, and vice versa. Unless otherwise noted, most of our discussion will be directed toward ritual activity.

Here's the concept—the timing of the whitetail rut centers around a narrow "ideal" window of time corresponding to specific dates on the calendar. However, the full moon nearest to the ideal breeding window and certain herd and environmental conditions can cause shifts in the timing and intensity of rutting activity, and perhaps even breeding, within certain "allowable" limits.

Now, let's explain what lies behind this concept, identify the major players in rut timing and try to put it all into a context you can take to the field.

BASIC BREEDING BIOLOGY

We'll start with some basic whitetail breeding biology. We'll go first to the root of the thing that controls the timing of the rut. Nothing about this whole process is random. In fact, the very survival of the species lies behind the timing of the rut. I'm talking about reproduction. More directly, the controlling factor in rut timing is fawn survival. You see, the timing of the rut is actually dictated by what happens 190 to 200 days *after* breeding, when the fawns are born.

Nature has selected a breeding time that results in a fawn drop when conditions are best for maximum fawn survival. That optimum window is narrower in some places than in others. In regions with harsh weather, such as the Canadian Northwoods, or potential natural calamities, like floods in the Mississippi River Delta, the window is quite narrow. Fawns born there outside the best time have a greatly diminished chance of seeing their first birthday. In mild regions largely devoid of extremes in weather or natural disruptions, like much of the South and East, the time of best survival is wider, but still limited. Cover, food availability, drought, floods, rain, snow and cold are all factors that can constrict the fawning window.

Given all this, environmental pressures have dictated a preferred window of time for fawning. Certainly, not all fawns are born during this time—nature doesn't bet it all on one toss of the dice—but the majority are. Though the preferred fawning window may be as long as two, three or even four weeks, the heart of that window, the ideal "centerpoint," is shorter. For our purposes, we'll call it a week. Moving forward 190 to 200 days will give us a corresponding ideal window of time for breeding. This is the time the deer herd "wants" to center its breeding around. In this discussion, the ideal centerpoint window for breeding will be synonymous with the "traditional peak of rut." We'll reference the traditional peak week throughout this chapter, not because there's any particular magic in a one-week designation but because it allows us to talk about the heart of the rutting window in specific terms.

The question arises: What signals the approach of this ideal time and marks its arrival? In short, how do the deer know it's time? It has to be something that doesn't change from year to year. It must be timed to the seasons since the climatic conditions affecting the fawning window are related to the seasons. It can't be weather since that varies from year to year. It can't be temporal environmental factors because they too change. It can't be the moon, at least not acting alone. After all, the moon repeats its cycle 12-plus times a year, making it a less-than-ideal *annual* trigger.

Plus, the timing of the various moon phases changes from month to month and year to year (phases do not correspond with calendar dates), making moon phases an unlikely candidate to be the trigger for precise rut timing. So, what controls the onset of whitetail breeding?

DAYLENGTH IS THE KEY

The thing that signals breeding startup is the same overriding fac-tor that triggers all the other changes whitetails undergo throughout the year—coat changes, antler growth, velvet-shedding, antler-casting, hor-monal changes, etc. I'm talking about the amount of light and darkness in a 24-hour period. We'll just call it daylength. It is the constant that cues, among a multitude of other things, the most important act in the whitetail's existence—propagation. Though daylength is constantly changing throughout the year, those changes are constant, predictable and tied directly to the seasons and a date on the calendar. This is an important point: *a specific date on the calendar equates to a specific daylength in the continuing cycle of shortening and lengthening daylength. Plus, daylength is directly related to the seasons; in fact, daylength determines the seasons. The beginning of each season is marked by a milestone daylength occurring within about one day of the same date each year.* No other influence is as constant as daylength or as important in controlling the whitetail cycle! This bears closer scrutiny.

Daylength And Our Calendar

Our calendar is based on the 365 days it takes the earth to make one revolution around the sun. (We're going to ignore the additional fraction of a day it takes to make a complete revolution that leads to a leap-year adjustment every four years.) During this trip around the sun, the earth remains in a constant 23.5-degree tilt to the sun. As a result of the earth's changing position in a revolution around the sun, the latitude at which the perpendicular rays of the sun strike the earth constantly and predictably changes on a north/south bases. Therefore, the northern half of the earth receives more sunlight when the axis is tipped toward the sun and less as the axis tips southward. The constantly changing angle of the earth's axis to the perpendicular rays of the sun results in our seasons and a pattern of consistently changing daylengths. This allows us to

All the hullabaloo about the rut is because it's the one time when big whitetails let down their formidable defenses and become vulnerable to a hunter's efforts. No wonder this is when most trophies are taken. Photo by Mike Biggs.

divide the year into days (dates) that represent specific daylengths and into natural periods we call seasons, which are each characterized by certain weather patterns. As a result, our calendar not only allows us to mark time based on a natural cycle (one trip around the sun), but it also means that *a certain date on the calendar stands for a certain day and night length, tying calendar dates directly to daylength and cyclic whitetail deer behavior.*

Let's complete the picture by relating all this to the four seasons in the Northern Hemisphere. The vertical rays of the sun reach their northernmost point on the earth's surface on June 21. This day, called the *summer solstice,* marks the beginning of summer and is the longest day (most hours of sunlight) of the year. At the other end of the spectrum, the *winter solstice,* when the vertical rays of the sun strike the earth at their southernmost point, occurs on December 22. This, the shortest (darkest) day of the year, begins our winter and is followed by progressively longer days until June 21. The sun is perpendicular to the equator twice a year in its north/south movement across the earth's surface. Both times mark the beginning of a season. The *spring equinox* occurs on March 21 and ushers in spring. The *autumnal equinox* marks the beginning of fall on

September 22. In the whitetail's light-controlled reproductive cycle, *the ever-shorter days following June 21 and continuing until December 22 bring specific and predictable biological responses*.

Over the centuries, deer in a given locale have developed an "internal clock" that initiates the breeding process at certain daylengths. That preferred daylength might be called the "macro-timer" for whitetail breeding. All evidence indicates that this macro-timer is genetically ingrained in deer at a given locale, having been arrived at over time by the fawn-survival requirements of the herd. Each herd is genetically predisposed to respond to changing daylengths at particular times in the annual cycle. Rutting time can be as early as August and September, which is true of South Florida, or as late as January and February, as is the case in parts of Mississippi and Alabama.

THE MOON—THE "LESSER" LIGHT

So, we find that the amount of light is a trigger in the timing of the reproductive cycle of the whitetail. However, daylight is not the only light source that figures into the equation. Moonlight also is a player in timing the rut. Think of it this way: *Daylength controls the preferred window and ideal centerpoint for whitetail breeding, but moonlight, especially the full moon, can cause minor shifts in the exact timing and intensity of the rut within the preferred window.* Before we get into the mechanics of the moon's effect, let's briefly see how the moon cycle and phases work.

The moon orbits the earth in a consistent, predictable pattern; thus, moon phases repeat themselves at predictable intervals, every 29.5 days to be precise. The months ("month" has its origin in the word "moon") of our calendar roughly correspond to the time it takes for the moon phases to repeat a full cycle...but not exactly. That's because our 12 months are set up to equal a calendar year (the time it takes the earth to rotate around the sun), which is actually about 12.4 moon cycles. Thus, moon phases are out of synch with our months and year. The end result is that moon phases don't line up with specific calendar dates or daylengths, meaning that the peak breeding window could fall on *any* moon phase in a given year.

The four main moon phases—new moon, first quarter, full moon and third quarter—are identified primarily by how much of the moon's

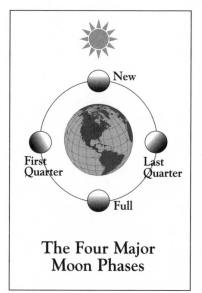

**The Four Major
Moon Phases**

lighted surface is visible. Of course, moonlight is simply reflected sunlight, the visible amount depending on the moon's position relative to the earth and the sun as it rotates around the earth during its 29.5-day voyage. It's reasonable to think of each phase as lasting seven days, the actual day of the phase and the three days before and after. Since moonlight (or the lack thereof) is the thing we believe to be a player in breeding activity, then logically the new and the full moons are the most likely suspects in the equation. (True, the moon's effect transcends mere light. Certainly, the gravitational pull of the moon has a very dramatic impact on the earth, especially ocean tides. Though I have seen for myself the effects moon-caused tides have on fish, I've never been able to carryover that effect to deer in a measurable way. I'll leave that argument for another day.) Let's take a look briefly at each moon phase.

The new, or dark, moon occurs when the moon is positioned between the earth and sun. Thus, from earth, we view the shadowed backside on the moon during the daytime. The new moon essentially rises at sunrise and sets at sunset, offering practically no reflected light at night. As the moon moves away from the sun to a more perpendicular angle to the earth, more and more of the lighted side of the moon is visible with each passing day. (Increasing moonlight is called waxing; decreasing, waning.) About seven days after the new moon, we arrive at the first quarter, when half of the moon is lighted and visible. The first-quarter moon rises about noon, stands overhead at dusk and sets about midnight, providing light only during the first half of the night.

When the moon moves all the way around to the far side of the earth relative to the sun a week or so after the first quarter, we get a full view of its lighted surface from about sunset to sunrise. This is the full moon. It sheds light on the earth throughout the night, and reaches meridian (its highest point) about midnight. After the full moon, nighttime light diminishes as the moon moves back toward the sun. The half-

Jim Skinner planned his first-ever hunt to Canada wisely. He was there during the traditional peak-rut dates, and his book-class 11-pointer was his reward. Photo by Carl Frohaug.

illuminated third quarter arrives about seven days later. This phase rises above the horizon around midnight and sets around noon, emitting light only during the second half of the night. It is at its highest point at sunrise. An easy way to remember when the four phases shed their light at night is: new moon, no light; first quarter, first half; full moon, all night; third (last) quarter, last half.

So, we come to this: While calendar dates are related to specific daylengths that are essentially constant from year to year, moon phases do not occur on the same date from year to year, and thus are not tied to specific daylengths. The fact is that a given moon phase can fall as much as two weeks either side of any fixed date. Worse yet, if you're trying to key off a specific moon, such as the Harvest Moon (which is the full moon hitting nearest September 22), then over the years, it is possible to have swings of up to 30 days in when that particular moon hits. That is too much variance in the timing of the whitetail rut and presents real problems with using the moon as a primary timer of something with the precise breeding requirements of the whitetail. The moon is just too much of a wild card in nature's scheme to be the overriding timing cue for the rut.

Does that mean the moon has no impact on the timing of whitetail breeding? No, it does not mean that. Rather, it simply means that whatever role the moon has is second fiddle to the more important constant—daylength. Yet, *since the timing of whitetail breeding is light-controlled, moon phases, particularly the brightest moon (full) and the darkest moon (new), introduce another light variable that I believe does have an impact on whitetail breeding.*

The Full Moon Wild Card

From my early adulthood, how the moon plays into wildlife activity has been both a mystery and a fascination for me. I've long known the moon had an effect on wildlife behavior. I probably first noticed that effect in fishing, especially the moon's influence on the timing of spawning. The old-timers in Florida, where I fished a lot during my youth, would confidently predict that thus and such fish would spawn on this or that full moon. As near as I could tell, they were usually right. I came to accept as fact that bass in that part of the world would spawn on the full moon of March, shellcrackers on the full moon of April and bluegill on the full moon of May.

When I first started deer hunting, I didn't think much about the moon but that quickly changed. The first thing that came to my attention was that distinct ups and downs in daylight movement appeared to be correlated to moon phases. Even as I was trying to figure that out, I graduated from college and became the managing partner of Burnt Pine Plantation, a 13,000-acre deer hunting operation in Central Georgia. The plantation became a veritable laboratory for whitetail study, and we collected data on everything imaginable. How the moon figured into deer movement, particularly rutting activity, was one of the things that fell under our scrutiny.

I soon began to suspect that there was a strong correlation between the full moon and the timing and intensity of rutting activity. I frequently observed rutting activity during all hours of the day during the full moon, making me suspicious that at least daytime rutting activity was enhanced by this moon phase. In time, night surveys, personal observations and a profusion of night-born running deer tracks, a sure sign of bucks chasing does, provided evidence of heavy nighttime rutting activity around the full moon. As data from the plantation swelled, I began to notice that a disproportionate number of mature bucks were killed near the full moon, strongly suggesting a link to the rut. This was especially so when the full moon hit near our traditional peak-rut dates but less so when the full moon hit a week or more either side of the magic November 3 to 9 window. With tangible evidence to rely on, we began to successfully predict heightened rutting activity around the full moon when it hit within a week of the traditional rut dates. Then, years into our program, we finally got hard proof that even breeding, not just ritual rutting activity, and the full moon were linked to a degree.

Georgia regulations call for a weeklong either-sex season between Christmas and New Year. This is when the plantation harvested the majority of the does necessary for management. Having a harvest universe of as many as a couple of hundred does allowed us to gather solid data on breeding dates. This was done by backdating the fetuses to determine when breeding actually took place. Over time, we saw clear, though modest, year-to-year shifts in peak breeding dates, really more like "bulges" forward or backwards within the same traditional rutting timeframe. It didn't take long to recognize that these shifts generally corresponded to shifts in full moon dates. That provided the hard proof we needed to verify what we had already observed in the field and in our harvests. The full moon not only affected the intensity of the ritual rutting activity, it also had a direct, albeit modest, impact on the timing of whitetail breeding. However, from all we saw, the full moon's impact on ritual rutting activity was greater than on actual breeding. In other words, the full moon would shift rutting activity further its way than it would shift breeding per se.

Since that discovery years ago, more research and time in the field have shed additional light on the full moon's effect on rut timing and intensity. I've had the opportunity to test the theories across the country in a wide variety of circumstances. Today, I've come to accept certain relationships between moon phases and rut timing and intensity as something I can apply to hunt planning with a high level of confidence.

Full Moon And The Rut

I said earlier that each moon phase could be viewed as lasting essentially seven days, the day of the phase plus three days before and after. That's certainly a logical way of looking at it, but it doesn't quite fit in the case of the full moon and the rut. The fact is that the full moon's effect on the rut seems to be greater toward the middle and end of the phase than at the front. The upswing in activity appears to start right before the moon fulls and continues a few days after. We'll look at a possible explanation of why that is so a little later.

Also, our discussions are aimed at hunting application, so we'll be mostly talking about ritual rutting activity as opposed to actual breeding. When important, I'll try to make the distinction. And, we'll be assuming all things are equal, which they seldom are. Outside factors other than the moon also affect the timing and intensity of the rut, as we'll see down the road.

Now, the impact of the full moon on the rut. To start with, everything I've seen says that *the full moon intensifies rutting activity when it coincides with our weeklong traditional peak of rut.* This is the best possible rutting scenario and results in an intense, well-defined rut of normal duration centered around the traditional peak-rut dates. While it is true that the full moon's effect can be slightly different when it hits toward the front of our traditional peak as opposed to the back, that is splitting hairs more finely than necessary. Suffice to say that small shifts can take place in the timing and intensity of the rut depending on where within the peak week the full moon falls. I will say this: I prefer earlier over later for reasons that should soon become apparent.

What happens when the full moon hits outside the magic rut window? It acts like a magnet on the rut, skewing it toward the full moon. To illustrate what happens, imagine a symmetrical bell-shaped curve when the full moon coincides with the traditional peak of rut. (In reality, a rutting curve would be "front heavy" since the rut, especially ritual activity, starts rather suddenly, peaks early and then tails off gradually.) When the full moon hits outside this peak window, imagine that the bell-shaped curve stretches, flattens and shifts toward the full moon, with the peak now lower and off center. The end result is that the full moon alters the timing, duration and intensity of the rut…but only within limits. Using the magnet comparison again, the further away from the peak-rut window the full moon falls, the less attraction it exerts on the rut, which makes sense remembering that daylength is the macro-timer. Conversely, the closer to the ideal time, the greater pull the full moon has on the rut.

How far away from the peak rut can the full moon exert influence? Remember, the furthest the full moon can fall from a specific date is roughly two weeks. In the case of our weeklong peak window, the full moon can hit as far away as about 11 days from either the beginning or ending date of the peak-rut window. That's close enough for the full moon to always exert some influence on the rut, i.e., spread it out and reduce its intensity, but from what I've seen, its power is considerably diminished when it falls a week or more away from the traditional peak dates.

Ok, here comes a bit of a curve ball: The effects of the full moon seem to be somewhat greater when it falls *before* the peak-rut dates rather than after. Actually, this is logical. Since daylength is the primary timer, passing up the macro-timer to get to the micro-timer doesn't make a whole lot of sense. When the full moon occurs in front of the peak dates, the micro-timer (moon) gets more of an open field and first shot at influencing the rut. (We also may be able to pin the greater influence of an early full moon on a biological explanation soon to follow.). The closer the fore full moon falls to the peak dates, the more the rut maintains its classic intensity, duration and form, even though it does shift forward at the cost of backside activity. The further away the fore-moon hits, the more the rut slides forward, spreads out, lowers in intensity and drops off on the backside, all of which cut into hunting opportunity. The changes in the rut we're talking about here are more than enough to cause a wise hunter to rethink his usual rut-centered timing.

For a long time, I suspected a full moon hitting *after* the traditional peak rut could delay or at least retard rutting activity, but I had trouble getting the goods on it. Now, I accept it as fact. The reason it took me so long to reach this conclusion is because an aft full moon doesn't have as dramatic an impact as an up-front one. Why? As we've said, the primary controlling factor, daylength, has had a chance to come into play before the secondary factor, moonlight, arrives on the scene. Plus, new data strongly suggest that the full moon's effect on the rut is delayed a few days before completely kicking in, pushing a late moon's effect even further away from the peak window, thus weakening it. (We'll talk about this shortly.) Still, a trailing full moon does have the same type of impact on the rut as an early one, but to a lesser degree. It seems to me that for an aft full moon to have an effect similar to an early moon it has to hit about three or four days nearer the traditional peak, but that comes under the heading of speculation. Whatever the degree, the impact is there and needs to be taken into account. Whenever a full moon hits within a week after the traditional peak rut, rutting activity starts at a slower pace, drops in intensity and carries on later than normal to overlap with the full moon.

Darkness, Light And Melatonin—The "Sleeping" Hormone

Why does the full moon have such an effect on the rut? The most obvious answer is light. The full moon illuminates the night, allowing deer to carry on their rutting activity in the quiet of the evening undisturbed by man and unhampered by darkness. True, deer can see much better at night than we can, but on dark nights, they still have visual limitations when trying to carry out the acrobatic maneuvers required in the rutting ritual.

I have long been convinced that most whitetail breeding takes place at night. Think about it. How many bucks have you ever seen in the actual act of breeding? Not many I bet! Of the hundreds and hundreds of bucks I've seen in the wild, I have only witnessed a double handful in the act of breeding. That alone leads me to believe that most breeding takes place at night. Certainly, daytime rutting activity can be intensified by the full moon, but I think what we see during the day is just the carryover from hot and heavy nighttime rutting escapades. I've sure seen plenty of evidence of that myself, and I'm not alone. The manager of a top South Texas ranch told me that when he drives around the ranch on full-moon nights during the rut, the sounds of fighting bucks, running deer and popping brush echo through the night as the rut is played out. Carroll Mann, a friend who until recently owned a ranch in the heart of Montana whitetail country, told me that on the full moon during the rut bucks chased does throughout the night in the meadow in front of his cabin, sometimes even waking him up with all their grunting, running and fighting. If heavy nighttime rutting activity is the norm during the rut-time full moon, then it doesn't take much of a stretch to imagine that better visibility from more light is part of the reason. But, I believe it goes deeper than that.

A bunch of highly suspect stuff has come out recently on the effect of the various moon phases on all kinds of deer activity. It's sometimes hard to separate the wheat from the chaff. Certainly, some of the best and most scientific information on the effects of the moon on whitetail breeding was published in the book *Solving the Mysteries of Deer Movement*, written by friend and ace deer biologist James Kroll, together with Ben Koerth. In their book, James and Ben delve into a possible scientific explanation of why the full moon triggers breeding activity. In their findings may lie some answers to the whys of all this moon and rutting stuff. Here, I'm going to try to give you a hunter's perspective of what goes on and what you need to know to turn this information into big bucks.

Ok, we've established that the timing of the whitetail reproductive cycle is tied to light, primarily daylength and secondarily moonlight. We have seen how deer at a particular locale are genetically ingrained to enter breeding readiness at certain daylengths. We have seen that the full moon tends to "bend" the rut its way. But why? How does it work? How do deer measure light? What happens biologically to trigger a response?

We know that deer have a very sensitive light-receptor called the pineal gland. This gland measures the light (actually, the amount of darkness) registered through the eyes and "communicates" its findings to the body through the production of a hormone called melatonin. We know it as a sleep inducer, but it also plays an important part in the regulation of day/night cycles and seasonal rhythms. Interestingly, darkness, not light, increases the production of melatonin. In whitetails, melatonin, or to be more accurate, the absence of melatonin, has a role in the release of sex hormones, including those that lead to breeding readiness. Now keep this in mind: *Darkness increases melatonin production; light reduces it, and the absence of melatonin at the right time of year can release sex hormones, trigger estrus in does and initiate breeding.*

Since melatonin is produced in greater quantities when it is dark, the production of melatonin increases on the new, or dark, moon. The greatest effect of that increased production comes into play during the days following the new moon, meaning during the first quarter. As the nights get brighter and brighter moving toward the full moon, melatonin production drops. James reports that artificial insemination studies have proven that the reduction of melatonin levels in does during the rutting window will trigger the onset of estrus. The removal of melatonin actually sets into motion a series of hormonal events that takes a few days to play out before bringing on estrus and subsequent breeding. So, the increased light, resulting in reduced melatonin, accompanying the full moon can initiate estrus in does and spark a flurry of rutting activity around and immediately following the full moon. This explains a number of things.

First, it explains why the full moon has such a dramatic impact on the rut—its light indirectly initiates estrus in breeding-ready does, the number of which depends on how close to the ideal breeding dates (daylengths) the full moon hits. If the full moon falls too far away from those peak dates, fewer does are in breeding readiness. If it hits closer, more does are ready and triggered into estrus. Thus, we see the workings of the pattern discussed earlier.

It is important to note that once the increased light of the seven-day full moon phase begins to reduce melatonin levels, it takes a few days before does enter estrus. In that delay, we find a possible answer for why the best rutting activity seems to crank up around the mid and latter part of the full-moon phase. The delayed response of the does also explains why a full moon hitting before the traditional rut dates has a greater impact on the rut than one falling after—the few days delay in coming into estrus puts breeding on the fore moon closer to the ideal daylengths and further away on the aft moon.

There also may be a practical understanding of deer movement coming out of this. I've known for years that daytime deer movement during the new moon tends to be good, especially during the prime early morning and late afternoon hours. I've also known that, with the very notable exception of the rut, daytime movement during the full moon tends to be poor. Remember, whatever else melatonin is, it is also a sleep enhancer. Countless people take the hormone to help them sleep. Is it possible that melatonin production, which increases on dark nights, pro-motes more rest and less movement at night during dark moons? If so, is it also possible that the light of day brings on renewed activity, especially during the prime early and late hours, perhaps by reducing melatonin lev-els or simply because the deer didn't move much at night? Conversely, is it possible that reduced melatonin production on bright nights results in less resting and more moving at night? Consequently, after an active night, wouldn't it be logical for the deer to rest more during the day, per-haps only to grab a bite around midday, as they seem to often do on full moons? All this would also explain why rutting activity intensifies during the full moon and is often so visible during midday hours—an increased number of hot does; bright nights of active rutting; resting after daybreak; midday rutting flurries; resting again late in the afternoon before an hot night on the town. There is a certain straightforward logic in it.

I also can't help but wonder if the pre-rut lull and post-rut recovery phases aren't connected to melatonin. It not only induces sleep, but an excess of it has been found to cause mood swings, tiredness and that "hung over" feeling the following day. In short, high doses of melatonin can dull daytime activity. Is it possible that the dulling effect of high levels of melatonin could contribute (along with other factors, no doubt) to the downtime so apparent during those two times bracketing the peak rut? The fact that the timing of both phases tends to shift around from year to year within about the same parameters as rutting activity certainly raises suspicions. Interestingly enough, both of these two low-movement times usually last about a week, the same as a moon phase. And, it may be no coincidence that these poor activity times seem to frequently overlap the first quarter, which follows the new moon and is the time of greatest melatonin production...and generally is the moon phase with the poorest overall deer activity. Interesting ideas worth watching.

OUTSIDE FACTORS AFFECTING THE RUT

We have talked about the two major predictable factors—daylength and moonlight—in the timing of the rut. A hunter can look ahead and predict how they may affect the timing and character of the rut. There are, however, other outside influences that can sway the timing of the rut, at least to minor degrees, and how the rut is played out. Some of these other factors can be identified in advance, such as hunting pressure and herd condition, and their effects anticipated. Others, like weather, are more short-term in nature and cannot be anticipated with any level of assurance. Yet, all of these factors figure into hunting strategies.

As we look at these factors, we're going to be mostly concerned about their impact on the intensity of rutting activity and not actual breeding, though some, like herd condition, can affect breeding. In most cases, their effect on breeding is minimal, but what they do to rutting activity can be dramatic. They can give at least the appearance of delaying, pausing or outright stopping the rut. Thus, we need to look into them and factor them into our fall planning.

Any trophy hunter worth his salt makes it his business to know when the rut hits. He must take advantage of this time of maximum buck movement, and he must understand the factors that affect exactly when and how the rut is played out. Then, bucks like this become a possibility. Photo by Mike Biggs.

Hunting Pressure

We've been over this before, but because no other outside factor affects the nature of the rut as much as hunting pressure, it bears repeating. Overall, the relationship between hunting pressure and rutting activity is simple: The higher the hunting pressure, the poorer the rutting activity. Excessive pressure brings both immediate liabilities and insidious long-term repercussions. Short term, heavy pressure drives the deer underground, so to speak, disrupting normal patterns, suppressing movement and crashing the rutting ritual, the very thing hunters depend on to put a mature buck in their sights. Longer term, when excessive pressure is exerted year after year, there no longer remains any hope of a "normal" rut. The sex and age structures of the herd are so screwed up that normal

191

whitetail social behavior becomes a thing of years gone by, resulting in an indistinct, low-intensity rut lacking visible rutting activity or its associated buck sign.

Temperature

Even when everything else is right, the wrong temperature can thwart rutting activity. What is the wrong temperature? Basically, anything above normal for that time of the year at that place stands to curtail rutting activity. Why? We're back to the deer's "comfort zone." Deer move best when the temperature is the most comfortable and invigorating for them relative to what they are used to and prepared to face. In the fall, when deer are all "dressed up" for coming winter, relatively cool temperatures feel good to them and spark movement. On the other hand, relatively warm weather is oppressive and curtails activity. It is possible for the temperature to fall below the comfort zone and cut into rutting activity, but this seldom is a problem, at least for very long. I'll take hard cold over hot any day.

Few things can so severely suppress rutting activity like unseasonably warm weather. Throw in high humidity, and you might think about going fishing. During such times, daylight rutting activity all but ceases and the rut becomes largely a nocturnal affair. I had just as soon to spend the weekend on the beach with my mother-in-law as hunt the rut, or any other time for that matter, during periods of unseasonably warm, humid (we call it muggy) weather.

Because of the role cooler temperature plays in deer activity, weather systems, specifically cold fronts, figure prominently into the rutting picture. Cold fronts—normally accompanied by cooler temperatures (obviously), lower humidity and high pressure, all things favorable for good deer movement—often trigger intense rutting activity. I've seen incredible turnarounds in rutting activity be swept in on the winds of a cold front countless times before, from Canada to Texas and Georgia to Montana. A recent Montana experience illustrates the triggering effect of fronts as well as any.

Several days into what should have been the rut, shirt-sleeve weather persisted and I hadn't found anything close to a shooter. I had tried nearly everything—rattling, grunting, aggressive still-hunts, stand-hunting clearcuts and scrapelines, hunting high and hunting low—but nothing seemed to work. Finally, the weatherman said a major cold front was rolling in, bringing with it several inches of snow and sub-zero temperatures. The mercury went from 60 above to 10 below overnight. After a short recoup time (about a day and a half) from the shockingly cold weather and snow, the big bucks came out of whatever hole they had been in! During the next six days, I was neck deep in big bucks. I shot a 155-point 10-pointer, watched my two hunting buddies from Georgia miss four, yes four, 150-class bucks and guided both my wife and oldest daughter to bucks in the 130s! Yes, temperature can impact the timing and intensity of rutting activity!

Often, cold fronts are followed by gusty, unsettled winds. When this happens, the best deer movement may await a settling of the weather, which usually comes a day or two after the passage of the front. Also, when a front is accompanied by a substantial amount of snow, it has been my experience that deer movement doesn't really crank up for a day or two following.

Drizzle

Like cooler temperature, a drizzling rain, or heavy mist, can trigger rutting activity, and as an added bonus, it makes deer less wary, even the jittery old bucks. Frankly, I don't know of a better time to be in the woods than during a drizzly day when the rut is underway. This is especially so when several warm days precede the coming of a drizzling rain, as is often the case. For some reason, drizzle incites aggression in bucks and puts them on the hunt for does. I've seen an explosion of trailing and chasing activity come with drizzles. I also have had some remarkable rattling days during the rut thanks to drizzles. One particular drizzly morning in South Texas, 16 mature bucks answered my rattling horns. All of them were big, and several of them put on shows with brush-beating displays of their own. I've never sensed such aggression from whitetails as was exuded that morning. I rattled in four or five of them more than once. One came back a second time with a six-foot mesquite limb tangled in his antlers, causing momentary cessation of my heartbeat and visions of my name by the world record non-typical. As I think back, several of my best bucks have fallen on just such days. Drizzle can, however, wear out its welcome. If a drizzle persists more than a couple of days, deer activity rapidly drops off. They just seem to get tired of it. So do I.

Extremes In Weather

Extreme weather of almost any kind can put a damper on rutting activity. Needless to say, severe storms will bring proceedings to a halt. So will heavy rain. In heavy downpours, deer will hold up in thick cover and cease almost all activity. I've sneaked into evergreen thickets in driving rains and found deer standing, slightly hunched with their heads hung, looking miserable and forlorned. Once rain stops, business usually returns to normal, or better, soon thereafter. I really like to be in the woods right after a lengthy heavy rain. The deer seem to revel in the relief.

A heavy snow will also drive deer into a holding pattern. Unlike rain, however, its effect may last for several days after the precipitation is over in extreme cases. Snow, you see, has sticking power...literally. A couple of years ago during the onset of the Montana rut, the northwestern part of the state was buried by a 24-hour-record 42 inches of snow! The rut had been progressing nicely, but with the snow, proceedings mired to a standstill. Only pure luck saved the season for me the morning after the big snowfall, but with friends in town to hunt, I had to keep slugging it out with the snow, which received two more feet of reinforcements a couple of days later, in an attempt to help them get a deer. After several days of hunting, we had nothing to show for our considerable efforts and had found precious little deer sign to encourage us. Then, I finally figured out what the deer were doing, or not doing. What I found was very interesting.

The deer were virtually trapped by the deep snow. Unable to travel long distances, they retreated to nearby timbered areas with a thick overhead canopy, where they held up. In these little enclaves, pockets of deer numbering from a handful to many dozens carried out a modified version of the rut. Whatever bucks were trapped with the group did the breeding. The dominance hierarchy went no further than the top dog in the local gathering. There was precious little traveling between groups of deer. Sign outside those pockets was almost nonexistent. Traditional rutting grounds I had hunted successfully in years past were practically devoid of tracks. In one instance three days after the last snowfall, I drudged nearly three miles across one of my favorite rutting hillsides and cut only two sets of tracks! Only after I began to locate the tightly bunched pockets of deer, mainly by following the few tracks I could find, did I find any evidence that the rut had resumed. All in all, I've never seen the rut so totally disrupted as it was by the dumping of nearly six feet of snow in less than four days.

Typically, extremes in weather only temporarily delay and/or alter normal rutting activity. I've seen flooding along major rivers disrupt and relocate rutting activity. In Canada, chinook winds, which are strong, warm winds coming off the east side of the Rockies, can last for several days and curb rutting activity. A couple of years ago, chinook winds gusting up to 50 mph persisted the entire week I was hunting the famed Mosquito Indian Reservation. Though it was the traditional peak of rut, 10 hunters only killed two bucks that week. One was mine—a big 9-pointer grossing 167. The other was a "mistake" buck shot during a desperation drive on the last day of the hunt. In most cases, the effects of heavy rain, high wind and the like pass quickly, allowing the rut to resume with catch-up fury.

Herd Condition

The physical condition of the deer within a herd can impact visible rutting activity and even breeding itself. When a herd is in poor condition, the start of breeding is often delayed and, once underway, breeding is less intense and more spread-out. This watered-down breeding cycle, now more widespread than ever before because of chronic overcrowding, is called a "trickle rut." There are also causes for short-term poor herd condition, such as drought, mast-crop failure, flooding and even disease, that can flatten out the rut in a given year. For instance, severe drought in South Texas or a poor acorn crop in an area with populations heavily dependent on mast often leads to poor deer condition and a trickle rut. During such pitiful ruts, I've even heard hunters declare that there was no rut at all that year. But, a full compliment of fawns was born the following spring so breeding did take place. It's just that hunters didn't see the ritual activity normally associated with the rut.

If all this seems too confusing, you can adopt the policy of my old hometown fishing buddy, Wilbur Pridgen. When asked about the best time to go fishing, his answer was always the same: "Don't worry about it. Just go every day and you'll be there when they bite." That'll work for deer, too!

Chapter Nineteen

Strategies for the Pre-Rut–Slow and Easy Does It

W HEN ERIC ALBUS STARTED describing his setup, I pressed the phone hard to my ear and took notice of what he had to say.

"Several of us ranchers decided to start managing our deer herd so we could get some age on the bucks. Our ranches lie along either side of the Milk River for about 12 miles. We've got several hundred acres of irrigated alfalfa fields. Most are isolated and adjacent to pretty big bush in the bends of the river. We haven't hunted the place in three years. We're seeing some mighty good bucks now and thought we'd take four or five bucks this year. You interested in coming?" Eric concluded.

Even as he was talking, my mind was processing the information and shaping the likely scenario. *Milk River. One of eastern Montana's best whitetail rivers. Open prairies surround the strips of whitetail cover along the river. Tremendous deer densities in those cottonwood bottoms. So many deer, in fact, that they have to depend almost exclusively on agriculture for food. Irrigated alfalfa...perfect. The deer will be concentrated on the fields. No hunting in three years. Pressure minimal. Deer will move and feed during daylight hours. This could be the place for an early season hunt.*

Right after velvet-shedding, the pre-rut starts out with the bucks still banded together. The bucks are calm and a bit naïve for a couple of weeks…until rising testosterone levels begin to charge them up for the coming festivities and make old buddies start looking at each other crossways. Photo by Troy Huffman.

When Eric first called and said he had a whitetail hunt I might be interested in, I had little reason to think I'd be able to work in another hunt in the coming fall. Unless there are extenuating circumstances, I always try to time my hunts to correspond with the rut, which normally starts in earnest the third week of November in Montana. Canada had already spoken for the last three weeks of that month. Trying to squeeze in another hunt around the rut didn't seem possible, and I couldn't rationalize in my own mind, let alone find an angle I could sell to my wife, being away from my family another week for a low-odds pre-rut hunt. But, what Eric was telling me was upping the odds of success on a late-October, opening-week hunt by the word. I still wasn't sure I could sell the deal to my wife, but even before Eric concluded, I knew the "extenuating circumstances" were right for a successful pre-rut hunt.

"Sounds great, but I've got to work out a few details on this end before I can commit," I finally answered, already thinking ahead to the hunt and about the line I would run by my wife. "If this works out, I've got several friends that might be interested. What do you think about opening week?"

"Should be fine. I saw plenty of big bucks last year on opening day. I was out watching the fields to be sure nobody came in on us. You know, though, the best time is later. We see the biggest bucks in the rut," Eric offered, clearly pushing for a later date.

"Yeah, I know, but I can't come then. But, this hunt sounds ideal for an early season hunt over the alfalfa fields. If we are very careful not to disturb the fields, we just might get a shot at some of the better bucks," I said, almost thinking out loud as I plotted strategy for the hunt I hoped would be forthcoming.

The day before the season opener in late October found five of us standing expectantly on the rolling prairie hills overlooking the Milk River bottoms. With a full two hours of daylight left, the distant alfalfa fields were already dotted with deer. If our strategy worked, the deer would be doing the same thing tomorrow at this time. We, however, would be among them...rifles in tow.

The stands were already hung. Eric and I had seen to that three weeks earlier. I had journeyed over from my across-state home in Bigfork to scout and build stands so we wouldn't have to disturb the area immediately before or during the hunt. We had carefully located the stands so we could get in and out without disturbing the deer. Our entire strategy revolved around not letting the deer know they were being hunted and keeping them blissfully on their feeding pattern. In fact, with a little persuasion, everybody agreed to lay off the main fields in the mornings for the first few days to minimize the chances of alerting the morning shift already out there feeding. The plan was to sneak in unnoticed during midday, hunt the prime afternoon hours and then slink out under the cover of darkness. We would spend the first half of the day hunting perimeter fields and the coulees in the open prairies.

It was a great strategy for pre-rut feeding bucks, and did it ever work! We looked over dozens and dozens of bucks during the five-day hunt, and all five hunters got shots at bucks over 150! Three of them were better than 160! But alas, the bucks seemed to be armor-plated! When the smoke cleared, we had only one buck to show for the fusillade, a 150-class 10-pointer I managed to kill after muffing the first shot. It was as though we were hunting in the Twilight Zone! A couple of weeks later, Randy Trice's low-150s 10-pointer also was recovered a mile away from where it had been shot, bringing to a conclusion one of the most bizarre hunts I've ever been a part of. Unfortunately, the only two deer recovered were the smallest two shot at!

The setup, however, was perfect for a pre-rut hunt and the strategy flawless. I still have no explanation for the outcome. Since the hunt was being videoed by Realtree Outdoors for their TV show and Monster Buck video series, the whole thing was captured on film. Otherwise, I might have thought it all a dream...or a nightmare!

PRE-RUT OVERVIEW

The pre-rut certainly has its pluses. Opportunity for success on big bucks does exist when everything is right, which frankly is seldom. Food and/or water drive movement during the pre-rut, and as whitetail patterns go, pre-rut feeding patterns can be somewhat predictable, though frequent food-source changes and nocturnal movement are often the norm. Also, the cool, crisp days of autumn, the brilliantly colored foliage and the sense of anticipation in the air make the pre-rut a most enjoyable time of year to chase whitetails.

The pre-rut can also be a trying time for serious trophy hunters. Mature bucks tend to be nocturnal throughout much of the pre-rut and become increasingly so as the period progresses. To make matters worse, pre-rut deer are very sensitive to hunting pressure, or any other kind of disturbance. At the least provocation, the deer, now in prime condition, will abandon daytime activity with Dracula-like steadfastness.

Having said all this, the odds of finding mature bucks are still generally better during the pre-rut than during the post-rut. However, when the goal shifts from simply mature bucks to top-end bucks, things change. The fact is that top-end bucks can be downright difficult to kill during the pre-rut. The biggest and the oldest bucks are especially nocturnal and secretive during this time. Often, they can live right among people totally undetected throughout the pre-rut, only to appear mysteriously later in the fall, oddly enough, often toward the tail-end of the rut or even during the post-rut. Though I rank the post-rut as the most difficult time to hunt

This 150-class 10-pointer, along with over 100 other deer, was on a classic pre-rut feeding pattern in an irrigated alfalfa field along north-central Montana's Milk River when I shot him. Photo by Eric Albus.

mature bucks, I put the post-rut ahead of the pre-rut for the biggest bucks, especially when major food sources are available during the post-rut. We'll discuss why later.

KEYS TO THE PRE-RUT

During the pre-rut, time, familiarity with the land and an understanding of deer travel patterns are all premium commodities. Unlike hunting in the rut, with its widespread and random buck movement, the pre-rut is characterized by passive feeding/resting patterns that are easily disrupted by hunting pressure. Hunting now requires patience, a deliberate approach and the location of spot-specific intercept points. Some serious scouting is called for. A game plan must start with the identification of major food sources, travel corridors (trails), bedding areas and the degree, nature and even direction of hunting pressure. But during the pre-rut, the must-find sign for me is the presence of big rubs, other than a reliable buck sighting, preferably by me. Big bucks are too scarce to hunt them blindly without some evidence one is around.

Because of all this, local hunters with an in-depth knowledge of the land and time to sort out a buck have a distinct advantage over visiting hunters with limited time. The Midwest is a perfect example of this. There, resident hunters stack up impressive scores on pre-rut (and post-rut) trophies, even when handicapped with regulatory weapons limitations. A visiting hunter could not hope to compete with those local hunters before (or after) the rut, but the odds would level out somewhat once bucks lay caution aside in favor of love.

The effects of pressure are more detrimental on feeding activity than on rutting movement, making pressure particularly onerous during times when bucks aren't blinded by passion. With or without major food sources, pressure disrupts normal daytime feeding patterns, makes old bucks nocturnal and forces the hunter to a tight, in-cover strategy. If where you hunt faces heavy pressure during the pre-rut, if possible, hunt elsewhere or stake your hopes on the rut. Your odds of success are just too long. Only if you know the area so well that you can anticipate the escape routes of rousted bucks will you have much hope.

The presence of identifiable, concentrated major food sources is the one thing that gives the pre-rut (and post-rut) hunter a real leg-up on connecting. But even in the absence of major food sources, almost any-place has feeding areas that receive more use than others. It'll behoove the hunter to search them out, even though they can be hard to identify. But because such dispersed or minor food sources aren't a must-hit place for a high percentage of area deer, it's helpful to know a shootable buck is in the vicinity rather than hunting blindly in an iffy place. I seldom invest hunting time in a modest feeding area without "big" cause.

In lightly pressured areas, even mature bucks can be taken while feeding in open food sources. In moderately pressured areas, really hot feeding grounds can be turned to an advantage, but don't expect a good buck to show up on open food sources before last shooting light or to remain in the morning much after the thrashers and mockingbirds cease their wakeup calls. When hunting food sources under moderate pressure, the best plan is to hunt in-cover trails and staging areas near the food sources or back toward the bedding area. The higher the pressure, the nearer to the bedding area you need to setup since increased pressure will cause mature bucks to hold tight in the security of their bedding area until low light or darkness.

When we talk about major food sources, we normally think about agricultural crops such as corn, soybeans, small grains, winter greens, alfalfa, sugar beets, clover, etc. However, in the absence of such agricultural attractants, other less obvious food sources can emerge as "major." In fact, some of what I call "in-cover food sources" can be every bit as good for big bucks as agricultural fields. For instance, in the South, wild grapes, or muscadines, and persimmons can be a real draw at times, especially during the early bow season. Clearcuts, particularly those at just the right age to provide lots of browse and ample cover to make the deer feel secure, are big-time deer attractants and one of the very best places to ambush mature bucks. And, of course, deer rush headlong to certain kinds of acorns. These natural food sources are deer magnets, and when acorn production is not so widespread as to disperse feeding activity all over the woods, acorn groves can be just the ticket for crossing paths with a whopper buck.

The closer the food source comes to supplying the bulk of the nutritional needs of area deer, the better it will be for hunting. When deer are very dependent on limited major food sources, as was the case when we hunted the irrigated alfalfa fields along Montana's Milk River, practically all area deer will end up feeding there. And, they likely will follow predictable bed-to-field, and vice versa, movement patterns that will get them to the fields early and keep them there late. Obviously, this makes for fine hunting, if the herd is not badly overcrowded.

TIMING A PRE-RUT HUNT

We have divided the pre-rut into three phases—the summer transition, core-area feeding and pre-rut lull phases. They are not all made equally when it comes to big bucks' vulnerability and your chances of scoring.

Summer Transition Phase

As we've said, the summer transition phase occurs during the first two weeks or so of the pre-rut, which usually starts up in September, depending on the part of the country. During this brief phase, the bucks, still in bachelor groups, continue on their summer feeding pattern, meaning they feed early and late on the best food sources around and rest in cool, protected places during the heat of day. Bucks feed heavily during this time and often appear on feeding grounds, especially major ones, early enough to do the hunter some good. Interestingly, bucks during the summer transition often exhibit the naivete characteristic of spring and summer, when they seem to be more trusting and tolerant of humans. This calmness and passiveness is probably more related to hormone levels than anything else, since the wired-up attitude brought on by increasing testosterone has not yet fully swept over them. If not harassed, these calm deer can be hunted right on the food source itself, even open agricultural fields.

Once located, bucks are now more predictable than at any other time of the season, provided the food sources hold out and pressure is low. But alas, there is a major fly in the soup—the season, at least firearms season, is not open during the summer transition phase over much of the country. Where whitetails can be hunted during this early season window, archers pretty much have exclusive rights. And, they take advantage of it! This is an excellent time for bowhunters to skewer a feeding trophy.

There are a handful of places that allow firearms hunting during this time. South Carolina is such a place. I've hunted deer there over soybean fields in late August and have had reams of bucks from which to choose. With an early September firearms season, northern Alberta also opens in time to get in on summer transition hunting. I've never hunted there then, but Scott Taylor, my outfitter friend in the Peace River Country, tells me he sees some fine bucks the first week or two after velvet-shedding. He says it's hard to convince hunters to forfeit the rutting time for a crack at these early season bucks, but it's something I want to try. After what I've endured in Canada during late November, hunting up there in shirtsheeves is mighty attractive! As good as it can be for mature bucks during this time, I've still found top-end bucks to be elusive then and anytime in the pre-rut.

Core-Area Feeding Phase

A couple of weeks into the pre-rut, aggression between mature bucks begins to mount and they begin posturing and vying for dominance. Tolerance of each other's company runs thin, and the bachelor groups begin to breakup. Bucks, especially the older ones, separate and retire to their own core area. Once there, they settle into a feeding/resting routine, thus initiating the core-area feeding phase.

I have seen situations where the hunting has been quite good during this time, but I've hunted the core-area feeding phase when I felt my chances of seeing a mature buck were something akin to the odds of the Atlanta Falcons winning the Super Bowl. What made the difference? You guessed it, concentrated major food sources. During my bowhunting years back in the South (Yes, I used to bowhunt a lot until one-deer limits caused me to opt for my 7mm Mag. in the belief I could take bigger bucks with it than with my bow.), major food sources were as likely to be white oak groves or persimmon thickets as soybeans, corn or winter greens. In fact, some of the in-cover food sources were where I launched most of my arrows. But still, the biggest bucks were scarce during the core-area feeding time. Good bucks, yes, but top-ends, seldom. There is just something about the elusiveness of the very biggest bucks, as fleshing out the now-infamous Milk River story I started this chapter with will illustrate.

For five days on that hunt, I sat on the same 50-acre alfalfa field. Twice prior to season, a 190-class 10-pointer had been seen in the field. That was reason enough to cast my lot there. Besides, I was seeing about 60 bucks a day, so many that it took me a couple of days to "catalog" all the different bucks. Eric Albus and his daddy, Loran, and the landowner, Terry Corban, had described several bucks they had watched feeding on the field earlier in the fall, and by the end of the third day, I had pretty well seen all of them...except the big 10. Still, I continued to hunt the field in hopes of the 190 finally showing up. When two more days passed without any new bucks making an appearance, I figured all the bucks using that food source were now accounted for. After all, only 75 acres of woods lay adjacent to the field and all 150-plus deer, counting does and fawns, were coming out of that one block of cover along the river. The alfalfa field was certainly the dining hotspot. The best buck I had seen was a low-160s 10-pointer. He was a regular visitor. A handful of 150-class bucks finished out the top group.

On the belief that nothing better was using the field, but still holding out hope the mystery 190 was somewhere on the ranch, I offered to take my buddy, Richard Jackson, to the field on the sixth morning to take one of the 150-plus regulars there. As luck would have it, the 160

Major food sources are a key to hunting the pre-rut. In areas where hunting pressure is low, it is possible to catch good bucks on open food sources at last light. These bucks are in prime pre-rut shape. Photo by Troy Huffman.

was the first good buck to show. We estimated the distance to be about 275 yards, and Richard lined up for the shot. The Realtree camera recorded exactly what happened next—the bullet struck low, creasing the brisket and passing through the fleshy part of the far side upper front leg. (Later, the distance proved to be 320 yards, resulting in a critical few more inches of bullet drop.) Knowing the buck was hit, we mounted a search, which really amounted to a deer drive, to try to recover the wounded deer. What followed was unquestionably one of the most amazing deer drives in recent times.

We stationed Realtree's Bill Jordan at the end of the 75-acre strip of riverside cover with two cameramen, David Blanton and Mike Robertson, by his side in the event the wounded buck should try to escape that way. Then, six of us began a slow directional search of the woods. The first few minutes were relatively uneventful, but as we started to crowd the deer toward the end of the strip, a veritable whitetail stampede threatened both drivers and standers with trampling. I literally sought refuge behind a big cottonwood as dozens of panicked deer poured back through the loose driveline. Bill, David and Mike caught the brunt of it and had whitetails practically jumping over them. Then, in the mist of whitetail pandemonium, the unexpected happened. A giant buck, one nobody had ever seen, burst onto the scene right in front of Bill and the cameras. Once the buck cleared the river of other deer, Bill made a raking shot on the buck as he quartered away at only 30 yards. The video image was clear—the 140-grain bullet struck the buck just behind the rib cage, passed through the chest and exited the off shoulder. A perfect shot...only the buck didn't go down. Indeed, he ran a half-mile across a field to the distant brushline and simply disappeared! Impossible, but it happened, adding another chapter to our Twilight Zone-like experience on that hunt.

From the initial description of the buck, I was certain it was the deer Richard had wounded. Even as David Blanton rewound the cameras there in the field so we could see the events that had just unfolded, Bill described the deer as very wide with at least 10, but probably 12, points. The 10-pointer we were searching for was 24 inches wide and certainly fit the bill. However, the instant I saw the buck on video I knew it was not the 10; it was a huge 25-inch 12-pointer I had never seen before!

My mind raced. Why hadn't I seen him during the five days I sat on this field? Had I somehow failed to pick him out among all the other deer in the field? No, not a buck that of size. Had he just moved into the area? Unlikely, since there was no surrounding pressure to move him. Or, had he been in the woods next to the field all along and simply been nocturnal? All I knew about top-end bucks told me that was the answer. That buck had remained secure in the brush day after day while all the other deer filed out of the woods to feed on the alfalfa. Was it simply a coincidence that the largest of some 60-plus bucks, many mature, in those woods was the only one, as far as we could determine, that did not expose himself during five crisp autumn days? No, it wasn't a coincidence. Top-ends are like that, especially during the pre-rut.

Still, 59 out of 60 ain't bad. And, that was made possible only by the presence of a major food source that provided the great bulk of the nutritional needs of area deer. Without that...well, there wouldn't have been over 60 bucks around to start with. And whatever reduced number of bucks would have been there, I would have been lucky to see 20 per-

cent of them! Major food sources make that much difference this time of
year!

For the most part, buck movement during the core-area feeding
phase is from their bedding area to feeding grounds and back again.
Fortunately, they do tend to lay down some sign, primarily rubs but also
some preliminary scrapes, where they spend the most time, which is in
their core areas, along travel routes and at major food sources. Even finding concentrated deer sign, such as tracks, droppings, heavily used trails,
evidence of browsing, etc., may not help a lot now since the sign may
have been made by does and immature bucks. Mature bucks don't intentionally hangout with the crowds, though they may feed on the same
food sources. For this reason, good buck sign is necessary to be sure that
what you're after is around.

In the absence of major food sources, there are other ways to gain
an edge. One is funnels or bottlenecks that direct an unusually high percentage of deer activity pass a particular ambush point. Finding such
places normally depends on the two other advantages we talked about
earlier—time and familiarity with the land—but an astute hunter can
often pick out such places on scouting runs or from topos and aerial photos. I had two or three such places back in Georgia on Burnt Pine, and
well before the bucks started making eyes at flashy does, I could count on
looking over several mature bucks in the course of a few sittings. One of
those bottlenecks was so productive that I had to limit the number of
bucks shot there for fear of shooting the age structure down in that area
of the plantation.

For consistent success during the pre-rut, some sort of advantage is
needed. Imagination may be required to find it. One of the things we did
at Burnt Pine was turn hunting pressure along our borders to our favor,
especially on heavily hunted opening week. There were certain tracts
adjoining us that we knew were going to see plenty of pressure, usually
right on our boundary. Because the direction of the pressure would be
from the outside moving toward Burnt Pine, it amounted to a slow, quiet
deer drive, the kind that works best for big bucks. Experience told us
where the bucks were most likely to go. All we had to do was sneak in
quietly, preferably quieter than the "drivers," and wait. Year after year, we
enjoyed extraordinary success doing this. In fact, the hunters posted next
to our "problem neighbors" experienced far greater success during the

If you can find a big buck on an undisturbed feeding pattern in the pre-rut, there's a chance of changing his address to your den wall. Bobby Parker, Jr. located this 185-point monster just before season and killed him on opening day in the very field he had seen him earlier. Photo courtesy of Bobby Parker, Jr.

opening week than did our hunters totally dependent on the rather slow natural movement of early season. A great byproduct of this strategy, at least for me as a deer manager, was that we got to harvest border bucks that would have eventually been taken by our plentiful neighbors…and the very presence of our hunters helped remind the multitudes where the property lines were, which they frequently forgot.

If I can't realize some sort of edge during the core-area feeding phase, then I either wait for the rut, look for a place that will give me an edge or do something I don't like to do—hunt tight. By this, I mean searching out the best in-cover sign I can find and sitting tight, hoping to catch a big buck on the move before limited visibility, few sightings and boredom get to me. I've hunted this way and killed big bucks, but it's a grind-it-out type of hunting. I like to have some visibility (perhaps that's my claustrophobia kicking in), frequent action and the knowledge that something is working in my favor. Unless I have big, hot buck sign to keep me chummed, I'll leave sitting in the thickets to somebody else.

Pre-Rut Lull

I don't really know for sure why this is (though you've read my theory in the chapter on timing the rut), but as the pre-rut period draws to a close, the homebody tendencies of mature bucks peak. They just seem to disappear. It truly is the lull before the rutting storm rumbling on the horizon. Now in prime condition and ready for the dance, perhaps they are all dressed up with no place to go...yet. Testosterone levels rising, food doesn't seem to hold the same appeal anymore. Something else begins to move front and center in their minds, causing them to forsake their usual feeding pattern and hang closer to home, taking out growing aggression on saplings and trees. Whatever the reason, during the last 7 to 10 days of the pre-rut, and sometimes even into the first part of the scraping period, bucks become nocturnal and reclusive, staying mostly in and around their core areas. I call this time the pre-rut lull, and I had just about as soon to be beat in the rear with a string of sun-dried catfish as hunt during this time.

If you must hunt now, you once again need an angle. We've talked about the old standbys, i.e., knowledge of the land, time, major food sources, bottlenecks, even "friendly" outside pressure. Now, I'll add one more situation that may be worth hunting, especially during the latter part of this phase—traditional scraping areas. These are the high-interaction social hubs where bucks make breeding scrapes and rubs year after year. As the scraping period of the rut approaches, bucks start making occasional scouting forays to such places, slipping in rather furtively and tentatively to begin with, usually at last light. If a hunter has previously located a traditional scraping area (as he must have since there'll be little or no current-year sign yet laid down to go by), he has a chance of meeting up with one of its users during the latter days of the pre-rut lull.

Without an edge, I seek out the best in-cover food sources or trails I can find with good buck sign and hope for the best. I often find myself with a couple of days of pre-rut lull on my hands during hunts timed to the scraping period. When I do, I am once again reminded of why I need to be at home raking leaves or washing my car during this quiet before the passion storm dawns. But, the good thing about the pre-rut lull is that it is the harbinger of great things to come—and rather suddenly at that!

Chapter Twenty

Strategies for the Scraping Period of the Rut–Let the Festivities Begin

MANY YEARS AGO WHILE HUNTING the Cameron Ranch in South Texas, a friend rattled in and shot a big buck standing front-on to him. As it happened, the bullet hit the wide-eyed buck in the neck and flattened him...for a few seconds. Before my elated buddy could get to the downed animal, the buck struggled to his feet and absconded, leaving behind no small amount of blood, hair and meat. A long and exasperating search failed to turn up the buck.

Less than a week later in almost the same place, another hunter was imitating the ruckus of an angry buck fight when a big buck burst onto the scene, his eyes rolled wide and nostrils flaring. A center-chest shot at rock-throwing distance put the buck down in a heap. The hunter hastened over to the buck and was shocked and a little sickened to see that almost a third of the thickness of the buck's neck about midway down was gone, replaced by a gaping wound. When he brought the buck to camp and told his story, everybody was astonished that the buck, now recognized as the same one my friend had shot a few days before, could

The scraping period is perhaps the best time to hunt one particular buck. For a brief time, they are on the move and somewhat predictable. I saw this Alberta 15-pointer very late one afternoon (too late to shoot) and went back to the same alfalfa field the next afternoon and killed him. Photo by Scott Taylor.

have survived such a ghastly injury. I, too, found it hard to believe the deer was still on his feet. But more than that, I marveled at the power of the rut! Here was a mortally wounded buck whose senses were so completely overwhelmed by the power of the rut that he ignored the pain and injury to engage in the rutting ritual, even as he practically died on his feet. And to further emphasize the sense-blinding grip of the rut, the buck met his demise charging into a fake fight only days after being grievously injured doing the same thing in the same place! That buck was smitten!

That event over 15 years ago taught me a lesson about the power of the rut I have never forgotten. When the long-awaited rut finally rolls around, which it does only once a year (that in itself helps explain its fierce intensity), the normally cautious, retiring whitetail buck becomes a bold, nomadic bundle of male hormones. Though it would be an over-statement to say that the quest for love causes bucks to throw all caution to the wind, the rut can cause even wizen old bucks, the kind that are darn-near unkillable outside the rut, to occasionally lower their awesome defenses and make mistakes I can turn to my advantage. Every year, I do my darnest to make the most of that fact.

As we've discussed, the rut can be divided into two periods—the scraping and breeding periods. The scraping period encompasses the preparatory ritual rutting activity leading up to actual breeding. Technically speaking, this time could be viewed as part of the pre-rut since breeding per se has not yet kicked off in earnest. However, during the scraping period, a buck's primary attention has shifted from feeding to breeding. From the hunter's standpoint, that's the deciding factor on how this period is viewed and the potential it holds to put a trophy buck in front of a hunter. We'll consider the rut to be the time when a buck's attention is diverted from survival, feeding and resting by the nemesis of clear-thinking, prudent behavior in males of every species—sex. That puts the scraping period under the heading of the rut.

THE OPPORTUNITY

Most activity during the scraping period is centered on the making and checking of scrapes near the high-activity areas of doe groups. Because much of the ritual activity takes place at night, the scraping period is not always an easy time to hunt trophy bucks. In fact, the symptoms of the pre-rut lull can carry over well into the scraping period, especially when unusually warm weather prevails. Still, big bucks are vulnerable during this time to patient, determined hunters. In fact, I consider the scraping period to be the very best time to find and hunt one *particular* buck. Why? Because big bucks are now more active and more prone to mistakes than previously, their travel pattern is predictable and, very importantly, they leave vital clues of their presence and pattern in the form of sign, i.e., rubs, scrapes and tracks. For a brief time right before breeding starts, that sign, specifically breeding scrapes and associated rubs, promises of a buck's imminent return, though one can only hope it will be during shooting hours.

The Dilemma
Scrape hunting is truly a matter of being in the right place at the

After making a scrape under the overhanging limb, this buck is now scent-marking the limb with his preorbital glands (in the corner of his eye). Scrapes are an important part of the whitetail breeding ritual and are hotbeds of scents that communicate all kinds of things to area deer. Photo by Mike Biggs.

right time. The right place is where a big buck is making or checking breeding scrapes and rubs or traveling to or from them. The right time is when he first starts doing it. It is the critical timing that presents a special problem for hunters. You see, by the time widespread sign is present in the woods, the most productive time to hunt that sign may well be past. Often, it's a classic case of "you should have been here last week." When bucks first start making and checking breeding scrapes, that is their most pressing priority at the moment and their activity patterns are somewhat predictable. But in a matter of only a few days, perhaps four or five, their priority begins to shift from setting a bait for does to the does themselves. With that, bucks begin to spend less time at their scrapes and more time on the move after prospective does, reducing the odds of catching them on their scrapes.

So, we have a dilemma. By the time we find an active scrapeline, the best time to hunt it could have passed. What's the answer? An astute hunter keen enough to pick up the first sign of serious activity may be able to overcome the problem by scouting likely scraping areas almost on a daily basis. But most hunters can't afford to burn up valuable time scouting as the rut heats up. Besides, much of that time could be spent looking for something that doesn't even exist yet. Plus, the time spent looking could be the very time you needed to spend on-stand to take advantage of the narrow optimum window of opportunity. And, tromping around and scenting-up a high-activity area can hamper daytime deer movement in the area to be hunted. Of course, you could depend on luck and hope to happen upon an active scrapeline at the right time. Or, you could sit on an established but waning scrapeline in hopes the buck wanders back through. I've done it both ways and killed bucks, but I've also spent a lot of time watching where bucks had been! There is a better way, a way that greatly improves your odds of being in the right place at the right time…and it doesn't have to eat into your hunting time! That better way is hunting what I call "traditional scraping areas."

A Solution—Traditional Scraping Areas

Traditional scraping areas are places where rut-struck bucks go year after year to advertise their presence and breeding readiness to local doe groups by making breeding scrapes and rubs. Contrary to popular belief, more than one buck usually uses such an area, although one may be dominant and the chief sign-maker. Both the local doe groups and the bucks hoping to connect with a hot doe from those groups are well aware of such areas long before the rut cranks up and the first serious rutting sign is laid down. True, scrapes and rubs will be made in places other than traditional scraping areas, but the other places don't offer the same advantage of predictability or similar odds that the dominant buck in those parts will show up there.

One of the real advantages of traditional scraping areas is that scouting for them can be done during the off-season. In fact, the best time to look for them is after season, when the sign is still clearly visible. In regions with little or no snow, immediately after season is the ideal time. In snow country, the time of choice is just after snowmelt. The earlier you go, the better the chances the scrapes will still be evident and the rubs will still be shining. Even summer and fall scouting for traditional scraping areas is possible, but the only sign still visible then is the time-dulled rubs.

How do you find and recognize traditional scraping areas? To start with, it has been my experience that traditional scraping areas are most common, or at least most visible, in places with a low buck:doe ratio and

This is a rub! The approaching buck is almost certainly not the only one that has contributed to the stripping of that tree. More than one buck will use "signpost" rubs like this. Big rubs are an important sign for hunters during the scraping period, and could point the way to a trophy. Photo by Troy Huffman.

a good buck age structure, i.e., locales with low to moderate hunting pressure. In heavily hunted herds with mostly young bucks, the normal behavioral patterns are disrupted and competition is reduced. Because of this, the traditional scraping areas are either so indistinguishable as to be hard to find or absent altogether. In such cases, hunters generally have to hunt whatever decent buck sign they can find and hope for the best.

Where pressure is light to moderate, traditional scraping areas will be present. You just have to find them. This takes some looking. Nothing replaces wearing out some shoe leather. If major food sources are present, I start my search there. Look for breaks and edges of some type. Small openings, logging roads, changes in cover or timber types and especially stream edges are all prime sites for traditional scraping areas.

When you find a traditional scraping area, it won't be hard to recognize. There will be lots of sign, most notably rubs and scrapes, but the one thing that will verify the identity of a traditional scraping area is the presence of rubs of varying age. There will probably be rubs on top of older rubs. I've seen stovepipe-sized trees rubbed nearly in half over the years. Scrapes obviously don't have the longevity of rubs, but even after evidence of scrapes has been erased from the ground, the telltale mangled limbs above them will still reveal their presence.

A traditional scraping area invariably has trails leading to and from it. The area is, after all, a social hub for deer during the fall. Study the area and try to figure out the overall travel pattern. Now's the time to decide on a stand site and perhaps even hang a stand. Walk the trails out, learn the terrain, determine the predominant wind direction, choose an approach route and clear a shooting lane if necessary. Write down what you've seen and decided. Have everything ready so you just walk in and hunt next fall…just as the sign is first being made! A recount of just such a hunt in Canada a few years ago will illustrate the benefits of this strategy.

The shroud of predawn finally gave way to the grey light of coming day. The formless surroundings of the frigid Northwoods slowly took shape. Scanning the area from my treestand with 10X Leicas, I could pull out the detail I needed to know if my strategy had worked. A dark blotch under a nearby spruce and another several yards beyond told me that it had. *Scrapes…just like last year.* More searching revealed two other fresh scrapes and rubs gouged deep in the bark of several poplars. The snow was pockmarked with tracks, some dragging across the surface of the six-inch deep snow. *They're doing it again. Just starting. At least a week before the startup of breeding. I'm just in time.*

I had found the area almost a year earlier during the middle of Saskatchewan's rut. Actually, my friend and outfitter Carl Frohaug had found the place. He had come back to camp with tales of a place so torn up with buck sign that he had become a bit concerned for his own safety, such was the destruction there. Knowing Carl was not the sort to be easily unnerved, I had to see this place for myself. I did…and experienced the same unsettled feeling, combined with excitement, that had prompted Carl to express his reservations about leaving his backside unprotected. The place was demolished. Poplar and spruce trees nearly as thick as my thigh had their bark shredded through to bare wood. Scars from rubs made in years past marred tree trucks in every direction. Several car-door-sized scrapes were churned clean of forest litter, the debris thrown 20 feet away. The musty scent of rutting bucks permeated the air.

I immediately began hunting the place, but since the sign was already showing evidence of age and the rut was raging, I knew I had already missed the main party and could only hope to catch the stragglers. Three days of vigilance only turned up a handful of small and intermediate bucks. In all likelihood, the dominant bucks had already broken off their normal travel patterns and were off who knows where courting a hot doe. Sure, a whopper buck could have walked into such a traditional scraping area as this any time, but I had missed the time of greatest opportunity. I filed that place away in my mind. Next year, I would be there when the bucks first started making the sign. Then, I would have my best chance of seeing the demolition crew.

Now, a year after first seeing the place, the many old scars on the trees reminded me just how hot this little semi-clearing in the deep forest could be. I had four days left for the right buck to make an appearance and for the scraping period of the rut to heat up. As I was about to find out, it wouldn't take that long.

As noon approached, the cold finally seeped into my bones and my muscles ached from hours of motionless sitting in the cramped stand. Besides, rental time on the three cups on coffee that had jumpstarted me before dawn had run out. I decided to climb down, but first, I would try another rattling sequence, having already rattled in a 140-class 10-pointer earlier that morning. I positioned my gun for quick access and began gently tickling the tines of the antlers together. Gradually, I picked up the tempo until I was twisting and turning the antlers together smartly. Perhaps 30 seconds into the process, I saw him coming at a fast trot. The rattling horns were immediately traded for my 7mm Rem. Mag. The buck abruptly halted about 60 yards away, his head and neck nearly completely obscured by two trees. I grabbed binoculars and tried to figure out exactly what he was wearing upstairs. *Huge body. Dark, heavy antlers but how many points?* Then, part of the rack briefly swung clear of the obscuring trees, revealing a heavy beam with four good primary tines standing! *A 12-pointer...if he has brows and the other side matches.* He gave me no time to find out.

The buck whirled around and trotted away a few yards before coming to a tentative halt at the edge of my vision. Only about a half-foot of the base of his massive neck was clearly visible through my scope. *No chance for a better look. Have to take him on the strength of what I've seen.*

Guy Shanks shot this palmated Montana buck at a traditional scraping area. Guy finds these areas in the early spring after snowmelt, and the next hunting season, he sets up on them before the new sign is ever laid down and then waits. This technique has enabled him to consistently kill big bucks early in the scraping period before others even find fresh scrapes. Photo by author.

The 140-grain Nosler Partition felled him where he stood. Scrambling down from the stand, I hurried over to find the largest-bodied whitetail I had ever seen. He was so enormous that I have no frame of reference for his size. After gawking at the 400-pound-plus buck, I finally got around to checking his antlers. The one side, as I had seen, sported six points; the other side five. *Umm, what you don't see always hurts you,* I reminded myself. Still, 11 long tines and good mass pushed his score into the 160s.

Location and good timing accounted for that immense buck. Location—traditional scraping area. Timing —the very front-end of the scraping activity. Had I been in the same spot a week or so later, as was the case the year before, I probably would not have seen that buck, even though I would have seen far more buck sign! Thus, we see the beauty of finding traditional scraping areas. It allowed me to escape the classic scraping period trap —waiting until the woods are sprinkled with wide-spread scraping sign before hunting that sign. By hunting a traditional scraping area, I got to the right spot before the scraping activity was in full swing and was present when the hot action went down, not after.

BIG BUCKS ON THE MOVE

The scraping period offers opportunity for big bucks even when not hunting a scraping area, traditional or otherwise, simply because older bucks are likely to be on the move, stirred by the breeding urge. Even hunting blind near major food sources and high doe concentrations holds promise, but I much prefer to hunt around big sign to booster my hopes that a shooter buck may be nearby. I particularly like hunting well-defined bottlenecks during the scraping period, especially those that lie between obvious feeding or scraping areas and bedding cover. Even though buck activity is picking up now, older bucks are still going to be mostly creatures of the night and setting up well back in cover is a good idea to hedge against their low-light tendencies. When I find a bottle-neck or funnel traversed by a trail laced with big sign, I confidently stick with it.

Before Saskatchewan booted nonresidents out of the farm country, I had just such a place. My stand was in the middle of a 600-yard strip of timber bordered on the east by a huge lake and the west by a vast, swampy grassfield. A quarter-mile north lay the endless Northwoods. To the south some half-mile, hundreds of acres of alfalfa fields were home to several doe groups, as well as a few resident bucks. Once the rutting urge began to cause bucks to start kicking up their heels, the alfalfa fields, or more specifically their associated doe groups, beckoned bucks from the security of the deep woods…down the well-rubbed trails and past my stand. Before getting the heave-ho, I shot a couple of good bucks from that stand and had several days where I saw 10 or more bucks in a sitting, which in Canada constitutes a veritable migration. The best time to hunt that stand was right at the height of scraping activity. I hunted it often during the breeding period and had some very good days, but activity was more erratic then.

Stand hunting, as you may have gathered, is the best way to hunt scrapes. It is critical that the area being hunted not be disturbed, which is one of the big pluses of scouting and preparing everything during the off-season. Depending on the setup, I am of the general opinion that your odds decrease the longer you hunt a particular stand, especially in tight quarters where the deer are sure to eventually pick you off. For this reason, I try to choose the very best time—both in terms of time of year and the days when deer movement is optimum—to hunt a promising scraping area.

While hunting this time of year generally calls for a deliberate and low key approach, there is a notable exception—rattling. Yes, the scraping period is one of the best times for this aggressive tactic. When hunting from a deer stand you figure to hunt over several days, rattle sparingly and rather passively, especially during the prime movement hours. Rattling, or grunting for that matter, repeatedly from a stationary position always has the potential of drawing attention to yourself but is particularly dicey when you're in the hub of deer activity and most likely in tight quarters. For this reason, when I suspect deer are on the move in the vicinity, I rattle or call only enough to entice them into the area but hopefully not enough to give them an exact fix on my location.

> *I am of the general opinion that your odds decrease the longer you hunt a particular stand, especially in tight quarters where the deer are sure to eventually pick you off.*

During midday hours or later in the scraping period when bucks are spending more time looking for does than checking scrapes, I will call or rattle with more frequency and vigor. In fact, one of my favorite late-scraping-period tactics, especially when I don't have a particular buck located, is to cover ground and rattle at every likely spot I come to. It's a good way to look over a bunch of country and, if the bucks are wired, a bunch of bucks. I've had my best luck rattling as fronts push in and the weather is changing. On one particular misty, drizzly day in South Texas in the late scraping period, I rattled in 16 bucks and they were all big!

TIMING WITHIN THE PERIOD

The scraping period, like the breeding period that follows, could have been broken into two parts—early and late. I didn't do this because essentially the same pattern is in place throughout the period, only the activity level accelerates as the period progresses. Moving into the second week, the bucks really begin to pick up the pace in their race for a breeding edge. All this activity builds to a fever pitch by the time wholesale breeding opportunities abound in deerdom, though once again, much of this activity is cloaked in darkness.

Now, it would be easy to assume that the last week is the best time since deer activity is on the rise, and that assumption would be right...unless you are hunting a traditional scraping area or otherwise have the pattern of a particular buck pegged. In which case, you are better off hunting early in the period before buck travel patterns start getting squirrelly. If you are coming into a place cold turkey, as so often is the case with the traveling hunter, the second week is much better. You have far better overall movement working for you and more mature bucks caught up in the festivities. Additionally, the cursed pre-rut lull can linger on well into the scraping period and can cause major headaches during the early days. Unless I'm onto something specific, give me the last week of the scraping period, which, by the way, is a great time for rattling.

HUNTING A PARTICULAR BUCK

I said earlier that the scraping period is my favorite time to hunt for a particular buck, and so it is. The truth is that travel patterns are no more predictable now than during the pre-rut, but there is a big difference—the older, bigger bucks are much more likely to be on the move and make a mistake. That alone gives the scraping period a big edge over the pre-rut. But even though the odds are better, killing a particular buck during the scraping period is still no give-me. Plus, the window of opportunity is quite narrow. I feel that the window of time when travel activity by mature bucks is greatest but before their pattern goes to pot in the quest for love is probably a week or less. Ideal weather, i.e., colder than normal or perhaps a passing front accompanied by a little drizzle, can extend and intensify activity. Plus, having somehow found a particular buck, either by sign, hearsay or, best yet, having seen him yourself, you can only hope that the part of his pattern you're privy to is a part he may repeat in daylight hours during the time you have to hunt him, or even that it is really a part of his pattern at all. And if you're hunting only sign, that he's a buck you want even if you are lucky enough to find him. There are a number of ifs, but the opportunity is there nonetheless.

All that said, there's nothing in whitetail hunting that I enjoy more than hunting a particular buck and there's no other time I'd rather do it than in the heat of the scraping period. Given time and a bit of luck, I always feel that if I can find a buck I can get him. Certainly, that doesn't always prove to be the case. (I have hunted a book-class 12-pointer in Tecomate Ranch in Texas for 28 days over three years, and I am yet to see him!) Still, I have been successful often enough during this unique window of predictable big buck activity so that I expect a happy outcome when time is sufficient and the circumstances seem right.

> *I have hunted a book-class 12-pointer on Tecomate Ranch in Texas for 28 days over three years, and I am yet to see him.*

Sometimes, it takes a while for the "train to finally come through." I hunted a particular 12-pointer (not the one mentioned above, not even on the same ranch) in Texas for three years before finally killing him when he was 9 1/2 years old about 200 yards from where I originally had seen him. A couple of years ago, I killed a 14-pointer in Montana after a three-year quest. Sometimes, however, success comes quickly. Like the mid-160s 9-pointer in Saskatchewan I saw on Wednesday and killed on Friday. Or, the Alberta 15-pointer I saw one afternoon and shot the next, which happened to be the last day of my 10-day hunt. Even with limited time left to hunt that buck, I was confident I'd get him because all the elements of success were there, as the following narrative of that hunt will show.

I was hunting the Peace River Country of northern Alberta. This is about as far north as whitetails live in numbers, and their survival is made possible by vast agricultural fields carved from even vaster wilderness forests. I was hunting with friend and outfitter Scott Taylor of Bearpaw Outfitting. While scouting some new country, he was first to see the buck. That same day, he and I found him again in the same alfalfa field just after legal shooting hours. I could only watch the huge buck through my 10X Leicas and look ahead longingly to the next day.

Scott and I had already seen enough of the area to know the buck would probably be back to this field. From our cursory lookabout, this was

There is nothing I enjoy more than hunting one particular buck. On rare occasions, one comes easy, but most of the time, I earn each one...if I ever get him at all. I hunted this buck three years before finally killing him at 9 1/2 years of age about 200 yards from where I had first seen him. Photo by Mark Lubin.

the only major food source for a couple of miles. We had seen the buck at a quiet, secluded spot in the back end of the huge field. Potholes and rolling hills even provided topographic cover for the deer as they exited the vast expanse of woods adjoining that part of the field, which lay to our east. With 50-foot hedgerows bordering both the north and south edges of the field (and nothing but fallow farmland, now turned snow-fields, beyond them), I had a perfect approach route to the action and an ideal place to setup a stand without getting too close to the deer activity. The bait was there in the form of several nervous does, which were being harried by a couple of intermediate bucks even as we watched. In fact, it was a jostling match between those two lesser bucks that had first attracted Scott's attention to the field and had drawn the big buck into sight. At the sound of the clacking antlers, the big buck had trotted over a hill into view of Scott's 30X spotting scope. Even from a distance of nearly a half-mile, Scott knew this buck was special as he watched the big intruder break up the fight and establish his dominance.

To further encourage me, a front was pushing in and snow was promised overnight to be followed by cooler temperatures. The next day was November 9, four or five days before the traditional startup of peak rut. We were in the middle of the scraping period. The buck was obviously making his rounds and full of himself. And, the field we had found him in seemed to be the best game in town for connecting with a willing doe-friend. It was a classic setup. I told Scott confidently, "Tomorrow, I'll get that buck." He nodded back with a knowing grin.

The game plan was simple. I didn't want to disturb the field at all, so I wouldn't try to put up a stand at night. Rather, I'd sneak down the backside of one of the hedgerows in the morning, which one depended on the wind direction, and check the field at daybreak. I figured I had a fair chance of catching him still in the field in the morning, but it was the afternoon that I staked my hopes on.

The morning hunt went perfectly. Just before shooting light, I slipped into position near the back of the field without making a sound, the wind stiff in my face. Even in the dim light of predawn, I could see big blaze marks on evermore trees as I neared the back of the field and the deep woods beyond. Two or three big, black blotches in the four inches of fresh snow along the edge of the hedgerow told of scrapes being worked just hours, perhaps even minutes before. Everything was just as I had hoped…only the buck I wanted was not in the field, at least that I could see. The rolling terrain limited my view. The morning ended with a tally of three does and one average buck. I needed elevation.

At 11 that morning, Scott provided that elevation in the form of a climbing treestand. Finding a sizable poplar in the north hegderow about 200 yards from the back of the field, the stand went up and I began my vigil, armed with my ultra-range .300 Weatherby for the 300 to 500-yard shot I expected.

The weather soon began to take a turn for the worse. Before long, 30-mph winds, stinging snow and plummeting temperatures reminded me that there was little between my perch and the Arctic other than some scraggly poplars and stunted spruce. Despite the brutal weather, over the next five hours my enthusiasm never faltered…but my outer extremities did. About the time I became convinced that a severe case of the shivers had robbed my ability to shoot, the two intermediate bucks from the day before topped a rise some 400 yards distant. I was sure the big buck would soon follow. I was equally sure I could do nothing about it in my frozen state. Twenty minutes passed and no buck. Ten more minutes and two does later, still no big buck. Time was running out. If I could have gotten to my watch, which had become impossible about an hour earlier, I was sure it would have told me I was down to my last few minutes of legal shooting time. As I pondered my plight in the fading light, I thought for the first time that I might not get the buck. Then, that thought was jolted from my mind!

> *At the sight of the buck, the cold instantly left me as I thanked the Good Lord above and thought to myself,* Oh, how I love hunting these things!

Movement to my right 75 yards up the hedgerow sent a shudder through me that wasn't from the cold. I couldn't believe my eyes. There was my buck, a mere 75 yards away, emerging from the hedgerow! I fumbled for my rifle—my 11-pound, super-long-range, 6.5-20X-scoped, sighted-in-for-350-yards rifle! Not only was my body numb and slow to respond, so was my mind. Besides not being able to hold the rifle steady, I couldn't figure out where to hold for a scant 75-yard shot! Somehow, my body and mind worked it out and the rifle went off, hardly audible over the roar of the wind. I thought the rifle had somehow misfired, but seemingly for no apparent reason, the buck slumped into the snow.

After exerting myself to the limit of my current physical state, thinking all the while of the fallacy of calling those stands "self-climbing," I mercifully reached the ground...and stumbled over to my 15-pointer, grossing 187! At the sight of the buck, the cold instantly left me as I thanked the Good Lord above and thought to myself, *Oh, how I love hunting these things!*

Such is hunting the scraping period of the rut.

Chapter Twenty-One

Strategies for the Breeding Period– Heart of the Rut... and Trophy Success

N OT MANY BIG BUCKS HAVE COME easy for me. Most are the product of planning and long hours of hard hunting. But occasionally, one just plain commits suicide and I just happen to be there when it happens. Invariably, it is during the heat of the breeding period when such gifts come my way, as was the case in Montana a couple of seasons ago.

I had just returned to my home in western Montana from an arduous, though successful, 18-day foray to Central Canada. At noon the next day, I was expecting longtime hunting buddy Chuck Larsen and New York friend Roberto Chiapelloni and his son, Gregory, to arrive for a Thanksgiving-week hunt, which always encompasses the very peak of breeding activity. I had several tried-and-proven areas to hunt in mind and wasn't worried about finding deer...until the storm of the century dumped nearly four feet—yes, feet!—of snow that night!

When I blundered upon this huge Montana buck, the only thing he had on his mind was the doe he was chasing. Not even my presence or four feet of fresh snow could distract him from his appointed rendezvous with his sweet-smelling girl friend. Only a 140-grain Nosler Partition from my trusty 7mm Mag. was able to do that. The power of the rut can dull the wits of the smartest and the biggest, as it did this 180-class 12-pointer. Photo by Debbie Morris.

When I awoke to the postcard surroundings, my party was already in the air somewhere between the East Coast and snowbound Big Sky Country so I couldn't abort the trip. I knew a major change of plans was called for. Roads were closed throughout the region, and the places I had hoped to hunt about 30 miles west of Kalispell would be inaccessible. Even if we could have reached my chosen places, which we couldn't, most of them called for a mile or two hike to reach prime country. In almost four feet of fresh powder, that was out of the question. We would have to hunt close by, and I would have to do some quick scouting to find accessible hunting spots nearby for four people. After plowing out my driveway, I donned my wading-in-the-snow garb and took off about 9 a.m. I had no intention of hunting, only scouting. But almost as an after-thought, I grabbed my rifle.

My first spot was a nearby meadow I wanted to check for sign. To reach it, I had to walk about 200 yards, which took me the better part of a half-hour. Exhausted and steaming under my heavy clothing, I finally got to the meadow, carelessly wallowing into the opening without checking it first. To my surprise, a doe was lunging her way through the snow about 125 yards away. Head low and tail straight out behind her, I knew a buck had her on the move. Tired from her struggles, she soon stopped and looked back. I waddled forward to take in more of the country behind her. There at about a 150 yards stood a huge buck. A quick check through my snowed-flecked binoculars told me two things—that he was as surprised to see me as I was him and that he was a shooter! I hurried to retrieve my rifle from its slung position, sure the buck was going to wheel around and disappear into the woods only 10 yards behind him. But instead, he did what a mature buck will only do when stupefied by the rut —he ran (or plowed) right out in the middle of that meadow, hot on the doe's trail and oblivious to me!

The 12-pointer grossed over 180…and was perhaps the easiest monster buck I have ever taken. He was more a victim of lust than of my hunting skills.

NO BETTER TIME

Without question, the best time to kill a trophy buck is during the peak of breeding. They move more often, travel farther, make more mistakes and expose themselves more frequently during daytime than at any other time of the year. A madness occasionally overtakes even the craftiest of the clan during the breeding period of the rut, and wise is the hunter who plans to be there to take advantage of this most golden of all hunting opportunities.

The great majority of the big bucks I've killed fell during what we hunters call the peak of rut, when breeding per se is underway. At this time, the bucks' main priority has become their quest for sex. They now spend most of their waking hours either rambling around the landscape in search of a hot doe or with a hot doe. Foolishness reigns and predictable patterns are out the window. The siren-scent of a ready doe is so powerful that it can lure even a mature buck into places no self-respecting whitetail would ever dare venture outside the rut, even right out into the bald open in broad daylight. I've even seen big bucks so addled by lust that

This whopper 10-pointer is ready to get down to business—rutting business. He is "flehmening," or performing a lip curl, to check the breeding readiness of the nearby doe. This is a common behavior in hoofed animals. It tells me the big buck is about to take leave of his senses. Photo by Mike Biggs.

they even bed down in the middle of a wide-open field with their honey. In fact, I've shot more than one buck caught in that miscalculation.

The truth is that if it weren't for the rut, precious few older bucks would ever be killed. Even in great big buck regions, like South Texas, Central Canada, the Northwest and the Midwest, hunting outside the rut would leave even competent hunters convinced few big bucks call the place home. The first time I hunted one of the best ranches in South Texas was just prior to Thanksgiving, nearly a month before the rut, and I came away wondering why it had such a lofty reputation. I scarcely saw any bucks, let alone any big ones. But a month later, I returned to the same ranch…and to a different world altogether. Big bucks seemed to be running everywhere. I've seen the same thing in Canada many times. On my little ranch in Montana, despite being right in the middle of big whitetail country, I only see the occasional big buck outside the rut. Then, once breeding fires up, big bucks show up I've never seen before. I

can't wait to get out every morning and see who's new in the neighborhood! That's what the rut will do. It pulls the big bucks out of hiding into
the light of day and stirs up the world of the whitetail.

WILD BUT RANDOM ACTION

If the breeding period has a drawback, it's that deer movement,
while great, is random. Whatever routine a buck might have had prior to
breeding is pretty much cast out the window. In the heat of the rut, a particular buck can be almost anywhere at any given time, drawn there by
breeding prospects that have developed somewhat randomly, at least as
far as we hunters are concerned.

It's not that a buck abandons his familiar country or leaves a particular area for good; it's just that at any given time he could be anywhere
in a rather large area, perhaps as large as several square miles. True, that
makes knowing where a particular buck may be less certain. But, what
good does it do you to know about where a buck is during, say, the pre-rut
if he steadfastly refuses to move during shooting hours? Not much! Even
though practically unkillable, it may make you feel better knowing he's
around. For my part, I had rather know he's moving about somewhere out
there, guard down and distracted, during the time I can send a bullet his
way. Besides, if a buck you're after is exposing himself while covering a
bunch of country, then there is a good chance that other bucks, some you
may not have known about and would like even better, are moving in
and out of your hunting territory, thereby offering you a chance to do a
little cherry-picking. Yes, pinpointing the approximate whereabouts of a
particular buck at a given time during the breeding period may be more
of a crapshoot than during other times, but you know what? Killing him
may not be!

While the micro-patterns during the breeding period are unpre-
dictable, the macro-pattern, or big-picture activity, is quite predictable.
And, a hunter can develop a strategy to take advantage of this big-picture
pattern. I could really simplify and shorten this entire discussion of hunting the rut by telling you to spend the most time possible hunting places
where you have the greatest chance of seeing the most deer. It's darn near
that simple. Get out there right in the middle of the most deer you can
find and wait for the old proverbial train to come through.

The timing of the rut varies across the country. Gary Schwarz claimed this book-class 12-pointer in the middle of South Texas' December rut, which is a full month later than the rut in most of the U.S. and Canada. Photo by Glenn Hayes.

So, strategy for the breeding period begins with finding concentrations of deer. Where the does are, bucks are sure to be nearby. If major food sources are present, start the search there. Look for evidence of heavy deer use, particularly rutting sign such as scrapes and rubs, scuff marks from buck fights and running deer tracks made during chases. I rely very heavily on fresh running tracks to let me know a hot doe is in the area. Rutting activity is sometimes concentrated in relatively localized pockets, perhaps because two or three does have come into estrus at the same time and have drawn a crowd. Search out these places. Often, several bucks, and perhaps even a couple of other does, will join in with a hot doe to form a sizable breeding party. Breeding parties can leave considerable sign, especially in snow, and may hang in the same vicinity for two or three days. If you can locate such a party, you may be able to look over several bucks.

AGGRESSIVE "SLIP-HUNTING"

Once promising deer activity and rutting sign are located, conditions will dictate which hunting method is best. However, when circum-stances allow, my preferred hunting method—and the one that I believe can be the deadliest of all during the peak of rut—is what I call aggressive slip-hunting. (I don't know how the term "still-hunting" came to describe slipping through the woods, but I've never cared for it. Stalk-hunting is a much more descriptive term, but because this often refers to sneaking on an animal that has been spotted, I have settled on "slip-hunting" as my term for the technique.) This method requires the right kind of country, plenty of room to roam and that the hunter possess considerable hunting skill.

The idea is to look over as much good habitat as possible at a pace that will allow you to see the deer before they see you. Certain conditions are best to accomplish this. First, the cover needs to be fairly open. If it is too thick, not only can't you look over much country, but worse, by the time you get close enough to the deer to see them, they will have probably already picked you off. Adequate distance tends to neutralize the deer's huge smell and hearing advantages. This makes the hunt more of a contest of sight, which a hunter has a chance of winning since he's alert and hopefully a rutting buck is distracted by thoughts of love. Generally, I consider less than 50 yards visibility to be too little for my slip-hunting taste. I prefer at least 75 yards. The more visibility, the faster the pace and the more country can be covered.

> *Whoever started the notion that rattling doesn't work once breeding starts was full of bull. I have rattled in some of my biggest bucks then.*

Ideal slip-hunting areas would also have travel routes through them that allow for quiet movement. Old logging roads, streambeds, firebreaks and the edges of fields, clearcuts and utility right-of-ways are likely prospects. Choose routes that provide some concealment and a diffused background. If possible, always look from thicker cover to thinner cover and from dark to light areas. Avoid a low sun in your face—not only can't you see, but you will also shine like a new penny. Hilly terrain offers the benefit of a concealed and silent approach as you peak over ridges, as well as the advantage of elevated views.

Slip-hunting during the rut is an aggressive form of hunting. The hunter should move quietly but quickly through likely country, looking for prowling bucks or breeding parties. His mobility and the deer's lack of awareness allow the hunter to take liberties not normally possible. I've followed trailing bucks and had them lead me to breeding parties. Several times, I shadowed breeding parties for some distance to get a better look and/or a shot at bucks involved in the chase. I've killed bucks this way that would have escaped unscathed had I been immobile in a stand. And countless times, I've walked up on shootable bucks staring at me in a lovesick stupor that would have been long gone outside of the rut.

Whoever started the notion that rattling doesn't work once breeding starts was full of bull. It does! I have rattled in some of my biggest bucks then. In fact, my favorite time to rattle is at the very height of breeding, when the bucks are the most excited and anxious. Rattling (and to a lesser degree, grunting) fits in perfectly with aggressive slip-hunting and with the charged state of the bucks during the breeding period. One of my favorite strategies is to walk, stop and rattle all day long. I generally rattle with lots of enthusiasm during the peak of rut, starting out with brush-rubbing and limb-breaking, moving into knuckle-bursting antler-rattling and ending with some serious ground-stomping using the butt of the horns. Then, I wrap the whole sequence up with two or three grunts. I'll wait about three to five minutes, grunt again a couple of times, wait another minute and then either start the sequence over again or leave for another place.

During the rut, the slip-hunter has extreme flexibility and can adapt to any new circumstance. He can change his course to accommodate a shift in wind or to take advantage of a ridge that offers a good view of promising country. If a buck is spooked, the hunter can try a quick maneuver to cut him off or loop around him. Upon finding hot sign or seeing a suspicious-acting deer, the hunter may choose to shift to a stop-and-go hunt, moving at a snail's pace, or perhaps to sit for a while at the base of a convenient tree. In snow conditions, he may pick up fresh tracks and follow them. Slip-hunting during the peak of rut is a wide-open field...and hunting in its purist form!

BREEDING PARTIES IN THE SNOW

Speaking of fresh tracks in the snow, I have developed a specialized snow-tracking strategy for the rut since moving to Montana. Though I'm

Bucks enter the rut in peak condition, like this bulked-up brute, but before it's all over, they may run, fight and worry off 25 or more percent of their body weight. Some may not survive the winter. Photo by Troy Huffman.

sure others have used the trick, I have never heard anyone mention it before, at least not as a defined hunting method. Granted, it is a specialized strategy that will only work under very specific conditions, namely brand new snow and fairly open country with room to ramble. The ideal setting is hilly country with relatively open cover, where the deer can be seen from a distance. As it happens, that's exactly what we have in much of western Montana.

The idea is to get out right after a fresh snow and cruise the woods or backroads looking for running deer tracks made by bucks chasing does. (Here in Montana, there are miles of quiet backroads traversing public land. While you can't hunt from the roads, you sure can travel them looking for tracks.) Once running tracks are located, it doesn't take a whole lot of woodsmanship to figure out if the tracks are those of a buck (or bucks) hot after a doe. The size of tracks themselves will usually tell the story. If not, the short, choppy strides or the zigzagging path will provide clues. I've even seen antler marks in the snow made by bucks sniffing where estrus does urinated or dripped down their hocks.

Occasionally, I come across a multitude of tracks made by a breeding party consisting of several bucks and perhaps even more than one doe. When this happens, things can really get interesting because of the competition between the bucks. I've had extraordinary luck trailing up breeding parties. Not only are the bucks in them usually distracted by each other as well as by the willing doe, they are fired up, making rattling particularly effective. On several occasions, I have rattled up two or three bucks from one breeding party. Rattling can also pull them out of cover you can't quietly enter.

Conditions are right for this technique only a few days each season at best. But when everything falls into place, I have confidence that I can find chases and look over some bucks. Just recently here in Montana, I cut two sets of fresh running tracks meeting all the requirements. I set out on them, moving silently in the foot of soft snow. Soon, the tracks dropped off the bench I had been slipping along. I eased to the edge of the bench and peered over. A doe, slightly hunched with her tail straight out, standard posture of a hot doe, was standing 60 yards away. Almost immediately, the buck came trotting out from behind a blowdown, intent on escorting his lady friend to quieter quarters. My Montana season ended when the 20-inch 10-pointer hit the ground.

OTHER PEAK-RUT BETS

Stand-hunting is an effective way to hunt the breeding season, but if you're going to burn time in one spot during this active period, do it in the right place. Again, the right place is where you can look over as much good deer country, with known activity, as possible. This is a great time to sit on utility right-of-ways, oil company seismic cutlines (senderos), clearcuts, intersections of woods roads or any place in the middle of high-use areas that provide extended visibility. I'll often hunt

places where I can see much farther than I can shoot in hopes of just seeing the buck I want. Then, I will move to him, either immediately on
foot or I'll set up a stand where he was as quickly as possible, especially if
he's got a hot doe with him, which increases the odds he'll stay in that
area for a day or two. I'll also hunt right on major food sources during the
rut, but only if they are quiet and secluded with hardly any pressure. A
concentration of does is a magnet to lust-driven bucks.

Earlier, I mentioned rattling and its effectiveness during the peak
of breeding. It is worth emphasizing again. Rattling works big time now.
The more violent, the better. Generally, I find the bucks to be more
charged up now and eager to answer the call. During the breeding time,
I've seen bucks come from as far away as a quarter-mile and I've rattled in
as many as 11 bucks at one sitting. True, some bucks are going to be with
does and hard to pull away from a sure thing. But, many bucks aren't
going to be connected-up at any given time and these are vulnerable to
rattling trickery.

I've often heard it said that you can't rattle in dominant bucks. I
don't buy that. Actually, I believe the most aggressive breeders, which are
often dominant bucks, are the ones most readily rattled in, assuming they
are not with does. Besides, the truth
is that frequently the very biggest
bucks are not aggressive breeders.
Instead, they often are passive,
opportunistic bystanders during the
rut. Such bucks aren't likely to come
to rattling, at least not directly into
the fracas. Because a disproportionate number of top-end bucks seem to
be of this passive mold, I think that has given rise to the notion that
dominant bucks (though what they really mean is the biggest) don't readily respond to rattling. In reality, dominant, active breeders and top-end
bucks are often two entirely different animals, as we'll discuss later in the
chapter on secretive super bucks.

> *During the breeding time,
> I've seen bucks come from as
> far away as a quarter-mile
> and I've rattled in as many as
> 11 bucks at one sitting.*

Grunting is also effective during the breeding period. In fact, it is
most effective now. Why? The guttural grunt that bucks make and
hunters try to imitate is usually made as an expression of sexual excitement. When chasing a doe or on a hot scent, they get so chummed up
that they express their excitement by venting a grunt. When we hunters

Aggressive tactics can be highly effective during the rut. After finding the running tracks of a breeding party in fresh snow, I tracked down this Montana buck. He hesitated long enough for a quick shot. Photo by Jennifer Morris.

fake that sound, we are in essence trying to convince nearby bucks that something in our direction has gotten a buck fired up and is worth checking on. If an excited buck is around to hear the grunt, he may come, especially during the breeding time when this sound is most often a part of the deer's world and when it might mean a ready doe.

Grunting, however, has two drawbacks. One, it has very limited range, probably not much over 100 yards in the most favorable conditions. Two, a buck usually has to be turned on before he takes any great interest in a grunt. I've grunted to dozens of bucks I could see as they went about everyday business that completely ignored the call. But when I see bucks switched on by hopes of connecting, there's a good chance I can get them interested in a grunt call. The range limitations and the need for a buck to be excited to respond make grunting an ideal tool to use in conjunction with rattling. Rattling is long-range, getting out several hundred yards, and has the capability to fire up even a relatively sedate buck at certain times. When a rattled in buck moves in close, the grunt call, which can be used without movement on the hunter's part, can be employed to tease the buck in for a look or shot.

For whatever reason, I find Canada to be a particularly good place to use the grunt call. Deer there seem to be particularly vocal. I especially like using the grunt call when stand-hunting in tight quarters. Unlike rattling, it's a passive, non-intrusive call that does not alert nearby deer or draw unnecessary attention to your location. There are times and places for both.

BREEDING PERIOD CHRONOLOGY

For our purposes, the breeding period is considered to last two weeks. In truth, breeding spreads over a much greater time span, but as hunters, we're most interested in the time we call the peak of rut, which lasts only about two weeks. Yet even within this two-week time span, rutting activity differs. As with the scraping period, I was tempted to divide the breeding period into two parts—early and late. I didn't mainly because the deer pattern and the requisite strategy are essentially the same early and late, but the intensity and character of the rutting activity are not. I don't, however, think the differences warrant dividing the period. Still, I want to point out the differences so you can factor them into your thinking. As I map out my own hunting strategy, these differences sometimes come into play and dictate the timing of certain hunts and places. It's worth a few parting comments.

The chances of killing a mature buck drop later in the rut...but I've always felt that the chances of killing a really big deer were better later in the rut than earlier.

To start with, weather, moon phases and other outside conditions can and most often do skew how the rut is played out. So here, I'm speaking in general terms. The first week of the two-week peak rut is the most chaotic time of the period. It is what we hunters generally call the peak of rut. When the first big wave of does comes into estrus, the bucks are frothing at the mouth to get after them and nearly every testosterone-charged buck hastens into action. Until this pent-up lust is partially satisfied, the rutting ritual continues at a breakneck pace, even though much of the activity takes place under the cover of darkness. The first week or so offers hunters their very best chance to see bucks and to kill a mature buck. With all the excitement, rattling really works well during the first week of the rut.

Into the second week, the hectic pace begins to slow, even if actual breeding doesn't. The fact is that the deer herd simply begins to wind down, tired from the frantic pace and days with little food. The intensity of competition lessens a little, especially among the subdominant bucks. The rut begins to settle into a bit more of an orderly process, with the dominant bucks controlling most of the hot does as they come into estrus. With fewer and fewer does receptive, there is a greater opportunity for the more aggressive breeders to get around to the hot does. Thus, while the number of chases drops and the number of bucks seen tends to be lower than during the first week, the average size of the bucks seen with the does generally is larger. The end result of all this is that the chances of killing a mature buck drop later in the rut, but if you do get lucky then, he may just be one of the better bucks in the neighborhood. For this reason, I've always felt that the chances of killing a really big deer were better later in the rut than earlier. However, I think there's another phenomenon at play late in the rut, and even into the first part of the post-rut, that makes this time the odds-on bet for those rare but real super bucks that don't actively participate in the rut. I'll discuss this more in the upcoming chapters on secretive super bucks and hunting top-end bucks.

For now, we'll close with this thought about the rut—just get out there amongst them!

Chapter Twenty-Two

Strategies for the Post-Rut—a Time of Hard-Earned Possibilities

O SAGE COUNTY, OKLAHOMA. BIG buck country from all I had heard. Now, five other excited hunters and I were about to find out. The 5,000-acre ranch, located in a U-bend in the Arkansas River, had not been hunted for years, and the reports we had received promised of big things. My only concern was the timing—early post-rut, the only time firearms season was open.

A scouting foray the afternoon before opening day told us the place was for real. Crop fields planted in corn, soybeans and small grain made up about half the ranch. The other half consisted of isolated wood-lots, broad hedgerows, a myriad of drainages fingering out from the Arkansas River and the riverbottom itself, which was nearly impenetrable both due to natural thick cover and the recent aftermath of one of history's most powerful tornadoes. Not only was the habitat all we could have hoped for, but the big bucks were there, too. Huge rubs marred trees on hedgerows and about every other type of edge. Desktop-size scrapes were

240

During the post-rut, bucks spend a lot of time bedded as they recuperate from the rigors of a demanding rut. This is not an easy time to hunt trophy white-tails, but opportunities do exist under the right conditions...for the patient hunter who understands post-rut patterns. Photo by Troy Huffman.

sprinkled around field edges and along hedgerows, but they were fading away from two or three weeks of neglect. Tracks like yearling cows dotted the soft earth of the fields.

When we gathered back at camp and compared notes, enthusiasm ran high. But, Dick Idol had more than tracks and rubs to talk about. He had seen a big non-typical...with a doe! The pair had gone into a deep draw just before dark. Since hot does were now few and far between, the odds were very good the buck would stick to her like hot on jalapeños. And since that buck was probably anxious to keep his prize away from other bucks, odds were he would still be in the draw come first light.

He was! And Dick started off the hunt with a bang...directed at a mid-170s non-typical! But from there, the realities of the post-rut set in and things got tough.

Over the next few days, we watched deer activity go from slow to almost nonexistent. About the only sightings were right a dusk, when it was almost too dark to judge or shoot. In the headlights en route to and from stands, we caught enough glimpses of big bucks to keep our hopes high. But between the approaching post-rut recovery time, unusually warm weather and the pressure we were exerting as we hunted and searched for just the right spot, the daytime activity had gone south, so to speak.

The last couple of days, we resorted to deer drives. It wasn't pretty, but by noon on the final day, we had managed to kick up and shoot a couple of decent bucks. We even pushed out a book-class monster by Steve Vaughn, my partner in WHITETAIL magazine, but alas, 350-yard running shots seldom do a kill make. As time ticked down, I ended the hunt with a respectable 10-pointer. The hunt concluded as so many post-rut hunts do—in frustration and desperation.

I am sorely tempted to say the post-rut is my least favorite time to hunt. However, I'm not so sure that's true. Undoubtedly, my attitude toward it is jaded by the fact that by the time the post-rut rolls around I'm as worn out as the bucks I'm hunting. And like them, about all I'm really interested in is rest and a good square meal or two. While the post-rut can be impossibly difficult to hunt, it is not without potential, in some situations. In fact, for someone with aims on a really big buck but who is prepared to go home empty-handed, and perhaps bored out of his gourd, the post-rut can hold promise.

Like the pre-rut, hunting pressure and major food sources are key players in determining hunting prospects. Both periods are characterized by feeding/resting patterns that are easily disrupted by hunting pressure and that are most evident when major food sources are present to concentrate feeding activity. In lightly hunted areas, concentrated major food sources are huge advantages for post-rut hunters. The more major, the better. Deer this time of year are in need of nutrition and energy to help recover from the rigors of the rut. A ready supply of good food is a very powerful magnet, but they won't come at any cost, unless they're desperate. Most visits will be at night, but with luck, some low-light action is possible.

Once the rut has lost its grip on deer on my Montana ranch, I will frequently see 20 to 30 deer feeding on my haystacks after dark, but usually, only a handful would have shown up before the stars were visible. Though deer may come in at all hours of the day in cold or inclement

About two weeks into the post-rut, the minor secondary rut may breathe a bit of renewed life into the exhausted bucks as young does enter estrus, but don't count on a resumption of widespread activity. Photo by Mike Biggs.

weather, most daytime visits normally occurs right before dark. Morning feeding is short-lived, with deer normally departing before there's light enough to make them out with binoculars. The fact is that post-rut deer, especially big bucks, lean to the nocturnal.

Pressure is the nemesis of daytime movement during the post-rut because any pressure exerted now falls on top of the cumulative effects of

One good thing about the early post-rut is that occasionally a real whopper will come tiptoeing around. Just such a buck, a gross 177 to be exact, wandered by Larry Woodcock's stand and paid for his indiscretion. Photo by Carl Frohaug.

weeks of previous hunting. It takes very little more to suppress movement or to drive deer into near-total hiding. By post-rut time, deer in general and bucks in particular are too tired, spent and shell-shocked to put up with a whole lot of aggravation. So, where pressure is high, unless you can find a quiet sanctuary, don't even attempt to stake your hopes on natural deer movement. Try to turn pressure to your advantage by either finding intercept points to cut off escaping deer or by pushing them yourself.

THE CRACKED WINDOW OF OPPORTUNITY

Earlier, I said the post-rut is not without possibilities. One of the things I was referring to is the fact that stressed deer will move to feed and expose themselves to some degree during the post-rut. Stress can be in the form of chronic nutritional stress, i.e., overcrowded deer populations, or from the high-energy demands of cold, as would be expected in northern climes. Keep in mind that deer, particularly big bucks, often enter this difficult time already stressed from the rut, sometimes severely so. To combat this stress, they have a couple of options. One, they can take in more calories to maintain themselves, that is, feed aggressively. Two, they can shift to an energy-conservation mode. Which of these two strategies they choose depends largely on where in the country they live, the availability of food and/or the time of year. Let me explain.

The part of the country is certainly one of the main factors governing how deer respond to post-rut/winter stress and how much daytime movement may accompany that response. Deer in warmer climates are adapted to an environment that does not normally have extreme cold for long periods of time and that supplies maintenance-level feed on demand even during the winter. Therefore, their strategy is usually to feed actively during the colder months, but because feed is usually there when they want it and the degree of cold does not place urgent demands on them, they usually feed without urgency and on their own schedule, which is most often at last light and at night. If, however, you interject *unusual stress* from prolonged bitter cold, chronic malnutrition from overcrowding or an especially competitive rut, even deer in warm locales will feed during the day and concentrate on major food sources.

In the Southeast and Texas, I've seen overcrowded deer populations bunch up on hot food sources in impressive numbers in broad daylight. And, I've seen Southern deer in balanced populations that normally stay put in cover during the day rush headlong to major food sources during the daytime when extended periods of cold and/or wet weather start to take a toll on their bodies. Plus, I've seen bucks on well-managed Texas ranches with low buck:doe ratios and loads of older bucks—conditions ripe for a highly competitive rut—hasten to winter food plots and corn feeders during the post-rut in an effort to rejuvenate their spent, neglected bodies. In each of the aforementioned cases, stress from one cause or another forced the deer into an unusual amount of daytime feeding activity a hunter can turn to his advantage.

In cold, harsh climes, how deer respond to winter's stress depends on the availability of food and, in part, the exact time of year. Let's address the issue of exact time of year first. In frigid, snowy climates, deer have adapted a strategy of retreating to thermal cover and holding tight to minimize energy consumption. The extreme case of this is known as "yarding," which is when deer congregate in a very small area and just "exist" through the winter. In most cold locations, classic yarding doesn't actually take place but the concept of moving to thermal cover and limiting movement still holds. (Even in the South, a watered-down version of this takes place, the degree depending on the availability of easy food.) They usually retreat to these yarding or holding sites as soon as the last remnants of the rut have concluded, which is almost always after hunting season. The deer have adapted this strategy because the place they live historically does not have sufficient, easily obtained food during the winter. The deer would burn up more energy attempting to feed than they would get from feeding, thus they limit movement to conserve precious energy.

The inherent pull to these thermal holding areas is indeed powerful. I've seen deer in Montana leave quality, readily available feed to head to their wintering grounds. Yet, given enough good feed, the pattern can be delayed, modified and, in areas with only marginally severe winters, perhaps even suspended. Thus, we see that the availability of food can sway the pattern. Interestingly, I've seen a super abundance of food make things hard on hunters because stress on the herd was so low that they only fed when they wanted to, which was usually at night.

Fortunately, even in places where deer are predisposed to shift to an energy-conservation pattern after breeding has run its course, nearly all post-rut hunting takes place when the deer are still in the active mode, though they are likely winding down, and somewhat stressed, from exhaustion and harassment. This brings us back to the importance of major food sources, which can actually *coax* deer into a hunter-friendly feeding pattern during what is otherwise a very difficult time to hunt big bucks. Thus, if conditions are right—major food sources, stress of some type and low hunting pressure—the post-rut can offer opportunity, albeit modest.

NO FOOD, HEAD TO COVER

Another way to enjoy a modicum of hope during the post-rut is to hunt thick cover. In most parts of the country, the woods are sparse and denuded. The leaves from the deciduous trees and bushes have dropped and the rest of the vegetation has been burned by frost or battered down by snow and rain. The protected areas where deer feel secure from intrusion are few and easily identified. The hunter with plenty of patience can set up on trails near such places and often wait out a post-rut buck. I've done it, but frankly, this kind of hunting drives me bonkers and the returns are marginal.

During my years at Burnt Pine, we had a weeklong bonus season beginning the day after Christmas, a full six weeks after the rut. Even the secondary rut was over by then. The deer usually were just returning to a feeding/resting pattern, though symptoms of the recovery phase still lingered. The deer spent most of their daylight hours resting in the thickest cover around, meaning pine thickets. Because some of the staff or I had been in the field everyday since October, we knew the approximate whereabouts of several good bucks. Since we entertained few deer-hunting clients during that week, I usually made it a point to hunt one of the known big bucks. Out of necessity, I hunted him in or just outside the thick cover in which I believed him to reside, based mostly on tracks and intuition since fresh buck sign was in short supply. For the better part of 20 years, I chased those thick-cover, post-rut bucks...and killed exactly two of them! That's not very good returns. True, I didn't hunt them everyday or all day long, though I doubt that would have helped much, but I did put in a lot of time in claustrophobic quarters.

I have faired better when hunting post-rut bucks in thick cover in more severe climates than Georgia has. Why? Again, the harsher conditions forced deer to move and feed more. In snow country, I've had the advantage of easy-to-read sign but that didn't make it easy. I have even had occasion to hunt deer after they were forced to bunch up in thermal cover by early deep snows. Despite so much snow that I could hardly walk through it, it took time to find the deer concentrations. Since they weren't moving, I couldn't find much sign until I got right on top of them. And, the places they picked to hold up weren't the kind of spots the casual hunter is going to just happen upon or choose to hunt on purpose. After finally finding their hideaway, tight cover, limited visibility and so many eyes made for slow, grueling hunting. Bump one deer and the whole area was shot. Anyway you look at it, success is going to come hard in the post-rut period without an edge of some sort.

EDGES AND HURDLES

Without the advantage of major food sources in the post-rut, you need some other type of edge or beginning point—familiarity with the area, the known whereabouts of a shooter buck, an undisturbed area or something that makes for high huntability, like right-of ways through thick cover. And, you'll need time, lots of it. Though bucks will completely relocate, especially late in the post-rut period, to prime food sources or wintering grounds, they do not tend to move very far once they settle into their winter home. This can make just finding the whereabouts of a shooter buck a season-eating endeavor without some insider knowledge, and even when you find him, there's still the problem of getting him to move during times that'll do you any good.

For a visiting hunter, all this makes the post-rut a difficult time to try his hand. This is why commercial hunting in the Midwest has been slow to take off, especially with gun hunters. Most gun-hunting there takes place in the post-rut, when deer activity has waned. Yes, there's often plenty of agriculture to provide food—too much, in fact. Food is in such abundance that the deer have little urgency and too many options. Local post-rut hunters have a great edge in both knowledge of the area and hunting time. Of course, the right friend or guide could give a visiting hunter a jumpstart, but my experience is that if I wait for someone else to find my bucks for me I might as well take up bird watching for all the big bucks I would kill!

You might have gathered that it is possible to successfully hunt a particular buck during the post-rut. Though I don't normally consider this to be an especially good time to hunt a particular buck, there is a chance of bringing the quest to a happy conclusion…if you've got him pinpointed or he's using a major food source.

WANING RUT—THE LAST BEST HOPE

The waning-rut phase is exactly what the name implies—the last of the significant rutting activity. This phase includes both tail-off breeding from the peak rut and the relatively minor secondary rut. Normally, you can expect the waning rut to run three to four weeks into the post-rut period. The level of rutting activity, or general deer movement, is not

Unless you are willing to push bucks from their beds, major food sources are the best game in town during the post-rut. The more major, the better. I shot this post-rut Midwest buck at last light on a winter wheat field. Notice how gaunt he is. The rut takes a toll. Photo by Chuck Larsen.

near that of the peak rut, but it's enough to offer hope. The strategy is basically the same as during the peak—hunt the doe concentrations, only now you have to stay nearer thick cover. You can't depend on the same types of blatant mistakes from mature bucks now as might have occurred earlier. Again, major food sources are a huge plus if they're around. You'll get bucks both hungry and horny there.

I mentioned the secondary rut, which falls toward the end of the waning-rut phase. The secondary rut begins roughly a month after the start up of the two-week primary rut, or about two weeks into the post-rut, and consists primarily of yearling and fawn does coming into heat. The significance of the secondary rut varies from one place to another. In healthy deer herds, it is more pronounced because a higher percentage of the younger does come into heat than in more stressed herds. In badly undernourished herds, I don't see much evidence of a secondary rut. Also, in very harsh climates, I have a hard time seeing much secondary rut activity, possibly because of the narrow fawning window there. At any rate, even in the best of cases, the secondary rut is but a pup compared to the he-dog primary rut. (There is also a tertiary rut about a month after the secondary rut, sparked almost entirely by doe fawns coming into estrus, but from a hunting standpoint, you can forget it.)

Because receptive does are now in relatively short supply, when a doe comes into estrus she's the queen of the ball and can draw quite a crowd. I once saw eight bucks lusting after a harried doe in the waning rut. Occasionally, at a time when everything else is quiet, you can find a local area with considerable rutting activity brought on by a hot doe or two. One of my most successful strategies during the post-rut is to actively seek out these few remaining breeding parties. Where I've had room to roam, decent visibility and reasonably quiet travel routes, I've had considerable success covering ground in search of either the sign left by these late season breeding parties or the participants themselves. The good thing about these parties is that they leave a lot of sign, primarily running deer tracks, at a time when relatively little sign is being put down. Plus, just the number of deer in the party increases the odds of seeing them. Once I locate a party, I comb the area on foot or set up a stand. It may take a lot of looking to find these parties, but sometimes you get lucky.

The one advantage the post-rut has over other periods is that *huge* bucks occasionally make an appearance then, usually in the waning rut. For me, that alone makes the period worth hunting, though I know my odds of benefiting from that fact are quite low. But, I've done it just enough to keep the hope alive. The pattern of over-sized bucks making occasional appearances actually has its beginning in the latter part of the breeding period and carries over into the waning-rut phase of the post-rut, and perhaps beyond. Though in this book I've spread this chunk of time over two periods based on overall patterns and hunting opportunities, the fact is that this entire time span, lasting about four weeks, represents the tailing off of breeding activity. In the upcoming chapter on secretive super bucks, we'll discuss in detail the possible reasons for the occasional appearance of huge bucks in the waning rut, so here, I'll just capsulize it.

As the rut winds down, breeding intensity wanes, buck travel diminishes and bucks, now beginning to tire and become somewhat sexually satiated, lose some of their aggression and amorous zeal. With lower aggression, less lust and reduced travel, the power of dominant prime breeders to suppress less dominant bucks seems to lose its grip. I believe this opens the door for some of the bigger-racked bucks, which are often less dominant (for reasons we'll discuss later), to snoop around. This "release" of big subdominant bucks even carries over into other parts of the post-rut. It's just that these other times don't usually offer the same opportunity to encounter them that a touch of rutting urge seems to bring out.

During my 20 years at Burnt Pine, most of our truly exceptional bucks were taken around Thanksgiving, despite a November 6 startup of peak rut. Hunter success for mature bucks was far lower then, but occasionally, we hit a home run. I've seen this same pattern everywhere I've hunted. In Canada, for instance, while the waning rut can be tough, some top-end bucks occasionally appear seemingly from nowhere at this time. Around my home in western Montana, rutting festivities kickoff in earnest about November 18, but the few giants that are killed in these parts each year nearly all fall the last few days of season, which ends around December 1. Actually, on my Montana ranch, I see the biggest bucks a week or two *after* season.

In South Texas, I customarily hunt a great ranch on December 10 through 17. This time encompasses the December 14 startup of peak rut. By mid-point of the hunt, rutting activity is going strong and I usually manage to shoot a solid trophy after looking over lots of mature bucks. But, the ranch manager tells me that the biggest bucks consistently emerge from the thick brush around and after Christmas, a time set-aside for the ranch owners. Hunting can be difficult then, but over the years, a disproportionate number of the truly exceptional bucks sighted and killed on that 100,000-acre ranch made their appearance as the rut tailed off.

Though the post-rut can be very tough, every once in a while a top-end buck will mysteriously show up then. That's just what happened on the King Ranch to Wallace Culpepper (right) and me in the early days of the waning rut. Both of these bucks grossed better than 170. Photo by Amos Dewitt.

THE RECOVERY PHASE—GOOD LUCK!

As I said earlier, it is not entirely accurate to call the recovery phase a "phase." Rather than a specific phase of behavior that occurs at a predictable time, it is more something that bucks just do as the last vestiges of the rut fade away, or soon thereafter. That *something* is disappear. The bucks, exhausted from weeks of physical exertion and abuse, seek a secluded place to recuperate. Many of the hard-drivers are probably nursing injuries, and most have dropped 20 to 30 percent of their body weight. Stiff and stove up, they walk like they're suffering from advanced arthritis. They may still be game for a last fling if a hot scent hits them in the face, but their enthusiasm for the chase has succumbed to the frailties of the flesh. As a result, they lay up in thick cover and begin to slowly recuperate. For how long? A week to 10 days is a good duration ballpark. The exact timing of this disappearing act varies, but it will happen sometime during the first month or so of the post-rut. I can tell you this much—if unseasonably hot weather sets in anytime during the waning rut, the symptoms of the recovery phase will likely be in full effect.

When the recovery phase does come, good luck! I would sure like to tell you about some wonderful strategy for this time, but alas, I don't know one, except deer drives. The best I can do is point you toward thick cover and suggest that you tell your wife you'll be late for supper...for a week or two. And, you might want to take a book.

POST-RUT FEEDING—A ROUTINE AGAIN

Much of what I said earlier in this chapter was directed toward this phase. The deer have now settled into a fairly predictable feeding/resting routine, though it might not include much daytime movement. The basic strategy is to hunt the food sources. In the absence of agriculture, one of my favorite post-rut haunts is secluded clearcuts. The right ones offer both good feed and enough cover to make even an old buck feel reasonably secure. If there are no obvious food sources, head to thick cover and hunt the best sign you can find, or a known buck. Use the first and last remnants of light and carry good optics. Beware of changing food sources, and feeding grounds beyond the borders of your property, even well beyond. Deer may travel (and relocate) long distances to prime feed this time of year. Don't be left behind hunting where the deer *were*. And, remember that deer are energy efficient during this time. Apply that concept to your situation and develop a suitable strategy. Then, just keep thinking *big*. That'll help ward off the cold and the boredom. If all else fails, gather up your hunting buddies and "push the bush." There's no better time for it than now!

> *Remember that deer are energy efficient during this time. Apply that concept to your situation and develop a suitable strategy.*

Chapter Twenty-Three

Little Things That Make a "Big" Difference

WHY IS IT THAT CERTAIN HUNTERS consistently shoot big bucks, while others, even when all things are equal, or appear so, only rarely, if ever, bring home an outstanding whitetail?

Of course, the first thing that comes to mind is that the consistent guys hunt better places. Certainly, that would make all the difference in the world. But here, I'm talking about people who hunt similar places, maybe even the same tract of land.

Perhaps, you say, the hunters who enjoy regular success put in more hours. No, eliminate that as a variable. Time in the woods is surely a major element in success, but in this scenario, time in pursuit does not differ.

Well, the successful guys are obviously more knowledgeable. They must know the most effective tactics, the best times and how to properly use calls, decoys, scents, etc. There's no denying that knowledge is critical in outmaneuvering savvy old whitetails, but I've seen a great disparity in

254

When it gets right down to the nitty gritty, some hunters have a knack for getting the job done. Others, however, seem to have an equal knack for NOT coming through in a pinch. Why is that? In the final analysis, it's often the little things that make all the difference. Photo by author.

success exist between hunters who were all overflowing with head knowledge about whitetails. Knowledge alone can't provide the answer.

Then, it must be experience, you say. When it comes to chasing big whitetails, experience is certainly right at the top of the requirements for success. But, even differing experience levels can't account for the difference in consistency I'm talking about here. I know hunters who come up short time after time even though they have just as much experience, in some cases even more, as the consistent guys do.

Why, then, do some hunters lay claim to trophy whitetails year after year, while others, seemingly with all the same advantages and

When you're pitting yourself against a big mature whitetail, you had better have your senses on full alert because you can bet he will...and he's better equipped! Photo by Troy Huffman.

opportunities, meet with less than stellar success?

I've often pondered that question, and the answer, to be sure, is neither simple nor particularly obvious. The obvious things—better places, more time hunting, greater knowledge and experience—are easy to spot. But after much contemplation and close observation of both the consistent and inconsistent guys, I've come up with some conclusions. Interestingly, it's often the little things that determine ultimate success, the seemingly insignificant things that are hardly noticeable at first glance. But, what a difference they make in the long run!

You may have noticed that I failed to mention skill as being one of the factors that could be eliminated. That's because skill is indeed a factor in creating the opportunity to encounter a trophy buck, in properly reacting to the encounter and, ultimately, in closing the deal. True, experience and time in the field do sharpen skills, but hunters with exactly the same experience and time in pursuit don't necessarily end up with the same skill level.

It's like two NFL running backs. Both may have been in the league the same number of years and have the same game time under their belt, but one may average 100 yards a game and the other only 25. When watching them play, there may be little discernable difference in their skill level. But when the game is over, the one has his 100 yards and the other his 25. And, the reasons for the difference may be as imperceptible as a dropped shoulder here or a stutter step there. Or perhaps, the ace runner has a slightly faster start, an edge in peripheral vision or a touch better balance—little things (call them skills, natural abilities, talents, whatever) that you may not even be able to see but that make the difference between stardom and mediocrity. It's the same in trophy whitetail hunting.

The skills of trophy whitetail hunting can be divided into two general categories—one, those needed to maximize the opportunity for an encounter and two, those needed to make good on the encounter once it is realized. Let's look at each separately.

CREATING OPPORTUNITY FOR AN ENCOUNTER

The first category, creating the opportunity for an encounter, includes the obvious and most-discussed factors of deer hunting—where, when, how—but here, we're more concerned with the less obvious but nonetheless vital elements that increase one's odds of bumping into a big whitetail. We'll begin our discussion at ground level.

Power Of Observation

One of the most essential of the neglected mysterious ingredients in the recipe for consistent whitetail success is also one of the most basic—the power of observation. The ability to perceive what's going on around them varies greatly among people. Certainly, the ability to focus attention and accurately observe is related to one's interest level in the activity. But, some people are just naturally unobservant, even when they are keenly interested in what they're doing. My wife is that way. She not only fails to see what's around her, but she has an uncanny knack for looking in the opposite direction when I try to point out something she should see. While this can be maddening to me, happily, it doesn't seem to bother her in the slightest.

I've hunted with guys who could share a motel room with a rhinoceros without realizing it was there. My brown bear guide in Alaska kept losing his rifle and would only notice it was gone when I would point out he was unarmed. I've walked through the woods with serious hunters who are oblivious to very apparent rubs, scrapes, trails and other sign critical to their hunt. I've watched longtime hunters let deer walk by their stand unnoticed while they daydream or even sleep. Some seem to become almost mesmerized after sitting, driving or even when walking for a while. One fellow I hunted with in Texas practically went into a trance as soon as the high-rack (an elevated, mobile deer stand mounted on the back of a pickup) started moving. He would become hypnotized by the road and stare ahead blankly, with no chance of seeing any deer that did not pass beneath the front bumper. The fact is that some people just do not keep tabs on what's going on around them...but some do.

The best hunters I know are keen observers. Not only do they see the obvious, they notice the little things—a barking squirrel, a flushing jay, the direction of tracks, a shift in the wind, the faint snap of a twig, the odd horizontal line, the misplaced color or the slight blur of motion. They are alert and focused, constantly gathering information from what they see, hear and even smell. Everything is potentially important—the backward glance of a doe, the body language of a young buck, running deer tracks, which side of the tree the rub is on, the musky smell wafting on the wind, the debris in a scrape...or the lack thereof. Hardly anything escapes their notice, no matter how seemingly insignificant.

> *The best hunters I know are keen observers. Not only do they see the obvious, they notice the little things.*

The last two bucks I shot in northern Saskatchewan illustrate the edge afforded by staying constantly alert. In both cases, I was hunting a localized feeding area directly in front of my tree stand. The woods were very thick on three sides, and I had little reason to expect to see a buck unless he came into the opening I was facing, except that big bucks seldom do what they are "supposed" to. Besides, if he did walk into the opening, I'd see him. That was a no-brainer. Thus, I was keeping a close eye and ear out for activity in the less conspicuous places, the kinds of places in which big bucks seem to show up.

In the first instance, I heard the faintest "whooshing" sound to my right. I stared for long moments in that direction and was finally reward-

Guide Phil Reddock (left) is one of the best whitetail observers I know. Nothing escapes his scrutiny. His cohort, George Cooper, can close the deal as well as anyone, as he did on this 24-inch 11-pointer grossing 166. Photo by author.

ed with a swaying spruce limb. My binoculars revealed the source of the commotion to be a buck working a limb overhanging a scrape. When he turned to walk away, I made out three heavy primary tines and a massive main beam. I scrambled for my rifle and shot the buck as he ambled through a small opening en route to departing.

In the case of the second buck, I saw a slight blur of movement... in exactly the opposite direction from the opening where the deer were feeding. I hastily set up for a shot just as the buck crossed a narrow lane affording three seconds of judging and shooting time. Neither of those bucks would now be on my wall had I been content to simply sit and stare straight ahead, oblivious to 75 percent of the coverage area. I killed them because I was paying attention, even after hours of nothingness. It pays to stay focused when big bucks are on the line.

The power of observation goes hand-in-hand with one's ability to see deer. Much has been written on the tricks that help see deer, i.e., watch for horizontal lines, movement and deer parts, not the whole animal. From my experience, the problem with most hunters is not that they don't know how to look for deer; it's simply that they *don't* look for deer. Why? They are poor observers and quick to lose focus.

From my own experience, I'm convinced many opportunities are squandered by unobservant hunters who are never even aware that a dream trophy was within their grasp. Over the years, I've been with many hunters who I'm certain would have let golden opportunities at big bucks slip away unnoticed had I not been there to point the deer out. Some of these bucks were practically in the bald open. On many occasions, my unseeing companions failed to ever see the buck despite my best efforts, which have included everything from manually pointing heads to actually aiming rifles while they looked through the scope.

One particular case of "assisted sighting" was particularly memorable. I was hunting with my daughter, Kristin, who has her mother's "power" of observation. After exhausting all conventional methods of showing her a good buck slipping through the late afternoon shadows some 100 yards away, I told her to shoulder the rifle and look through the scope. I then reached around from behind and, sighting down the barrel, began to slowly move the rifle around in the direction of the buck. I told her to let me know when she saw the deer so I could turn loose and let her steady up for the shot. As I was moving the rifle, she simultaneously shouted, "there he is," and fired. The only thing greater than my shock that she had shot was my surprise that the buck was stone dead!

Inquiring Mind

For the hunter, it's not enough just to observe; he must also process that information and apply it to the hunt. This is where some hunters, even those who are keen observers, come up short. They fail to respond to the things important to the hunt that they do see, or simply fail to recognize their significance.

Just recently, an experienced hunter and I walked into an area in Canada that was torn up with big rubs and scrapes. After casually commenting on the sign, he climbed back on his snowmobile and left in search of a "good" stand. I killed a big buck there two days later! While hunting the late rut in western Montana, I bumped into a hunter who said he had just seen two big bucks chasing a hot doe in a nearby clearcut. He sadly reported that they had disappeared into the woods before he could get a shot. When I asked him why he hadn't waited around for their possible return, he said he was a "walker" not a "sitter." Now, let's see—a hot doe in the late rut being chased by at least two big bucks in a remote clearcut. I like "walk-hunting" too, but I became a "sitter" that afternoon...but only for about two hours thanks to a 150-class 8-pointer!

The truly successful trophy hunters have inquiring minds. They are constantly processing new information, trying to figure out the whys and wherefores of what they see. They are thinking all the time in an effort to put what they observe into context. As new facts come to light, they adapt their strategy. Every piece of information is a possible clue to where, when and how they will encounter their next trophy buck.

> *The truly successful trophy hunters have inquiring minds. They are constantly processing new information, trying to figure out the whys and wherefores of what they see.*

Nothing is dismissed out-of-hand without first processing it and factoring it into the equation.

Sometimes even good hunters can fail to act upon the obvious... and it can cost them. A couple of years ago I was hunting on a large Texas ranch with a friend who was after a book-class 10-pointer that had been seen a few afternoons earlier at a remote tank (pond). This tank, because of severe drought conditions, was the only water source within a two-mile radius. Since the rut was underway and the temperature was crowding 90 degrees, bucks were watering there in impressive numbers. My friend had hunted the tank steadfastly for three mornings. He had seen a myriad of bucks, but the lure of the vast ranch and a touch of impatience wouldn't allow him to sit at the tank all day, despite encouragement to do so from both his guide, Phil Reddock, and me. Then, on the fourth morning at the waterhole, my friend shot a mid-150s 10-pointer. That very afternoon found me at the tank.

Given the facts, hunting the tank in the afternoon seemed a logical strategy. The tank held the only water within miles. Because of the demands of the rut and high temperatures, the bucks had to drink frequently. Most buck traffic at the waterhole, at least in the morning, was between 9 and 11, meaning that after a hard night and early morning of rutting the bucks were drinking before bedding up for the day. The tank

If you were overlooking the Peace River valley in Alberta, where this picture was taken, what would you see? Just pretty landscape? Or, would you "see" the lay of land 3-dimensionally and then be able to pick out potential whitetail bedding areas, travel corridors, funnels, access routes to the tabletop farmlands, edges between habitat types and possible hunting routes overlooking strategic areas? If your answer leans to the latter, you may have the power of "mental mapping," a great asset in trophy whitetail hunting. Photo by author.

had not yet been hunted in the afternoon. It seemed logical that there would be an afternoon flurry of buck visitations as they left their bed and prepared for the evening festivities. And finally, the big 10-pointer had been seen in the afternoon. An hour before dark that very day, my 140-grain Nosler intercepted the 170-class 10-pointer.

Mental Mapping

I first began to notice it way back in my bass guiding days on Alabama's Lake Eufaula. A few guides seemed to have a knack for locating fish, even in unfamiliar water; others seemed to stumble around blindly, and without much success. Oh, the "stumblers" could catch fish well enough once they got on them, which they usually did by following the "finders," so it wasn't a question of knowing how to actually fish. It was really just this simple—some could find fish and some couldn't. Why?

Over time, I began to understand the answer, at least one of the biggest ones. It seems that the finders had the unique ability to "see" the bottom of the lake 3-dimensionally. The stumblers, on the other hand, saw only a sheet of surface water. Both groups had the advantages of depthfinders, pre-impoundment aerial photos, topo maps and, of course, shoreline topography to help reveal what was underwater. But for some reason, the stumblers couldn't seem to envision the lake floor beyond the flash on their depthfinder. They simply couldn't put together a coherent mental picture of the bass' environs that would help reveal travel patterns, feeding areas and spawning grounds. Their vision was largely limited to what they were looking at that moment, which was usually miles of glimmering surface water.

On the other hand, the mind's eye of the finders saw the lake bottom in 3-dimension, as though the water was transparent. They "saw" river and creek beds, underwater islands and humps, ditches, submerged timber, outside bends in channels and shallow flats. Upon "seeing" these features, they could envision how bass and baitfish related to this structure at various times of the year and under various conditions. Thus, they could anticipate the bass' whereabouts and narrow their search, rather than blindly exploring the whole lake. This ability to see in 3-dimension and to apply it to bass movement kept them in high odds places and largely eliminated wasted time in dead water.

Try as one may, the ability to mentally see 3-dimensionally can be learned only to a limited degree. It is largely a natural ability that one either has or doesn't. It's not surprising that nearly all the great bass pros possess this ability. Recently, I read with interest that one of the traits sought in candidates for the U.S. Delta Forces, one of the military's most elite special forces, was the ability to mentally map terrain in 3-D.

This ability comes in degrees to be sure, but I've met some folks who *really* don't have it! They may be skilled in all other areas of the hunt, but when it comes to figuring out the lay of the land and what the bucks are doing, they are severely handicapped. As you would expect, those without this ability invariably have a bad sense of direction. My good friend and longtime hunting buddy, Jim Goodchild, falls into this category. Forget envisioning the lay of the land; Jim has trouble finding the stand he hunted the day before! In Jim's own words, "My house is a mighty big place to me." But as a hunter and a shooter, Jim is one of the best; he just needs help finding his way around the woods…and back home again. I've known many others like that, including my daddy.

Certainly, the ability to quickly envision the lay of the land 3-dimensionally has to be one of the greatest assets a trophy whitetail hunter can possess. As with bass fishing, it is an indispensable tool in finding big bucks. Those who have this ability can study maps or aerials then walk a piece of property and have a pretty good mind's eye view of the lay of the land and, assuming a thorough understanding of the white-tail, what the deer movement patterns are likely to be. With this knowl-edge, they can anticipate deer bedding, feeding and rutting areas and the travel routes to and from such areas, thus allowing them to focus both their scouting and hunting time in high-use spots. Even when hunting unfamiliar property, they can quickly size up the place and narrow in on the most likely places to intercept big bucks.

MAKING GOOD ON THE ENCOUNTER

Now, our second category—making good on the encounter. In my opinion, the most common failings of experienced whitetail hunters occur once a trophy buck finally has been spotted. Far too often, the wheels come off somewhere between the time the buck is sighted and the killing shot is made. When this happens, all the advance planning, time invested and skills applied in creating the opportunity are lost.

> *Far too often, the wheels come off somewhere between the time the buck is sighted and the killing shot is made.*

It's like a football team that plays hard all game and then, on the final drive of the game, fights and scratches to get into position for the winning field goal…only the field-goal kicker has little chance of getting the ball through the uprights! What good is all the work that went into getting the ball within field-goal range if the kicker can't make the three points? Well, it's exact-ly the same in trophy hunting. All the work that goes into creating the opportunity is worthless if the last step is botched.

Trophy whitetail hunting is unique among all big-game hunting in its difficulty in converting a sighting into a kill. The real challenge in hunting most animals is finding them. Once that's accomplished, delivering the fatal blow is usually not that difficult if the hunter is reasonably competent. But, the trophy whitetail presents a unique challenge once contact is made, a challenge almost as daunting as finding him in the first place. That's because of the nature of the beast. I know of no other animal as nervous, as quick to respond to potential danger, as adept at using cover to disappear or as unlikely to expose himself in the open or in good light. And in most cases, he sees the hunter first, or is in someway clued in. Chances at trophy whitetails are often through some type of cover and involve an alerted animal on the move. To make matters worst, the opportunities are normally measured in seconds and occur in dim light. Add the fact that the very rarity of big buck sightings assures that the hunter is going to be fighting an adrenaline overdose, and you have the reality of trophy whitetail encounters—they are seldom easy!

So, here's the problem. Upon seeing a trophy, the hunter has to very quickly identify the animal as a shooter, position for the kill and deliver a fatal shot, often at a partially obscured or moving buck in dim light. Speed and mistake-free performance are called for. If you move too slowly, the window of opportunity closes. If you move fast but make a mistake anywhere along the way, the hunt is over. In my experience, the majority of would-be trophy hunters cannot consistently pull it off. I believe converting a sighting into a kill is the Achilles' heel of most serious hunters.

Let's now look at some of the little things that make the difference between success and failure once the buck is in sight. They can be divided into three main areas—judging, positioning for the shot and making the kill.

Judging Quickly

Upon sighting a potential trophy, the first thing the hunter has to do is determine whether or not the buck is indeed a shooter. The clock is running so the decision has to be made quickly. That can't be done if the hunter doesn't know how to judge deer. I marvel at hunters who set very specific size standards and then go searching for that animal...without having any idea of what it looks like. It would be like going to the Atlanta airport to meet Joe Bob without having a clue what Joe Bob looks like. I know serious trophy hunters who simply cannot judge bucks and who are as likely to let a big buck pass as to shoot a small one. Most often, however, while frozen in their indecision, they let the opportunity slip away, whether the buck is a shooter or not.

An investment of time and effort is a prerequisite to becoming competent at field judging and scoring. I know of no other way. And, speed is of the essence. The quicker you size up the buck and decide he's the one, the more time you've got to set up and shoot. Practice and study are required. Pictures in magazines and books help, but better yet, visit taxidermy shops and check stations. Learn to score deer and actually tape as many as you can. This will help imprint upon your mind the relative appearance of certain dimensions. Of course, the ideal is to study bucks in the field at such places as game reserves, state parks, wildlife refuges, etc.

While on the subject, quality binoculars are critical in judging deer. Most often, what a buck is wearing on his head will be little more than a guess without good glasses. Even if fairly close, big bucks seldom are in the open and in good enough light so that the naked eye is sufficient to size up the rack. Besides, small details—an inch here or there, a broken point, an extra tine or two—often determine whether or not a buck meets the grade. That kind of detail can't normally be discerned without quality specs.

Positioning For The Shot

Between the time a buck is identified as a shooter and the time the bullet leaves the barrel, if it leaves the barrel, is what I call positioning for the shot. It is simply making the moves necessary to get into position for the finale. Sounds easy enough, doesn't it? Well, it may be...or it may require some fast thinking, risky moves and some fancy footwork. It just depends on the situation. The options may range from just turning quietly in a deer stand, to running 100 yards to cut off a buck, to grabbing a set of rattling horns in an effort to lure a buck back into view, to doing nothing at all while the buck makes his next move. But whatever it involves, the elections made go a long way in determining the outcome of the encounter, and I'm amazed how often bad decisions muck up the deal.

Possibly more than any other aspect of the closure, positioning for the shot is an art, or a knack, or perhaps even a natural ability. It's part of that mystical hunter's instinct, when a person knows instinctively from

People spend lots of time and money for a crack at a big buck like this long-beamed 11-pointer I shot in South Texas. Unfortunately, despite the fact that everything in hunting boils down to making a killing shot, many hunters are woefully ill-prepared to finish the job when the time comes. Photo by Dick Idol.

long years of experience with the whitetail what needs to be done to bring the encounter to a happy conclusion. Call it what you will, but some folks have it; some don't. It surely can be learned to a degree, but it's a gift when somebody is really good at it. Some hunters just seem to know what it takes to get into position for the kill, no matter how complicated the moves may be. Others seem to have a penchant for consistently making exactly the wrong moves.

While making the right moves after a shooter is seen is sometimes as easy as lifting the rifle and shooting, that's seldom the case with trophy bucks, even for stand-hunters. Usually, there's ample room for mistakes. For instance, even on relatively easy chances, some hunters blow the deal simply by moving too fast or at the wrong time, thus giving themselves away. The mistimed lifting of a bow or rifle for the shot is a notorious point of disaster. Little noises, too, can ruin give-me deals, even the rustle of clothes, the snap of a twig, the squeak of a stand, the creak of a cold

A happy George Tomkins traveled thousands of miles for the chance at a buck like this 150-plus 8-pointer. When the pressure was on, he quickly judged the animal, positioned for a shot and put the bullet in a vital place. Sounds easy enough, but the wheels all too often come off after the animal is in the "kill zone," nullifying all the effort that went before. Photo by author.

bow, the clack of an arrow falling off the rest or the click of a rifle safety. Whitetails don't miss much, and the smallest, most innocent mistake can spell disaster.

Often, significant maneuvering is necessary to turn a sighting into a kill, especially when still-hunting or plying any of the more aggressive tactics, like rattling, grunting, deer drives, etc. This is where more than just *not* making a mistake is called for. The hunter may well have to make a quick judgment call and then execute some type of aggressive maneuver to salvage a marginal opportunity. Athletic ability, woodsmanship, keen observation skills, thorough knowledge of the animal, a cool head under pressure, decisive thinking, mastery of various hunting techniques and plain old hunting instincts can all be important in this critical area of trophy hunting. The consistency with which a hunter scores on these marginal opportunities is one of the most telling traits of the great hunters versus the so-so ones. So rare is any crack, no matter how marginal, at a trophy whitetail that the hunter must be prepared to convert even the most difficult ones.

Making The Shot

After eliminating where and when one hunts, knowledge of the whitetail and hunting experience as variables, I believe the single greatest factor separating consistent trophy hunters from those who aren't is the ability to make the shot under a wide range of conditions. As I said earlier, a degree of difficulty is the norm with shots at trophy whitetails. Givemes are rare, but even they are muffed with regularity.

Certainly, one's propensity toward buck fever is a big factor in the outcome of a shot. Buck fever can be debilitating. I've experienced its blinding grip myself, and I've seen more than my share of it in my hunting companions. It's almost impossible to overestimate its power to bring low those severely inflicted. I've seen victims rendered motionless in its grip, fire harmlessly in the air and suffer mental lapses, even to the point of insisting they shot and killed the buck when they never even pulled the trigger.

Among trophy hunters, its effects are usually less obvious but still can be disastrous. For instance, years ago I bowhunted frequently with the Southeastern U.S. broadhead champion. When target shooting, he could stack one arrow on top of another out to 60 yards with boring monotony. If ever anybody should have been lethal on deer, it was this guy, but alas, when it came to shooting live critters, he was a basket case. As I recall, he missed 16 deer before finally killing his first…with an errant head shot intended for the lungs, I might add!

Another friend I frequently hunt with is an ace on the range and on varmints. He's generally a sure shot on whitetails, too, but ever so often, especially when under pressure late in the hunt or when the shot has to be rushed, he suffers "mystery misses." For no good reason, he simply misses shots he normally would make with ease. It's nothing more than a subtle but insidious form of buck fever, causing him to momentarily lose control of his shooting disciplines and instincts.

Buck fever is best dealt with by experience and forced discipline. The experience has to be gained one experience at a time, with buck fever hopefully becoming less of a nemesis each time it is faced. The forced discipline is just that—forced. Even after all these years, I nearly always have to force myself to remain calm and methodical when the time to shoot arrives. I've never found anything better than the old standby—two or three deep breaths—to calm me down and help regain some semblance of control. I still have to force each step, from finding and using a solid rest to picking an exact spot on the deer to squeezing the trigger. I haven't stopped becoming excited when I'm about to shoot a big buck (and hope I never do); I've just learned to keep buck fever from becoming the master of the moment...most of the time!

Buck fever is an understandable part of trophy hunting and a justifiable reason for blowing shots, but the same cannot be said for the lack of shooting skills. There is no excuse for any hunter bent on shooting deer to venture forth without sound shooting skills honed by hours of practice on the range. Yet, with the general hunting public, poor shooting skills are almost the norm rather than the exception. Even many trophy whitetail hunters cannot consistently make shots requiring much more than the most basic skills. Frankly, I don't understand this, not considering the time, effort and perhaps money required for even an infrequent chance at a trophy buck. Why make the investment if you aren't able to close the deal when the time comes?

> *Buck fever is an understandable part of trophy hunting and a justifiable reason for blowing shots, but the same cannot be said for lack of shooting skills.*

Shooting shortcomings take several forms. Some hunters simply never practice shooting; some don't even bother to sight-in their rifle. This is the worst. While others may sight-in every year or two, they make no further investment in developing their shooting skills. Therefore, though they take to the woods with a gun capable of shooting where it is aimed, they have no idea of what it takes to accurately place a bullet under field conditions. They don't understand that a rifle is a precision instrument that puts a very small bullet exactly where aimed and nowhere else. It will not kill anything in the general direction of the shot just because it's loud and kicks a lot.

Besides the obvious need for practice, the keys to shooting a rifle well in the field are using a rest whenever possible, trigger control and familiarity with the rifle and its capabilities. I instinctively find and use a rest when setting up for a shot. It takes dire circumstances for me to shoot offhand. I know I can't hold steady without a rest. Rifle shooting with a scope, which I assume all serious trophy hunters employ, is a learned, mechanical discipline. It's a step-by-step process, and resting the rifle to take out the tremors is a vital part of the process. Skip it and the success of the shot is put in serious jeopardy.

Trigger control is the process of controlling the squeeze of the trigger so that the rifle goes off at the right instant without being jerked off the target. This is another critical part of the process. With practice, a shooter can develop a feel for exactly when sufficient pressure has been applied to break the trigger. Coupled with a solid rest, this allows a hunter to form an accurate sight picture at the time of discharge and confidently tell where the bullet hit, a very helpful advantage known as "calling the shot."

Trigger control can only be developed on the range under benchrest conditions using proper ear and recoil protection. When shooting loud, bucking centerfire rifles, nearly everybody's natural tendency is to close their eyes and jerk. Stopping this urge takes some doing. My favorite way to teach trigger control is for me to do the loading for the shooter and occasionally give him an empty gun, without him knowing it. If he jerks, and I almost guarantee he will unless he's experienced, it will be evident to all when he dry fires. Not knowing whether or not the gun is loaded does wonders for trigger control. Besides, embarrassment is a great motivator.

The last aspect of good field shooting is familiarity with the gun (or bow) and its performance. This, of course, brings us back to practice and time with the gun. Different guns handle and shoot differently. Spend enough time with your deer rifle so that using it becomes automatic. Know where it shoots at various ranges, when the trigger is going to break and that, given any reasonable shot at a trophy whitetail, you and your rifle can get it done. After all, ultimately, the only connection you have to that buck and the only thing that can bring a hunt to a successful conclusion is that little projectile you send downrange. If the bullet fails to do its job, everything that has gone before is for naught. It is just another one of those overlooked "little things" that can make a "big" difference in success…literally!

Chapter Twenty-Four

Rattling, Calls and Scents– Beyond the Basics

T HE BRIGHT, NEAR-NOON SUN HAD not taken the chill off the cold, blustery morning. A front had moved through Georgia the day before and, after drenching the countryside, had dropped both the temperature and humidity by more than 60 notches. I had seen several deer earlier that morning while still-hunting before the wind picked up. Now, as I moved to a better vantage point overlooking the third clearcut I had checked in the last hour, I knew the deer had already bedded down. No matter. My plan took that into account. I knew that bucks often bedded in open areas with low ground cover on bright,

With imagination, rattling horns, as well as calls and scents, can be used in a multitude of ways to fool even wise old bucks. Photo by author.

cold days like this. If a buck was bedded in this clearcut, I might be able to get him to show himself.

I soon reached the elevated knob on the high side of the 30-acre clearcut. Three years earlier, pine seedlings had been planted to replace the harvested trees, and the young loblollies, along with a healthy stand of sweetgums and briars, provided chest-high cover for deer. A streambed lined with thick brush and a smattering of oaks wound through the pine plantation and added to its deer appeal. I leaned my rifle against a nearby tree, reached for my rattling horns and began thrashing them together, lightly at first then harder. I had no intentions or expectations of rattling a buck in, but I had every hope that the end result of the rattling would be a buck in my sights!

I was only on my second rapped knuckle when I saw a doe's head peering over a clump of briars about 125 yards away. Then, a flash near her drew my attention. I went immediately for my binoculars and found a very good buck looking through a tangle of briars alternately at me and the doe, obviously unsure where the ruckus had come from. I could see enough to know he was a shooter but not enough to get a shot. I again grabbed my rattling horns and gave them a vigorous shaking. The 10-pointer tensed, stared hard in my direction and then took two, just two, steps to his right to get a better view. He got it...so did I!

CREATIVE RATTLING

In the minds of many hunters, rattling horns, grunt calls and scents fit into a nice little stereotype of how they are to be used and are of little value outside that basic usage. That, however, is simply not the case. With some imagination, the value and usefulness of these deer-hunting tools can be expanded far beyond their traditional place in the whitetail woods.

"Rattling" conjures up visions of a wide-eyed buck rushing head-long toward an awaiting hunter. That certainly happens (though perhaps not as often in reality as in print), but over the years, I have learned that rattling has a far broader use than simply calling in bucks, as the Georgia buck illustrates. I wasn't trying to call that buck to me. Under the circumstances, that was unlikely to happen. I was simply trying to get any buck bedded in that clearcut to stand up and expose himself. Deer are curious, and they like to identify the source of unusual sights, sounds or smells. The sound of fighting bucks was enough to warrant a passive look-see but not an all-out investigation. That passive look-see was all I needed to turn an unsuccessful morning into a memorable one.

With some imagination, the value of these deer-hunting tools can be expanded far beyond their traditional place in the whitetail woods.

I've used rattling horns to get bucks to expose themselves in many different situations. One of my favorites is to slip along ridges, bluffs or hillsides overlooking good deer habitat that offers some visibility, even if just a few holes or small clearings, and rattle every 200 or so yards. The object is to get a buck to expose himself as he moves around to check out the mock fight. Often, a buck will stop in clear view since he is trying to get a look at the combatants. And if he can see you, chances are you can see him.

In the right place and at the right time, this technique is a great

Just before and during the rut, aggressive bucks sometimes rush headlong into a fake fight, but there are many other ways to effectively use rattling rather than simply trying to lure deer in. Photo by Mike Biggs.

way to look over a lot of bucks. On a ranch I hunt in South Texas, a 40-foot-high escarpment runs north and south for five miles through prime deer country. I frequently spend the morning (when the sun is at my back) walking the lip of this bluff and rattling. Though the escarpment serves as a physical barrier to actually rattling the bucks right to me, some bucks do come running to the base of the bluff. Most, however, stay back in the brush and tiptoe around in an effort to get a look at the source of the fracas. With the sun at my back and full on the deer, they shine like a light and any movement is quickly picked up, especially when reflective antlers are involved. I've looked over as many as 20 bucks in a morning on this ranch using rattling horns to draw out the deer.

One of the good things about this technique is that it works even in places where bucks don't respond particularly well to rattling horns. Though they aren't prone to come running, the curiosity factor is still there and they may invest a few steps into taking a peek at what's going on. The setup doesn't require a hill or a bluff; any place with decent visi-

Rumor has it that top-end bucks don't respond to rattling. Don't you believe it! I rattled in this 180-class 11-pointer in Saskatchewan. Photo by author.

bility has potential. As we saw earlier, clearcuts, which are just about everywhere, are great places to ply this tactic.

There is one particular set of rather odd conditions where bucks, especially big bucks, can sometimes be lured into sight using rattling horns that is worth mentioning. For some reasons on cold, windy days following the passage of a front during the peak of the rut, a unique opportunity exists—not necessarily to call bucks in on top of you but to get them to expose themselves, albeit at a distance. Contrary to the normal view of ideal rattling conditions, this tactic calls for a fairly stiff wind, say 15 mph or more. Plus, I've had my best success in the heart of the breeding period when the bucks are hard after does. Generally speaking, not as many bucks respond to rattling under these conditions as they might during calmer winds and the more traditional rattling time just prior to breeding, but the chances of a top-end buck showing up now seem to be better.

The setup is critical. To start with, you need extended downwind visibility of at least 100 yards and preferably 200 to 300 yards. The best "lanes," like senderos, utility right-of-ways, old logging roads, etc., have enough cover to give a buck some security when he moves into them. Next, good deer-holding cover must border the downwind view, if for no other reason than to insure that the buck you hope to draw out can hear the horns you're clashing together above the wind.

I start the rattling sequence slowly, as I always do to keep from startling nearby deer, but quickly escalate the tempo to imitate a violet battle, both because serious fights take place this time of year and because the volume has to be sufficient to carry a long distance in high winds. I'll usually rattle for about two minutes then lay the horns down and wait for at least 15 to 20 minutes. The wait is an important part of this tactic because it seems to take bucks quite a while to show themselves. Perhaps it is because of the extra caution they show during periods of high wind. Or, maybe it is because it takes time for a buck to work his way well downwind of the mock battle. Whatever the reason, patience is called for.

Most of the bucks, especially the big ones, responding to rattling under these conditions tend to show up a considerable distance downwind, usually 100 yards or more, thus the need for extended downwind visibility. Many times, I had them sneak into view 200 or 300 yards away. This is perhaps the most unusual aspect of this tactic. I don't know why they tend to investigate the ruckus from so far away. Maybe the high wind gives them the unique opportunity to check out a fight from a safe distance by swinging well downwind and using their incredible nose. I personally think this is why rattling under

> *I have a theory that old bucks have a "protected space" and are reluctant to violate it when approaching potential danger.*

these conditions tends to be particularly effective for big bucks. I have a theory that old bucks have a "protected space," so to speak, and are reluctant to get any closer to potential danger than that protected space, which may well be 100 yards or so. Whatever the reasons, I have several convincing proofs on my wall that this tactic works for big bucks.

The fact is that nearly all the top-end bucks I've ever rattled in and shot have come under these conditions, many at distances of over 200 yards. The widest buck I have ever taken, a 28 1/4-inch 10-pointer, fell to this strategy after chasing him around the South Texas Brush Country for four years. I have shot two big Canadian bucks while rattling in wind so strong that I could hardly even hear the banging myself. Both slipped into the downwind alley nearly 200 away a half-hour or so into the session, only to snap their heads around and look straight toward me. Big Georgia and Montana bucks have made similar miscalculations in the wailing wind.

Noise, like scent and visibility, can be masked to a degree, and rattling horns can be used to accomplish this.

Another way I use rattling horns other than just to call bucks in is what I call "noise-masking." Deer have three basic defense senses—smell, sight and hearing. Considerable effort has gone into the development of masking scents designed to cover human odor. And, camouflage is intended to hide you from the deer's sight. But, what about masking a hunter's sound? Much has been done to quieten clothes, boots and even gun stocks, but unless a hunter sits perfectly still, he will inevitably make some noise—brush rubbing against clothes, limbs breaking, leaves crunching, etc. Mobility is an important part of my hunting strategy and some noise is inescapable. But, the noise doesn't have to always give me away. Noise, like scent and visibility, can be masked to a degree, and rattling horns can be used to accomplish this.

When trying to slip up on deer, any noise can potentially give you away. It works this way. A deer hears an unidentified sound and becomes alerted. He focuses his full senses on the direction of the noise. Now tense and alert, any further suspicious noise, not to mention movement or scent, can cause him to depart posthaste. On the other hand, a reassuring sound, a masking sound if you well, following a suspicious noise can put the buck at ease and cause him to lower his defenses. This is where rattling horns come in.

I've tried mooing like a cow, grunting and various other disarming mimics, but the best option I've found to mask a errant noise is to use rattling horns to imitate a buck rubbing brush. When I snap a limb, hook the brush with my rifle barrel or whatever, I'll often knell on the spot and start lightly rubbing nearby brush. Not hard and not long; just enough to convince a listening deer that I'm a buck ambling along and doing buckish things. Then, I'll sit there a few minutes to allow time for things to settle down and to give a buck a chance to ease over and check out the competition. That's an important side benefit of this tactic—not only can it mask an errant noise, it can also call in a curious or aggressive buck!

This fine Montana buck, shot by Pete Dunckle (left) with help from Frank Dykstra, never had any intentions of "coming in," but the ruckus rousted him from his bed and caused him to move into sight for a shot. Rattling is more versatile than most hunters realize. Photo courtesy of Pete Dunckle.

Depending on the situation, outright rattling and/or grunting can also be a part of the cover-up initiated by a miscue.

Another way rattling horns can be employed is to stop a buck and/or make him look your way so he can be judged or shot. I prefer to use rattling horns for this purpose only when the buck is some distance away or if I already have the horns in my hands. When a buck is close by, the movement involved in rattling can draw attention, especially since the buck is sure to be looking your way after you rattle. There's also the problem of the time needed to pick up the antlers, rattle and put them down. For all these reasons, if a buck is nearby and time is short, I'll usually whistle or grunt to stop a buck I want to look over. Whistling, however, does have the disadvantage of potentially alerting the deer, and grunting has limited range and is sometimes ignored by a preoccupied buck. Rattling, if it can be done without giving yourself away, almost always has the desired effect and, compared to grunting, has the advantage of range. I've seen bucks respond to rattling well over a quarter-mile away.

A deer's nose is his life...literally. With it, he finds girlfriends, communicates with other deer, detects enemies and locates good vittles. It's very hard to completely fool such an incredible "instrument" of detection, but it can be "messed" with to the advantage of the hunter. Photo by Troy Huffman.

GETTING THE GOOD OUT OF CALLS

Grunt calls definitely have a place in whitetail hunting, but as a means of calling in trophy bucks cold turkey, I frankly think too much is expected of them. In my opinion, grunt calls are most useful when used to reassure or calm a suspicious buck and when used as a close-range coaxer on a buck that has been previously excited by rattling, the smell of a hot doe or the challenge of another buck. As for reassuring and calming, the grunt call can be used to mask a mistake, as discussed earlier. I also mentioned that a grunt call could be used to stop a buck or make him face you for a better look. Now, I want to briefly focus on what I feel is the best use of a grunt call—a close-range coaxer for an excited buck.

I have grunted at countless bucks that were within sight of me. Most just looked briefly my way. Some ignored the call altogether. A few ambled in my direction in what might be called a passive response. Only a mere handful came toward me with any sign of enthusiasm. Almost without exception, the bucks that did respond had already been excited by something. You see, the sound of a grunt in itself is generally not enough to excite a buck and elicit an aggressive response. The smell of a hot doe will do it. So will the sight or sound of another buck rubbing bushes or two bucks fighting, which rattling mimics. But, a grunt alone in no other context is seldom enough to initiate a positive response from a buck. For grunting to be effective with any consistency, the buck has to be turned on. This is why the breeding period is recognized as being the best time to use a grunt call—the chances are better then that a grunt will fall on the ears of a buck charged up by the rut.

> *For grunting to be effective with any consistency, the buck has to be turned on. This is why the breeding period is recognized as being the best time to use a grunt call.*

Given all this, I have found grunting to be of consistent value in three situations—and then primarily to coax a buck in a few steps or to hold him a bit longer. The first is when hunting active scrapes. The bucks are excited and expectant when they come into scraping areas, and a well-placed grunt can be just the ticket to entice a buck into view for a shot. The second time is when you know something is going on in the area that would excite a buck—a chase, a buck fight, red-hot buck sign, etc. The odds of a turned-on buck being nearby are simply better under those circumstances. The last is when rattling. Let's take a closer look at this one.

A buck responding to rattling is sure to be excited. Often, he will hurry over in the direction of the fight, usually trying to work his way downwind if there is any, and then stand and listen to determine the exact nature and whereabouts of the racket. When a buck is in close, more rattling can be tricky because of movement and because it tends to give away your position too precisely. This is when a grunt call is most valuable. A light grunt or two can reassure a tentative buck of what he has heard and, hopefully, coax him in the last few steps. I've done this many times and employee the grunt call as a regular part of my rattling ruse. Very often, bucks have quickly materialized after a grunt or two that

I'm absolutely certain I would not have seen had I been armed only with rattling horns.

USING SCENTS SENSIBILITY

Like the grunt call, too much is expected from scents, especially the buck lures, which usually claim to be made from the urine of estrus does. I do occasionally use a masking or cover scent in an attempt to partially counter the deer's far superior nose when hunting tight cover. But, the whitetail's nose is too acute to be completely fooled all the time. I was reminded of just how amazing their sense of smell is just this past season in South Texas. The rancher had put out some corn on a sendero to draw in some does for harvest. I was scouting an area about a quarter-mile away and downwind of the corn. A mid-sized buck crossed an opening downwind of me, and I knew he would shortly catch my scent. But before he reached my scentline, he threw up his head, sniffed and started running in my direction. He passed about 30 yards to my right and continued his trot out of sight. *The corn*, I thought, though I found it hard to believe he had smelled it from a distance of nearly 500 yards in the light breeze. I hurried to the sendero to see if the buck was there. He was…merrily gobbling up the kernels of corn! A nose like that is hard to fool!

My favorite way to use buck lure is not as an attractant at all. It is to stop bucks momentarily, usually out of curiosity, in places where they would normally pass by too quickly to judge and/or to shoot.

Besides masking and cover scents, I've tried buck lures of every kind in hopes of finding one that would magically draw in big bucks. Though I've had a few encouraging experiences, a couple of which were quite dramatic, a foolproof buck lure remains but a dream. Buck lures do, however, have their place. As with grunt calls, they work best when a buck is already excited, which makes scrape-hunting an ideal time to use buck lures. Some hunters even use buck lure to make up their own "mock scrapes" by scratching out a scrape in a likely place and saturating it with the stinky stuff. This tactic does have some merit, but I'm not sold on it for big bucks. I prefer to use buck lure on existing scrapes, but not for the purpose of attracting the buck to the scrapes. He's already coming to the scrapes, or I wouldn't be there to start with. I use buck lure for the purpose of luring a buck to or stopping him in a particular spot at or near the scrapes for a look or a shot. I also use it around scrapes to mask my scent if I go over to check for sign, which I do very sparingly once I commit to hunt a place.

Actually, my favorite way to use buck lure is not as an attractant at all. It is to stop bucks momentarily, usually out of curiosity, in places where they would normally pass by too quickly to judge and/or to shoot. When hunting trails, logging roads, utility right-of-ways and such, where deer are likely to cross relatively narrow openings too quickly for me to get the job done, I'll frequently lace the likely crossing spots with buck lure. A buck ambling across will usually nose the buck lure, allowing time to judge and shoot. I have used this tactic quite successfully many times. It is especially useful when hunting narrow lanes in the kind of thick cover big bucks like so well.

Often in my pursuit of big whitetails, the time comes when I like, or even need, to take more than a passive role in the hunt to make things happen. I do this by covering a lot of country, reacting to sign, sightings and circumstances and trying to make deer expose themselves. Rattling horns, grunt calls, buck lures and a double dose of imagination are the tools of the trade. With them and some old-fashioned hard work, you can go a long ways toward making your own luck!

Chapter Twenty-Five

Dressing for Hot Action in Extreme Cold

I WAS BORN AND RAISED IN SOUTH
Alabama, right on the Florida line. I received my college education at
Auburn University, also in South Alabama. I spent the first 25 years of
my working life in Middle Georgia. I started my serious trophy hunting
career, at least my traveling career, in South Texas. In short, I've spent
most of my life where the temperature and the humidity during much of
the year seemed to be in daily competition to be the first to reach the
three-digit reading...and where, I might add, any given breath could
consist of 5 to 10 percent gnats.

I know what hot weather is. Cold weather, on the other hand, I
always had figured as anything much under 50 degrees. I was a warm-
weather person, plain and simple...without any plans to ever change
that. When I moved to Middle Georgia, which I did only after being
assured it lay south of the Mason-Dixon Line, I figured that was as far
north as this South Alabama farm boy would ever go. In fact, I made a
commitment to that effect, along with two other now infamous "I will

Cold-weather hunting certainly brings its own challenges, and at times, its own unique rewards. To effectively hunt harsh climates, you must dress so you can somewhat comfortably endure long hours in frigid weather. Every part of the body, from head to toe, literally, must be protected. This Saskatchewan buck, by the way, was the heaviest whitetail I've ever killed, or seen. His live weight was right at 400 pounds! Photo by Carl Frohaug.

never" statements I made in my foolish youth.

The first was: I will never live in Atlanta, where I ended up living for 10 enjoyable years. The second was: I will never join a Baptist church, which I not only eventually did, but I also became, of all things, a Baptist deacon! And lastly, the biggie: I will never live north of Atlanta, which was already a compromise from my previous "I will never live north of Montgomery" declaration.

I now live in Montana...by choice! It's cold in Montana, much of the time far below my previous "cold" mark of 50 degrees. In fact, I wasn't there long before finding out there really is a reason for that minus part on the thermometer. Nowadays, I also spend considerable time every fall in Canada chasing big whitetails. It is really cold in Canada, colder than

I ever dreamed possible. But, big deer live there so...

My northern excursions first began in 1982 with a deer hunt to Manitoba. There, I quickly realized that dressing for brief morning lows in the 30s had very little in common with weathering a day in the snowy wilds where the high may never see zero, as was the case the entire week I was there!

I went knowing that Manitoba would be colder than Georgia so I simply took more of my Southern attire. That's when I discovered that an extra pair of insulated underwear, a second flannel shirt, an extra pair of socks, a pair of foam-lined gloves and a fleece-lined baseball cap wasn't upgrade enough to handle that kind of weather. I also found out that you can't get enough layers under regular-sized clothing and boots to insulate you from the cold...and still move. Lord knows I tried on that trip. I lay-ered-up with everything I owned or could borrow. With my outer layer stretched as taunt Mama Cass' girdle, I promptly found out that not only could I not move, neither could my blood. That's when I learned the car-dinal rule of staying warm—never restrict your circulation!

Sometime later, just when I began to get a grip on dressing for an active day afield in extreme cold, Saskatchewan and Alberta muddied up the water. They passed laws restricting non-resident hunters from moving around in the bush without a guide/outfitter within handholding distance of them. (Those laws have now been relaxed somewhat, especially in Alberta.) That pretty much relegated non-residents to stand-hunting, which meant long hours of inactivity in sub-zero weather. After trying that a time or two, I was once again faced with coming up with a way to combat a whole new level of cold. Now, after several years, I am happy to report that I have met with some success.

I am including a chapter on dressing for the cold in this book because some of the biggest whitetails in the world are in very cold cli-mates. If you can't stay out there with them, you aren't likely to kill them. Staying reasonably warm and comfortable is an essential beginning strategy up there, whether in the upper Midwest, Central Canada or the deep forests of the Maritimes provinces. Here, I want to focus on inac-tive hunting in extremely cold weather. Even when temperatures are in the single digits, staying warm is not very difficult when the hunter can stay on the move.

Much has been written about the virtues of layering in recent years…and rightfully so. Layering is the concept of wearing several layers of clothing, rather than one or two heavier, more bulky layers. Multiple layers make for efficient insulation, can be added to or shed in keeping with conditions and generally allow for less bulk and greater mobility. An active body is a great furnace and adequate layering will hold in the heat generated quite nicely. But, long hours of motionless hunting in frigid temperatures present some unique problems since the need now is for maximum heat retention when relatively little heat is being generated. The concept of simply layering is not enough.

As I said earlier, the cardinal rule of staying warm is to maintain good circulation. This is especially true for the extremities. Restrict circulation to the feet, and they're going to be cold. Same for the hands, arms and legs. The head, too, is an extremity, but restricted circulation to the head is less a problem since it is usually signaled by difficulty *breathing*. Since the extremities are the first to feel cold's icy grip, let's start with them.

FEET AND HANDS

The feet, along with the hands, are undoubtedly the most cold-sensitive part of the body—and the part most often affected by poor circulation. It's easy to see how this happens. When a hunter shops for a pair of boots, what size does he request? Usually his shoe size. As he tries on the boots, he'll normally don one pair of socks, generally the handiest pair regardless of thickness. If the boots don't hurt his feet on a quick jaunt around the room, all is well. Before taking to the cold woods, he cinches up the laces good and tight. Eventually, he climbs into a cramped deer stand and pulls his feet up under him, creating acute angles at the knees and ankles that restrict blood flow to both his legs and feet. Pretty soon, his feet are cold. He figures more insulation is the answer so the next day he's back with an extra pair of socks stuffed into his boots, further cutting off circulation. The only good thing is that he doesn't have to suffer too long before his feet become numb.

Cold feet long have been a problem for me. I had just about resigned myself to the inevitability of it when I discovered an answer—actually answers. First, boots must be large enough to comfortably (loosely) accommodate the whole of whatever you put in them. In cold weather, I always wear at least two pairs of wool and/or insulated, high-tech synthetic socks, one medium weight and one heavy. Frequently, I will even add a second heavy pair. All this, of course, necessitates a larger-than-usual boot. So for sitting boots, I buy a pair *two* full sizes larger than I normally wear. You'll feel silly when trying them on, but when your feet are toasty in sub-zero weather, you'll get over feeling silly.

With adequately large boots in hand, the next thing to avoid is lacing them too tightly. Even if they have to be laced fairly tight for the walk to the stand, loosen them once there. When sitting, the tendency is for the boot to cut into the front of the foot at ankle height, thus crimping circulation. Loosening the laces will greatly help this problem. And, though legroom is limited in a stand, try to avoid sitting with your feet pulled far back under you since this restricts blood flow at the knee and the ankle. At least, stretch your legs occasionally.

Which boot is best for extreme cold? Actually, there are countless boots that will serve quite well. Just be sure to purchase high-quality boots designed for bitter cold. Since cold weather is so often accompanied by snow, most extreme-weather boots tend to be the rubber-bottomed, felt-lined models like those made by L.L. Bean, Sorel, Cabela's and LaCrosse, to name a few. I've spent many an hour shodded in these boots. Provided they are plenty big, they are fine. If they are the least bit tight, they can restrict circulation at the ankle when the foot is at an acute angle because of the rubber/leather seam and because the rubber bottoms tend to stiffen in extreme cold. Also, be certain that the boots are insulated on the bottoms by something other than just the felt liner. The liner compresses and loses much of its insulating qualities. Air spaces (waffling), foam or insulated innersoles are all ways of preventing cold-creep from the bottom of boots.

Just by happenstance, I found a boot, probably more accurately called a mukluk, that eliminates the binding problem. I prefer this particular boot to any other I've tried, but only when sitting for long periods of time in weather that would send penguins packing. They are too "sloppy" on the foot for good walking. The exterior of this boot is made of tightly woven, water-resistant nylon rather than the traditional leather tops and rubber bottoms. Actually, the outer shell, and that's all it is, is little more than a supped-up, knee-high basketball shoe. The boot's flexibility and its interior "working parts" are the secrets to its warmth.

My best Canadian buck, an Alberta 15-pointer grossing 187. Photo by Scott Taylor.

The gang...until the rutting urge kicks in. Photo by Mike Biggs.

Late afternoon on wintergreens. Photo by Mike Biggs.

Rebecca Schwarz with her dad and her 160-class 8-pointer. Photo by author.

A special moment between Dave McClure and his book-class Peace River 10-pointer. Photo by author.

Two velvet-antlered bucks facing off—an unusual sight. Testosterone levels are undoubtedly rising. Photo by Troy Huffman.

I shot this gnarly old buck in the forested foothills of western Alberta. Photo by George Cooper.

No waiting, no thinking—it's shooting time. Photo by Mike Biggs.

I don't like neck shots, but... Photo by Mike Biggs.

Though I've taken bigger, this 180-class 28-incher is still one of my favorites. Photo by Corey Rowland.

After three years of hunting him, I finally caught up with this 12-pointer at age 9 1/2. By then, his rack was much smaller than it had been when I first saw him at 6 1/2. Photo by author.

All manner of scent is being laid down by this scraping buck. Photo by Troy Huffman.

George Cooper is a big man, but even he can't diminish the size of this wide Saskatchewan buck. Photo by author.

A big buck with his face stuck in an agricultural crop—a picture of the future of deer management. Photo by Troy Huffman.

There's nothing like the moment you first walk up to a trophy. Photo by author.

At 192 6/8, this is my highest scoring buck. The length of his tines is remarkable—from brows out, they measure 5, 13, 12 and 10 inches! Photo by Mark Lubin.

Trouble for the doe…and for the buck if I were there. Photo by Mike Biggs.

The only double-main-beamed buck I've ever shot. Photo by Glenn Hayes.

Like it or not, some of the biggest bucks in the world are in bitter cold regions. If you want to hunt them, you have to go where they live...and face the same severe conditions they face. Photo by Troy Huffman.

The boot is called a Chimo boot and is made in Quebec expressly for use by the Canadian military and Royal Canadian Mounted Police in the Far North. Chimos feature a thick waffled "floor" to provide a trapped air space to prevent transferring the cold directly to the feet. This is then topped with a thick wool insole. Next, comes the heart of the boot—a double-layered wool liner. This liner is actually two wool liners of mid-chin height sown together to provide both added thickness and a buffering air space, i.e., the layering effect. I normally augment this arrangement by wearing three pairs of socks. Thus adorned, my feet can stay acceptably warm for extended periods in the coldest conditions. Chimo boots are available from Douphin Army and Navy Store, 434 1st Avenue Northeast, Douphin, Manitoba R7N 1A9.

There is another boot similar to the Chimo and apparently just as warm, perhaps even warmer. Frankly, I've never tried it, but everyone who has swears by it. I'm speaking of Northern Outfitters EXP Boots (P.O. Box 700, 14072 S. Pony Express Rd., Draper, UT 84020). Like the Chimo, the top portion is nylon (Cordura) rather than rubber, providing good flexibility. The boot is insulated all around with 1.5 inches of open-cell polyurethane foam and features an additional thermal insole and a moisture control screen. I've been in camp during bitter cold times with guys wearing these boots, and they raved about their performance.

Before leaving the feet, I should say something about the large, insulated coverall booties, the kind you carry with you until you arrive at the stand and then pull on over your hunting boots. As cumbersome as they are to carry, put on and take off, they do work well.

Now for the hands, a most vulnerable extremity to cold. For a long time, I tried every conceivable type of glove to preserve dexterity in biting cold, largely without success. I finally settled on a pair that is excellent when the temperature is 15 degrees or warmer. These gloves, sold by Cabela's, have a ragg-wool exterior, are insulated with 100 grams of Thinsulate and are made waterproof and windproof by a Gore-Tex bladder. It is even possible to shoot with them on, though I don't recommend it. They are about as warm a glove as I've found, but they are not nearly as warm as good mittens.

I avoided mittens for a long time because they are cumbersome and must be removed to shoot, or to do just about anything else. But for keeping warm in numbing cold, nothing beats mittens. They retain more heat than gloves, since their external surface area is much less, greatly reducing heat loss. Plus, the fingers literally warm themselves even with the little heat they generate. There are many excellent mittens on the market. I prefer the large snowmobile-type mittens that extent almost to the elbow over the smaller wrist-length versions. Also, I buy over-sized mittens that will allow room for a pair of wool or polypropylene glove liners and the use of the chemical hand-warmer packets (more on these momentarily) so popular with snow skiers. The reason I sometimes use glove liners inside the mittens is not for warmth while in the mitten but for short-term protection when I remove my hands to glass, shoot or do whatever. Even brief exposure in sub-zero weather can quickly numb bare hands and render them useless.

I've recently tried the tube-type hand-warmer muff. The one I used was made by Cabela's, had a fleece exterior and was insulated with Thinsulate Lite Loft. My hands stayed warm into the mid-teens. When I used the chemical hand-warmer packets with the muff, even sub-zero temperatures posed no problem. However, because the muff doesn't allow the use of the hands at all without removing them from the protective warmth, I prefer mittens.

Just a word on the chemical heating packets. Recent years have brought a proliferation of these disposable little marvels, each generation working better than the previous. They flat work, providing clean, odorless heat for hours, some even all day. When placed in reasonably warm gloves, as long as they are a bit oversized, they will keep your hands quite comfortable in bitter cold. In mittens, the cold-hand problem can be completely eliminated with heating packets. I've also used the type designed for boots. While they help, they tend to be a bother when walking and don't have the longevity of the larger hand and body packets.

THE HEAD

It has often been said, "the best way to keep your feet warm is to wear a hat." There's truth in that statement. Keeping the head warm does wonders for keeping the rest of the body toasty. A lot of heat can be lost through the head if it's not properly protected. For the deer hunter, keeping the head warm comes at the cost of compromised hearing and sight, at least to some degree. But if it's cold enough, that can seem like a small enough price to pay.

To be honest, I've never found a perfect solution for the head, certainly not an all-in-one answer. I don't particularly like hoods that are attached to coats. They limit side-to-side vision, both by physically blocking it and because the hood usually doesn't turn with the head when looking to the side. If that weren't enough, every time you turn your head the "noise" of your head rubbing against the relatively stationary hood is transmitted directly to your nearby ears, effectively deafening you. Plus, most hoods are uncomfortable when used for long periods because they tend to bind and put constant down-pressure on your noggin. However, some of the garment makers have finally figured this out and are making much better fitting hoods now. If you plan to use a coat-attached hood as primary protection, be certain the hood is properly designed, not an afterthought.

While I've found no single answer, I have managed to put together a combination of apparel that gets the job done nicely, even if the end results make me look so ridiculous that my mama wouldn't claim me. But then again, I seldom bump into her in the sub-zero wilds. The beginning point of my headgear is an insulated cap with earflaps. I prefer one with a bill to help keep snow and rain off my glasses, to block the sun and to help shield my face when deer are near. The cap I wear mostly is insulated with Thinsulate and lined with Gore-Tex, which in freezing weather is far more valuable as a wind-stopper than as a water barrier. The earflaps, which fold up and snap over the top of the cap when not in use, are lined with warm-feeling simulated shearling, a feature I really like. But, the cap is just the beginning.

Next comes the full-length facemask. I've used two different types. One has holes cut for the eyes and mouth and comes with a raised nose ridge. This one has a wool-blend body with a Polarfleece face. The other, made with an inner lining of polypropylene and an outer shell of wool, has a single big slit for the eyes. Because I wear glasses, I prefer the latter, plus it allows for a better view. I wear the facemask only when necessary, which is just about anytime the wind is in my face or the temperature is 10 degrees or below, and I'm never without it. Often, I'll pull it over my cap for added warmth and for added coverage on my neck and face. When I want full-face protection, I put the facemask on first then snug my cap down on top of it, a most ridiculous-looking arrangement.

The last item for keeping the head warm is so wonderfully effective and versatile that I'm surprised it took me so long to discover it. (Actually, my wife showed it to me.) It is now standard equipment on my cold-weather forays. I'm speaking of a wool scarf. When my wife gave me her six-foot-long, eight-inch-wide lamb's wool scarf, I suddenly found the missing element necessary for upstairs warmth. There are other neck-warming garments available, like pullover neck sleeves and even turtle-neck underwear, but I haven't found anything as versatile as a lengthy scarf.

My standard use of the scarf is to simply wrap it around my neck a couple of times and then tuck the tails down my coat collar. It's amazing the warming effect this has, both by warming the neck, which is a source of considerable heat loss, and by acting as a seal to prevent heat loss from the upper body. Additionally, the scarf can be spread out and part of it pulled up on the lower face for protection there, leaving the eyes unencumbered. The scarf is especially effective when used in combination with the insulated cap with earflaps and will eliminate the need for a

When sitting for long periods in subzero weather, you want to wear all the clothes you can get on...at least right up to the point where you can no longer move well enough to hunt. Heavy outer clothing, especially, tends to restrict freedom of movement, but the Raven Wear outfit I have on here is about the least restrictive I've tried. Photo by Brent Mitchell.

facemask except in the coldest weather. A scarf can literally make the difference between a barely tolerable day in the cold and a quite comfortable, thank you, day in the frigid netherlands.

THE BODY

Now to the body. Layering is obviously the byword. I start with two pairs of insulated underwear. One pair is medium weight and the other is heavy or expedition weight...and a size larger than the first pair to fit over it. In bitter weather, I often wear a third top. I prefer tops with two buttons at the collar so I can release some body heat when active. Many materials will keep you warm, and almost any of the new space-age synthetics are jam-up. Look for something that is, obviously, warm, wicks away moisture and tends to slide on the skin so that it doesn't bind when sitting, walking or raising your arms.

After the underwear comes the intermediate garments. For me, that begins with a shirt and pants made of wool or one of the wool-like synthetics such as Worsterlon. (In the severest cold, wool is still my choice.) Then, I wear some type of layering sweater or jacket (even a vest will serve here) for the purpose of sealing the upper body from heat loss. I look for a couple of things here. One, it must be sufficiently light and flexible to allow easy movement when the outer garment(s) is added. The Polarfleece-type materials really shine here. Wool, especially wool sweaters, and down can also work well in this application. Two, the jacket or sweater should have some type of breathable wind barrier, like Gore-tex, Windstopper, Dry-Plus or some other such fabric, especially if the outer coat doesn't have windproofing. A breathable, windproof membrane greatly enhances the heat-retention of a garment, especially in windy conditions. If it's really cold, I'll sometimes wear a down vest under the windproof jacket or sweater for extra warmth.

There's a reason I normally prefer windproofing as part of the intermediate layer as opposed to the outer garment. That reason is noise. In the past, windproof membranes have been somewhat "crinkly," thus movement renders more noise than is tolerable at close quarters in the almost supernaturally quiet Northwoods. However, newer versions of windproofing are very quiet, almost noiseless. So, the option does exist to include the windproofing in the outer garment, but you must choose the right material.

On to the outer garments—the heavy artillery, if you will. Layering in several relatively thin layers definitely works, but when sitting for long periods in numbing cold, plain old bulk is called for to keep out the cold and hold in the warmth. To do this, I rely on either bib-type overalls in combination with a heavy parka or full-length coveralls. No matter how well insulated, I don't like regular waist-height pants as well as bib overalls or coveralls because pants tend to allow the cold to permeate the cold-sensitive kidney region just above the waist. I suppose my preference leans toward the bib/parka combination over full-length coveralls. Bibs and a parka are easier to get on and off, offer a bit more flexibility and don't tend to bind as much as coveralls when sitting. However, coveralls are certainly fine.

Besides the obvious need to be adequately large, the outer garment must be both warm and quiet. It's the quiet part that is often the limiting factor. Down, for instance, is still about the warmest thing going for its weight, but down garments have traditionally been noisy because of the nylon liner used to hold the down in place. Nowadays, some down outer garments have been quietened down considerably by using noise-dampening fleece-type exteriors and/or by employing softer, quieter liners for the down. For both down and windproof garments, just be sure about their decibel level before going to the woods. A garment that's a little noisy in the store is going to sound like a rushing river in the silent Northwoods. New garments, especially, tend to be noisy. A little breaking in, or a washing when appropriate, usually will quieten them down.

Wool is very quiet, and as a parka exterior, it's hard to beat. Combine wool with an insulating material like Thinsulate, and you've got a very functional outer garment. I wore just such a parka for years in Canada, and it served me well. My only complaint about wool outer coats is weight. Thick wool is heavy, so much so that it restricts movement somewhat. Worsterlon and fleece are also good exterior materials. They are both very quiet and, if insulated with the right stuff, can be adequately warm. Actually, the list of acceptable materials for outer garments is long, but after trying many alternatives, I didn't think I would find anything I liked better than my wool/Thinsulate coat...until I found Raven Wear.

A few years back, a friend named Brantley Kemp, who researches whitetail stuff more than anyone I know, told me about a lady in Alberta who was making clothes especially for hunting that frigid land. Knowing that Canadians as a group hardly give notice to weather that would make my blood ice up, I figured I had better look into clothing that the natives thought was warm. Brantley gave me the number for Raven Wear, and I called owner Susan Hindbo and ordered the "Rifle Hunter Anti-Freeze System." The name itself was enough to make me fork out the nearly $500 for it. For my money, I got a parka, bib overalls, a watch cap and Susan threw in a vest. The garments had a fleece exterior and were insulated with a lining of thick sherpa, a synthetic material that looks and feels like soft lamb's wool. One of the first things I noticed about these garments was their weight. Despite being encouragingly thick, the parka was much lighter than my wool/Thinsulate coat, and a whole lot less cumbersome and restrictive.

For years now, I have used Raven Wear almost exclusively on my

Canadian excursions, as well as a bunch in Montana. The warmth-to-weight ratio is excellent. Susan puts really big pockets everywhere you need them, which I like, and cuts the fit so the garments are roomy enough to go over a stack of other clothes. As you would expect with fleece and sherpa, Raven Wear is almost totally silent. While many other garments are warm and quiet, the thing that sets Raven Wear apart is the freedom of movement allowed by the soft, relatively light material. The only beef I ever had with Raven Wear was that on windy days or when riding ATVs or snowmobiles to stands, the wind would penetrate the garments. A couple of years ago, I suggested to Susan that she look into adding a quiet windproofing of some kind. She did so and now offers as an option ComforMax® IB Wind Barrier, a thin, soft, windproof fabric that stays quiet even in extreme cold. With that addition, I don't know of a warmer, more comfortable, less restrictive outer garment with which to take on sub-arctic weather. Susan offers a wide variety of garments at Raven Wear in many popular camo patterns, as well as in white and blaze orange. She can be reached at Raven Wear, Box 411, Caroline, Alberta Canada T0M 0M0.

Obviously, it takes less to keep warm from the waist down than it does from the waist up. For this reason, the lower body garment, in the case of the bib/parka combo, can be somewhat lighter and less bulky than the parka. In other words, there is greater latitude in selection. For years in Canada, I wore bibs with a cotton exterior and Hollofil insulation. They kept me warm in all but the most miserable weather. If my parka had been the same material, I probably would have chattered my teeth to nubs long ago. Since I've been wearing the Raven Wear bib overalls, a cold lower body has not been something requiring much attention.

All this garb should be enough to keep you fairly warm for quite a while in biting cold, but if you stay inactive long enough, the cold will somehow seep through. There is, however, one more move to keep the icy tentacles at bay beyond depending only on what you wear to the stand. That move is carry an add-on level to be put on once in the stand. Not having to walk with it on opens up all kinds of options for staying warm.

One of the first things I tried was a sleeping bag. As for keeping warm, it worked great. But, there were some problems, like standing up, turning around, getting into and out of it, keeping it in place when unzipped and using my arms for glassing, rattling or shooting. A sleeping bag just wasn't designed to accommodate the needs of a hunter, but the concept of an insulated full-body suit is certainly valid. Seeing the need for such a product, Cabela's came out with their Canadian Coversuit, described in their catalog as a "sleeping bag with suspenders," an apt description. I immediately gave this a try. The suspenders, along with some additional features, made it more practical that a traditional sleeping bag, but there was still room for improvement.

A relatively new product called the Heater Body Suit made by Heater Clothing, Inc., (1600 Granite St., Winston Salem, NC 27107) has pushed the envelope even further. The Heater Body Suit, which retails for about $250, is basically a big set of heavily insulated coveralls designed to go over everything, boots and all. Instead of being a bag, the suit has legs, allowing some mobility in the stand. It's fairly easy to get on and off. Once in place, the suit offers full-body coverage all the way up to the neck and is very warm and quiet. I have spent many all-day vigilances in Canada snuggly bundled in this get-up without ever getting cold. We had two Heater Body Suits in a Saskatchewan camp of eight one year when the mercury almost lost itself in the little bulb at the bottom of the thermometer. Fisticuffs nearly broke out every morning over who was going to get to wear one of the suits that day. They work.

One of the best features of this suit is the quiet, easy-open zipper that can be unzipped instantly simply by pushing out on the suit from the inside, allowing quick use of the hands for glassing, shooting or whatever. Suspenders keep the suit from falling down when opened for action. The suit comes with an extra pair of booties that goes over your hunting boots before inserting them into the suit. These booties serve to both insulate and keep the suit clean. The outfit can be rolled up for carrying and weighs about three pounds. Like any such add-on layer, the Heater Body Suit is a bit of a pain to lug around and get on and off, but when the goal is to stay warm and functional during long periods in numbing cold, a little inconvenience is a small price to pay.

It's an inescapable fact that some of the largest bucks in the world live in bitterly cold climates. Donning all the garb we've discussed, chore though it may be, should make the frigid temperatures at least tolerable. If it doesn't...well, have you considered South Texas?

Chapter Twenty-Six

Strategies for Top-End Bucks

I AGONIZED OVER WHAT TO DO about the buck before me. Now that the red Texas predawn sky had bled out to the pale gray of first day I could see him clearly, and he was big! As I watched him stand guard over his doe, I argued the case in my mind.

Shoot or hold out for something better? Only the second day of the hunt. Five more to go. The best rutting activity should still be ahead. But wow, he's good! I can only take one buck, though. Is he the one? Light's better now. I'll look him over one more time.

Though the buck was 150 yards away, my 10X Leicas gave me a 15-yard look. The spread was the most eye-catching feature of his all-around impressive antlers. He was wide...at least 26 inches. His mass was good but not extraordinary, about 17 inches of circumference measurements per side. The squared-off rack assured long beams, probably around 25 inches. The brow tines were average, maybe four inches. His G-2s, however, were exceptional, perhaps a foot. His G-3s were slightly shorter, near 11 inches. Then came the rub—he had a five-inch G-4 on his right side but was slick on his left.

The missing G-4 four was the only reason the buck was still standing vigil over the doe, but was that reason enough to hold out for something better? After all, the 9-pointer scored in the 160s. That's a trophy by any standard, but I knew the vast thorn brush of this fabulous ranch

When hunting top-end bucks, you're only after the biggest of the big. Top-enders like this 192 6/8-point non-typical I shot in South Texas represent a tiny percent of the total buck population. Photo by Mark Lubin.

held the potential for even better bucks. With utmost reluctance, I played the long odds and moved on in search of that veritable needle in the haystack—a top-end whitetail.

If trophy hunting is the graduate course of deer hunting, then hunting top-end bucks is the doctorate course of trophy hunting. A hunter after a top-end buck must maintain the opportunity to kill the biggest buck around for the longest possible time, but that opportunity comes at a cost. Lots of bucks, sometimes even trophy bucks, must be passed up without any assurance that a top-end buck will ever come along. In fact, it is entirely possible that a top-end buck may not even live in the immediate area you're hunting. Time, hard work and dogged determination, not to mention considerable skill and experience, are necessary to make the odds of success worth all the effort, frustration and perhaps even monetary expense.

What exactly is a top-end buck? To answer that, let's go back to our definition of a trophy—a buck at least 3 1/2 years of age with antlers large enough to rank him among the better bucks consistently harvested in a given area. Under that definition, a mature buck representing the top, say, 10 to 20 percent of area bucks (of all ages) could rightfully be considered a trophy. The more demanding a trophy hunter is, the lower the percentage becomes for what he considers a trophy. If you take this concept out to its ultimate end when, say, less than five percent, perhaps even as low as two or three percent, of the buck population qualifies as a potential shooter, then you've moved from simply hunting trophy bucks to hunting top-end bucks.

(In the next chapter, we will talk about an animal I call the "secretive super buck." This buck is not only an anomaly in antler size, but more importantly, he is also an anomaly in behavior. The secretive super buck's shy, reclusive nature, even to the point of not actively participating in the rut, makes him a unique animal. While he is a part of the overall universe of top-enders, in this chapter we are really only concerned about the biggest of the big within the context of "normal bucks," those that follow the typical behavioral pattern of mature whitetail bucks, which are plenty reclusive enough.)

The challenge of hunting top-end bucks should be apparent. Hunting any mature whitetail buck is hard enough. In *trophy* hunting, the target elevates to include only those mature bucks that are larger than average. When hunting *top-end* bucks, you're after only the biggest of the trophy bucks. As you move further up the latter in size, not only are there fewer animals to hunt, but they are increasingly more difficult to hunt. By the time you get to top-end whitetails, you're hunting the rarest and the smartest member of one of the most intelligent clans in the animal kingdom! That's challenge enough for anybody, and the fact is that hunting top-end bucks is not for everybody...or even for all times and circumstances. Let me explain.

FACTORS INFLUENCING SIZE GOALS

I enjoy the challenge of hunting big, smart bucks. I set my size goal as high as the place and circumstances allow. I'm always after trophy bucks, but circumstances don't always allow me to hold out for top-end bucks. Several factors determine how far up the relative size latter I set my goal. Obviously, the place is the primary consideration in terms of

To have any hope of bumping into a monster like this, a hunter must do something to greatly enhance his odds. Chance alone won't cut it when your sights are set on top-end bucks. Photo by Mike Biggs.

absolute size, but here, we're talking about relative size in comparison to what's there. Among the factors that influence my relative size goal are the time available, the huntability of the place, the level of deer activity and the bag limit. Let's briefly consider each.

Time is an essential ingredient in hunting top-end bucks. Even in the best of circumstances, you cannot reasonably expect to quickly find such a rare and reclusive animal as a top-end whitetail. It can happen but don't count on it. The best plan is to do all you can to swing the odds your way and then allow as much time as possible for your number to come up.

The huntability of the place plays heavily into your chances of ferreting out a top-end buck, assuming he is there to start with. Some places are plain hard to hunt. Thick cover, rough terrain, swampy conditions, an absence of major food sources, unbroken tracts of homogenous cover and even being limited to small parcels of land can add a degree of difficulty that makes holding out for one of the biggest bucks around a fool's game.

The level of deer movement greatly affects your chances of shooting a top-end buck. We've already seen how crucial proper timing relative to the fall movement patterns is to the outcome of a hunt. If timing is bad, goals need to be lowered. Weather conditions, hunting pressure, food sources, etc., are all factors to be considered. Then, we have the all-important rut. When hunting top-end bucks, being there when the rut is underway is paramount, unless unique local circumstances override the norm. The rut is about the only time wise old bucks are stupified enough to give us hunters a chance.

As for the bag limit, if I'm limited to one buck, I want to hold out for the biggest buck I've got any kind of reasonable chance to bring home. If two bucks are possible, I may well shoot the first buck I see that meets my trophy standards, and that I like. However, when it comes to filling the second tag, I would keep my 7mm Mag. silent to the last minute in hopes of finding a top-end buck.

TO SHOOT OR NOT TO SHOOT?—THAT IS THE QUESTION

Now, let's put all this together. Hunting top-end bucks is risky business. Even for the best of hunters, there are situations—too little time, poor deer movement, hard to hunt cover, etc.—when the odds are stacked too heavily against him and a choice has to be made. Should he lower his size standards to a level more realistic for the circumstances or continue to hold out for a top-end buck and be prepared to go home empty-handed? There are no right or wrong answers. I've done it both ways. Sometimes my decision worked out well; other times I've regretted my course. That's top-end hunting.

I bring all this up because I've seen the question of what to shoot plague some hunters. Many hunters today have killed enough bucks that their goal is no longer to shoot just any buck. They want a whopper, the bigger the better. And in many places, they are limited to one buck, making the choice of what to shoot an anxiety-wrought experience. I know hunters who set their standards at the very top-end and steadfastly refuse to shoot a buck that doesn't measure up to what amounts to unrealistic expectations. To a man, they are the most frustrated hunters I know. They go year after year without shooting a buck, all the while the tension builds and the enjoyment of the sport seeps away. Oddly, a common trait of these self-abusing individuals is that when the pressure finally builds enough they eventually end up shooting a substandard "mistake" buck while under the blinding influence of anxiety. Even when they do kill a top-end buck once every three coons' ages, the satisfaction hardly offsets the misery of the futile in-between years.

On the other hand, I know those who earnestly desire to be a trophy hunter and long to shoot some of the bigger bucks available to them. But alas, they cannot restrain their trigger finger. When the first nice buck comes along, he's history. Immediately, they regret shooting the buck and wish for another chance, realizing they have squandered opportunity. They, too, are frustrated hunters, but frankly, not as much so as our first example. They at least have the satisfaction of frequent success, even if it's not everything they had hoped for.

My approach lies between these two extremes. I enjoy the sport of deer hunting too much to set unrealistic goals for myself that are certain to bring frustration and all-too-frequent failure. Besides, although it is not politically correct to say it, the kill is integral to the ultimate success and satisfaction of the hunt. Yet, I have no interest in shooting young or substandard bucks. Trophy-sized antlers hold a great fascination for me, as do the animals that carry them. So then, a balance. My strategy is to stay right on the outer edge of realistic probability for success. To do this, I take the time available and the circumstances under which I'm hunting into consideration and set my size goal as high as I think I have a reasonable chance of achieving. As time and circumstances change, so may my size goal.

In recent years, I admit my tendency has been to hold out longer for top-end bucks, especially when I have the luxury of time. Commonly, I'll devote a certain period of time to hunting top-end bucks, and if not successful during that time, I'll readjust my standards. This plan often results in passing up bucks early in the hunt that meet my personal trophy standards, only to wish later on for another chance at them. Of course, passing up acceptable trophies leaves the window open for an even larger, maybe much larger, buck that may indeed come along later. It is that hope that motivates me to devote a substantial amount of my hunting time to top-end bucks. You see, there is a nagging truth that keeps echoing around in my head: As long as my tag remains unfilled, I have a chance to kill the biggest buck in the woods!

DON'T LIKE THE ODDS? LOAD THE DICE!

When I purposely started hunting top-end bucks, it soon became obvious that I needed an edge of some sort to have any hope of acceptable consistency. General hunting techniques and strategies weren't

Chuck Larsen, my old hunting buddy, was lucky enough to have caught a glimpse of this 186-point non-typical early in a hunt. He then hunted the buck relentlessly until he showed up there again. Finding the whereabouts of a top-end buck represents a giant step toward incurring a taxidermy bill. Photo by author.

enough for animals so wary and rare. Obviously, my first move was to hunt the very best places at the very best times and to learn as much as I could about the unique animal that is the mature whitetail buck. But still, I needed to find a way to somehow focus directly on top-end bucks or to do something to improve on the sorry odds of encountering one. Over time, three different scenarios began to take shape that could significantly improve my chances, and yours, of tagging top-end bucks. Let's look at them.

Hunt A Known Big Buck

The first and best scenario is hunting a known top-end buck, preferably one that you have laid eyes on yourself. When you hear of a big buck from someone else, check it out carefully. More times than not, the supposed whopper buck sightings I've followed up on have been disappointing. Obviously, this strategy depends heavily on intensive scouting, both in-season and out. Ideally, the buck would have been seen more than once. Multiple sightings narrow-in on his range and can give valuable insight about his travel patterns. Also, a single sighting might have no relevance to where the buck should be hunted. The closer to the actual hunting time you have verified sightings, the better. Bucks can change their range and travel patterns considerably from one time of the year to another.

Once you're onto a top-end buck, the time has come to figure him out and come up with a plan to kill him. This can be tricky. You want to learn all you can about the buck without disturbing him. If you harass him too much, you run the risk of moving him out of the area, changing his travel pattern or making him nocturnal. For this reason, I do as much advance "scouting" as I can with topo maps and aerial photos or from a distance using binoculars before hitting the ground to look for sign, usually during midday and in places where I'm not likely to blunder into the buck. A top-end buck won't tolerate many mistakes, but you've got to burn the necessary boot leather to nail down his pattern. I consider facing off against one particular giant whitetail buck to be near the very pinnacle of hunting challenges and experiences.

Hunt The Biggest Sign Around

The second scenario is like the first, except that instead of hunting a known top-end buck you're hunting exceptionally large sign *possibly* belonging to a top-end buck. This is a distant second choice to having seen the buck but beats hunting blindly by a country mile. One big plus is that when you find the sign you've already got a leg up on patterning the buck, though much work remains to be done. One minus is that big sign does not always translate into big racks, especially top-end racks. But short of seeing the buck, really big sign, especially out-sized rubs, is the most promising indicator available that you may be onto a top-end buck.

Just to keep things in their proper perspective, remember this: If you do everything right and catch up with an old buck making big sign and he turns out *not* to be a top-ender, that doesn't diminish the accomplishment and certainly doesn't mean he's not a trophy, at least to you! When you hunt down a mature whitetail based on unraveling his pattern from sign, you will have the satisfaction of knowing, whether or not you pull the trigger, that you earned the right to a "prized memento of a highly valued personal accomplishment," as one dictionary defines "trophy." For me, just knowing I've outmaneuvered an old whitetail on his home court is often trophy enough…and with an unburned tag still in my pocket, I get to try to do it all over again!

"Inventory" Lots Of Bucks

The last scenario does not depend on having already located either a buck or promising sign. It is a strategy dependent on math. The idea is that if you look over (what I call "inventory") enough bucks, the odds are that one of them eventually will be a top-ender. It works like this: Since top-end bucks represent a certain percentage of the buck population, say two percent (1 in 50), then if you could look over 50 bucks, the odds say one of them will be top-end. Or if you could see 25 bucks, you would have a 50 percent chance that one of them would be a shooter, and so on. (Actually, since trophy bucks, and especially top-end bucks, are much harder to encounter than lesser bucks, the math doesn't work that way, but we'll assume it does to keep it simple.) Following this logic, the more bucks you can look over, the better your chances of finding a top-end buck. The objective, then, is to come up with a way to see lots of bucks and let the numbers work for you. Doing that very thing (in places with really big bucks) is a major part of my top-end strategy. I am always looking for an angle, some type of edge that will allow me to inventory lots of bucks so that the rather daunting math of top-end hunting will swing more in my favor.

Sometimes, special situations exist that allow hunters to inventory an extraordinary number of bucks. For instance, an undisturbed major feeding area may attract a high percentage of area deer. Where baiting is legal, as in Saskatchewan, Texas and a few Southeastern states, the potential to attract deer can be considerable, especially where no agricultural crops or other concentrated food sources compete. Unique topography or cover layouts may funnel large numbers of deer through a bottleneck where they can be observed. Perhaps a shooting lane of some type transverses one or more major deer travel routes. Occasionally, bucks respond particularly well to rattling, allowing lots of bucks to be seen in a short time. Waterholes in hot, dry country may lure in lots of bucks. Any of these special situations could allow a hunter to inventory a high number of bucks, and when I find such unique situations, I am quick to take

While hunting one of the best ranches in South Texas, I looked over 140 bucks before shooting this 170-class 10-pointer. Hunting top-end bucks often requires passing up many good trophies in hopes of finding an outstanding animal. Sometimes, it means going home empty-handed. Photo by Bob Zaiglin.

advantage of them.

There are times when you have to be rather creative to look over any number of mature bucks. Such was the case in Central Canada a few years ago. A scheduling conflict had forced me to move my hunt forward to the late pre-rut and the earliest beginnings of the scraping period. Typical of that time, daytime deer activity was light. After several days of trying all the usual things (not just me but also the seven others in camp), it was obvious that a change of some sort was called for. I lay in bed that night mulling over the situation.

The best buck sign is around the many alfalfa fields. No surprise there. But, the mature bucks are not coming into the fields in the evenings until after legal shooting hours. In the mornings, they are leaving at first light, but with the legal shooting time being 30 minutes before sunrise, some are apparently staying in the fields just long enough for a shot. There's a window of perhaps minutes to catch big bucks in the fields in the mornings. I would have to be set up well before daybreak to take advantage of that tiny window. But, which of the dozen or so fields with big rubs should I stake my five-minute hunt on? If only there was a way to know which fields had a big buck loitering around to daybreak. Umm, the moon is approaching the third quarter. It's bright during the latter part of the night. There's enough snow cover to provide a good background in the moonlight. What if I got out well before dawn and sneaked into the fields one at a time until I found a big buck? Then, I could retrieve my rifle and set up before daylight. If he stays late enough, and if he's a shooter, I just might make something happen.

As it turned out, that strategy worked perfectly. During the next several days, I looked over 20 or more bucks before finally shooting a book-class monster. I was even able to put three other hunters on bucks I had seen during the morning twilight minutes on fields. The strategy was simple: Unarmed and traveling light, I would slip into the fields and glass their occupants in the dim moonlight. Though I couldn't precisely judge antler size, I could easily distinguish mature bucks from other deer by their body size and the dark "mass" above their heads. If the deer looked good enough, I would return to the truck, gather my gear, ease into position before daylight and wait. A couple of times, the old boys slipped out before shooting light, but most of the time, they dallied just long enough for me to make out their size and to shoot...if they had been what I wanted. It was truly amazing to see how they would leave the field right on cue at first light, well before most hunters would ever think of getting on-stand.

When special situations exist that allow you to inventory lots of bucks, not only have the mathematical odds of encountering a top-ender increased, but just seeing lots of bucks guarantees plenty of plain old fun. Unfortunately, because these special situations to look over a multitude of bucks are unique, they can't be counted on. So, I have come to rely on a strategy that allows me to take matters into my own hands to create the opportunity to encounter more bucks even if a "special situation" doesn't exist. That strategy is aggressive "slip-hunting."

Though we've already discussed this strategy, a recap is warranted here. The idea behind aggressive slip-hunting is to cover as much good deer country as possible at a pace that will allow you to see the deer, at least many of them, before they see you. The ideal setup calls for fairly open cover (visibility of 75 or more yards), relatively quiet travel routes, lots of room to ramble and, preferably, deer distracted by the rut. Flexibility and keen observation are required. The pace, the route and even the tactic of the moment will have to change frequently to suit the cover, terrain, walking conditions and deer sightings and sign. If conditions are right and the hunter does his part, this is an excellent way to inventory lots of bucks.

I frequently employ this strategy in western Montana and average seeing about five bucks a day. In a week's time, if my legs hold out that long, I should see around 30 bucks. The odds are good that one of them will be a top-ender. In South Texas, aggressive slip-hunting, often combined with rattling, will net an average of perhaps 10 sightings a day. If I use a high-rack (an elevated platform mounted on a vehicle, a South Texas invention) to inventory bucks, my daily sightings may increase to 15 or 20 bucks. In a week, that means I may be able to pick from more than 100 bucks! Even if I'm hunting a top-end buck that represents only a mere one percent of the population, you can see that my odds of bumping into him are quite favorable.

Aggressive slip-hunting could be described as having a twofold objective, although if the first one is met the second is moot. The first is to shoot the buck when you initially encounter him. I've been lucky enough to do this on a number of occasions, but sometimes, this aggressive style of hunting results in a poor chance for a shot. There may not be sufficient time; the buck could be on the move; there may not be a rifle rest handy; and so on. (This is particularly true with the Texas high-rack, which is of more value in finding a buck to hunt than in providing an opportunity for a shot.) That's okay. At least you've seen him, which is the second objective. Just having found a top-end buck puts you light years ahead of the game…and back to our first and best scenario—hunting a known buck!

Now, back to the Texas hunt that started this chapter. Was passing up the big 9-pointer a good decision or not? I got lucky on that hunt. With time running out and the 9-pointer haunting my every thought, I shot a 23-inch 10-pointer that just missed the record book! He was the 140th buck I had seen that week and, from the way my legs felt, came on the 140th mile I had covered!

Chapter Twenty-Seven

The Mystery of the Secretive Super Buck

T HROUGHOUT MY HUNTING CAREER, a singular aspect of the whitetail deer has intrigued me more than any other. Specifically, why is it that bucks with truly exceptional racks often behave so differently from "normal" mature bucks? Too often to be coincidence, these bucks are more secretive, sedentary, passive and nocturnal than other mature bucks. They seem to leave relatively little sign, and rare is the time when they are caught chasing does, making rubs and scrapes and doing the other "buck things." When, or more accurately if, their presence is known, it is usually through a chance encounter or simple fluke.

A giant, super secretive, darn-near unkillable buck—sounds like a myth or perhaps the contrivance of a bunch of over-imaginative hunters with too much camp time on their hands. But, the fact is that such animals do exist. True, they're not common anywhere, but they do show up from time to time, especially in herds with good age structures. For me, these secretive super bucks represent one of whitetail hunting's greatest mysteries and add a most intriguing aspect to our sport.

In all likelihood, this is a classic secretive super buck. He is certainly super! Adan Alverez killed this 239 5/8-point non-typical on Texas' King Ranch in January 1998. The buck was shot in the post-rut, was relatively small-bodied (field-dressed just over 100 pounds), didn't appear to be an aggressive breeder and is the product of a herd with lots of older age-class bucks—all characteristics of passive super bucks, one of nature's most intriguing animals. Photo courtesy of Adan Alverez and North American WHITETAIL.

I've spent long hours mulling over the matter in an attempt to understand what makes these mysterious bucks tick. Why do they exist? Why are they so big? Why do they behave so differently? I've discussed these questions with the best deer hunters and the most respected biologists on the continent. I've studied the animals ceaselessly, keeping notes on both my own observations and those of others. I've tested theory after theory against the realities trying to find fits. Though important parts of the puzzle surfaced from time to time, for years my best attempts to come up with an overall explanation that really worked were thwarted. Sure, it would have been easy to buy into the claims of some that these bucks were so smart that they realized, perhaps by looking at their reflection in a waterhole, that they had whopper antlers and that hunters were after them, and thus they behaved differently. Unable to accept that theory,

Secretive super bucks are "anomalies" in both antler size and behavior, but certainly not all exceptionally large bucks behave in a passive, secretive manner. Some are "normal" bucks, doing all the things you would expect an active prime breeder to do, including chasing the girls around. This 186-point nontypical was hot after a doe when I shot him. Photo by Steve Spears.

my search continued for something that made sense. Now, I believe I'm onto something.

I don't claim to have all the answers, and my theory is just that— a theory. But, it pretty well matches up with the facts and seems to account for many of the unique aspects of secretive super bucks. If the theory is correct, at least we'll know what we're up against when we set our sights on the biggest of the big and the slipperiest of the slippery. Let's begin this discussion by better describing the buck we're talking about.

WHAT IS HE AND HOW IS HE DIFFERENT?

Our animal is unique in two ways—exceptional antler size and abnormal behavior. Certainly, not every buck sporting whopper antlers fits our description of a secretive super buck, nor does every buck that behaves abnormally. Some giant bucks exhibit classic behavioral patterns for mature whitetails, though frankly, not as many as you might expect. And, some bucks with mediocre antlers may well have an "eccentric" lifestyle much like the secretive super buck, but without the outstanding antlers, nobody notices. In this discussion, we're concerned only with bucks that are anomalies both in antler size and behavior. Let's look one by one at the traits and behavioral differences of these bucks.

The antler size of the bucks we're concerned with is outside the "normal" size parameters of a herd. Statistically, such over-endowed bucks hardly exist in a herd. They are very top-end bucks that represent only one or two percent, if that, of the *older* age-class bucks and only a fraction of a percent of the *total* number of bucks in a herd. By no means are all of them B&C bucks, though many bucks in the record book undoubtedly fit the bill. And, size alone doesn't make it. But when a buck not only breaks rank with the *size norms* for antlers, but also breaks rank with herd *behavioral norms*, then he's our boy—the secretive super buck!

The traditional cornerstones determining antler size are age, nutrition and genetics. Of these, age and nutrition can be eliminated as factors unique to secretive super bucks. Their exceptional antler size is in comparison to other mature, similar-aged bucks within the *same* herd. And, all the deer within that herd have access to the same feed, so better nutrition isn't the answer either. Genetics can partially explain the *size* of our bucks but not their behavioral differences. Given all this, something other than age, nutrition and even genetics must be at play, at least in regards to behavior and perhaps even size.

Super secretive bucks seem to be primarily byproducts of herds with good buck age structures. At first glance, simple math would seem to account for this. The more older bucks, the greater the odds that one of them is going to be a giant, perhaps even a secretive one. I think that's part of it, and the fact that many of these bucks are really old, say 7 1/2 or 8 1/2, would seem to argue that their existence is just a function of getting enough of them into the upper age classes for the odds to kick in. But, I think it's more than just that. In fact, I believe that a high number of mature bucks—specifically, the competition between them—is largely responsible for creating the conditions necessary to turn out at least some of these super bucks, as I'll explain later.

Our mysterious bucks are very secretive and rarely seen on the move during daylight hours. They don't appear to range over long distances. In fact, *most of their time seems to be spent in relatively small, secluded areas.* These bucks actually appear reluctant to enter high-use deer areas, but they are occasionally seen shyly lurking around the periphery of such areas. To make matters worse, they leave relatively little buck sign. What sign they do leave tends to be localized and is usually in the form of less-than-impressive rubs. Their sedentary lifestyle accounts for why encounters with these bucks usually are the result of a fluke or of somebody hunting in an offbeat way or place. It's easy to see why they can live right under man's nose without ever being seen.

While locating and seeing one of these bucks can be most difficult, once contact is made *they sometimes appear passive and calm and don't exhibit the hair-trigger jitters characteristic of mature whitetails.* Of the few such bucks I've killed, nearly all stood and stared calmly as scrambled to get off a shot.

Seldom are they seen participating in classic rutting activity, such as chasing or trailing does and making rubs and scrapes. Where hunting season overlaps the rut, most mature bucks are killed because of some type of rutting behavior, particularly chasing and trailing does. Yet, few of the truly great bucks are killed while engaged in aggressive rutting activity. Most have entered the Great Hereafter under extenuating circumstances of some sort. This tells me something is weird about these giants of the species.

Along those same lines, *secretive super bucks appear to seldom fight.* When in the presence of other mature bucks, which doesn't seem to happen often, they appear submissive, despite superior headgear. Their lack of aggression probably is the reason why, even after the rut, their antlers are seldom chipped and broken, as is the case with most bucks. On the rare occasion they do get into a scrap with another mature buck, they seem to invariably come out on the short end. Texas photographer Mike Biggs captured a classic case in-point on film when he caught a super 185-point non-typical and a bullish 125-class 8-pointer in a skirmish. The larger-bodied 8-pointer quickly defeated the much bigger-antlered 13-pointer. Recently, I saw some awesome video footage shot at night in a cornfield in Illinois that featured a 220-class non-typical mixing it up with a 150-class 10-pointer. The more aggressive 10-pointer won.

Interestingly, *secretive super bucks tend to be smaller in body size than many other mature bucks. Additionally, they normally lack the bullish, masculine features of a prime rutting buck and can be "steerlike" in appearance.* Sometimes, they are sleek and fat, even during and after the rut, and I've even seen a few that had dewlaps. Occasionally, they have dried patches and strips of velvet still on their antlers well into the fall, even late in the rut. My friend, David Shashy, from Ocala, Florida, filmed just such a buck on a Texas ranch we were hunting. After shooting his buck, David retired with his video camera to an out-of-the-way food plot and recorded nearly an hour in the life of what appears to be a classic secretive super buck. Despite the fact that the rut was in full swing, the huge 10-pointer was sleek and steerlike, clearly lacking the musculature characteristic of a rutting buck. He even had a distinctive dewlap to accompany his sagging belly. To top it off, black, dried velvet covered most of his tine tips and hung in strips from several spots along his ample beams. David described the buck as being very calm and lethargic. The fact that he was later killed by the ranch owner's wife very near the food plot points to a homebody nature characteristic of secretive super bucks. The buck, by the way, grossed 173!

A most telling fact is that *many of these bucks are either infertile or have low virile semen counts.* In fact, some super bucks even have obvious testicle damage. A program was initiated a few years ago in Texas to collect semen from super bucks immediately after they were harvested for the purposes of artificial insemination. However, the program was soon abandoned because the virile sperm count of most of the super bucks was too low for dependable conception. And, a few were altogether sterile.

A disproportionate number of the super bucks are non-typical. I'm not saying that more of these bucks are non-typical than typical. Typicals far outnumber non-typicals in any herd, but the normal relationship of non-typical to typical is heavily skewed in favor of non-typicals when it comes to super bucks. Interesting, I believe that most of the top all-time non-typicals fall into the category of secretive super bucks. Many were not killed by conventional tactics that depend on voluntary deer movement. In fact, a surprising number of world-class non-typicals weren't even killed by a hunter, or known to exist until they were found dead.

Consider, for instance, some of the very biggest non-typicals of all-

Many of the all-time great non-typicals surely fit the mold for secretive super bucks. In fact, a disproportionate number were either found dead or killed as a result of forced movement, as was the case with Iowa's 282-point Raveling buck pictured here. Photo by Dick Idol, courtesy of North American WHITETAIL.

time. The world-record St. Louis buck was found dead, practically in downtown St. Louis. We have no evidence he was ever seen alive. The No.2 Hole-in-the-Horn buck from Ohio was killed by a train on a military base and was unknown until found dead by the tracks. The only two other 300-point-plus bucks we have hard evidence of are known only from sheds, one set from Minnesota and one from Kansas. Neither buck was ever killed. The unofficial No.4, scoring 288 4/8 and also from Ohio, was found dead by a rabbit hunter. The former world-record 284 3/8-point buck from Hill Country Texas, long believed to have been killed by Jeff Benson, now is believed to have actually been found dead based on compelling new evidence. The 282-point Raveling buck from Iowa was killed as a result of forced movement on a deer drive. The list goes on.

(By the way, the Raveling buck has long been considered the "biggest buck ever killed by a known hunter," but he recently lost that title to a 295 6/8-point Mississippi non-typical shot in 1995 by Tony Fulton. Tony shot the new No.3 when the buck ran into a wheat field at last light. Whether he was pushed out or moving on his own I don't know.)

Interestingly, when a true giant is killed in areas not usually known for huge bucks, it is almost invariably a non-typical. Take, for instance, Florida and South Carolina, states not known for big deer. Florida has one B&C, a non-typical, and South Carolina has three B&Cs, two non-typicals and a typical. Alabama has only four typicals on record against six non-typicals. The Texas Hill Country, noted for vast numbers of relatively small deer, probably best illustrates the point. This region has practically no record typicals to its credit but has booked over a dozen non-typicals, some of which are high-ranking.

One characteristic of these bucks that long baffled me is that *they tend to show up late in the rut, if they show up at all.* Their occasional appearance late in the rut doesn't neces- sarily mean they are engaging in blatant rutting activity; in fact, they rarely are. Yet, more often than any other time, they occasionally loiter around in daylight hours toward the tail end of rut, which certainly is not the best time for general rutting activity or to kill a mature buck.

> *One characteristic of these bucks that long baffled me is that they tend to show up late in the rut, if they show up at all.*

Interestingly, the second best time to happen upon a super buck is during the post-rut, especially in cold climates when major food sources are pre- sent. Through our big deer pipeline, we at *WHITETAIL* magazine see the pattern of late season appearances played out every year across North America. They just don't tend to show up often during the peak of rut- ting activity.

So, we have painted a picture of a giant buck that behaves well outside the norms of classic whitetail behavior, particularly, and this is key, during the rut. You see, the behavior we've described for the secre- tive super buck—secretive, sedentary and largely nocturnal—is really not all that different from the behavior of *any* other older age-class buck *out- side* the rut. But when passion seizes them during the rut, normal white- tail buck behavior changes drastically and even seasoned old bucks typi- cally let down their guard somewhat. However, when it comes to secre- tive super bucks, even *during* the rut their usual cautious, reclusive behav- ior doesn't change much, making them darn-near unkillable.

THE BENEFITS OF NOT ACTIVELY RUTTING

So, we come to the crux of the difference in the secretive super bucks—they don't appear to aggressively participate in the rut. It is this singular aspect that separates them from other "normal" over-sized bucks, but does the lack of active participation in the rut really explain their unkillability and why so many true giants seem to fit this description? Quite possibly, but it takes some explaining to put the whole picture together. That explaining needs to start with a review of the rut and how it affects bucks behaviorally and physically.

By nature, old bucks are cautious, secretive animals. Only when feeding on major food sources during the summer months and perhaps during the winter stress time are old bucks likely to be reasonably visible. Otherwise, once the bachelor groups breakup in the early fall, the older bucks are pretty much loners, spending most of their time in a familiar, well-defined core area. Much of their movement is at night or in protective cover. But for most bucks, this secretive lifestyle takes a dramatic turn once the breeding urge takes hold, changing their attitude, priorities and behavior.

The changes are first manifest in attitude, specifically increased aggression and restlessness. They start rubbing and mock-fighting bushes and small trees. In time, through both exercise and the steroid effect of testosterone, they build up their bodies to prime condition, as characterized by thick, bulging necks and heavily muscled shoulders. Soon, wanderlust sets in. They begin expanding the time and distance of their travels as they check out various doe groups and begin making scrapes and rubs at these and other locations. At this point, their priorities shift from food and security to the irresistible lure of the rut. From now until the end of the rut, an old buck's cautious nature is compromised and he is vulnerable.

As breeding time approaches and the expanded ranges of mature bucks overlap more frequently, buck fights become more common. Feeding and resting take a backseat to traveling, scraping and jockeying for hierarchical position. The pace becomes increasingly frantic until the first big flurry of does finally enters estrus, sparking what seems like chaos in the whitetail world. The older bucks aggressively compete for breeding rights—seeking, trailing or chasing does long hours each day. With a hot doe as the prize, serious fights, some ending in injury and even death, often mark encounters by bucks of equal status.

Between the rigors of the rut and the neglect of food and rest, active breeders may lose as much as 25 to 35 percent of their body weight. Their health is often further jeopardized by injuries from fights. I have seen many bucks with serious puncture wounds around their head and neck made from the slashing tines of rut-driven opponents. As a result of all this, active breeders often emerge from the rut emaciated from hunger and overexertion and perhaps badly battered, resulting in "post-rut mortality" losses among active breeders of up to 25 percent in competitive herds.

Given this summary of the rut, what would happen if an older buck *didn't* actively participate in the rut? Two obvious things come to mind. One, he would continue to exhibit his reclusive, sedentary nature right on through the rut. Two, he would come through the rut time with most of his fat reserves and body mass intact, and without the battering experienced by active breeders. As a result of his reclusive lifestyle and better physical condition, he would be less likely to die from either a hunter's bullet or post-rut mortality. Plus, he would be better able to make it through the trying winter months and into spring in good shape, which may account in part for the exceptional antler size of some rut-shy bucks. Let me explain.

We know that a buck's body condition going into the spring, when nutritious food again becomes available, is a key factor in antler growth. Spring is when antler growth begins, and a good start to this process is vital for antlers to realize their full potential in the four short months they have to grow. In order to insure the buck's survival, nature directs spring nutritional intake first to body recovery and second to antler growth. In most cases, winter's cold and/or lack of quality food prevent a rut-stressed buck from recovering then. In fact, depending on the region, their condition usually worsens. So, when the warm days of spring bring a renewed food supply, the body gets first dibs on the nutrition.

If the buck is a prime breeder, much of the initial nutrient intake goes to refurbishing a gaunt and spent physical frame, cutting into what's available for antlers during the vital beginning antler development stage. Being more observable than wild bucks, the price paid in antler growth is frequently seen in older penned or game-farm bucks. When one of these

The thick neck and massive shoulders tell me this is a prime breeder pumped up by testosterone, but typical of many such deer, he has only modest headgear. The rigors of actively participating in the rut can adversely affect a buck's subsequent set of antlers. Photo by Troy Huffman.

bucks, even one in his prime antler-growing years, suddenly gains dominance or is given free reign to breed a high number of does, it is common for the increased stress of being an active breeder to take such a toll on his body that his next set of antlers either fails to increase in size or even drops off. I've also seen this scenario played out a number of times in the wild with aggressive, peak-aged bucks I have kept track of from year to year. The great physical toll of the rut makes it hard for all but the most genetically superior prime breeders to attain giant status and explains why the vast majority of prime breeders fall well within the normal size range of mature bucks in a herd.

Interestingly, younger bucks, 2 1/2 and 3 1/2, that achieve dominance or access to breeding rights normally don't experience this antler leveling or decline because of the overriding influence of moving a year closer to a peak-antler age, and because they probably weren't active breeders the *year before*. Actually, younger bucks often show a sudden jump in antler size when becoming dominant, but whether this is age related or somehow associated with achieving dominance per se I cannot say for sure, though I suspect it's some of both.

In the case of bucks that don't suffer the physical deprivation of the rut and enter spring in good shape, a higher percentage of their nutritional intake is directed toward antler growth during the critical first weeks of spring, giving them a big edge in realizing their maximum antler potential. *If such passive bucks carry genes for big antlers*, and obviously not all will, then they may be on their way to becoming a secretive super buck. Yet, there may well be something else involved as well.

WHAT'S BEHIND PASSIVE BREEDERS?

The question arises: Why don't these bucks get in on rutting festivities? The quick answer is that they don't achieve dominance. And frankly, that appears to be true. But, most normal subdominant bucks sure make every attempt to spread their genes and expend considerable energy in their efforts. However, I find little evidence that the bucks we are talking about ever make a sincere attempt to compete in the breeding ritual. That's not to say they wouldn't take advantage of a lonely, lovesick doe if an easy opportunity arises, but they sure don't seem to pay the price required to actively participate in the rut. Even if they are *chronic* subdominants, despite superior antlers, why don't they make an earnest effort to breed like other bucks, dominant and subdominant? Before we try to answer that question, let's discuss the dominance issue.

The Dominance Issue

In healthy herds with lots of older bucks, dominance most often is claimed by bucks in the prime breeding ages of 4 1/2 to 6 1/2 years. These "prime breeders" are usually the most aggressive, most muscled and biggest bodied, but they may well *not* be the biggest antlered. In fact, they often aren't. I'm amazed how frequently the local bully carries only modest headgear. Of the many serious fights I've watched between mature bucks, most were eventually won by the bigger-bodied buck. In some cases, the bigger-bodied buck also had bigger antlers. If so, he usually won. If the bigger-bodied buck had smaller antlers, he also usually won. If the bucks were the same body size, the most innately aggressive buck nor-mally came out victorious. The outcome didn't seem to depend on antler size. The truth is that for some reason dominant bucks very often seem to be barrel-chested 8-pointers with an attitude.

Recently, some very interesting new information has come to light regarding the effects of dominance in whitetails. We've long known that dominant bucks keep subdominants from having unrestricted access to breeding rights through physical challenges and intimidation. Most expe-rienced hunters have seen subdominant, or satellite, bucks trying to horn-in on a dominant buck's doe while the old man threatens or chases away the would-be interlopers. But, what we haven't known is that dominant bucks can actually *suppress* the rutting *urge* and *activity* of at least *some* subdominants by leaving chemical secretions on rubs, in scrapes and even in their tracks. So great is this suppression factor on some subdominants that it can cause them to behave almost as though they were not actively participating in the rut at all. Clearly, dominance suppression doesn't have such a dramatic effect on all subdominants, but for whatever reason, its impact on some bucks appears to be most telling.

Dominant bucks, and even challenging wannabes, have two dis-tinguishing characteristics. One, they are heavily muscled and bullish. Two, they are active and aggressive. As for their bullish features, bucks are not naturally like this all the time. They work themselves into this state only as the rut approaches. Their muscles swell and bulge just like those of a pumped-up athlete on steroids. As for their aggression, simply put, they have an attitude. Circling in that peculiar stiff-legged sidling walk, with hackles up, ears back, back humped slightly and eyes rolled, they are quick to threaten any competing buck. In these two characteris-tics—pumped-up muscles and aggression (both lacking in our super buck) —we get a hint of the presence of another factor I think is key to unrav-eling the mystery of the secretive super buck. That factor is male hor-mones, primarily testosterone...or in the case of secretive super bucks, the lack thereof.

Hormones At Work

We know that testosterone, which is produced by the testes and adrenal glands, plays an important role in both buck behavior and antler growth. We know that *increased* testosterone levels trigger the onset of rut and causes bucks to be more aggressive, masculine, active and lustful. By contrast, we also know what the *lack* of male hormones can do to an animal's temperament and behavior. Take, for instance, a male dog that is too aggressive, high-strung or far-ranging. What's the normal procedure to calm him down, keep him at home, reduce his competition with other dogs and, most notably, curb his aggression? The answer is castration. What does this do? It cuts back greatly on the production of testosterone. As a result, the dog becomes a passive homebody, usually growing fat and sleek, and is less masculine, competitive and aggressive. (Castration works the same way on cattle, explaining why bulls are made into steers when maximum beef production is the goal.) Sounds familiar, doesn't it? In fact, it sounds just like our super buck!

Additionally, we know that testosterone plays an essential part in antler development, velvet-shedding and antler-casting. We also know that hormonal imbalances can cause weird things to happen to antlers. For instance, the often strangely shaped, velvet-covered antlers of "stag" and "cactus-horned" bucks are products of hormonal imbalances caused by testicle injury or castration. Even in bucks that do develop hard antlers, we know that injury to one or both testes can prompt wild, accelerated (and often non-typical) antler growth. And, the evidence points toward the same thing being true, to varying degrees, of bucks with low testosterone levels *without* obvious testicle damage. Interestingly, it is a documented fact that an occasional buck, especially an older buck that should have long ago demonstrated his genetic antler traits, will suddenly grow a non-typical rack that breaks his previous antler conformation pattern. Such sudden, dramatic departures are unlikely to be triggered by either genetics or nutrition, but hormone changes could definitely be the culprit.

Occasionally, an older buck that should have long ago demonstrated his genetic antler traits will suddenly grow a non-typical rack that breaks his previous antler conformation pattern.

Assuming hormonal imbalances do play into our secretive super buck theory, bucks could bear the affliction for most or all of their lives or they could be thus inflicted later in life. Hormonal imbalances and related fertility problems may be more common in deer than we realize. Having been raised on a cattle farm, I know that low fertility can be an occasional problem with bulls and can smite the best of them, even at an early age. I'll never forget traveling from our Alabama farm to Texas to buy a remarkable young bull of renowned lineage, only to discover several months later that he was practically infertile. I've known of or seen prime-breeding-aged bucks that seemed to fit our description of a secretive super buck. Well-known deer biologist James Kroll killed a 6 1/2-year-old, 190-plus non-typical in East Texas that definitely fit our formula—he only had one testicle! I have killed a 5 1/2 and 6 1/2 that sure fit the bill. Undoubtedly, hormonal imbalances, and secretive super bucks, are not limited to very old bucks only.

Probably more common than lifelong hormonal imbalances are those that accompany the aging process. In the animal kingdom, it is natural for older males to become less sexually active, accompanied by much lower testosterone levels, and to retire to a sedate, solitary life. In deer, these older bucks often are said to be "on the mend" when, relieved of the stress of competing in the rut, they gain weight and become steerlike in appearance.

> *It is natural for older males to become less sexually active...I believe it is very possible that they also may experience a big jump in antler size.*

Given superior genetics, I believe it is very possible that they also may experience a big jump in antler size, assuming they aren't too old to garner in the necessary nutrition. In all likelihood, this is the scenario when an oversized non-typical rack suddenly springs forth from an older buck that hitherto had a basic typical frame. Yet, I don't think late-life hormonal changes produce *only* big non-typicals. An occasional on-the-mend typical with superior genetics may well suddenly blossom into a great typical when relieved of rutting stresses, assuming good nutrition is available. I have killed three bucks I believe fit that category, and all were 7 1/2 or 8 1/2 years old.

THE THEORY IN A NUTSHELL

From all this, we can develop a theory. In a population with lots of mature bucks, an occasional buck with superior genetics comes along that because of a hormonal imbalance and/or inherent subdominant tendencies (they go hand in hand) does not actively participate in the rut.

Some over-sized typicals also fall into the secretive super buck category. This book-class King Ranch 8-pointer had all the characteristics. Note his slender neck and almost feminine appearance. There was no evidence that he was an active participant in the rut. Photo by Amos Dewitt.

Thus, he maintains the characteristic caution and secretiveness of older bucks throughout the breeding period, greatly reducing his vulnerability to hunters. Because this passive buck, whose rutting urge and activity is suppressed by dominant bucks, does not endure the tremendous physical rigors of the rut, he goes into the spring in far better shape than active breeders. This allows him to put more of the critical spring nutrition into antler growth rather than body recovery, giving them a leg up on realizing his genetic potential. Plus, antler growth is somehow further enhanced by the hormonal imbalance itself. The outcome of all this is that rare top-end whitetail called the secretive super buck.

THE DISCOVERY OF THE "MISSING LINK"

Before we put the theory to the test, I want to relate how the last critical piece of the puzzle first came into my possession. It's funny how a little something can suddenly roll back the confusion and make everything fall into place. For me that little piece of information came while hunting on Gary Schwarz's El Tecomate Ranch in South Texas in 1995. I already knew that the secretive super buck did not actively participate in the rut and that hormones played into why, but there were a few things I couldn't make fit. Something else was needed to flesh out my theory on these bucks and pull all the elements together. That something else—a better understanding of the effects of dominance—came in an unexpected way.

Gary had caught glimpses of a huge, wide non-typical (later named "Heart Attack") in February 1993 and again a year later almost to the day. Recognizing the buck as exceptional, Gary began hatching a plan in the spring of 1995 to corral the buck in an enclosure in hopes of spreading his superior genes to the fullest extent possible. The only problem was that it was almost impossible to see the buck, much less keep track of him, despite the fact that he apparently lived in a narrow, pie-shaped corner of the ranch with high fences on two sides. Undaunted, Gary simply ran a gameproof fence across the remaining leg of the triangle. Then, the gate left open, he set an inviting table just inside the enclosure (besides a 20-acre lablab food plot that was already there) and waited.

In July 1995, a set of big tracks joined those of the many does already inside the enclosure and the gate was immediately closed. But soon afterwards, photographer Glen Hayes was staked out at a nearby waterhole *outside* the 80-acre fenced area and guess who showed up—the big non-typical. The gate was opened and the waiting game was on again. In October, another set of big tracks passed through the opening into the fenced area and, on the strength of a recent possible sighting of the non-typical near the entrance by a ranch hand, the gate was again shut. The vigilance for the big non-typical began.

Gary, Glen Hayes, then-ranch manager Mike Hehman and friend Roy York spent hours in search of the mysterious buck. To the disappointment of all, the only buck they saw was a big-bodied, mature 9-pointer scoring around 140, presumably the first buck that had gotten into the pen back in July. He and the 14 or so does entrapped with him were frequently seen moving in the brush or feeding on the lush lablab food plot. But, weeks of searching turned up no sign of the non-typical. When I showed up for a hunt on December 17, the peak of rut, Gary had become very doubtful that the non-typical was in the trap.

Finally, almost resigned to the fact that the non-typical had eluded their capture, Gary gave Roy the go-ahead to hunt the 9-pointer, which was aggressively engaged in rutting activity, figuring there were better bucks on the ranch to breed the does in the enclosure. Amazingly, Roy hunted the 9-pointer hard for three days before finally getting a shot at him. While looking for the mortally wounded buck, Roy saw, you guessed it, the big non-typical, right there in the 80-acre enclosure where he had been for nearly three months completely undetected!

The incredible events up to this point fascinated all involved, especially me. I was seeing a secretive super buck scenario played out right before my eyes in a relatively controlled setup. But, what happened next did more than fascinate me—it provided an invaluable piece to the secretive super buck puzzle that went a long way toward allowing me to fill in some of the most troubling gaps.

Within a matter of days after the 9-pointer's demise, the hitherto invisible, reclusive, timid, nocturnal non-typical suddenly began showing up regularly. He was seen chasing does, feeding on lablab, moving around during daylight hours and doing all the things a mature whitetail buck does during the rut, which was now into its second week. Everybody was shocked. After months of being completely invisible, the big buck had shucked his inhibitions and seemed determined to catch up on missed time—all this immediately after the death of the bullish 9-pointer. (Incidentally, the 9-pointer was 7 1/2 and the non-typical 6 1/2.)

Why? The answer seemed obvious—the 140-class 9-pointer was dominant over the 200-class non-typical and had been suppressing his rutting urge and activity. Sure, I knew about dominance and intimidation, but what I was familiar with depended on some type of direct contact. I had always felt that the dominance of one buck over another was pretty much limited to the time and place of contact. However, the events on Tecomate Ranch proved me wrong.

So great was the suppression by the 9-pointer over the non-typical that the larger-racked buck seemed afraid to show his face during daylight hours and appeared to have abandoned all attempts to participate in the rut. This was not just a *contact* suppression; it was a pervasive suppression of rutting urges and behavior that lasted beyond any direct contact. Just the presence of the dominant buck, and undoubtedly the scent he left through various means, changed the entire behavioral pattern of the sub-dominant non-typical. With this revelation came possible answers I had long sought in the understanding of both the creation and the behavior of the secretive super buck.

Since the events on Tecomate Ranch, I have furthered my under-standing of the power of dominance suppression through conversations with leading biologists and the findings of recent studies on dominance and scent communication in whitetails. Everything I've learned validates what we saw occur with the big non-typical. Specifically, when, and this is an important *when*, an inherently passive buck is involved, a dominant buck can exert so much sway over him that his rutting urge, movement and even his testosterone levels can be suppressed! If such a chronic sub-dominant is carrying the genes for giant antlers, then we may well have the basic formula, at least one of them, for the secretive super buck. I said "at least one of them" because, while dominance suppression is certainly a major player in the super-buck phenomenon in prime-aged bucks, I think age can also lead to an older, on-the-mend buck ending up in the same subdominant position with much the same outcome.

Which comes first in the relationship between hormones and a passive nature—low testosterone levels followed by a timid nature or a timid nature leading to lower testosterone levels? I don't know the answer, and perhaps it doesn't really matter. The fact is that dominance and submission appear to be somehow related to hormone levels and all this contributes to the existence and behavior of our buck. So, with this added to our data bank, let's test what we know, or hypothesize, about dominance, hormones and rutting impact against the known characteris-tics of the secretive super buck (perhaps another good name for this sub-dominant buck is "super beta") and see if it all begins to make sense.

TESTING THE THEORY

We've well established why secretive super bucks sport antlers of exceptional size so we won't cover it again. Let's now go down the list of

This super-wide non-typical has all the earmarks of an on-the-mend old-timer with hormones running a bit amok. Photo by Mike Biggs.

other traits and see if our theory will explain them.

They seem to be byproducts of herds with good buck age structures.
Besides the obvious math involved, the competition between mature
bucks certainly contributes to the creation as super bucks. How? The
more mature bucks, the greater the competition. Greater competition
causes more of the passive *mature* bucks, not just younger bucks, to be
suppressed by the dominance of aggressive prime breeders. The more passive mature bucks there are that *don't* actively participate in the rut, the
greater the odds that one of them will be genetically superior and emerge
as a secretive super buck. In herds with lower competition, the passive

mature bucks have a better chance of participating in the breeding rites by default. As rutting bucks, they are pulled down physically, reducing their chances of achieving full antler potential. Plus, their testosterone levels are undoubtedly elevated by the very act of participating in the rut, causing them to lose whatever advantages lowered hormones mean to enhanced antler growth.

The value of large numbers of older age-class bucks was driven home to me back in the '80s when I had the wonderful privilege of being one of the first to hunt the vast, newly opened King and Kenedy ranches. I had the run of tens of thousands of unhunted acres and was able to look over literally hundreds of relatively naïve bucks. I expected the ranches to be full of really big bucks, but that was not what I found. The ranches were full of *old* bucks, but the vast majority grossed in the 120s and 130s. A 140 was very big on either ranch, and anything over 150 represented less than one percent of the buck population. But then as now, out of that vast pool of older age-class bucks, a giant occasionally pops up that has no business being there. On my first King Ranch hunt, I was lucky enough to take such an animal—an 8-pointer scoring over 170. And just last season on the King Ranch, Adan Alverez pushed the size anomaly envelope to an all-new level when he shot a monster non-typical netting 239 5/8 points! My buck certainly fit the behavioral mold of a secretive super buck, and I have no doubt that the Alverez buck did as well.

They are secretive and largely nocturnal. Let's see, they aren't players in the rut and they are suppressed by dominant bucks—is it any wonder that super betas lay low even when the breeding festivities are underway? Dominance suppression also explains why they are sometimes seen lurking around the periphery of high-use deer areas but seem reluctant to enter such places. They are intimidated by the prospects of encountering a dominant buck.

Once contact is made, super bucks often seem calm and passive. Hormones are at play here. If, as we suspect, our bucks have reduced levels of testosterone in their bloodstream, the end effect is a calmer, more sedentary, passive animal—similar to Old Fido when his manhood is removed.

They are seldom seen engaged in classic rutting activity and leave little buck sign. Again, it's because they simply don't play the rutting game, at least to the degree other bucks do. This also accounts for why they make so little buck sign and why they seldom mix it up with other bucks. As passive bystanders, they have no ax to grind or the impudence to grind it.

Secretive super bucks are often smaller in body size and usually lack the bullish features of prime breeders. The reason for the lack of masculinity is fairly obvious—without testosterone to spur them to activity and pump-up their muscles, they retain a rather sleek, slender-necked, feminine appearance. The smaller overall body size is more difficult to explain and is by no means a given in every case. Still, it happens too often to be disregarded. The best answer I can come up with is that dominance is often determined by body size. A smaller buck has less chance of rising to dominance. Thus, the odds say that bucks with relatively small bodies are more likely to be relegated to a subdominant position...and to the antler-size advantages that passive living appears to bring. Or, perhaps they are smaller in body size simply because they *don't* bulk up from the combined effect of testosterone and exercise, as do active breeders.

A disproportionate number of super bucks are non-typical. In the beginning, this fact led me to suspect that hormones were involved. I knew that hormonal imbalances contributed to non-typical antler growth. When information came to light that many of the true giants, especially non-typicals, were only marginally fertile or sterile and that some actually had testicle damage, then I knew hormones were at work and understood why so many secretive super bucks were non-typicals.

And finally, they tend to show up most often late in the rut. The reason for this appears to stem from dominance suppression, or more precisely, its decreasing impact as the rut wears on. It works like this: When the rut first comes in, testosterone levels are at a peak in dominant bucks and they are very aggressive, amorous and active. Competition is keen, and dominance suppression is now in full effect. As the rut wears on, dominant bucks, their sex urge partly satiated and exhausted from physical exertion and the lack of food, begin to lose their zeal, which, interestingly, corresponds with a reduction in testosterone levels. They spend less and less time pursuing the remaining receptive does, as evidenced by the slowdown in visible rutting activity toward the end of the rut. This leaves an opening for hitherto suppressed subdominants, including passive super bucks, to slip around, perhaps in hopes of catching an easy doe. The mere fact that they are less likely to come into either direct or scent contact with aggressive dominant bucks late in the rut somewhat lifts the weight of suppression from the passive bucks. Plus, having sat out the frenzied early rut, they are not suffering from exhaustion as are the prime breeders. As a result, shy subdominants can sometimes be caught cautiously prowling around in the late rut, or even the post-rut.

There you have it—the theory tested against the known and suspected traits of the secretive super buck. Does it all make sense? I think so. It is true? Possibly. Is there more to it? Probably. If the theory is basically correct, then the concept that only three factors—age, nutrition and genetics—affect antler size may need revamping. This theory makes a case that a buck's participation in the rut (or lack thereof), hormonal balance and dominance status, all of which are interrelated, may also factor into antler size. True, these factors rank well below the three established cornerstones in importance, but nonetheless, they shouldn't be ignored, especially the dominance issue. Why? It may be possible for the private landowners to "manage" the effects of dominance by manipulating the buck age structure to better achieve certain harvest objectives, but that's a topic to be covered in another book. For now, it's enough to know that these factors appear to contribute to the existence of one of the most fascinating and mysterious of all whitetails—the secretive super buck, alias super beta.

A STRATEGY FOR SECRETIVE SUPER BUCKS

Boy, this is going to be short! Intentionally going out cold turkey after a secretive super buck is something akin to just showing up at a Yankees ballgame with aspirations of being asked to start at third base. Unless you have good reason for such hope, it ain't gonna happen. In the case of secretive super bucks, they are just too rare, not to mention too hard to kill, to intentionally set your sights on shooting one…unless you have the single best reason to have hope—a firm lead on the whereabouts of such a buck.

You see, about the only way to intentionally go after one of these animals with *any* hope of scoring is to hunt a known buck. If you hang around country with lots of older bucks long enough, sooner or later you might get a reliable lead on the whereabouts of a secretive giant, or perhaps even catch a glimpse of one yourself. Then, if you have lots of time and are reasonably certain of his location, you just might have a long-shot chance of catching up with an "unkillable" super buck. You'll have to camp out on top of him, probably with little buck sign to encourage you, but there's a chance. It's really this simple: *Finding the whereabouts of a secretive super buck increases your odds of killing such an animal astronomically!* Still, he's a long way from dead even when you know where he lives.

The only other hope of deliberately putting a super beta on your wall is to hunt a place where you can look over lots and lots of older age-class bucks and let the numbers work for you. Frankly, such places are very rare. The only places I've ever hunted like that were the vast, lightly hunted King, Kenedy and Piloncillo ranches in South Texas and a couple of riverbottom ranches in eastern Montana. At most places I hunt, it is impossible to see enough older bucks too ever have any kind of odds of crossing paths with something as extremely rare as a super beta.

> The great majority of secretive super bucks are killed as a result of nothing more than blind luck, meaning anybody, anytime, anywhere can kill one.

The only other advice I might offer for hunting secretive super bucks is to concentrate your efforts in the latter part of the rut, or strangely enough, perhaps even in the post-rut, especially in cold climates. He's most likely to expose himself *after* peak rut.

In closing, I want to point out the two things I like best about secretive super bucks. One, the great majority of them are killed as a result of nothing more than blind luck, meaning anybody, anytime, anywhere can kill one. You never know. Two, there are countless secretive super bucks in the minds and dreams of deer hunters everywhere. They haunt our thoughts and add an element of mystery to the sport that I hope the cold light of facts, logic and knowledge never burn away!

Chapter Twenty-Eight

All-Purpose Sporters

WHAT DOES SHOOTING HAVE TO DO with strategies? A lot! The whole purpose of *everything* boils down to making a killing shot when that rare and precious opportunity comes along for a trophy whitetail. Just seeing a trophy whitetail, no matter what the circumstances or distances involved, is hard enough, so I want to be able to make a killing shot under the widest possible circumstances. That calls for advance preparations—that's strategy!

You must go to the field with the right equipment for the job and be capable of using it. Here, I want to talk about choosing the right equipment for the job. I'm going to assume you will become proficient in the use of the equipment once chosen, though experience tells me many won't. Still, you know what it takes—lots of practice, serious practice—and the problem seldom is not knowing how to practice; it's just taking the time to do it.

The last few years have brought tremendous changes in the hunting world, particularly in the shooting scene. The quality and variety of shooting-related products have never been better. A dazzling array of rifles, optics, ammos and support products, some of which have taken advantage of space-age technology, now adorn the shelves of sporting-

After many years of service, this is still my favorite rifle...alongside perhaps my favorite buck, a 180-class 28-incher! The rifle is a custom 7mm Rem. Mag. built on a Remington Model 700 action with a fluted stainless steel barrel. It is topped with a 3-9X Swarovski scope mounted on low Leupold rings. When I do my part, it has always gotten the job done. Photo by author.

goods stores. Many of these products are designed for very specific jobs, reflecting the increasing specialization and sophistication of the hunting market, particularly the whitetail market, which is, after all, the engine that drives the North American hunting industry. Whitetail hunters have taken advantage of all this and have become much better armed, and not just for hunting at what we might term "traditional" ranges of 300 yards or less, but also for "long-range" shooting out to 500 yards. Nowadays, not only do hunters have a wide selection of topnotch sporters, but there's a whole line of rifles, ammo and equipment aimed at the growing long-range market. In fact, so many and varied are the choices of today's hunter that the process of picking out the "right" rig for the job can be rather daunting.

So, I want to try to simplify the selection process in this and the following chapter. My goal is not to pick brand names, though by necessity there'll be plenty of that. Rather, I mostly want to discuss the principles that should guide choices, or least that guide my choices. You may or may not agree with my opinions. That's fine. At the least, what I have to say may cause you to think, perhaps leading to one or two "improvements." If you're a serious trophy hunter, any helpful hint is sure to be welcome.

In my mind, there are two distinct types of rigs out there. One, those intended for traditional hunting at ranges out to 300 yards. We'll call these "sporters." Two, those designed for extended ranges of 300 to 500 yards, which we'll simply call "long-range" rifles. I don't mean to imply that sporters won't perform beyond 300 yards or that long-range outfits won't dispatch a buck at less than that distance, but certain elections have to be made in order for these two types of rifles to be best suited for their intended purpose. In those elections, their crossover suitability is likely to be compromised. True, it's possible to come up with a rifle that'll serve both purposes to some degree, but if you aren't careful, what you'll get is an El Camino—neither truck nor car, it'll serve either purpose fairly well but neither excellently. (Actually, with a bit of compromise in maximum range, a pretty good El Camino may be possible, as we'll see at the end of the next chapter.) With that, we'll start our discussion in this chapter with sporters.

WHAT'S A SPORTER?

John raised my rifle to his shoulder and took aim, first at one rock then another, trying the rifle on for size. "This is the best feeling rifle I've ever had in my hands," he said, still snapping from one "target" to another. "It's almost like an extension of my body. Where can I get one like it?" he asked, lowering the rifle to give it the once over again.

Taking my rifle back, I glanced over at his leaning against the benchrest. I saw immediately why he thought my gun felt so good. His rifle had a stock as crooked as a dog's leg and was topped off with a cheap 4-12X scope mounted on high "see-through" rings.

Ah, I thought to myself, no wonder he thinks my gun is something special. When he slaps that outfit to his cheek, his eye probably centers up on the back of the bolt, certainly not on the scope and probably not even on the hole in the see-through rings. He has to lift his face clear off the stock and crane his neck to bring his scope into play…and undoubtedly gets smacked in the jaw on the shot for his trouble.

Many hunters are armed with rigs ill-suited for the job. Some are leftovers from days gone by, when rifles still had the carryover design for use with iron sights. Some outfits are just plain sorry, and were from the outset. Some are products of bad elections or intentional, but unwise, compromises made by the owner, or the previous owner who pawned the piece off on the guy now in possession of it. Some would be fine for certain situations but are poorly suited to their present use. Some are even ok for the job but poorly suited to the individual employing it. What, then, are we looking for in an ideal sporter?

First, let's decide what we need from a sporter. This is the general-purpose, everyday rifle in the deer hunting arsenal. It may be called upon to go everywhere and perform in every conceivable habitat and hunting situation. While it may be possible to work with it out to ranges of 400 yards, let's limit the practical working range to 300 yards for reasons that'll soon become clear. From stands to stalks, from mountainside treks to wading a flooded riverbottom, from jump-shooting in pine thickets to precision shots across a cornfield, whether 30 yards or 300 yards, this gun has to be capable of consistently getting the job done.

The rifle must fit so well that its use is almost instinctive. When it snaps to the shoulder, the sight picture must be gained instantly so the shot can be made quickly at an animal that may be there for scant seconds or on the move or perhaps somewhat obscured by brush. It has to be light enough to carry but needs sufficient heft to steady-up for long or offhand shots. A fairly quick second, third or fourth shot would be nice. A scope is mandated for the kind of work it'll have to do. A variable is best so the magnification can be low enough on the bottom side to quickly get on close and/or moving targets in tight cover but high enough on the upside to allow for exact bullet placement at 275 yards in fading light. The cartridge must be adequately powerful to handle the worst-case scenario likely to be encountered, like a quartering-away shot across a big soybean field. And, it must be flat enough to take most of the guesswork out of a 300-yard shot…while the bullet closely hugs the line of sight en route. The bullet itself must hold together on a 20-yard shoulder shot when zinging along at nearly three times the speed of sound but still expand and penetrate when plodding along at three football fields' distance.

Behind that tree stands a very wide basic 10-pointer with double drop-tines on this left beam! Though I don't know what's on his right beam, what I can see is enough to get him shot, but it will take precise bullet placement. This type situation is why I don't want much bullet deviation above the line of sight at mid ranges, thus I've settled on a maximum sight-in height of two inches at 100 yards. Photo by Mike Biggs.

ACTIONS

I freely admit that I'm a bolt-action man. True, other actions also will work, as long as the rifle is dependable, has a good trigger and shoots straight. Single-shots meet the test and can be aesthetically pleasing, but why limit yourself to one shot when chasing once-in-a-lifetime animals? Autos and pumps are faster than bolt-guns but generally aren't as dependable, accurate or sleek. The same thing can be said about lever-actions. This leaves the bolt-action as the top preference.

What bolt-action is best? It's your choice. I've seen fine sporters built on every make and model of bolt-action. Personally, I like the new pre-64-style Model 70 Winchester and the Remington Model 700, but there are plenty of others just as good. Almost all the actions made by major manufacturers are dependable and capable of good accuracy with some tweaking. Frankly, it's a good idea to have a competent gunsmith touch-up the action, bedding and trigger on any factory rifle. Often, the action is not concentric, the locking lugs don't make even contact, the bedding is restless and the trigger pull is so heavy that it almost takes two fingers to release the firing pin. For a bit more money, some major gun manufacturers will put together dressed-up, finely tuned versions of their standard offerings in their custom shops. I have several rifles from Remington's custom shop, mostly their Custom KS (Kevlar) Mountain Rifles, and have found them to be excellent.

If an all-out custom rifle is more to your liking, there are countless good gunsmiths out there who can make high-performance rifles. Most of my principle hunting rifles are custom, mainly because I like to put together exactly what I want and they seem more special to me when I help design them. I recently completed two custom projects that were the products of weeks of strategizing. One was a .300 Win. Mag. sporter on a pre-64 Winchester Model 70 action designed for elk, Canadian whitetails and light African hunting. That rifle was a collaboration between two fine gunsmiths—Tim McWhorter (McWhorter Custom Rifles, 1549 Howell Rd., Doerun, GA 31744) and one of the foremost Winchester Model 70 experts in the country, D'Arcy Echols, (D'Arcy Echols & Co., P.O. Box 421, Millville, UT 84326). The other, a long-range rifle, was a .300 Weatherby Mag. built on a reworked Remington 700 action by Tim McWhorter. The sporter saw heavy action in Africa last year and did all I asked of it. The long-range rifle has already accounted for several big whitetails, a couple of which I would not even have attempted a shot at with a sporter.

STOCKS

Before we talk about stocks, first some terminology. The comb of a stock is the top portion of the buttstock, the part on which your cheek rests, or should, when aiming. The "drop" of a stock, according to today's industry standards, is essentially the distance from the centerline of the bore to the top line of the comb. Drop is usually measured in two places, the nose of the comb, which is the beginning of the comb just behind the grip, and the heel of the comb, which is the end of the stock. But since I prefer a straight buttstock with little or no drop between the nose and the heel, the drop at the comb as I will use it basically refers to anywhere along the comb, but especially to the place where the cheek makes contact.

In the old days when iron sights were the thing, the drop had to

be considerable so the eye would align with the iron sights sitting immediately atop the rifle. Since "that was the way it has always been done,"
even after scopes, which are mounted much higher than iron sights, came
out the change to less drop by gun manufacturers came harder than getting the straight scoop out of a politician. Because custom gun makers
were bold enough to break tradition and raise the comb so a guy could
nestle his cheek firmly against his stock and still see through his scope,
custom guns gained the reputation in the early years for having a "good
feel." You see, a key element in quick, accurate, comfortable shooting—
the kind that is more instinctive than calculated—is having eye/scope
alignment when the cheek is firmly snuggled-up against the comb of the
stock. Otherwise, the shooter has to raise his face off the stock and crane
his neck to see through the scope, losing the constancy of a standard
anchor point and the stability of firm cheek-to-stock contact, which tactical shooters call the stock or cheek weld. Plus, instead of getting
"pushed" by the recoil, a shooter in this hiked-up position is likely to get
smacked smartly on the cheek or jaw, which does nothing to improve
accuracy or shooting skills.

The Monte Carlo comb was a Californianized attempt to address
the low-comb problem by sticking a hump on the buttstock to elevate the
eye. While it did help, it was uglier than sin and a difficult-to-achieve
solution to a very simple problem. The simple and attractive answer was
to just raise the comb by reducing the drop, i.e., make the stock
straighter, which over the years has been done by most manufacturers,
though compromise still permeates the industry.

Even the cheek piece is tied to the drop-at-comb problem to a
degree. If the comb is at the right height, which in my opinion is nine-
sixteenths of an inch below the centerline of the bore, there would be no
need for any add-on pieces to the buttstock, assuming the comb is of sufficient thickness to provide good cheek support. Still, I find a tasteful
cheek piece to be aesthetically pleasing, and if designed properly, it can
give additional support to the cheek and face.

Some stocks have a little "castoff," which is nothing more than a
slight bend in the stock to help put the shooter's eye in better alignment
with the scope. While not required, it sure doesn't hurt, especially in
stocks with thicker combs. D'Arcy Echols routinely puts about a quarter-
inch castoff in his rifles, and they fit exceptionally well.

Beyond the practical sighting needs of the buttstock, we are all free to choose whatever shapes and designs we like in a stock. But, the material from which the stock is made may be a bit more of a functional issue.

If you had told me a decade or so ago that I would like, even prefer, synthetic stocks, I would have thought you were heavy on the wacky weed. I loved the warmth and beauty of nicely figured and crafted walnut on something as dear to me as a good hunting rifle. When synthetics first came out, I saw them as little short of an abomination to the nobility of fine rifles. Then, like the cross-eyed, snub-nosed, semi-bobbed-tailed pointer I once had that could find more quail than any other birddog I ever hunted with, I began to see and admire the utilitarian aspects rather than be stumbled by the ugly. Now, I behold a certain functional "beauty" in a clean-lined synthetic stock that's a part of a gun that shoots in the same place day after day, rain or shine!

The advantages of synthetic stocks lie in their lightweight and stability. Being lighter than wood, the weight saved in the stock can be put into other parts of the gun that may contribute more to performance...or just left out to make the rifle lighter. For all practical purposes, most (but not all) synthetic stocks are impervious to warpage from moisture, sun and time, a most important asset. The problem with many synthetics is that they tend to be noisier, some more so than others, than wood when branches and whatnot rub against them.

In fairness, I must point out that with some bedding work and the right finish, conventional wood stocks can be made stable enough to perform quite well under practically all conditions. And, laminated-wood stocks are essentially as stable as synthetics, but they tend to be heavy. On rifles where weight is not much of a consideration, i.e., long-range and big-bore rifles, laminated stocks offer the stability of fiberglass and the warmth of traditional wood.

SCOPES

First, I want to go back to the sighting-plane discussion as it relates to mounting a scope. If having the eye very nearly aligned with the scope when the cheek contacts the comb is desirable in a sporter, and it is, then the height of the scope is obviously a part of that equation. It's safe to say that a scope can't be mounted too low for a good sighting plane, but it certainly can be mounted too high, at least for fast sighting and a secure, natural anchor point. Thus, a low scope is called for, especially in a sporter.

How low? As low as is feasible, given the dimensions of scopes suitable for trophy whitetail sporters. I prefer a height of about 1.5 inches above the centerline of the bore, which works out to about seven-eighths-inch of base and ring height above the receiver on most rifles. To achieve that, you pretty much have to go with low rings on most scope-mounting systems, such as Redfield, Leupold, Burris, etc. Unfortunately, many of the more popular scopes today won't fit on rifles with low rings. Either the objective bell won't clear the barrel or the bolt won't clear the eyepiece, dictating higher rings. However, if a scope mandates higher rings than mediums on your sporter, you may want to reconsider your choice of scopes. Depending on the rifle and mounting system, low rings will usually work with scope objective diameters of less than 38mms and mediums with less than 44mms.

I prefer variable scopes. There was a time when some gun experts browbeat variables as not being as accurate or dependable as fixed-power scopes. Well, you can forget that. You may prefer a fixed-power for your own reasons, but it shouldn't be because you think variables won't cut it for serious whitetail hunting. If I hunted one type of habitat all the time and all my shots were at predictable ranges under controlled conditions, I might opt for a fixed-power scope for simplicity and because they tend to be a tad cheaper, brighter and smaller. But, I don't hunt one habitat type and the circumstances under which my shots come vary from one end of the spectrum to the other. One day, I may be sitting on a scrapeline in a spruce thicket in Saskatchewan, straining my eyes to see 75 yards. Soon afterwards, I may be in Alberta looking over a square-mile alfalfa field or in Montana slipping through cutovers, where a shot can come at a running, walking or standing deer at distances ranging from 50 to 300 yards. You get the picture. Varying cover conditions, distances, shot circumstances and levels of precision and speed require varying power settings on a scope. Otherwise, a guy with a do-it-all rig, which a sporter needs to be, is going to be rather limited at one end of the spectrum or the other...or compromised throughout.

What range of power is best? On the low side, I don't want the bottom-end magnification to be higher than 3.5X. That level of magnifi-

Jim Goodchild of Atlanta, Georgia, shot this 150-class buck at a distance of 200 yards with his Remington Custom KS Mountain Rifle in 7mm Rem. Mag. His scope is a 2.5-8X Leupold, a fine choice. Photo by author.

cation, and lower, allows for a good field of view and quick sighting in tight cover or on moving targets. On the topside, 6X would be my minimum, but my preference would be 8 or 9X for the precision sometimes needed in long or fine work. I don't see any need for more than 10X, but I have no problem with scopes that deliver more power as long as the low-end setting doesn't exceed 3.5X and they'll fit on at least medium rings. Often, the objective lens on higher-powered variables must be so large to transmit enough light at the top setting that the scope won't fit on low and sometimes even on medium rings, mucking up the desired sighting plane. Plus, weight and length normally increase with upside power. So, variables ranging from 1.5-6X to 3.5-12X are the ticket for trophy whitetails. Obviously, such ranges as 2-7X, 2.5-8X, 3-9X and even 2.5-10X are fine choices…as long as they'll fit on low or medium rings.

Now, a word on what is normally called "light-gathering" capabilities. However, since scopes only transmit available light, not *gather* it, we're simply going to use the term "brightness" to describe how well you can see through a scope in low light, when most big whitetails are shot. With today's higher-quality scopes, brightness is not something you need to worry a great deal about because the manufacturers have already taken it into account and provided more than adequate capabilities for hunting in the lowest legal light. But, some general guidelines for better brightness may be helpful.

Only three factors are of real concern regarding brightness. One, the quality of the lens. Simply put, the better the glass you're looking through, the better you can see. Two, the coating on the scope lenses. To keep it simple, uncoated glass reflects a lot of light, preventing it from reaching the hunter's eye and allowing him to see better in dim light. Coating scope lenses with special chemicals greatly reduces light reflection, allowing more light to pass through the scope. The better scope manufacturers coat all lenses, both those on the outside and inside, and actually put multiple coats on each lens so that the full range of light wavelengths will be transmitted. Poorer quality scopes have only one coat or multiple coats only on outside lenses.

Three, the diameter of the objective lens affects how much light enters the scope. However, in quality scopes of the power we are talking about for sporters, the difference in brightness between, say, a 42mm and a 50mm objective lens is not as much as you might first think. In fact, below 6X, the difference between 42 and 50mms is hardly discernable to the human eye. When magnification is higher than 6X, then the additional brightness of the larger objective lens does improve the sight picture, all else being equal. Why is this?

A factor comes into play called the "exit pupil," which is essentially a measure of the amount of light being transmitted through the scope to the eye. When you hold a scope at arm's length, you can see a clear aperture in the ocular, or eyepiece, lens. This is the exit pupil, and it can be measured, usually in millimeters. An easier way to determine the size of the exit pupil is by dividing the objective lens diameter by the magnification level, i.e., a 42mm lens divided by 6X results in an exit pupil of 7mms, which happens to be all the light the human eye can utilize! An exit pupil greater than that is wasted on us, explaining why the diameter of the objective lens only affects brightness at the higher power settings. And, the sad truth is that as we age our ability to use even 7mms of exit pupil erodes to the point that about 5mms is our usable limit since how much our pupils will dilate gradually diminishes, explaining why older folks have trouble driving at night. As a result of reduced pupil dilation with age, us baby-boomers don't even get the full benefit of larger diameter objective lenses even at higher magnification. Plus, 5mms is about as much as even young eyes can use during the dim early and late light when old bucks seem to show themselves.

What does all this tell us? That we're probably not gaining much from large diameter objective bells, say over 42mms, at sporter magnification levels. For example, a scope with a 42mm objective bell set at 8X has an exit pupil of 5.25mms, which is a bit more than studies have shown we can use in dawn/dusk light. Even a 36mm objective bell exceeds the 5mm test at 7X. By the way, the notion that scopes with 30mm tubes are brighter than those with one-inch tubes doesn't really hold water. If the quality and the objective bell diameter are the same, the exit pupil and the corresponding brightness on scopes with one-inch tubes and 30mm tubes will be the same.

I mention all this because it might cause some to rethink their choice of scopes, leading to picks better suited to sporters, meaning a scope in the right power range with an objective bell that will allow for reasonably low scope mounting. In my opinion, you lose more than you gain when unnecessarily large diameter objective bells force you to mounts higher than mediums. My favorite whitetail rifle carries a 3-9X Swarovski (one-inch tube) with a 36mm objective lens, and I've never had a buck I could see and judge in dim light with binoculars that I could not shoot with that scope. The cardinal rule in scope buying is: Get the very best scope you can afford. Nothing beats quality in optics!

CARTRIDGE

What cartridge for sporters? Let's first set some minimum parameters regarding what we want it to do. In my first book, *Hunting Trophy Whitetails*, I did just that in detail and see no reason to deviate from the parameters set then. Let's review them here without going into the lengthy explanation of why I set them. For serious trophy whitetail hunting, a sporter cartridge should hustle at least a 120-grain bullet downrange at a minimum muzzle velocity of 2,700 feet per second (fps) and

The rifle is only as good as the person behind it. Time on the range is essential to good shooting. Don't skimp on shooting practice. Photo by author.

should impact at 300 yards with no less than 1,300 foot-pounds of energy. The bullet-weight minimum relates both to penetration and downrange energy requirements. The muzzle-velocity minimum is dictated by both trajectory and downrange energy requirements. The 300-yard energy minimum of 1,300 foot-pounds is a bit arbitrary but comes from years of hunting experience and seeing hundreds of deer-sized animals shot.

From these parameters, we get our range of acceptable trophy cartridges, starting with the .25-06, which just makes the bullet-weight and 300-yard energy requirements. The 7mm-08, 7x57 and .308 make the cut but not by a whole lot. Then comes the ones I consider serious contenders—264 Win. Mag. , .270, .280, .284, 7mm Rem. Mag., .30-06 and .300 Win. Mag. Of course, the Weatherby counterparts and similar proprietary cartridges will likewise do the job. Personally, I want my sporter to shoot at least a 140-grain bullet at better than 3,000 fps, explaining why the .280, 7mm Rem. Mag. and .300 Win. Mag. are my favorites.

Frankly, in a sporter, I don't see much need for some of the .30-caliber super magnums now on the market, unless the goal is to stretch the range well beyond 300 yards, which is where they shine. The more powerful of the whitetail-class cartridges I have mentioned are plenty flat enough and pack more than sufficient punch at 300 yards. In a sporter, anything beyond the .300 Weatherby Mag.—and there are lots of them now—is overkill…for the hunter, not the deer! But if having to pick up your hat and refocus your eyes after every shot is acceptable, more power to you!

BULLETS

The only connection you have to the ultimate success of a hunt is the bullet. On it rides the payoff for all the planning, money and hard work. Since the bullet is the only representative you've got to send to the closing, doesn't it make sense to select the best bullet possible to bring the matter to a quick, happy conclusion? I guess the passive attitude toward bullet selection stems in part from the fact that most any big-game bullet from an adequate cartridge will kill a buck under *most* circumstances. Plus, all too often, even when a bullet fails to perform properly, the hunter has so many other things to blame it on that he can't isolate the problem.

Well, not all bullets are the same. They are not all designed to do the same thing. Even among those that are, some do it far better than others. However, it is usually true that more than one bullet, whether you're talking about brand name, weight, design or "model," will ink the deal with equal finality. Still, you must choose one that will perform well, and in the case of a sporter, it must do so under a wide range of conditions. And, therein lies the challenge in selecting bullets for sporters.

If every deer you shot were the same size, at the same range and hit in the same place from the same cartridge, then you could pick the perfect bullet for that particular job and get speculator results every time. But when you change one or more of those variables, the outcome could well change. Of course, in real hunting situations, you don't necessarily know what any of those variables are likely to be…but you still want the bullet to kill quickly—whether the buck weighs 150 pounds or 300 pounds, is 30 or 300 yards downrange or is standing broadside or quartering away. That places demanding requirements on a sporter bullet. Let's look at an example of just how demanding.

As velocity increases, the physics of bullet impact change at an accelerating, not linear, rate. For instance, a 180-grain bullet traveling at

2,700 fps from a .308 smacks home with 2,900 foot-pounds of energy, while that same 180-grain bullet from a .300 Weatherby Mag. leaves the barrel at 3,200 fps (19 percent faster) and strikes with 4,100 foot-pounds of energy. That's 40 percent more energy than the .308, even though the velocity is only 19 percent greater! Relative to bullet construction, that's a huge difference in terminal dynamics and stresses.

And, the problem is not limited to different cartridges. Because of range variances, it exists within the same cartridge…and can manifest itself on any given shot. For instance, at 30 yards, a 165-grain bullet from a .300 Win. Mag. arrives at 3,200 fps (3,750 foot-pounds of energy), but at 300 yards, that same bullet has slowed to a modest 2,475 fps (2,240 foot-pounds). In delivered energy, that's a 67 percent difference! So, under such varying conditions, how can one bullet do it all—stay together and penetrate at super-high velocity yet open up rapidly at much slower speeds? Let's see.

I'm going to start out talking mostly about what we'll call "standard-grade" bullets, as opposed to the more expensive "premium-grade" bullets built for enhanced performance, which we'll discuss later. For bullets in the calibers of concern to whitetail hunters, a couple of general manufacturing trends are of interest. One, the lighter bullets in a particular caliber are designed for smaller big-game animals, thus they tend to be "softer" and expand faster, sometimes providing spectacular kills on whitetails. However, the downside, and a very serious one, to the lighter bullets is that even on whitetails their penetration can be poor, especially at high velocities. This can result in wounded animals. In contrast to lighter bullets, the heavier bullets in a particular caliber tend to be designed for larger big-game species, thus are more stoutly constructed, resulting in slower expansion and greater penetration. That's a good thing …up to a point. Whitetails are not very heavily built, and if a bullet fails to expand much, it can punch through the animal and expend its energy en route to the next county, failing to quickly dispatch the animal. For whitetails, you want both expansion *and* penetration.

Also, manufacturers are forced to pick a velocity range at which a particular bullet will perform best on the animals most likely to be shot with it. Designing a bullet for the "average" means that performance at the extremes (faster or slower velocities, bigger or smaller animals) is likely to be less than perfect. Most standard-grade bullets in our grouping of

This shot is why I want plenty of power and bullet penetration in a trophy whitetail cartridge. With the right rifle and a good rest, I would not hesitate to take this shot, even out to 300 yards. Photo by Mike Biggs.

whitetail cartridges are designed to perform quite nicely at, say, 50 to 150 yards when starting out around 2,600 to 2,900 fps. The problem really comes when velocities exceed 3,000 fps, which I want my whitetail rifles to do. Many standard-grade bullets aren't designed to impact at that kind of speed, and unless they have enough weight to assure decent penetration, they occasionally fail to kill cleanly at close ranges. Because of this, I stay away from lighter standard-grade bullets when velocities push 3,000 fps. I've seen too many "blowups" at close ranges.

So, here we are. The lighter bullets—like the 130-grain in .270, 140 in 7mm and 150 in .30 caliber—may come apart at close ranges at high velocities. And, the heaviest ones—like the 160-grain in .270, 175 in 7mm and 220 in .30 caliber—may not open up well enough for a clean kill at longer ranges. Plus, moving all the way to the top of the bullet-weight ladder in a caliber will result in a considerable reduction in velocity, cutting into trajectory. While I'm not the velocity manic I once was, I am reluctant to give up too much velocity both for trajectory reasons and for the undeniable "shock power" that super velocity brings.

Obviously, compromise is called for, at least if the solution is a standard-grade bullet. That compromise is the medium-weight bullets in a caliber—like the 150-grain in .270; 150 or 160 in 7mm; and 180 in .30 caliber. These weight bullets, assuming they are big-game bullets made by reputable manufacturers, are usually heavy enough, both in terms of weight and construction strength, to hold together at close ranges and magnum velocities but are still capable of reasonable expansion at long ranges and reduced speeds. I must emphasis, however, that not all bullets, not even standard-grades, are the same. For instance, boattails as a group expand more rapidly than do the conventional, squared-off versions. And, some bullets are notoriously fast-openers while a few will darn-near pass through a deer from stem to stern with little discernable expansion. Choose wisely.

There aren't many things in which you can have your cake and eat it too, but bullet selection may be an exception. There is a way to insure penetration even at close ranges and high velocities and still have a bullet with a soft enough front-end to expand at the longer distances. I'm speaking of "premium-grade" bullets specially designed to retain a high percentage of their weight for deep penetration even when impacting at hyper velocity, while still opening up rapidly even at knuckle-ball speeds. To be sure, attempts are made to varying degrees even in standards bullets to accomplish this but cost prohibits pulling out all stops. In premium bullets, the cost of success is certainly greater, sometimes much greater, but in my opinion, having a bullet that will both penetrate and expand dependably under a wide range of conditions is worth the extra cost. After all, how many times do I shoot at trophy bucks every year? I can practice with standard grades and then sight-in and hunt with premium grades without getting a call from my banker.

Because penetration is assured even in the lighter big-game premiums, bullet weight isn't as great of a concern in whitetail hunting as with standard-grade bullets. For instance, I have shot 140-grain Nosler Partitions, one of the best of the premiums, for years in my .280 and 7mm Rem. Mag. and never had reason to change. I shoot the 140-grain in my .280 by choice so I can keep the velocity up. But in my 7mm Rem. Mag., I shoot the 140-grain bullet only because it is more accurate in my rifle than the 150-grain, which is the bullet weight I prefer in that cartridge because of big Canadian whitetails and the occasional elk I run into when hunting whitetails in Montana.

All kinds of techniques are used to accomplish the specialized performance in bullets. Nosler and Swift use a partition between the front and rear lead core. My experience with the Swift A-Frame has all been good but is limited to game bigger than whitetails. But with the Nosler Partition, I've shot hundreds of big-game animals from Africa to the Yukon and most points in between and consider it to be as good a hunting bullet as there is. The front-end opens rapidly at all ranges, and depending on the caliber and bullet weight, it'll peal back to the partition and retain 50 to 60 percent of its weight and keep on truckin', becoming virtually a mushroomed solid. I've got a drawer full of recovered Noslers that are ad-quality mushrooms. The only knock on the Nosler Partition is that it is not the most accurate bullet in the world, but it is accurate enough for hunting at sporter ranges. Most of my rifles will shoot a minute angle or so with them.

Other manufacturers have approached the "controlled-expansion" challenge from a different angle. Some, like Trophy Bonded, have developed special processes to bond the lead-alloy core to the jacket so the bullet will mushroom but not come apart. Barnes has eliminated the lead core altogether in their X-Bullet by making the projectile of solid copper. Winchester's Fail Safe Bullet features a solid copper-alloy nose in front of a notched hollowpoint cavity to assure expansion and a steel insert to protect the rear lead core for deep penetration. The list goes on. I've tried most of these premium-grade bullets to some degree, but personally, I always seem to come back to Nosler Partitions when I'm seriously chasing big whitetails...or big anythings!

Just because a bullet is premium grade doesn't make it a good whitetail bullet. I've found some of them, especially the heavier ones in calibers above .270, to be slow to open on whitetail-sized animals. Clearly, many are designed for animals larger than whitetails. Magnum velocities help promote expansion, but the problem is still there at longer ranges. For this reason, I normally lean toward the lighter and middle-weight premium-grade bullets—like 130 and 140 grain in .270; 140 and 150 in 7mm; and 165 and 180 in .30 caliber. This elevates velocity, helping both expansion and trajectory, and assures that the bullet is designed for lighter big game such as whitetails. The premium construction should guarantee weight retention and penetration even at close ranges and high velocities. In my experience, the greater concern with premiums is expansion, not penetration, so be sure to choose the right one for the job. If in doubt, use Nosler Partitions until you can find something better...if it exists!

SIGHTING-IN AND TRAJECTORY

Now, I want to talk about sighting-in and trajectory for sporters. (When we talk about long-range rifles, the ball game changes.) We'll start with trajectory, or the flight path of a bullet. I'm certain you know that a bullet begins to drop from the time it leaves the barrel and that the line of sight is perfectly level. In order to keep a dropping bullet near the line of sight for the greatest possible distance, scoped rifles are set up so that the line of sight and the bullet path intersect twice. This is accomplished by aligning the scope so that it is angled ever so slightly downward toward the barrel. This allows the dropping bullet to cross the level line of sight. The first time is when the bullet crosses on its ascent, normally somewhere around 30 yards. The second time occurs when the bullet crosses the line of sight on its descent. This second crossing is called the point of aim or dead-on sight-in point, which occurs, for instance, at 250 yards with my 7mm Mag. when sighted in two inches high at 100 yards.

Once the bullet falls below the line of sight, we call this "drop" and we hunters get real concerned about it. However, drop is not the only deviation off the line of sight—so is the "rise" *above* the line of sight. What affects the amount of rise? Several factors, like sight-in point, height of scope, velocity and bullet ballistic coefficient. For now, I want to focus on the sight-in point.

We all know the sight-in point affects downrange drop, but it also plays a big role in midrange rise. You see, the higher your sight-in point at 100 yards, the less the drop at 300 yards but the greater the deviation above the line of sight. The zenith of that rise is called "midrange trajectory," though instead of being halfway to the "dead-on" point, it occurs about 55 percent of the way. For instance, say a .30-06 is sighted in two inches high at 100 yards and is dead-on at 225 yards, the bullet will reach its highest point above the line of sight, in this case about three inches, at about 125 yards.

Why would rise be of interest to a whitetail hunter? For the same reason drop is. Think about it, if you are shooting at an animal 300 yards away and your bullet is going to strike three, four or five inches below the point of aim, you certainly need to be aware of it and compensate accordingly. A vertical variance of four or five inches in where the bullet hits can make the difference between a fatal hit and a wounded or missed deer. So, while it's easy to see why drop of a few inches can be important, why is it so often overlooked that rise above the line of sight can be just as problematic, particularly in whitetail hunting?

Let's explore why rise must be considered. First, there's the obvious problem of simply shooting too high on midrange deer because deviation above the point of aim isn't taken into account. This happens more than you might think. After all, most deer are shot in the middle ranges, 75 to 175 yards, where the bullet is significantly above the line of sight, mathematically increasing the likelihood of a problem with bullet rise. I have seen several bucks missed or wounded because hunters, concerned about bullet drop, sighted-in their rifles three or four inches high at a hundred. As a result, the midrange trajectory was so high that they missed relatively easy shots at nine-iron distances. I saw one hunter miss three 150 to 200-yard shots at antelope in one day because his sight-in point was 300 yards (3.5 inches high at 100), resulting in a midrange trajectory of five inches...enough to clear the backs of two antelope and shave the third.

Because I prefer a high-shoulder shot to all others (two-thirds to three-quarters of the way up the body inline with the front leg), I am particularly concerned about rise above the line of sight. A hit just three or four inches higher than the point of aim can end in sleepless nights and endless "what-ifs." On more than one occasion, I have flirted with disaster, only to be saved my the fact that too high a hit on a high-shoulder shot still shocks the spine and provides a chance for a hasty finishing shot.

Compensating for rise to hit midrange targets is not the only thing to think about. Another big concern, especially in whitetail hunting, is the potential for bullets deviating too much from the line of sight to be deflected by brush. Whereas most long shots, where drop is a factor, are taken at deer standing in the relative open with little to interfere with bullet flight, close and midrange shots are often taken at animals in some type of cover. Many times, only part the animal is in the clear. Often, the only route to the vitals is through a hole in the cover, sometimes only a few inches in diameter. This calls for precise shooting—both in terms of bullet placement and allowance for the flight path of the bullet. Since obstructing brush may be just below or above the line of sight, it is necessary either to consciously calculate the bullet's deviation from the line of sight, something difficult to do in the excitement of the moment, or to minimize that deviation so that it seldom causes a problem. The latter is my solution, explaining why I try not to have a midrange trajectory greater than three inches in whitetail sporters. A sight-in point of two inches high at 100 yards accomplishes this and serves as a compromise between the needs of midrange and long-range.

A two-inch-high sight-in point works well throughout the range of velocities and distances we've established for trophy whitetails. At our minimum velocity of 2,700 fps, a .308, for instance, so sighted will be 10 inches low at 300 yards. That still allows for a hold-on-the-body aim at 300 yards, considering that a buck's chest-depth is from 18 to 22 inches. With a starting velocity in excess of 3,000 fps, the 300-yard drop can be cut in half, which is far preferable. I like to hit where I'm aiming without a whole lot of extrapolation. The heated rush of getting a shot off at a big buck is not the best time to be doing math. My old faithful 7mm Mag. is only three inches low at 300 yards when sighted-in two inches high at 100 yards. I can just hold a little high of center and let fly.

I'm aware that many writers recommend sighting-in three inches high at 100 yards. In most cases, they are basing that recommendation on the need to shoot at the longer ranges often encountered in the relatively open West. Even my personal favorite writer, Jack O'Conner, favored a three-inch-high sight-in point. But, he hunted mostly wide-open spaces. Other than the Coues whitetail of the hilly Southwest deserts, he shot only one other whitetail, a 10-pointer in Idaho, that he ever wrote about. But, hunting trophy whitetails is altogether different from Western hunting. And, if you sight-in your sporter more than two inches high at 100 yards, sooner or later it will get you into more trouble than sighting-in lower would. In fact, in most whitetail cover, particularly in the East, a sight-in point of dead-on at 100 yards or one-inch high would probably be even better than two high.

THE IDEAL SPORTER RIG

Ok, what's the ideal sporter rig? Mine would be a 7mm Rem. Mag. (or .300 Win. Mag.) built on a reworked Remington 700 action (or pre-

George Cooper has good reason for grinning like the old proverbial "mule eating briars"—he made a 200-yard offhand shot to kill this 150-class 8-pointer. George is an excellent shot because he practices a bunch. His rifle is a .300 Win. Mag. sporting a 3-9X Zeiss scope. Photo by author.

64-style Winchester Model 70). The trigger would be set to break at 2.75 pounds with no creep. I would stick a 24-inch, fluted barrel on it (without a muzzle brake so I could preserve my hearing and that of those around me) and put a Teflon finish on all the metalwork. I would drop all that hardware into a straight synthetic (fiberglass) stock adorned with a conservative cheek piece. I would paint the stock with rough-finish paint and/or have checkering cut in for improved grip. The drop at the straight comb would be nine-sixteenths-inch; the length of pull would be 13 5/8 inches; and I would have a quarter-inch of castoff in the stock. I would mount a 3-9X Swarovski (or Zeiss) scope (one-inch tube and 36mm objective lens) on two-piece Leupold bases and low rings. The whole outfit would weigh 8.5 pounds unloaded and without the sling. I would shoot handloaded 150-grain Nosler Partitions at a muzzle velocity crowding 3,200 fps and sight-in two inches high at 100 yards. For over 12 years, I have had just such a sporter, and despite trying and owning many others, I always grab my old faithful when serious whitetails are on the line.

Chapter Twenty-Nine

Long-Range Rifles

I HAD ALWAYS THOUGHT OF MYSELF
as a long-range shooter. After all, I could hit game with reasonable proficiency out to the far-distant ranges of 250 to 300 yards, and perhaps even 350 yards if pressed. Oh, I had killed a handful of animals even farther. I once lobbed a 150-grain bullet from a .30-06 at a big 13-pointer that had stopped to catch his breath on the far horizon after I had already missed him twice on a dead run at a couple of hundred yards. To my shock and his surprise, the bullet dropped right into his ribcage. I don't know exactly how far he was, but the bullet fell at least three feet! In Tanzania, I fired on a roan antelope at an impossibly long distance after several futile attempts to get closer. After a "sighter" from my .300 Win. Mag., the second bullet hit him in the heart! My crosshairs were a half-body-depth over the 750-pound animal's back, meaning at least five feet above his heart! I freely confess that with both the 13-pointer and roan, I was operating more on their bad luck than on my good shooting. The truth is that I should not have taken either shot.

But with those two memorable kills to bolster my confidence, along with plenty of 250 to 300-yard kills and a sprinkling of other

The laser rangefinder read 393 yards when I pulled the trigger on my .300 Weatherby Mag. scoped with a 6.5-20X Leupold to bring down this double-main-beamed 13-pointer scoring 172 points. Sighted-in 3.5 inches high at 100 yards, the holdover was only five inches at that range. Photo by Glenn Hayes.

fringe-distance successes, I answered Gary Schwarz affirmatively when he asked if I could handle long shots back in 1995 before my first visit to El Tecomate Ranch. Having no context for his question, I thought to myself, *I probably can hit 'em as far away as the next guy,* which was true... as long as the next guy wasn't Gary Schwarz!

When I arrived on Tecomate in Deep South Texas, I soon learned why Gary had asked me that question. His hunting strategy was (and still is) one of low impact, which he effected by setting up tripod stands at the intersection of three or four senderos (cutlines through the brush). His stands were completely surrounded by brush; in fact, the senderos didn't even start for more than 75 yards from the stands. Then, the 30-foot-wide open strips extended through the dense brush for at least 500 yards, sometimes more! Because of the height of the brush, about the closest shot one could hope for was 100 yards and the longest looked like it might be in Mexico!

For four days, I hunted in fear of seeing a shooter beyond my range, which was where most of the bucks seemed to pop out of the brush. For the first time since I blundered upon a pair of rowdy Cape buffalo in Africa while stalking a lesser critter of some kind, my 7mm Rem. Mag. seemed woefully inadequate for the task assigned it. Finally, on the fifth day, a "suspect" buck quickly crossed one of the senderos en route to another, obviously patrolling for a lady friend. I prepared for the shot...if the buck proved to be as big as he had looked. He stepped out about 300 yards away. I shouted above the modest wind in hopes of stopping him for a better look and perhaps a shot. When he balked, I snatched a quick look and decided to shoot, figuring a big buck within range was worth four or five bigger ones just over the curve of the earth.

> *Upon the shot, the buck hit the ground...then jumped up and left. I knew from experience that a long chase usually follows such a reaction.*

Upon the shot, the buck hit the ground...then jumped up and left! I knew from experience that a long chase usually follows such a reaction. After a cursory search, finding only a little blood where he had gone down, I returned to the camp...heartsick and wishing I had taken up Gary's offer to use that monstrous-looking thing he called a rifle sitting in his gun case.

Thanks to Mike Hehman and his trail dog, we found the buck, a 160-class 11-pointer, a couple of hours and many thorn punctures later. When the celebration subsided, I got down to business...that of finding out about the man-sized rifle Gary had had made for hunting those endless senderos of his. (Gary had graciously offered to let me keep hunting for a mysterious 12-pointer that showed up on helicopter surveys but never on the ground.) My pride and 7mm aside, I wanted to know more about a rifle capable of reaching out 500 to 600 yards.

Gary explained the need to minimize the impact of hunting pressure on relatively small ranches. (Tecomate is about 3,000 acres.) That required minimizing contact with the deer. That required distance, and distance required a rifle that could dependably kill at ranges well beyond the capabilities of a standard sporter. That's where Tim McWhorter came in. Tim was, and remains so today, Gary's head guide, as well as a world-class gun maker. When Tim first came to Tecomate as a hunting guest, he and Gary struck up a friendship and put their heads together to come up with a rifle/cartridge combination to handle Gary's long-distance hunting demands. Tim was already making precision long-range rifles but mostly for competition shooting. Because of the high-stakes nature of hunting Tecomate's huge whitetails, Gary wanted *lots* of velocity and power. (This was before today's powerful, long-range wildcat, proprietary and commercial cartridges were readily available.)

What Tim eventually came up with was a classic long-range rig chambered for a cartridge they named the .30 T-Raptor, the "T" standing for Tecomate. Tim fashioned the T-Raptor from a .404 Jeffery case. The 14-pound rifle sported a 6.5-20X Leupold scope, grouped three shots in one ragged hole and zinged a 180-grain bullet down the senderos at better than 3,400 fps! With it, and a Leica Geovid laser rangefinder, low-impact hunting became a reality on Tecomate...except, that is, for the deer on the receiving end of the T-Raptor!

That briefing behind me, the next day Gary and I went afield with the T-Raptor for demonstrations. A couple of does and javelina later—at ranges from 400 to 500 yards!—I was convinced. Once the Leica determined the distance, the rest was a matter of mechanics—a solid rest, a *little* allowance for drop and wind and squezzzze. It was obvious that there was another world of long-range shooting beyond what sporters could reasonably be asked to do. I knew then that another kind of rifle, a very specialized one, was soon to find its way onto the whitetail scene. In the words of Will Smith when he was flying that awesome alien spaceship in the movie, *Independence Day*, I said to myself, *I have got to get me one of these!*

And, get me one I did, or at least a modified version of it. Before I left Tecomate, Tim had my order for an across-the-county rifle. Knowing I would be using it in a wide variety of places and circumstances, I made a few changes, which we'll discuss later, but the concept was the same. And, it definitely ain't a sporter!

Let's look at the various elements that go into the makeup of a long-range rig. Before we start, I should point out that long-range shooting was made feasible by the availability of laser rangefinders, which are capable of ranging an object within plus or minus a yard or two out to several hundred yards. Without these instruments to gauge precise distances, shooting at deer four, five or six hundred yards away is a fool's game. Bullet drop is just too great at those distances and is worsening at an ever-increasing rate. If you misjudge the distance of a deer standing over a quarter-mile away by even 50 yards, which is not only easy to do but very hard *not* to do, a dead-steady hold could still result in a bad hit or miss. The parabolic trajectory of bullets at that range leaves precious little room for error in distance judging.

THE HUMAN ELEMENT

Before we launch, I want to point out that the equipment we will be talking about is capable of greater performance than most people, including myself, are capable of getting out of it. In the hands of the right person, there are rigs capable of hitting the kill zone of a deer with shocking frequency out to 1,000 yards. In fact, a military-sniper-rifle maker I know assures me that consistent "kills" out to 1,500 meters are entirely possible under the right conditions with a rangefinder and knowledge of how to dope the wind and mirages. That, my friend, is a mile! That same guy is a hunter himself, and when he goes hunting, his "trophy" standards are not based so much on size as on distance—he won't shoot if the animal isn't at least 800 yards away! He killed a New Mexico elk last year, on video I might add, that was nearly three-quarters of a mile away! And just moments before writing this, he called to tell me that he and two (amateur) friends had just collaborated on a four-shot group at 600 yards that measured six-tenths of an inch!

Now, having said all that, you can forget it. Shooting at those distances has nothing to do with hunting. Such extreme ranges are well beyond any hunting application...and the ability of 99.99 (you can take those "9s" out as far as you like) percent of whitetail hunters regardless of the equipment. Besides, hunting conditions aren't conducive to judging and setting up for a shot at such great distances. Plus, we ordinary humans have nerves, emotions and, in the excitement of seeing and deciding to shoot a trophy animal, heartbeats revved up by overdoses of adrenaline that often put inches onto our groups even at *normal* ranges. At ranges measurable as parts of a mile, those inches become feet and the average deer hunter has no business even attempting such shots.

From a hunting standpoint, I can assure you that the weak link is not likely to be the gear—it will be the user. Shooting a scoped high-powered rifle is not an innate talent; it is a learned skill. Practice, prac-

It is essential to know exactly where your rifle shoots at various ranges, which requires time behind a benchrest. Long-range shooting demands skills developed through lots of "trigger time" on the range. Photo by Gordon Whittington.

tice and more practice is called for. Long-range shooting, in particular, is a precision sport requiring skills that can only be developed by what my sniper-rifle-maker friend calls "trigger time" on the range. Plus, the hunter must have an intimate knowledge of the trajectory of his rifle at various ranges and under various conditions. And, he must know what he and his rifle in tandem are capable of. Then and only then is he ready to start shooting at game...within the envelope of reasonable long-range hunting distances. And, what is that?

For the vast majority of us serious trophy whitetail hunters, who I would assume come into the long-range arena already quite proficient with a rifle, I think the limit of long-range attempts should be around 500 yards. And, that's only after the requisite trigger time on the range. Believe me, 500 yards in the field is a very, very long way off!

Until I started fooling with long-range rifles, the idea of shooting at a buck 500 yards away, assuming I could even tell he was shooter, normally would not have even crossed my mind. Now, it may cross my mind but it won't come to pass unless everything is just right for me to judge the animal, solidly set up for the shot, take a deep breath and let half of it out, focus my concentration, lock on the animal and squezzzze the trigger. When I pull the trigger, I want to *know* I've done everything within my power to kill that animal cleanly and quickly. Everything—wriggles, nerves, heartbeats, jerks, inaccuracies in the rifle/bullet, etc.—is exaggerated by distance. Shooting at extended ranges must be a methodical, mechanical process precisely controlled throughout by the hunter. No shoot-and-hope deals here. Nothing can be left to chance. Instinctive shooting does not play a role here, as it might in sporters. Allow me to illustrate.

Let's just say the kill zone on a whitetail is 10x10 inches. (I know it's a little bigger, but let's go with it for illustration purposes.) At 500 yards, hitting a 10x10 area requires a two-minute angle, or a two-inch group at 100 yards. The truth is that most hunters I know can't consistently shoot a two-inch group on paper from a benchrest on a calm day. Yet, to kill a big buck standing 500 yards away, they have to find a solid rest (no bench available), figure out the range to something they can hardy see, remember the drop, dope the wind (even a modest 10 mph wind can move a bullet 20 inches), control a pounding heartbeat and make the shot before the deer steps into the brush! That's asking a lot, but it is possible, given enough practice and the right gear.

THE OVERVIEW

What do we want a long-range rig to do and what basic parameters should guide our choices? For our purposes, we want it to be capable of hitting and killing big whitetails at distances of 300 to 500 yards. To have the "flatness" we need for that kind of range, we need a muzzle velocity topping 3,000 fps and a sight-in point that will maximize downrange trajectory (unless we have a way of quantitatively compensating for drop at various ranges, which we'll talk about later). For the downrange power needed to make clean kills, a bullet with plenty of weight that'll expand at reduced velocities is called for. We need to clearly see what we're shooting at, so a high-quality scope with adequate magnification is needed. Obviously, we also want the rifle to be capable of getting the job done closer than 300 yards when that time inevitably comes. That adds to scope and bullet requirements. The rifle should be heavy enough to steady-up for precise long shots but light enough to carry back and forth to the stand. Above all, it must be accurate, i.e., capable of shooting half-inch groups at 100 yards! To round out the long-range kit, a laser rangefinder is useful, if not essential, to judge distance; a set of quality binoculars and/or spotting scope is mandated to judge trophy quality; and some type of aid in resting the rifle is a very good idea.

For our purposes, we want a long-range rig to be capable of hitting and killing big whitetails at distances of 300 to 500 yards...above all, it must be accurate, capable of shooting half-inch groups at 100 yards.

As we move into our discussion of the various components and options in long-range gear, I should point out that this field is virtually exploding with innovative new high-tech products, far too many for me to cover them all...or even know about them all. As I was doing my research for this chapter, I was amazed by the proliferation of specialized products aimed at the emerging long-range market—from rifles to cartridges to scopes and everything in between. High-tech has hit the shooting industry and will change much about our sport. Because some of this new stuff is yet to be proven and because there would be no end to this chapter if I tried to cover it all, I'm going to try to stay away from brand-name mentions. Still, a certain amount of it will be necessary for illustration purposes and because my experience may lie with a particular product. But, know that there are always other options...and new ones on the way. All this said, there are certain principles we can establish to guide our decisions and this is where I want to focus.

THE RIFLE

As with sporters, the make of rifle you choose is a personal decision. The type of action is less limited. Bolt-actions are far and away the favorite among the long-range clan, but a good single-shot will also work since speedy follow-up shots are seldom in the cards. You can go factory, semi-custom or custom. (I define semi-custom as either a production rifle, as opposed to a special order, made by one of the smaller, specialty gun builders or a significantly reworked factory rifle.) Nearly all the major manufacturers now make factory versions of long-range rifles, and some of them are excellent. The only one I have much experience with is the

Remington Sendero, which is of near-custom quality, though a little fine-tuning is helpful. When working at ranges up to and beyond a quarter-mile, it's a good idea to have any factory rifle "cleaned up" by a competent gunsmith. A little smoothing here and there, a bit of bedding touchup and some trigger work really make a difference. Often, factories just can't take the time for the fine work needed to wring out the last ounce of performance in a rifle. Triggers, especially, need attention, largely because liability has forced gun makers to set the trigger at higher breaking points than a long-range shooter can live with.

There are a great many semi-custom and custom gun makers now turning out long-range rigs. If ever there was a reason to go this way, long-range shooting would seem to be it. The tricks of the trade are many, and a professional can squeeze out the last bit of accuracy and even speed from a rifle/cartridge combination. Plus, there are many details in setup and fit a man with know-how and time can incorporate that will help you satisfactorily ink the deal when a big buck is standing on the far horizon.

I recently worked with two gun makers—Tim McWhorter and D'Arcy Echols (addresses given in previous chapter)—on custom projects and gained great rifles and lots of knowledge from those guys. But, many others pros are out there. Some of my friends have rifles made by long-range pioneer Kenny Jarrett (383 Brown Road, Jackson, SC 29831) and think they have the best. I've heard glowing firsthand performance reports on cross-country rifles built by Lazzeroni Arms (P.O. Box 26696, Tucson, AZ 85726), David Miller Company (3131 East Greenlee Road, Tucson, AZ 85716) and Brown Precision (P.O. Box 270-R, Los Molinos, CA 96055). Many of the semi-custom and custom gun builders also have access to wildcats or have their own proprietary cartridges that will put up better numbers than most anything commercially available, with the notable exception of Weatherby's new .30-378.

Because accuracy is such a premium in long-range rifles, there are a couple of after-market barrel treatments worth mentioning that can enhance accuracy and barrel life. I'm speaking of electro-chemical polishing and cryogenic tempering. Either or both treatments can be applied to your rifle. They are not prohibitively expensive, and either or both can tighten groups on some rifles considerably. BlackStar Accurizing (11501 Brittmoore Park Drive, Houston, TX 77041) is the place for the electronic smoothing of barrels. The cryogenic treatment, which involves deep-

My daughter, Jennifer, used Gary Schwarz's 14.5 pound long-range rifle to make a 250-yard shot down a sendero to kill this fine drop-tined buck on El Tecomate Ranch. In the excitement of a hurried shot, the extra weight helped steady the rifle. The buck fell where he stood. Photo by author.

freezing the barrel to relieve stresses and to smooth and toughen the steel, is the purview of Cryo-Accurizing (1160 South Monroe, Decatur, IL 62521). In long-range work, the extra accuracy these treatments may be able to deliver could pay off someday in the field, assuming your rifle isn't all it should be to start with.

Opinions about the right size and weight of a long-range rig are many and varied. Essentially, there are two schools of thought. One, it should be light enough to also serve as a sporter. Two, it should be purely a long-distance firearm, and thus should be heavy enough to settle in firmly on the rest and absorb some of the inevitable tremors emanating from a nervous hunter. I lean more toward the latter, though I don't want it any heavier than necessary for good stability. I know that there are very accurate light rifles in long-range calibers that have the potential to shoot just as precisely at great distances as heavier ones. But, "potential" doesn't kill a deer; reality does. And, reality is that a heavier rifle will steady-up and shoot better under field conditions than will a light rifle.

For that reason, not inherent accuracy, I prefer some weight in a long-range rig. There's also the added benefit of heavier rifles not kicking as hard as lighter ones shooting the same cartridge. That translates into better accuracy, and probably more trigger time on the range.

How much weight is enough? I think the ideal compromise between carry-weight and shooting-weight for the scoped rifle is somewhere around 11 pounds. To increase barrel stiffness without adding too much weight, I like to flute the barrel, which shaves off about a half-pound, making the gun less barrel heavy and a bit easier to carry on a sling. Frankly, a heavier gun would be more stable, but in the places I hunt, I often have to tote the thing, along with all the other paraphernalia for long-range shooting and long hours of sitting, for several hundred yards. If it were much heavier, better field accuracy wouldn't do me any good because I would leave it at home anyway. My friend, Gary Schwarz, prefers a heavier gun, but most of his hunting is on Tecomate Ranch, where he can drive to within a couple hundred yards of his tripods. If your situation allows for a heavier rifle, you would not regret the extra weight when shooting time arrives.

> *I think the ideal compromise between carry-weight and shooting-weight for the scoped rifle is somewhere around 11 pounds.*

On most sporter magnums, 24-inch barrels are standard, but on long-range rifles, the standard length is 26 inches. This squeezes out the last bit of velocity by making better use of the slow-burning powders employed in the big-capacity cases needed to push a reasonably heavy bullet at high speeds. The longer barrel is a bit cumbersome, especially when tipped by a muzzle brake, to move around in tight quarters. Still, for long-range shooting and maximum velocity, you need the added length. Many sniper rifles carry 30-inch tubes.

I mentioned muzzle brakes, so I'll address them now. True, muzzle brakes do reduce muzzle jump and recoil, but heavy long-range rifles tend to moderate these maladies anyway. As a matter of personal preference, not so much a functional issue, I don't like them. They are too loud. Not only do they bother me when I'm shooting, but anyone around who is so unlucky as to be in a worse position than I am when behind the buttstock is likely to be nearly deafened.

My long-range rifle has a screw-on muzzle brake, which can be removed and replaced with a standard tip. The first time I ever shot that gun, it was equipped with the brake. I was on a rifle range that had a very low metal roof angling down just in front of the muzzle (a very bad roof design for a range). I had on full ear protection, but when I fired, I thought someone had hit me squarely in the nose, so great was the concussion of the report off that roof. The guy next to me jumped up from his bench and staggered away, shaking his head and opening his mouth wide in an attempt to relieve the pressure on his ears. Everybody else on the range stopped what they were doing and looked my way…accusingly. For myself, I was busy checking to see how badly my nose was bleeding. By unanimous consent, I removed the muzzle brake and haven't put it back on since. Guides, in particular, hate them since they are often the most direct recipient of the ear-splitting report. Since I often "guide" my family, I don't have them on any of my rifles. Kick I can handle, but I draw the line on blowing out my sinuses and eardrums.

A crisp, light trigger is particularly important on long-range rifles. Mine is set at 2.5 pounds. That's light enough. Any lighter might get me in trouble on cold days or when I'm hyped up by the sight of a whopper buck.

The stock on a long-range rig should be sufficiently stout to complement the overall bulk of the gun. My preferences lean the same way as they do on a sporter—straight, sleek lines, no Monte Carlo comb, perhaps a small cheek piece and minimal drop at the comb, i.e., nine-sixteenths-inch. I like a forearm undersurface broad enough to provide a stable resting surface for shooting, but I don't like a flat fore-end that's uncomfortable to grip. Because scopes are often mounted higher on long-range rifles than on sporters, it does not hurt for the comb to be a bit thicker and rounder to provide a little more elevation, a tad firmer contact point and a little less of a smack on recoil. With the thicker comb, a bit of castoff in the stock will aid in eye alignment.

SHOOTING STRATEGIES AND SIGHTING-IN

Before we go any further, you have a decision to make regarding your shooting strategy. How do you want to compensate for bullet drop—and to a lesser degree, wind drift—in long-range shooting? There are essentially three strategies from which to choose. One, you can dial-in a scope-setting known to be correct for that rifle and load at that particular distance and hold dead-on the target. We'll call this the "dial-in" method. Two, you can use dots or lines inside the scope calibrated to span specific minutes of angle (MOA, i.e., one inch at 100 yards) to aid both in distance estimation and sighting at extended ranges. This we'll label the "MOA" method. Three, you can sight-in the rifle in the most advantageous way to maximize downrange trajectory and then holdover (good old Kentucky windage) based on the bullet's known trajectory at various ranges. We'll refer to this as the "holdover," or "point-blank," method.

Out to about 500 yards, the holdover method works quite nicely. Beyond that distance, a decided edge goes to the dial-in and, to a lesser degree, the MOA methods. For hunting purposes, with our limit of 500 yards, any of the three will work. I lean toward the simplicity and practicality of the MOA and holdover methods. Yet, I think you're going to see more and more people eventually go to the dial-in drop allowance once scopes with precision adjustments and trajectory/scope-adjustment charts (and computer programs) are more readily available… and once ranges begin to creep out farther, as I fear they will. Here, I will focus primarily on the lower-tech alternatives, though I will discuss the use of range-compensating scopes briefly.

Dial-In Shooting

With both the dial-in and MOA shooting strategies, specialized scopes are required. In dial-in shooting, the scope, called a range-compensating scope, must have remarkably accurate external adjustments. Don't confuse this type of scope with the long-available, popular-priced scopes with external adjustments. I'm talking about a precision, costly instrument designed to move the point of aim exactly according to the calibrations. Very few scopes presently available can do that accurately enough for the exacting demands of long-range shooting, though several make the claim. A few scopes have good repeatability, meaning that a certain number of clicks always moves the point of impact a certain amount, but the clicks don't (always) correspond to the advertised calibration. That's an acceptable solution for someone who is willing to spend enough time on the range to learn exactly the number of clicks needed for various ranges. Of course, what you really want is both repeatability *and* accurate calibration. On that count, the general consen-

The tools of the trade. A long-range rifle, a sandbag, a spotting scope and a stand with a steady rifle rest. The only thing missing is a laser rangefinder, which was around my neck when I snapped the photo.

sus is that Night Force scopes currently lead the way. Some shooters I know use the Leupold Mark 4 scopes to good effect, though the scope's repeatability has a better reputation than does the accuracy of its calibrations. Other scopes also are reported to work well, but I am reluctant to name them since I don't have firsthand knowledge of their performance. The point is that they are available and more are on the way.

Once you've put together the right dial-in gear, all you need to put this system to practice is a big buck at a known range (that's where the laser rangefinder comes in), an intimate knowledge of your rifle's trajectory at various ranges and the number of clicks needed to move the scope's point of aim to the desired distance, the latter two elements being the tricky parts. To get that information, you need time on the range and some basic math skills, or a ballistics computer program…then time on the range. Once you have it all figured out, just hold dead-on and squeeze. This long-range strategy works and is about the only way to accurately shoot at varying ranges much beyond 600 yards. Kentucky windage and any other form of guesswork just doesn't cut it at those distances. The fact that most elite military units primarily use range-compensating scopes for their extreme-range work speaks to the effectiveness of this strategy.

MOA Aids In Shooting

The MOA method involves a dot (or dots) sized to represent certain minutes of angle or a series of lines, called stadia wires, spaced to represent specified minutes of angle. Besides aiding in sighting, this method also has the added benefit of being a reasonably accurate way to gauge distances. When employing this method, the magnification of the scope must be fixed since the dots and wires are scaled to a specific magnification. (A variable scope can be used, but when using the dot or wires, the scope must be set on maximum power. Even a fixed intermediate-power setting won't do because the scope can't be set *exactly* on an intermediate power.) To use the range-finding feature of this method, you have to know the chest-depth of the animal you are hunting.

With a fixed magnification and a known chest-depth, a dot or the span between wires of a known MOA allows the user to scale the chest-depth of the animal and determine the distance. For instance, let's assume that the dot or stadia wire represents three MOA (which means it spans three inches per 100 yards, thus, six inches at 200 yards, nine inches at 300 yards, and so on) and that it covers three-fourths of a whitetail believed to be 20 inches deep in the chest. Three-fourths of 20 inches is 15 inches. To determine distance, simply divide the number of inches indicated by the dot or wire, in this case 15, by three (the MOA of the dot or stadia wire) and you get the answer in hundreds of yards. In this case, the answer is five, telling us the deer is standing 500 yards away. Now, if we know the number of inches spanned by the dot or stadia wire and we know the drop of the bullet at the distance the deer is standing, then we can use the dot or wire as a sighting reference to compensate for drop, or perhaps even as an aiming point for a dead-on hold, depending on the setup.

I have had considerable experience with a single, center-crosshair dot, mainly in varmint shooting, and found it to be somewhat useful as a rangefinder, but I didn't like it as a sight. It covered too much of the target and didn't lend itself to the precision I like at long ranges. There are several other types of dots and circles available, perhaps the most useful of which are the Mil. Dots Leupold puts in their Mark 4 scopes. Mil. Dots are simply a series of tiny dots that replace the fine crosswires in duplex reticles. Each dot (four in each direction from center) is spaced to represent 3.5 minutes when the scope is at maximum power. When the target is a known size, the dots can be used both as ranging and sighting aids. The concept is exactly the same as with stadia wires, so what I'm about to say about the wires also applies to Mil. Dots, though I feel stadia wires are easier to see and use in the field.

The fact that most elite military units primarily use range-compensating scopes for their extreme-range work speaks to the effectiveness of this strategy.

Until recently, I had never used stadia wires, but when D'Arcy Echols tells me something works, I listen. He really likes stadia wires both as a rangefinder and a sighting tool to compensate for long-range drop. When he offered to send me a scope with stadia wires to try, I eagerly accepted. The scope he sent me was a 4.5-14X Leupold sporting stadia wires that had been installed by Dick Thomas (Premier Reticle, 920 Breckinridge Lane, Winchester, VA 22601, 540-722-0601) for a cost of around $125. This particular scope had two wires positioned just below the horizontal reticle at a distance of three MOA when the variable was on full power. Plus, it had a single vertical stadia wire (also three MOA) on either side of the upright crosshair to aid in compensating for wind drift. Frankly, I didn't like the vertical wires. They tended to confuse the sight picture. After trying the horizontal stadia wires, both as a range-estimator and sighting aid, I concur that this is an excellent way to go.

As a range-estimator, D'Arcy said that he had tested the stadia-rigged scope against laser rangefinders on deer and antelope and, with experience, had found it to be accurate to within 25 yards out to 500 yards. Armed with my laser rangefinder, I immediately ran my own tests on the scope's rangefinding qualities on the many whitetails on my Montana ranch. After some practice, I was surprised by its ranging accuracy and simplicity. Of course, the key is knowing the chest-depth of the animal you are trying to range. Of the areas I hunt most frequently, these general measurements would apply: the Southeast and South Texas, 18 inches; the Northwest, 19 inches; Central Canada, 21 inches.

The stadia wires are not only accurate range-estimators, they also are excellent sighting aids, if you know where your rifle is shooting at various distances, which is a necessity with any system. For instance, say a buck suspected of having a 20-inch-deep chest is standing across a alfalfa field. You put the horizontal crosshair on his back, and the first stadia wire hits him just slightly over half way down...12 inches, you figure. Divide 12 by three and you get four...400 yards, that is. Conveniently, say your rifle is sighted-in to be 12 inches low at 400. You just use the first stadia wire as the horizontal crosshair and let fly. At 500 yards, that same rifle in a .300 Win. Mag. would be about 30 inches low. A quick calculation tells you that 30 inches at 500 yards is six MOA (30 divided by 5). Happily, the second stadia wire is three MOA below the first, or six MOA down from the horizontal crosswire. To hit the 500-yard deer, hold dead-on with the second stadia wire. This is a very neat system that is surprisingly quick and accurate with a little experience...and all that from two simple wires. Of course, stadia-wire sighting works wonderfully in combination with a laser rangefinder, too.

Even the point where the coarse crosswire changes to the thinner wire on duplex crosshairs can be scaled to a specific MOA on the range at maximum magnification and used as a rangefinding and/or sighting aid. Other mechanical aids also have been worked into scopes for such purposes, but they are all variations off a central theme. Most work to some degree, though some only help in rangefinding, but I have not found anything simpler or more effective than stadia wires. And when a big buck is standing way out there, simple and effective is not a bad combination.

Kentucky Windage...But Not Too Much!

Even simpler, and still quite effective, is sighting-in in such a way as to maximize downrange trajectory by keeping the bullet near the line of sight for the greatest possible distance. There are essentially three factors that affect downrange trajectory—one, the sight-in point; two, bullet velocity; three, bullet ballistic coefficient. That's also pretty much their order of importance. The general idea is to shoot a streamlined, relatively heavy (for its diameter) bullet at a high velocity (over 3,000 fps) that is sighted-in for the longest possible distance (300 yards or more) that won't cause bad midrange trajectory problems. We'll talk more about velocity and ballistic coefficient when we get to our cartridge and bullet discussions. Here, I want to discuss sighting-in.

Let's come at this through the backdoor by setting certain parameters, a wish list if you will. Then, we'll see what they tell us about the ideal sight-in point for holdover shooting. We'll start with deviation above the line of sight. After all, no matter how long a shot you prepare for, shorter shots are sure to come, and our instinct is to aim straight at close-up animals. A couple of years ago in Canada, I set up on a half-mile-square alfalfa field with my long-range rig *hoping* to get a shot as close as 400 or 500 yards. When the buck I was after walked across a corner of the field about 150 yards away headed to a thick willow slough, I hastily got off a shot just before he disappeared over a knoll. In my rush, I forgot to allow for rise, which was nearing its zenith at that range. Luckily, my center-shoulder hold resulted in a spine shot. The buck went down but required a finishing shot. My rifle was about 4.5 inches high at that distance. An inch or two higher, and I would not have gotten that buck.

Deviation above the line of sight does make a big difference. That's the reason my personal maximum for allowable midrange trajectory is five inches. This guideline serves as a major determining factor in my sight-in point. Anymore than five inches, and sooner or later, a rushed shot will result in a missed or wounded animal. Less than five, say four, wouldn't hurt my feelings if I could get acceptable downrange performance, which in holdover shooting I define as being no more than 24 inches low at 500 yards. With 24 inches of drop, I can holdover the buck's back a distance of about half his chest-depth, which is easy enough to gauge, and still kill the animal cleanly. Much more than that, and the guesswork gets a little shaky.

A maximum rise of five inches and a maximum 500-yard drop of 24 inches pretty much dictate a velocity of about 3,100 fps. If I throw into the formula a minimum bullet weight of 150 grains to guarantee enough downrange power (I'll explain later), then some stringent requirements have been placed on a long-range rifle dependant on estimated holdover at 400 and 500 yards. That's ok. When using Kentucky windage to shoot at a deer as far away as 500 yards, you must have stringent parameters to reduce the guesswork to acceptable levels. Otherwise, you had better be a good tracker or take failure well.

Given our parameters—a maximum midrange trajectory of five inches, no more than 24 inches of drop at 500 yards, a velocity bettering 3,100 fps and a bullet weight of at least 150 grains—then we can come up with a sight-in point for holdover shooting. It'll probably come as no surprise that the ideal sight-in point for long-range rifles is from 3 to 3.5 inches high at 100 yards. With a velocity of 3,100 fps, three inches will put the bullet dead-on target somewhere around 300 yards and 3.5 high will hit the bull's eye at about 325 yards. More than 3.5 inches high at a hundred on most rigs will result in greater than five inches of rise, thus becoming the limiting factor.

Though I have seen this trajectory path punched out on paper many times at the range, just to be sure of the exact numbers I called D'Arcy Echols, knowing he knew folks with a computerized ballistics program who could run the numbers precisely. (The ballistics tables I had didn't quite jive with my desired sight-in points.) I gave D'Arcy the specs from my .300 Weatherby Mag.—180-grain Nosler Ballistic Tip, 3,200 fps, 3.5 inches high at 100—and he promptly called Nosler's Mike Harris, who kindly ran the numbers through the company computer. The ballistics table Mike generated for a 3.5-inch-high sight-in point is shown. I found it to be very interesting.

500-Yard Ballistics Table

(180-grain Nosler Ballistic Tip, 3,200 fps, sighted-in 3.5 inches high, 325-yard zero, maximum deviation above line of sight is 4.88 inches at 183 yards.)

Distance (yards)	0	50	100	150	200	250	300	350	400	450	500
Velocity	3200	3113	3027	2944	2862	2782	2702	2625	2550	2475	2402
Energy	4092	3872	3662	3463	3274	3092	2920	2755	2538	2448	2305
Path	-1.55	+1.44	+3.53	+4.67	+4.81	+3.89	+1.85	-1.33	-5.87	-11.69	-18.93

How did we do against our trajectory parameters? At 3.5 high, we get a maximum rise of 4.9 inches at 183 yards, about all we can tolerate. The dead-on point is 325 yards, and the 500-yard drop is 18.9 inches. All our guiding parameters were met, including striking energy, which at 500 yards came in with room to spare at 2,305 foot-pounds. Sighting-in three inches high (Mike also ran those numbers) affects the downrange numbers a little but still meets our parameters. The bullet reaches its zenith of 4.2 inches above the line of sight at 171 yards and falls back on target at 305 yards. At 500 yards, it's 21 inches low, two inches lower than the 3.5-inch sight-in point. The only liability to attain that two inches of "flatness" is an extra three-quarter-inch of rise. That's a tradeoff I would make, which is why I think a sight-in point of 3.5 inches high at 100 yards is the ideal compromise for holdover shooting.

Let's translate this into practical guidelines for aiming points when hunting. But remember, this is the trajectory of my .300 Weatherby Mag. so sighted. Your rifle will undoubtedly differ. Whatever it is, you must find out before you take to the field. Now, my sighting rules of thumb for that rifle. If the buck is within 275 yards (where the bullet is still about 2.5 inches high), I aim for the heart. That gives me the maximum kill zone *above* the aiming point to account for high impact. From 275 to 350 yards, I hold for a center-shoulder shot. If he's 350 to 425 yards (where the bullet is about 8 inches low), I hold for a high-shoulder shot, about three-fourths of the way up. Now comes the Kentucky windage. At 450 yards, I hold even with the top of his back. At 475 yards, (where the bullet is about 15 inches low) I hold a quarter-chest-depth over his back. When shooting at 500 yards, I holdover his back a half-chest-depth.

Before moving on, I should say that sighting-in 3.5 inches high is less critical when using stadia wire or a range-compensating scope because both of these methods depend on quantitative means of accounting for drop at various ranges. The sight-in point for those methods should be something that lends itself to easy-to-remember numbers or, in the case of stadia wires, a point that allows the stadia wires to coincide as closely as possible to 400 and 500 yards. The point is that with those two shooting strategies other factors need to be considered, but in most cases, you're still going to want to get all you can out of the trajectory before you have to start compensating, meaning 3 to 3.5 inches high is likely where you'll end up.

One more thing. It is a widely held belief that, all other things being equal, scope height can make a big difference in downrange trajectory. I, too, once believed this to be the case. Well, it does make a difference, but not much of one. D'Arcy asked Mike Harris at Nosler to compare the trajectory of a 180-grain bullet traveling at 3,200 fps sighted to hit three inches high at 100 yards from a medium-height scope mount versus a super-high mount. At 500 yards, the rifle with a medium-height scope will hit just over one inch lower than the rifle with super-high scope mounts. That's not much difference; in fact, it's about one-fifth MOA. You can't hold that in the field. This leaves the only justification for high mounts in the fact that they allow the use of scopes with larger objective lenses that will improve brightness at *higher* magnification.

SCOPES

Again, I prefer variables. Even long-range rifles will occasionally see close-up or in-cover duty, requiring low-end magnification in the 4 to 6X-range. On the top-end, magnification can be as high as a shooter would like...unless he's using MOA stadia wires (or dots). As I said earlier, using stadia wire requires a fixed magnification, which dictates that variables be turned to the highest power setting. Because mirages can badly distort the image at high magnification under certain conditions, the practical limit of magnification when using stadia wires is about 14X to avoid mirage problems. On scopes not equipped with MOA stadia wire, they can be set on any magnification if mirages (and brightness) are not a concern. However, I doubt if much is gained with magnification over 16X. I have a 6.5-20X Leupold on my rifle and usually end up hunting with it set somewhere around 15X for better brightness and clarity. (I do use the higher magnification at the range, though.) A 3-12X is about minimum, but something with 4 to 6X on the bottom and 14 to 16X on the top is about ideal.

Back in our discussion of scope brightness in sporters, we concluded that at sporter magnification levels scope quality was more important than anything else, including the size of the objective bell. Likewise, in scopes for long-range shooting, nothing beats quality, but at the higher magnification levels needed for precise faraway work, the size of the objective lens does become an important consideration in brightness. Remember our discussions on exit pupil—that it could be determined by dividing the diameter of the objective bell by the magnification level and that the most exit pupil we humans can use is 7mms but, practically speaking, about all we hunters can take advantage of is 5mms.

In sporters, with their working magnification "average" of, say, 7X, lens diameters of 36, 40 and 42mms all still yield exit pupils of 6mm or better, well above the practical usable number of 5mms. But in long-range scopes, the working magnification "average" is, say, 12X. On a 42mm objective lens, that yields an exit pupil of 3.5mm. It quickly becomes apparent that objective lens size does matter in high-magnification scopes. As a rule of thumb, I want to have an exit pupil of at least 4mms in low light when at 10X. That means a minimum objective diameter of 40mms for my long-range scopes. If you want more light dur-

This is an 8-pointer! Gun maker Tim McWhorter of Doerun, Georgia, shot this 158-point buck on El Tecomate Ranch with his own proprietary cartridge, a .30 T-Raptor, one of several super .30-calibers capable of pushing a 180-grain bullet downrange at 3,400 fps. Photo by author.

ing the dim early and late hours, you'll have to either settle for less magnification than 10X or buy a scope with a larger objective lens. My 6.5-20X Leupold has a 50mm lens that gives me a 5mm exit pupil at 10X, or allows me to go to 12X to net a 4mm exit pupil. Do the math for yourself to decide what you want.

I once asked a shooting expert about that mysterious thing called parallax. After a long and complicated explanation, I still didn't know what it meant and how it would affect me as a shooter. Finally, with the help of D'Arcy Echols and Leupold, I've got a partial handle on it. This is Leupold's explanation: "Parallax is the apparent movement of the target relative to the reticle when you move your eye away from the centerpoint of the eyepiece. It occurs when the target does not fall on the same plane as the reticle."

What does that mean to you? Essentially, that parallax can cause a deviation between where the crosshairs are "looking" and the sighted-in point of aim, leading to inaccuracy. At short distances, the parallax effect has very little impact on accuracy, but at the long ranges we're talking about in this chapter, it can make a difference of an inch or more. Therefore, on long-range rifles, it's a good idea to buy a scope that can be adjusted to eliminate parallax at a given range. Most high-magnification scopes come so equipped.

CARTRIDGES

Let me start by saying that if you're using one of the calibrated drop-compensating aids, such as stadia wire or a dial-in scope, the trajectory of the cartridge is less important than when the holdover method is used. After all, many sniper rifles and 1,000-yard competition rifles are .308s, which lob a 180-grain bullet at a mere 2,700 fps, but these users aren't depending on holdover to arc the bullet into the target. They have ways of precisely compensating for bullet drop. But, the holdover method does require a flat trajectory to minimize guesswork. Plus, in hunting, we are not only concerned about hitting the target, but we also want to make a clean kill on a animal that we may or may not hit perfectly. That calls for considerable striking energy—more, in my opinion, than is needed in a sporter where ranges are closer and where exact bullet placement is likely to be better.

The fact is that every potential for error is multiplied at extended ranges (even a one-inch group at 100 yards becomes a five-inch group at 500 yards). One of the few ways we have to compensate for the crap-happens factor inherent to long-range shooting is plenty of striking energy. For my money, I like to have at least 2,000 foot-pounds of energy at 500 yards. That pretty much dictates a 150-grain bullet leaving the muzzle at around 3,100 fps, meaning that the 7mm Rem. Mag. and the slightly more powerful 7mm Weatherby Mag. are about the minimum cartridges I would even look at for long-range trophy whitetail hunting. And, the truth is that if I were forced to use a 7mm I would opt for one of the more powerful 7mms, like the 7.21 Lazzeroni Firehawk or 7mm STW, either of which can run a 160-grain bullet downrange at something better than 3,200 fps. But, I'm not forced to choose a 7mm, so I would go to my first preference—a hot .30-caliber cartridge.

Considering downrange energy, frontal area, velocity, bullet weight and shootability, the powerful .30 calibers are my choices. It could be argued that going even larger, to the 8mm or .338 calibers, would give you more of a good thing, and if you want to go that way, fine. I don't think it's necessary for whitetails. Plus, you may give up something in shootability, and perhaps in velocity. For my money, .30 caliber is where it's at. But, which .30-caliber cartridge?

The .300 Win. Mag., which pushes a 180-grain bullet along at about 3,100 fps (handloaded), is where I would start looking. A slightly better choice is the .300 Weatherby Mag., which can get 3,200 fps out of the 180-grain. Then, we move to some hot new numbers, like the .300 Dakota (it is based on the .404 Jeffery case and is virtually identical to Tim McWhorter's .30 T-Raptor), .300 Jarrett, 7.82 Lazzeroni Warbird and the new speed king, the .30-378 Weatherby Mag. These cartridges are all capable of velocities topping 3,200 fps with 180-grain bullets, going all the way up to 3,500 fps in the .30-378.

So, which one? It's your choice. Any of them will do the job. The difference in 3,100 and 3,500 fps at 500 yards is about four inches in drop and 600 foot-pounds of energy. A difference, to be sure, but you have to decide if it's worth the cost. The more powerful you go, the more of a lickin' you're going to take. If you go with a wildcat or proprietary cartridge, expect to pay more and perhaps have a harder time getting brass. I chose the .300 Weatherby Mag. for shootability and for availability of brass. A 180-grain bullet at 3,200 fps has served me very well so far. And, I don't dread going to the range with it, but I wouldn't want much more of what it dishes out!

BULLETS

A long-range bullet must be extremely accurate, fast expanding and able to penetrate well enough to kill cleanly from various angles and distances. That's asking a lot of a bullet. Just the extremely accurate requirement eliminates many bullets from consideration since we've said the bullet/rifle combination must be capable of half-minute accuracy. The fast-opening part, necessary because of the .30-30 speeds at which it must expand at long distances, puts a bunch more out of contention. And, we need adequate penetration, not just at long ranges but also for the closer shots. How do we get all that? The answer is: Find an inherently accurate big-game bullet known to open rapidly and choose a relative heavyweight in that bullet. In the 7mm, that means at least 150 grains but preferably 160. In the .30 caliber, the preferred weight is 180 grains and 200 would not be a bad choice in the super magnums.

What make of bullet is best? I don't know that I can answer that, but I can tell you what I use and which ones are preferred by dedicated long-range shooters I know. I use Nosler Ballistic Tips and so do most of the guys who take their long-range shooting seriously. The Ballistic Tip has an extremely hard polycarbonate tip that both becomes a wedge on impact, disrupting the front of the bullet for fast expansion, and prevents accuracy-robbing tip damage in the magazine from heavy recoil. Nosler and Winchester have recently joined forces to make supreme bullets under the name Combined Technology and are making a version of the Ballistic Tip, called the Ballistic Silvertip, that sports a special coating intended to reduce fouling and friction, thus increasing velocity. Though I haven't used it yet, it should perform as well as the Ballistic Tip.

> *Ballistic coefficient affects velocity retention, which affects trajectory and down-range energy.*

Another bullet favored by those in the know is the Sierra Game King. Both the Nosler and Sierra are renown for their accuracy and are quick to open, so quick in fact that you *must* use the heavier weights if they are to hold together at the hyper velocities of sub-100-yard shots. No doubt, other bullets will do the job. Hornady makes a 162-grain 7mm and a 180 and 190-grain .30-caliber Boat-Tail Spire Point bullet that should be excellent for long-range work. Using sporters, I've shot many deer with Hornady Interlock bullets and have found them to be accurate and fast to expand, but I have not used them as part of my long-distance shooting mix.

The requirement for a relatively heavy bullet goes a long way in addressing something I want to briefly mention. That something is ballistic coefficient, which is a measure of a bullet's aerodynamic efficiency, or simply put, how well it flies and retains its velocity and energy. Ballistic coefficient is essentially a function of bullet sectional density (weight for its diameter) and shape. Though I'm certain this doesn't need to be stated, long-range shooting requires pointed-nosed, streamlined bullets. Of course, sleek boat-tail bullets are the stereotypical long-distance projectile, but all else being equal, the boat-tail shape in itself doesn't make all that much difference. The real ballistic-coefficient battle is won in over-all shape and weight versus diameter. If you pick a pointed-nose bullet, called a spitzer, that is relatively heavy for its caliber, then you've pretty well covered ballistic-coefficient concerns. Why even be concerned about it in the first place?

Ballistic coefficient affects velocity retention, which affects trajectory and downrange energy. Because sectional density is a big part of ballistic coefficient, it is possible for a heavier bullet in a particular caliber to start out slower than a lighter bullet and actually end up faster at some distant point. For instance, let's take a .30-caliber 150-grain Nosler Solid Base (ballistic coefficient of .393) and start it off at .300 Weatherby velocities, i.e., 3,400 fps, and compare it to a 180-grain bullet (ballistic coefficient of .491) of the same make and from the same cartridge leaving the muzzle at 3,200 fps. At 400 yards, the 180-grain bullet is actually going faster than the 150-grain bullet. At 500 yards, the trajectory difference is negligible. Around the 600-yard mark, the 180 is actually flatter and becomes increasingly so as the range increases.

The distance at which the ballistic (trajectory and/or energy) advantages of a bullet with a greater initial velocity give way to the superior flight efficiency of a slower bullet with a higher ballistic coefficient is what I call the "ballistic crossover point." Beyond that point, the bullet with the better ballistic coefficient has everything going for it, regardless of its initial velocity. This is why the ultra-range shooters prefer heavy, high-ballistic-coefficient bullets like the 200-grain in the .30 caliber. The military has even developed special high-density bullets with ballistic coefficients topping .800 for shooting at distances well beyond 1,000 yards. At such extreme ranges, ballistic coefficient is of far greater concern than squeezing out the last bit of velocity. Yet, out to 500 yards with spitzer bullets, the crossover point where ballistic coefficient becomes more important in *trajectory* than initial velocity is seldom reached. So, practically speaking, assuming decent spitzer hunting bullets are chosen to begin with, ballistic coefficient is not a major concern relative to trajectory...but it is relative to striking energy and wind drift.

Continuing the same 150-grain (3,400 fps muzzle velocity) versus 180-grain (3,200 fps) comparison, let's look at 500-yard energy. The 150 arrives with 1,639 foot-pounds of energy compared to 2,055 for the 180. That's an energy difference of 25 percent! And not only that, the extra weight of the 180 guarantees better penetration, which is vital for the occasional close-up shot. Fortunately, because long-range setups typically are somewhat in the open, most deer shot at sporter ranges with a gun intended for 300 to 500-yard shots are in the clear and allow enough time to pick the shot. Still, go with the heaviest bullet that'll give you the desired trajectory. It'll pay off in the long and short run...and shot!

The impact wind has on a bullet at long distances is amazing. I consider wind drift a far more difficult factor to deal with than drop. After all, drop is consistent; wind is not. Even when you can estimate wind speed where you are sitting, it may not be the same 450 yards away where the buck is, or anywhere along the bullet's route. Anyway you shake it out, wind is a wildcard you can only partially compensate for. And, some of the places where long-range shooting is most likely to be called for, like the Plains and Prairies, Central Canada, South Texas and hills most anywhere, tend to be particularly windy. Many of my hunting days in eastern Montana have featured 20 to 30-mph winds. In fact, once when hunting along the Milk River, I shot at a buck standing 325 yards away and failed to compensate for a 30-mph crosswind. I hardly even scared him. (As luck would have it, the miss was recorded for all to see on Realtree's Monster Buck IV video.) Fortunately, the buck gave me a second shot at about 300 yards. Facing almost straight toward me, I held a full 15 inches into the wind, completely off his body, and finished the sordid affair.

How much does wind affect bullet flight? A bunch, but ballistic coefficient (and higher velocity) does make a difference in how much. Let's go back to our 150 versus 180 comparison. The 150-grain bullet, ballistic coefficient of .391, will be blown off course by a mere 10-mph wind 6.2 inches (Number Three *Nosler Reloading Manual*) at 300 yards and a whopping 18.4 inches at 500 yards. The 180-grain bullet (ballistic coefficient .491) fairs better but is far from being immune to wind drift. At 300 yards, it suffers 5.3 inches of drift, and at 500 yards, it's off course by 15.6 inches. Even in a modest 10-mph wind, the drift in either case is enough to result in a wounded or missed deer. And, the amount of wind drift increases proportionate to the increase in wind velocity, i.e., a 20-mph wind moves a bullet twice as much as a 10-mph wind. That means that a 20-mph crosswind can move a bullet off course by almost three feet at 500 yards! The wind is a very serious problem for long-range shooters. High velocity and high ballistic coefficients help, but you have to either

Long-range rifles are made to order when hunting places like large agricultural fields, where the buck of your dreams could walk out at any range. The keys to making the shot out to as far as 500 yards are knowing the distance, having a solid rest and being armed with an accurate rig you are intimately familiar with. Then, the last step—pulling the trigger—should be a practiced, mechanical process…if you can beat back buck fever! Photo by Troy Huffman.

record or remember the wind drift for your rifle at various ranges…or better yet, don't shoot at extreme distances in strong winds.

GEAR

Back in my baseball days, I used to encourage my pitcher and aggravate the opposing batter with the chant, "You can't hit what you can't see." That also is a truism in trophy whitetail hunting. Certainly, that saying applies to scopes, but here, I want to change it a bit and apply it to viewing optics, i.e., binoculars and spotting scopes. Our revised version is: "You shouldn't shoot at what you can't see…and judge."

The purpose of long-range shooting, at least in this discussion, is to extend the distance at which a trophy whitetail can be harvested. The problem is being able to recognize a trophy at extreme distances. I can tell you from experience that judging antlers in the kind of detail I like from a distance of 400 or 500 yards is not easy with the best binoculars. I use 10x42 Leicas, which are as good as they come, and I can't always tell what is atop a buck's head when he's beyond 400 yards well enough to make a shooting call. For this reason, I've had to incorporate additional magnification into my long-range-hunting daypack. My solution is the handheld Zeiss 20X spotting scope with a stabilizer. It really is a remarkable piece of equipment. When you press the stabilizer button, the vision-destroying quakes that accompany high magnification are taken out. Gary Schwarz uses the 20X Zeiss binoculars with the same stabilizing system and swears by them. Personally, I like the monocular better because the binoculars can't be adjusted for width and don't fit my eyes.

There are many other ways to go. Certainly, standard spotting scopes will work if you can set them up. Several folks I know attach spotting scopes to blank rifle stocks and that works well, even if it's cumbersome. And, there's always the possibility of using the rifle scope if the magnification is high enough, like 14 to 20X, for the final detail work after you've identified the buck as a suspect. The point is that you have to come up with a way to judge at the distances you hope to shoot. Otherwise, you will be handicapped, and sooner or later, you'll be kicking yourself for making a mistake on a deer you didn't want or for passing up one you did.

This long-range business requires that you know the distance. The MOA stadia wire or dot is one way to estimate range, but a far better way is the use of a laser rangefinder. These wonderful instruments are able to measure distances to within a yard or so in an instant. There was a time when they were very spendy, and some still are. But, Bushnell changed the rangefinding landscape a few years ago when the company came out with its popular-priced Yardage Pro 400, so named because it could measure distances out to 400 yards. Under hunting conditions, however, I found it to be more of a 300-yard rangefinder. That's just the distance at which the long-range shooter needs to start, not stop, his ranging work. Still, it was useful with a little creativity. But then, Bushnell came out with the Yardage Pro 800. Now we're cooking! Even though I find it to be more of a 600 to 700-yard tool, that's still plenty for 500-yard shooting. At about $450, this thing is a bargain.

For the most serious shooters, there is yet another step up in rangefinders to the Leica Geovid, which can read distances beyond 1,000 yards. At about $3,000, it ought to do wonders and it does. Swarovski also makes a rangefinder of similar quality and price. There are other rangefinders on the market that also work well. Swarovski even makes a 3-12X scope with a laser rangefinder built-in. If you're serious about long-range shooting, get a quality rangefinder.

Before you shoot at something a quarter-mile away, determine the trajectory of your rifle/bullet combination and write it down, preferably in 50-yard increments, especially beyond 350 yards, but at least in 100-yard increments. It's a good idea to tape the data to your stock, rangefinder or something you'll have with you when banging away at a deer across the valley.

Long-range shooting requires a solid rest. Depending on the hunting situation, there are many ways to prepare in advance. A bipod mounted to the front sling stud is one that will work well in certain situations, like open-country hunting from the ground. But, be certain to check your rifle's point of impact with the bipod in place because the upward pressure of the bipod can change where the bullet hits in some rifles, especially those that don't have free-floated barrels. When hunting from a stand, I prepare the rest before I ever commit the time to sit there. A small sandbag is a standard part of my long-range ditty bag. Think about the rest ahead of time and work out what you are going to do. Makeshift rests are usually fine with sporters but not so fine in the precise environment of long-range shooting.

One other thing. This hasn't got anything to do with gear, but it is essential advice for way-off shooting. Mark the exact spot the deer was standing when you shot, whether he runs or drops in his tracks! Horror stories abound about shooting a deer on the far mountain, way down the cutline, out in the clearcut or wherever, only to never find a trace of the deer once the hunter reaches the "spot." Things look different once you hit the ground and start walking. When a buck is 300, 400 or 500 yards away, it's very easy to mismark the spot by a hundred yards or more.

Just last year, a friend made a great 400-yard shot on a buck standing in a sendero in South Texas. He knew he hit him from the reaction and the telltale "thump." He confidently jumped down from his stand and went to retrieve him. Six hours later, no trace of the deer had been found. Certain that he had missed or only barely wounded the deer, he returned to the same stand the next morning and soon saw a gathering of

caracaras, a type of scavenging bird common in South Texas. He promptly joined the gathering…and found his 160-class 10-pointer lying in the
brush only 10 yards off the sendero. His six-hour search the day before
had been spent well short of where the buck lay! It happens all the time.

Mark the spot exactly…with clear landmarks! Better yet, if someone is with you, mark the spot and have them, or you, stay behind as a
spotter to guide in the retrieval process. Perhaps best of all, use your laser
rangefinder to mark the distance to the deer, and then, once recovery is
underway, range back on your stand. I won't do you much good to be able
to shoot over the curve of the earth if you can't find what you kill!

THE IDEAL LONG-RANGE RIFLE

There's plenty of room for varying opinions on this topic, but here
are my thoughts. As with sporters, I would build my long-range rig on
either a reworked Remington Model 700 or Winchester Model 70 action.
I would screw-in a 26-inch, fluted barrel, without a muzzle brake, though
most such rifles have one. I would set the trigger at a crisp 2.5 pounds. I
would select a straight, somewhat beefy, high-quality synthetic stock with
a nine-sixteenths-inch drop at the comb and a 13 5/8-inch length of pull.
Using two-piece Leupold bases and dovetail rings, I would mount a 4.5-
14X Leupold Vari-X III with a 50mm objective lens. (Yeah, I know
50mms forces me to high mounts, but I want the added brightness for
low-light hunting. I wouldn't, however, begrudge anybody choosing a
40mm objective lens to go with medium mounts.) I would have Premier
Reticle install two horizontal stadia wires spaced to three MOA. (If I did
not go with the stadia wires and depended on the holdover sighting
method, I would opt for the 6.5-20X Leupold with the 50mm objective
lens. The added magnification might occasionally help in judging and
would be handy for precise target shooting on the range. If I went with
the dial-in method, I would choose a 3.5-15X Nightforce scope, which
has a 56mm lens. I would elect one of their several reticle options that
include some type of MOA dots or lines for backup aids in ranging and
sighting.) I would choose a .300 Weatherby Mag. (handloaded) and shoot
180-grain Nosler Ballistic Tips at 3,200 fps. The whole setup, unloaded
and without a sling, would weigh about 11 pounds. I would do whatever
necessary—including electro-chemical polishing and/or cryogenic

tempering—to get half-inch accuracy out of it before going to the field.

THE ACCEPTABLE "EL CAMINO"

In our discussions of sporters, I said that a compromise between a sporter and a long-range rifle might end up being an "El Camino" that is neither fish nor foul. That's true, but what if that El Camino turned out to be essentially a sporter capable of 400-yard shots? Such a rifle might well prove to be practical and useful…as long as little or nothing is given up on the sporter-use side. Well, with a few modifications to our sporter specifications, that's possible.

First, we'll install a scope, perhaps something in the 3-10X class, with a single four-MOA horizontal stadia wire. We'll go to either the .300 Win. Mag. or .300 Weatherby Mag. for plenty of downrange wallop. We'll stick with the Nosler Partition, or some other premium bullet, to assure good penetration at high velocities on close-up shots. (The accuracy of the Partition is marginally sufficient for 400-yard shots in very accurate rifles.) We'll be sure the rig has adequate weight, say 8.75 to 9 pounds, to steady up for the longer shots while still being light enough to be handy as a sporter. We'll maintain the two-inch-high, 100-yard sight-in point. That will put the bullet about four inches low at 300 yards and, interestingly enough, about 16 inches low at 400 yards, which just happens to be four MOA, the same as the stadia wire! Plus, at 16 inches at 400 yards, four MOA is close enough to the chest-depth of most deer to be very useful as a range-estimator. With this setup, a trophy hunter would be quite well equipped for almost any opportunity out to 400 yards…without undue sacrifice at the more important sub-200-yard distances. Not a bad El Camino!

Chapter Thirty

Trophy Hunting– the State of Our Sport

I'M SURE YOU'VE FIGURED OUT BY now that this book was written for *serious* trophy hunters, among whose ranks I am proud to be counted...most of the time. Trophy hunting is a noble and honorable sport. But as so often is the case with popular and sometimes high-stakes endeavors, a darker side to trophy hunting has begun to emerge. It threatens to do harm to our sport from within and certainly stands to further tarnish our already shaky image in the eyes of the non-hunting public, something we can ill afford. But before looking at the concerns, let's look at some of trophy hunting's many positive attributes.

The fact that trophy hunting, i.e., the pursuit of *mature* bucks ranking among the area's best, requires selectivity is the foundation for some of the sport's greatest advantages, both for pursuer and pursuee. We'll start with the hunter, who is not just hunting *any* deer—he's after only a small part of the total buck population. He must be prepared to work his way through a number of lesser deer to find the one he wants. This selectivity has advantages for all concerned.

We're at a crossroads in private land deer management. We can take a direction aimed at restoring our herds to a healthy, natural state, leading to bucks like the one on the right. Or, we can continue on our present course and live with overcrowded, buck-depleted herds, where the buck on the left would be considered huge. I know how the deer would vote. Photo by Mike Biggs.

A MORE RESPONSIBLE HUNTER

To start with, hunting relatively rare and elusive animals increases the hunter's challenge and interest in the sport, especially if he has killed lots of bucks previously. The increased difficulty level also forces him to become more skilled, knowledgeable and better equipped, leading to a more capable, responsible hunter. Plus, the need to be selective makes him more disciplined, cautious and deliberate, thus a much safer hunter. And as a trophy hunter's involvement in his sport grows and his standards rise, he becomes more committed, not only to hunting but also to protecting and managing the species, often through the expenditure of considerable time and money.

Given all this, the dedicated trophy hunter is a true sportsman who puts more into his sport than he takes out. He is informed, involved and at the forefront of conservation and management issues affecting the whitetail and its habitat. He is willing to invest his time and resources, not just lip service, into the protection of the species and the pursuit of his sport, which for him is often a year-round endeavor. Because of his keen interest and active participation in the sport, the trophy hunter often seeks the chance to share his expertise and time afield with those of less experience and opportunity. This aspect of trophy hunting is very good for the sport, especially where children and women are involved.

Trophy hunting is a relatively non-consumptive sport. A trophy hunter's success is measured in the quality of the experience and in the quality, not quantity, of the animals he takes, or simply sees. He spends far more time watching and studying deer en route to that special trophy than does the indiscriminate hunter, who may end his hunt at the first sight of exposed bone. Because a trophy hunter passes smaller bucks, he leaves more bucks to grow older and bigger, or more for the less selective hunters to take. Anyway you look at it, trophy hunting is good for the sport. But, is it good for the whitetail? A resounding "Yes!"

GOOD FOR THE SPECIES

Trophy hunting and its associated trophy management are indeed good for the species. Why? Let's contrast trophy management to traditional "chicken-in-every-pot" management, and the answer will become clear. We'll start with the way many states have traditionally "managed" their herds.

The norm throughout much of the country has been heavy, indiscriminate buck pressure and an inadequate doe harvest. In too many places, does receive special protection but any buck that comes along is immediately converted to venison, resulting in a poor buck age structure and buck:doe ratio and too many deer. Such shot-out buck populations experience a breakdown in the whitetail social structure, and if this condition continues long-term, the genetic health of the herd will deteriorate. The logical end is a out-of-balance, overcrowded population of stunted, disease-prone deer, leading eventually to die-offs.

Perhaps worst of all, overcrowded deer populations can so severely damage the habitat that it can take *years* to recover, even after deer numbers are reduced. Many fail to realize this because even in over-browsed habitats there seems to be plenty of green vegetation for a green-vegeta-

This is what deer hunting is all about—good friends sharing special moments in a wonderful sport. Photo by Glenn Hayes.

tion-eater like the whitetail, but what the causal observer fails to realize is that not all vegetation is created equal from a deer's nutritional or palatability standpoint, not even close. The most nutritious and palatable plants are called preferred foods. They're the ones that make healthy, prosperous herds...and the first to go when there are too many deer.

The next tier in plant preference is secondary foods. Though less nutritious and/or palatable, deer can nonetheless survive on them, but at the cost of body and antler size and perhaps reproductive rates. By the time deer numbers are so high that secondary foods are in short supply, or virtually eliminated, the herd is in danger of having starvation and disease step in to indiscriminately reduce the population.

Tragically, when die-offs occur from gross overcrowding, deer numbers often fall well below the level the land could originally support. But even worst, long-term overcrowding causes a serious reduction in the land's original carrying capacity. In most such cases, the preferred foods have been all but eliminated and the secondary foods have taken a severe beating. With these plants so drastically reduced, the remaining undesirable plants invade the niches previously occupied by the primary and secondary species, making their recovery slow and difficult, even after deer numbers have plummeted. And, the rebound of the desirable plants is further hampered by the desperate need of the remaining deer, which are quick to gobble up preferred or secondary plants as soon as they make an appearance. So, unless the herd is reduced and maintained well below carrying capacity for *years*, severely over-browsed habitat may never regain its former productivity.

Trophy management, by contrast, calls for keeping deer numbers in *balance* with the habitat (through an aggressive doe harvest) and promotes the long-term health of both the deer herd and the habitat. Management practices are directed at *enhancing* the habitat, which benefits nearly all the other wildlife species that share the land with the whitetail. The sex ratio and buck age structure are maintained in proper balance by a selective buck harvest and a doe harvest roughly equaling that of bucks. This results in a competitive rut, assuring that the best genes are passed along. All in all, *trophy management recreates a natural, balanced whitetail herd* like that which existed before man disrupted the balance by killing off the natural predators and altering the sex and age structure through a harvest heavily weighed toward bucks. If deer could vote, they would cast their ballot in favor of trophy management and its natural, balanced herds rather than the overcrowded, out-of-balance, buck-depleted herds waiting to crash that are so prevalent today across the country.

Now, before moving on, our above discussion left hunters and landowners dealing with the long-term effects of overcrowding with only a most unpalatable option—reduce their herd size for years to allow time for the desirable browse species to recover. Not a pleasant prospect. Is there a better solution? Yes. Food-source management. As we've discussed, this is a management strategy aimed at elevating the nutritional plane of the property through agricultural plantings and/or direct feeding. The beauty of this program, when intensively applied, is that more, bigger and healthier deer are possible...while the natural habitat *improves* because of the relief provided by the crops and/or supplemental feed! Yes, it requires money, time and commitment to pull off, but *serious* trophy hunters are just the folks committed enough to make it a reality, as they are doing across the country right now. And, everybody and everything, right down to the lowly blue-winged warbler, benefits.

THE FEW BAD APPLES

While there's plenty good about trophy hunting, some bad is creeping in, too. With the swelling interest in trophy hunting and the prestige, and occasionally even monetary rewards, associated with shooting a record buck or accumulating a notable collection of outstanding heads, the ugly side of human nature has started to surface in our noble sport. Whether its deer hunting, horseracing or tiddlywinks, anytime the stakes are high and personal gain is there for the taking, the unscrupulous step beyond the bounds of legalities, ethics and common decency and blacken the eye of all associated with the activity. Sadly, this element has infiltrated the ranks of trophy whitetail hunting.

In recent years, the mentality among the scoundrels has become kill at any cost. Too many would-be trophy hunters have stepped far outside the bounds of sportsmanship and even legality in their attempt to claim a spot in the whitetail limelight. This has been seen all too often among the high-profile "experts." Like the well-known Illinois hunter who recently was caught trying to pass off a buck he shot on a game-farm in Missouri as a wild buck he took in Illinois. Or, the famed Kansas hunter with a wall full of supposedly bow-killed giants who recently saw his bucks removed from the record book under allegations they were shot illegally. Then, there's the now-infamous Canadian outfitter who both shot and guided clients to an outrageous number of monster bucks, only to see his star fall when he was found to have gained his fame largely from illegal hunting of every imaginable kind, including hunting from an airplane. The list of sorted tales goes on.

In some cases, the perpetrators didn't even shoot the bucks they

Let us never forget that the meaning of "trophy" lies in the eyes of the beholder. Bryant Wright shot this fine 9-pointer, and as his first deer, he couldn't have been prouder if it had made the top 10 in B&C. We trophy hunters can't let "trophy snobbery" ever rob the joy of such successes. Photo by author.

tried to use to lift themselves to stardom. Perhaps the most publicized such case involved a Texas banker who sewed the stolen rack of a giant Canadian non-typical on the head of a freshly killed Mexican buck in an attempt to claim for himself the new Mexico non-typical record. Then, there was the fellow from Alabama who weaseled a set of record-book sheds from a "friend" in Georgia, attached them to a buck and claimed to have shot the new Alabama state record. There are many more such tales.

The illegal or fraudulent taking of big bucks is not limited to well-publicized cases only. Countless instances occur across the country every year. Poachers increasingly pursue big bucks wherever they are found, refusing to allow posted signs and landowner rights stand between them and a big buck. The fervor for notoriety makes trophy bucks fair game wherever and whenever they are found, in-season and out. At *WHITE-TAIL* magazine, we have become reluctant to jump on the story of a huge buck right after it is killed for fear that time will reveal the buck was taken illegally. The same is true when a new "expert" emerges with an incredible collection of big bucks. We've found that when something comes our way that seems unbelievable, it usually is *unbelievable*! For instance, I recently was told about a guy in South Texas who had supposedly rattled in and shot a phenomenal number of 160-plus bucks near where I hunt. The story was too fantastic to accept so I did some checking, which soon revealed that the guy was a notorious poacher on a famous unhunted ranch.

There seems to be no limit to what someone will do. In Athens, Georgia, for instance, a popular tame buck in a small public pen was arrowed to death and his head removed the day before bow season. A couple of years ago, a friend shot at a 190-class 10-pointer in Canada. Upon the shot, the buck ran a short distance over a hill and out of sight before dropping near a country road. The hunter picked up the blood trail and followed it to where the deer had fallen. There, the foot-deep snow told the story. The buck had been picked up by someone who had apparently been standing for a while along an old fence just off the road. The story could have ended there but it didn't. That night, word got out that an American in another camp had killed a giant buck. My friend went over to see the deer, and lo and behold, there lay his buck. When confronted, the offending hunter didn't even deny that he hadn't shot the buck, but even after two days of tense negotiations, he steadfastly refused to return the buck to its rightful owner. The giant buck meant more to the deer thief than morality, sportsmanship, legality or common decency, and that has become the case all too often today when a big buck is involved.

A QUESTION OF FAIR CHASE

Along the lines of a trophy at any cost, it seems more and more people are willing to buy a trophy under any circumstance for any price. Last season, I got a call from an "outfitter" who wanted me to come *shoot*, not hunt, a 25-inch 10-pointer with double drop-tines in exchange for a story. He went on to say that a half-day was all it would take, most of which would be spent on pictures. Then, he concluded his spiel by asking for my FAX number so he could send me a photo of the buck. After a couple of questions, I found, as suspected, that this buck was nothing more than pet on a 150-acre, essentially coverless game farm. As tactfully as I could, I told him I wouldn't touch that deal with the proverbial 10-foot pole.

The demand for trophy bucks has given rise to a disturbing new trend—canned "hunts" for game-farm bucks on fenced enclosures so small and devoid of cover that the *shooter* is guaranteed to go home with a buck, complete with ear tags, a veterinary certificate and wire-fence-blunted antlers. The envelope has even been pushed to the point that put-and-take hunting for big bucks is here. This kind of ego-massaging goings-on may be "shooting" or "collecting," but it is *not* hunting. Nor does it have anything to do with game management—game-farming, possibly; feedlot overseeing, maybe; but deer management, forget it. It is now even possible for a "hunter" to shop for his big buck in brochures like shopping for clothes in a catalog. The only question is why would he want to? Why not shoot a Holstein? At least his family would get more meat and our sport would be spared the guilt by association with something that, in fact, is not even hunting.

More and more, fair chase is going to become an issue in trophy hunting. If we don't address it and police ourselves, then those outside the sport will. Need proof? The U.S. Congress recently took up a bill that would have prohibited the shooting of big game on fenced areas of less than 1,000 acres. Great day, 1,000 acres of the right habitat is large enough to hide half the Chinese army and larger than scores of fenced operations around the country trying to legitimately manage for better whitetails. It's time we wake up and take care of our own house or politicians and anti-hunters will do it for us.

The fact that the politicians focused only on the game-proof fence as the culprit tells me they don't understand the fair-chase issue. A high-fence is just one of many management tools available to help game manager's achieve better results. True, a small fenced area can so restrict a deer's escape options that fair chase is compromised. How small is too small? That depends on many factors, foremost being cover and topography, but 1,000 acres is certainly enough country for savvy old bucks to elude hunters, unless it looks like moonscape.

The truth is that we now have the "management" technology available—artificial insemination, genetic manipulation, hormonal implants, intensive feeding, game-proof fencing, animal husbandry techniques, to name but a few—to push us over the fair-chase edge if we choose to abuse these tools. But, managing deer is like driving a car—just because it'll go 120 mph doesn't mean we should drive it that fast, and just because an irresponsible few have high-speed crashes doesn't mean we shouldn't drive cars! We have the management knowledge and tools to enable us to return our long-abused herds back to their *natural*, healthy, balanced

Kristin Morris did everything right en route to tagging this beautiful Montana 8-pointer and is justifiably happy with her accomplishment. We must encourage the younger generation to enjoy our sport to the fullest if it is going to continue to prosper in the future. Photo by author.

state, which is good for all concerned. The challenge is to do it *while* maintaining not only fair chase, but also the aesthetics and mystique that make whitetail hunting the wonderful sport it is. We must be responsible managers. And, we can't let a few "reckless drivers" blacken our eye with the very things that offer us, and the deer, hope for a better future.

SOUR GRAPES

Unhealthy, even ugly, competition between hunters is another unfortunate side effect of the rush for success in trophy hunting. This competition can manifest itself simply as sour grapes when one hunter is more successful than another or as overtly as outright sabotage of stands, equipment or property by the jealous hunter. Even in its less insidious form, the one subjected to the pettiness is robbed of some of the joy of his accomplishment and the wonderful experience of sharing it with others. The greatest loser, however, is the guy on the giving end. He has missed the whole essence of the sport—the one-on-one challenge of hunting a great and worthy animal in nature's arena and the privilege of sharing his adventures, successful or not, with others...and having others share theirs

This is not the sun setting on trophy hunting; it's the dawn of a new and better era...if we all do our part to assure the health of our sport and the whitetail herds across North America! Photo by Mike Biggs.

with him. Misguided competition places emphasis on the kill and inches of antler rather than the sport, time in the field and shared experiences with good friends or family. The pressure competition exerts can make us forget about sharing the hunting experience with the less fortunate or young. That would be the greatest failure in deer hunting.

As trophy hunting has increased in popularity, the term "trophy" has become more synonymous with "really big." Certainly, I relate to this. But frankly, when it gets right down to it, I still like the definition that says a trophy is a "prized memento of one's personal accomplishment." You see, I *do* believe "trophy" is in the eyes of the beholder. If a hunter is proud of his buck, regardless of the size, nobody has the right to say that deer is not a trophy. I say this because defining a trophy purely on size has given rise to another disconcerting aspect of trophy hunting—"trophy snob-bery." If a buck doesn't meet the standards of the trophy snob, both the hunter and his game are belittled and scorned, sometimes in mean-spirit-ed terms but more often in subtle, condescending ways. Regardless of how, it's wrong, and I believe it is detrimental to the sport since it tends to especially discourage and demoralize the young and inexperienced, who must eventually carry the hunting banner.

Several years ago, my youngest daughter, Kristin, shot her first buck, a spike with one antler broken off. Nine years old at the time, she was ecstatic about her great fortune. When we got back to the Burnt Pine lodge, where about 15 hunters were gathered recounting the afternoon's hunt, she ran in, beaming with pride, and announced to all that she had shot a "1-pointer!" Everybody present showered her with the appropriate accolades, except for one particular sorehead.

Upon walking out to the hanging pole and seeing the buck for himself, he strolled over to Kristin and said accusingly, "You shot a *yearling*." Then, he turned and walked away, in apparent disgust. Kristin, who fortunately didn't know what the word "yearling" meant, gave him with a puzzled look, shrugged her shoulders and then continued to revel in the praises of the gallery. I watched him walk back to lodge, considering whether or not I was going to exercise my privileges as owner. But when I heard Kristin begin to recite her story yet again, I turned back to her. The beaming face told it all—that 1-pointer *was* a *trophy* to be proud of and nobody could tell her, or me, differently!

Despite a few kinks yet to be worked out, trophy whitetail hunting is alive and well, with its best years still ahead. When I look back over my 30-plus years of chasing big bucks, I marvel at how far our sport has come. Back in the 1960s, when a deer track was cause for excitement, at least in my part of the world, and a sighting made for a successful season, I could not have possibly imagined that whitetail hunting would evolve into the national obsession it is today. But, even more amazing to me is that, by the grace of Almighty God, I have been allowed to make this wonderful sport a big part of my life, even my career. And, I never take my good fortune for granted. I appreciate every day in the field, every deer I see, every place I hunt, every new friend I meet who shares my passion and every buck that comes my way. I feel a great responsibility to share what I've learned and experienced with others so they, too, can fully enjoy this marvelous sport…thus this book. And if God so wills it, I'll continue to pursue trophy whitetails and enjoy the wonder of it all until Lord Jesus calls me home.